Information Hunters

Information Hunters

When Librarians, Soldiers, and Spies
Banded Together in World War II Europe

Kathy Peiss

OXFORD
UNIVERSITY PRESS

OXFORD
UNIVERSITY PRESS

Oxford University Press is a department of the University of Oxford. It furthers
the University's objective of excellence in research, scholarship, and education
by publishing worldwide. Oxford is a registered trade mark of Oxford University
Press in the UK and certain other countries.

Published in the United States of America by Oxford University Press
198 Madison Avenue, New York, NY 10016, United States of America.

Library of Congress Cataloging-in-Publication Data
Names: Peiss, Kathy Lee, author.
Title: Information hunters : when librarians, soldiers, and spies
banded together in World War II Europe / Kathy Peiss.
Other titles: When librarians, soldiers, and spies banded together in World War II Europe
Description: New York, NY : Oxford University Press, [2020] |
Identifiers: LCCN 2019015762 | ISBN 9780190944612 (hardback) |
ISBN 9780190944636 (epub) | ISBN 9780190944629 (updf)
Subjects: LCSH: World War, 1939–1945—Confiscations and contributions—Europe. |
World War, 1939–1945—Military intelligence—United States. |
Books—Europe—History—20th century. | Intelligence service—United States—
Information services. | Acquisitions (Libraries)—United States—History—
20th century. | Cultural property—Protection—Europe—History—20th century. |
Librarians—United States—History—20th century. | World War, 1939–1945—
Destruction and pillage—Europe. | United States. Office of Strategic Services. |
Library of Congress Mission to Germany.
Classification: LCC D810.C8 P45 2020 | DDC 940.54/8673094—dc23
LC record available at https://lccn.loc.gov/2019015762

3 5 7 9 8 6 4 2

Printed by Sheridan Books, Inc., United States of America

For Peter
Once again, and always

CONTENTS

ACKNOWLEDGMENTS

I began this project knowing little about the history of books, information, the military, or intelligence. I am grateful to many individuals and institutions who have helped me pursue this work over a number of years. Fellowships from the American Council of Learned Societies, the Radcliffe Institute for Advanced Study, and the John Simon Guggenheim Memorial Foundation supported my research, and a Dean's Leave from the School of Arts and Sciences at the University of Pennsylvania gave me time to write. A Gilder Lehrman Foundation Fellowship and Hoover Presidential Library Association Travel Grant facilitated visits to collections. For archival materials, I thank the British Library, Center for Jewish History, Herbert Hoover Presidential Library, Hoover Institution Library and Archives, Library of Congress, National Archives at College Park, The National Archives (UK), New York Public Library, Wisconsin Historical Society, and the archives and special collections libraries at Columbia University, Harvard University, Massachusetts Institute of Technology, Princeton University, Stanford University, Trinity College, University of Illinois, University of Pennsylvania, University of Regina, University of Virginia, and Yale University. I am indebted to librarians and archivists George Boziwick, Kyle DeCicco-Carey, Miles Crowley, Tim Driscoll, Ernest Emrich, Michelle Gachette, Ed King, Larry MacDonald, Melanie Meyers, Harry Miller, Jim Moske, Josephus Nelson, Richard Peuser, Chris Prom, Matt Schaefer, Elizabeth Seitz, Joe Weber, Sarah Wipperman, Craig Wright, and Penn's Interlibrary Loan staff.

I am especially grateful to the extraordinary librarian-scholars at the University of Pennsylvania, who have been engaged with this work and assisted me in so many ways: Lynne Farrington, Mitch Fraas, Arthur Kiron, Bruce Nielsen, Nick Okrent, John Pollack, and Daniel Traister. Library historians Alistair Black, Maria Gonzalez, Miriam Intrator, and Boyd Rayward gave me needed guidance in a new field.

Many individuals directed me to sources, suggested readings, and provided advice, including Mark Bergman, Roger Chartier, David Engerman, Astrid Eckert, Ronald Granieri, John Hench, Nathan Ensmenger, Hemant Shah, Nancy Sinkoff, Melissa Teixera, Judith Vichniac, and Noam Zadoff. Others offered insightful comments on chapters and presentations: Ayelet Brinn, Kevin Boyle, Andrew Cayton, Sarah Barringer Gordon, Arthur Kiron, Amy Offner, Simon Richter, Sophia Rosenfeld, Dan Schiller, Katrin Shreiter, and Beth Wenger. I am grateful to Billy Coleman, Rebecca Cutler, Simon Ertz, Laura Freeman, Raquel Kirby, Josef Nothmann, Vanessa Smith, Aro Velmet, and Binghao Zhao for research assistance; thanks especially to Leead Staller, Elizabeth Vaziri, and Shane Wilson. I have benefited from audience questions and remarks when I have presented my work at the American Library Association Library History Round Table, the Institute of Historical Research (London), King's College London, Radcliffe Institute, St. Joseph's University, Smith College, University of Delaware, University of Illinois, University of Melbourne, University of Michigan, Woodrow Wilson International Center for Scholars, the Yale Program in the History of the Book, and at Penn, the History Department's Annenberg Seminar, the History and Sociology of Science Workshop, the Wolf Humanities Center, and the Workshop in the History of Material Texts.

I was fortunate to discover several family members of those who had participated in the collection and preservation of books during the war. I am deeply grateful to Susan Josephson for sharing a portion of her father Glenn Goodman's unpublished memoir; reading it shed new light on the restitution effort. Eric Andersson told me family stories about his great-aunt Adele Kibre, which illuminated a woman of mystery. Alex Zuckerman, with Miriam Intrator's kind assistance, allowed me to read the letters of his father, Jacob Zuckerman. I also appreciate conversations with Yvonne Pine and Robert Sargeant. Early in the project I met Frederick and Eleanor Kilgour, who welcomed me to their North Carolina home. Finally, thanks to Saul and Joanne Pasternack for hosting a dinner with relatives who told stories about Reuben Peiss; to Susan Goldschmidt Ellis for sharing photographs and a home movie; and to Barbara Grossman, who copied a handful of Reuben's letters and photographs.

My editor Susan Ferber followed this project for many years, and her editorial work and encouragement have been invaluable. My agent Lisa Adams lifted my concerns and made some key intellectual contributions to this work. It has been a great pleasure to work with them. My revisions were guided by the insightful reports of three anonymous reviewers for Oxford University Press. I am also grateful to production manager Jeremy Toynbee, copy editor Michael Sandlin, and indexer Alexander Trotter.

I owe special thanks to a handful of friends and colleagues. Bruce Kuklick supported me in this project from the beginning. His questions, suggestions, and readings of my work have made this a better book. Jennifer Rodgers also helped in innumerable ways, including sharing sources from her own work and commenting on the full manuscript. Conversations with Antonio Feros, Judy Gerson, Sally Gordon, Stephanie McCurry, Barbara Savage, and Susan Strasser inspired and enlightened me on many occasions. My husband Peter Agree has sustained me in this work and in life, in ways great and small. His curiosity about people and insight into the past, his attention to every page, his daily support and love mean everything to me. I am grateful beyond words.

Information Hunters

Prologue

This book grew out of a chance discovery of an online memorial to an uncle I never knew. Reuben Peiss had been a librarian at Harvard when World War II began, and like many in academia, he was recruited into the Office of Strategic Services, the nation's first intelligence agency. As a field agent based in Lisbon and Bern, he developed a network of book dealers and private individuals to acquire timely publications for intelligence analysis. When the Allies pushed into Germany, he worked with documents-gathering teams to uncover records of war crimes, caches of Nazi propaganda, and book collections buried in caves and mines. After the war, he headed an overseas mission of the Library of Congress to acquire works published in wartime Germany and occupied countries for American research libraries. When he returned, he worked in the State Department and taught at the library school of the University of California, Berkeley. Plagued with chronic illness, he lived a short life, dying in 1952 at age forty.

The memorial, posted on the University of California website, took me by surprise. My parents had never told me much about my father's oldest brother. I had never read the book he translated, Alfred Hessel's *A History of Libraries*; on my bookshelf sat a rare Spinoza volume he had once owned. When I asked about his secret activities, my mother exclaimed, "Oh yes, Reuben was a spy!" But there were few memories and no letters or photographs. It did not take much searching, however, to find a paper trail, an extensive correspondence with leading American librarians, OSS colleagues, and military officials. An e-mail to the man who had recruited him led to a phone conversation and a visit. When I met eighty-nine-year-old Frederick Kilgour—a pioneer in information science—he was spry and quick-witted, answering my questions with the caginess of an old intelligence agent. There were other traces, too, that made Reuben Peiss come alive. In the Library of Congress, teletype rolls—still marked secret and requiring declassification—reproduced conversations with his boss across the Atlantic, revealing the cadence of his everyday speech and his anxiety as he faced the urgent challenge of his mission in Germany. Relatives shared their few personal letters, photographs, and even a home movie that had been transferred to videotape. Filmed without sound in the summer of 1945, it showed Reuben Peiss with his closest childhood friend, then an army doctor, the two men in uniform, smoking and chatting at an army installation in Bavaria. Most evocative was a lengthy tribute from leading lights in the library field, published not long after Peiss's death in a memorial edition of *A History of Libraries*. These men remembered their colleague not only as a professional but also for a rare set of personal qualities—a combination of physical weakness and mental courage, a sharp intelligence and self-effacing sense of humor, an embrace of high culture and low, from Whitehead and Spinoza to Groucho Marx. I recognized these family traits and, wanting to know more, I dug into the archives.

Reuben Peiss was the eldest son of Russian Jewish immigrants, Alexander Peisachowitz and Rose Pasternack, who came to the United States in the early twentieth century, met, and married. When Alexander died in 1924, Rose raised their four children in Hartford, Connecticut, working as a milliner and receiving help from her brothers. Reuben Peiss, a stellar high school student, earned a scholarship from the city to go to Trinity College in 1929. He was like other day students there, many of them Jewish "strivers," who lived at home, held jobs, needed financial aid, and were relentless in their pursuit of higher education—a source of tension at a college where affluent Protestant fraternity men dominated campus life.

When he graduated, he received a fellowship from Trinity to attend Harvard University for a year of postgraduate work in philosophy, studying Spinoza and Jewish thought with the eminent scholar Harry Austryn Wolfson. Yet Harvard, too, was inhospitable and exclusionary, offering little support to Jewish students. Peiss graduated with a master's degree in 1934, but without further funding, he suspended his doctoral work. His class photograph shows a young man dressed in a formal suit, with vest and watch chain, a shy smile and direct gaze behind round metal glasses—the well-bred look of someone trying to fit in.

Needing to earn a living in the midst of the Great Depression, he began teaching at Hartford Federal College, a community college founded as a federal emergency relief school by the Works Progress Administration. The experimental college struggled to stay open, as critics attacked both its progressive curriculum and the faculty's leftwing politics. In 1937, Peiss decided to become a librarian, attending an accelerated program in library science at the University of Michigan. His colleagues would later extol this choice as one that recognized the affinity between "philosophy as the love of knowledge, and libraries which are the repositories of knowledge."[1] The truth is likely more prosaic. The future of the federal college was grim, he could not advance in academe without a PhD, and as the family's oldest son, he felt a duty to help his mother and siblings.

In the fall of 1938, newly credentialed, he looked for work. Times were still hard, and there were few openings. He returned to Harvard as a low-level employee in the library, hired on temporary funds for a special project, the revision of the *Union List of Serials*, a massive guide to the periodical holdings of the major libraries across the United States and Canada. The first edition of the ULS, published in 1927 after a decade of labor, was a remarkable achievement in the age before computers but was riddled with inaccuracies and "ghosts," as the librarians called false entries. Work on a second edition began in 1937. Harvard contained many libraries and specialized collections, each with different personalities and practices, from fussy to slipshod. "The magnitude of the task . . . has surpassed all expectations," Peiss observed, and the librarians sometimes despaired of completing it.[2] To break up the routine, he pulled catalog cards that fetched a laugh, with such titles as *Kansas Knocker: A Journal for Cranks* and *National Nut News*.

After the United States entered the war, his friend and coworker, Frederick Kilgour, went to Washington to work for the OSS, which actively recruited scholars and specialists from the Ivy League. Kilgour's assignment was to organize an overseas program to acquire enemy publications. He needed seasoned librarians, he wrote his former boss, Harvard Library director Keyes Metcalf, and preferred men ineligible for the draft, "a mild 4-F such as Reuben," whose academic knowledge, library experience, and fluency in several languages made him an obvious choice. Metcalf endorsed the suggestion: "I know that he is restless and anxious to do his share in the war."[3]

Reuben Peiss jumped at the chance to join the OSS and travel abroad. Arriving in Lisbon in September 1943, he quickly picked up the language and became attuned to the "machine gun" rate of speaking. The city was remarkable in its difference from every place he had known—its narrow streets and steep hills, the day full of sunlight and "night fragrant, with star-studded skies." He marveled at the courtesy of the Portuguese, the strong family feeling, even the women with "enormous baskets of fish on their heads, striding along with magnificent posture." He also saw the poverty and "deplorable squalor" behind the picturesque scene, and the "very deep strain of sadness running throughout life here." In Lisbon he acquired publications from Germany and occupied countries, an open activity that at times drifted into clandestine work. At the end of 1944, when the border between Switzerland and France opened up, he went on to the OSS post in Bern, with trips to London, Paris, and Geneva. "I have been seeing the world, and it has been an exciting experience indeed," he wrote his aunt.[4]

Few letters record how he felt about those experiences or reveal his inner life. He remained single over the years; family members fleetingly mention a college sweetheart and a rumored affair with a Parisian woman, but nothing more. His feelings occasionally overcame him—his outrage over perceived antisemitism in the treatment of his brother, and the pain, visible in his handwriting, when his young sister died of leukemia. But his correspondence usually moved along easier registers—work, books, people, and immediate problems to solve.

His colleagues saw the slight librarian-scholar as a man who could get things done. Transferred to Switzerland, Peiss presented a calling card to legendary spymaster Allen W. Dulles from H. Gregory Thomas, OSS chief in the Iberian Peninsula, inscribed with a note of introduction. "He is a remarkably good man and I am sorry to lose him," Thomas wrote in tiny script, "I am sure you will find him most useful."[5] That card survived the war, deep in an accordion file at the National Archives. In postwar Germany, Peiss was known as a scrounger, the military's term of approval for someone who knew how to cut through red tape or work around it. He felt no compunction walking up to the American proconsul of Germany Lucius D. Clay in the breakfast line to chat about a problem with book acquisition. General Clay, in turn, gave him an unintentional promotion by addressing him as "Doctor."

Over the years, Peiss's exploits remained vivid to those he worked with. "It's strange the things one remembers," commented composer Ross Lee Finney about his wartime intelligence experiences. "There was someone named Reuben . . . his work was always top secret and the less I knew about it, the better." In a telling recollection, librarian Scott Adams, a colleague on the Library of Congress Mission, described the epic retrieval of books for American research libraries in Leipzig in the Soviet zone of occupation. Peiss was a "little wisp of a Jewish lad out of Harvard," a "little 135 pound Spinoza scholar," who "organized a convoy of something like fifty American Army trucks and drove them behind these Russians' lines into Leipzig," managing to "snap all this stuff up and get it back so that it could be delivered."[6] Adams embellished a true story—there were only four trucks and the Soviet administration cooperated with this mission—telling it as a librarian's version of Clark Kent and Superman.

Reuben Peiss loved mysteries, and he bequeathed one to me. Uncovering his life became an obsessive search for clues buried in archives and hidden in plain sight. He led me into a world of American librarians, archivists, collectors, scholars, and soldiers, galvanized by the war to acquire and preserve the written word. His life pointed me toward a bigger story, one largely untold, of American mass collecting missions and how they mattered in a cataclysmic war.

Introduction

Shelved in library stacks or consigned to storage, the publications date back to the 1930s and 1940s, some even earlier. Written in many languages, they include everything from government documents and newspapers to underground pamphlets and pulp fiction. After World War II, two million foreign books and periodical issues landed in the Library of Congress and leading American research libraries. Another 160,000 volumes looted from European Jews made their way to Jewish seminaries and other repositories in the United States. Thousands of microfilm reels filled with enemy periodicals and other materials, once avidly studied by US government officials, are now scattered, uncatalogued, and even up for auction on the internet. Rarely do library catalogues give readers a way to discover the origins of these works. Only a stamp, bookplate, label, or handwritten notation hint at their travels. At once abundant and unrecognized, these are the vestiges of an unprecedented American effort to acquire foreign publications and information during World War II and its immediate aftermath.

An unlikely band of American librarians, archivists, scholars, spies, and soldiers went abroad to aid the Allies' cause, their war work centered on books, documents, and print culture. They traveled to neutral cities around the world to gather enemy publications and followed advancing armies into the shattered war zones of Europe, capturing records in a massive program of confiscation. In the final months of the war and onset of the occupation in Germany, they seized Nazi works from bookstores and schools, unearthed collections hidden in cellars and caves, and grappled with the consequences of mass looting and dislocation of countless books. Improvising library techniques in wartime conditions, they contributed to

Allied intelligence, safeguarded endangered books, restituted looted ones, and participated in a policy to destroy works containing Nazi and militaristic content.

This book uncovers these worlds of collecting—in the spy-ridden cities of Stockholm and Lisbon, in liberated Paris and the rubble of Berlin, and in German caves and mineshafts. It explores what collecting meant to the men and women who embarked on these missions, and how the particular challenges of a total war led to an intense focus on books and documents.

At the outset of this devastating conflict, no one could have foreseen that book collecting—the domain of bibliographers and bibliophiles—would turn into a government commitment to mass acquisitions. In the end, librarians' and collectors' skills, expertise, and aspirations aligned with American military and political objectives. The participants carried with them a strong commitment to winning the war, felt revulsion against the Nazi regime, and shared the confidence that America would rescue endangered civilization. Yet underlying this sense of national purpose lay uneasy questions about the ethics of acquisition, the rights of the victors, the relationship of reading and freedom, and the justice of restitution.

Why did collecting come to be so important in the American fight in World War II? The answer lies in the very nature of books and printed texts, and in the particular character of the war. Books serve readers in many different ways: as sources of useful information, as forms of communication, and as material manifestations of knowledge and cultural tradition. In a total war, these general attributes became terrains of battle. To fight the enemy required the mobilization of knowledge, which produced a sweeping commitment to intelligence gathering, including the "open source" intelligence gleaned in publications. It also demanded ideological confrontations that sharply contrasted freedom and fascism; German books and other media were seen as carriers of Nazi propaganda that must be eliminated. Modern warfare's assault on civilian life also prompted new attention to preserving books and other cultural material. Only at the end of the war was the Third Reich's pillaging of European culture fully exposed, yet many Americans had already embraced a sense of responsibility for rescuing the records of European civilization.

One other development helps explain these wartime mass acquisitions projects: changes in the world of libraries and scholarship. Library science had begun to explore new approaches to information and technologies of reproduction such as microfilm, which could be used to disseminate enemy publications for intelligence purposes. Social scientists in communications and educational psychology now examined books and reading for their social and ideological effects, which influenced how postwar planners addressed the problem of books in occupied Germany. Even more important, wartime mobilization encouraged new aspirations among major libraries to achieve national leadership and international prominence through the development of foreign holdings. Libraries had partnered with the government before—the Library War Service in World War I, for example—but the breadth and depth of this relationship was new and far reaching.[1]

The American acquisition of enemy publications and records was not an entirely new phenomenon in World War II. Armies had long seized enemy records and taken war booty from the field of combat. Commanders gathered information opportunistically, seizing letters and reports when they could. In the midst of the Civil War, the US War Department issued rules of land warfare, officially called General Order No. 100 but known as the Lieber Code, after its author, jurist Francis Lieber. This statement of principles became the basis for such later international agreements as The Hague Conventions of 1899 and 1907. Devised in a war that devastated civilian populations, the Lieber Code addressed how armies should handle various forms of property, including intellectual and cultural materials. Significantly, it initiated a commitment to cultural preservation, requiring military forces to protect libraries, art, and scientific collections from looting and destruction. Yet it also authorized the removal of such materials in instances of military necessity and for the benefit of the conquering nation. The Union Army seized many Confederate records at the end of the war; these were archived, and many were later published. Similarly, during the Philippine-American War, the United States confiscated three tons of documents and established an Insurgent Records Office in Manila to house and examine them; in 1902, the records were sent to Washington. In World War I, the military created an intelligence division, known as G-2, to acquire and handle captured materials. American participation in the war was relatively short, however, and attention to enemy records dropped after the armistice.[2]

On the eve of World War II, the US government had a limited and uncoordinated capacity for gathering such information. The Federal Bureau of Investigation compiled dossiers on domestic threats, increased surveillance, and intercepted mail. American embassies reported on foreign developments, and the armed services strengthened military intelligence. However, compared to Great Britain and Germany, which had long-standing intelligence services, the United States was far behind. As the international crisis mounted, President Franklin D. Roosevelt and others came to believe they needed to enlarge and centralize intelligence gathering and analysis. In July 1941 Roosevelt directed William "Wild Bill" Donovan to build a civilian intelligence operation, which became renowned as the Office of Strategic Services.[3]

Initially Donovan's agency was called the Coordinator of Information, a significant name, for it was this new attention to *information* that led to the first wartime collecting missions. Although espionage and secret operations would come to play an outsized role, the fledgling agency focused on the prosaic task of gathering and analyzing non-secret publications and documents. Donovan turned to Librarian of Congress Archibald MacLeish for practical aid and institutional support. Out of their relationship came the plan to send librarians, antiquarians, scholars, and microfilm specialists to neutral cities around the world, acquiring foreign publications for intelligence purposes. Later, after the D-Day landing, such collecting became militarized. Army units known as T-Forces—often with the OSS participating—scoured "targets" for records and publications of consequence for military operations, intelligence, the prosecution of war crimes, and the postwar occupation.[4]

The idea that open sources would yield information needed to win the war was an arresting one, not necessarily self-evident. Unlike the interception and analysis of coded messages (signals intelligence), publications were openly available and often not timely. Yet over the course of the war, publications transmuted into valued intelligence—indicated, ironically, by the fact that they became classified information, were removed from public access, and often remained secret long after the war was over. In the process, librarians and scholars turned into unlikely intelligence agents, who applied their professional knowledge to the clandestine war and the larger effort to defeat the Axis.[5]

This was an unparalleled relationship between the government, military, and American libraries, one that libraries embraced not only out of patriotic duty but as an opportunity. Already they felt that the nation's research libraries were inadequate to the needs of modern researchers and government, a sense heightened by the naval war in the Atlantic that had largely suspended the international book trade by 1940. Imagining a new role for American research libraries as repositories of the world's knowledge, MacLeish and others argued that every important foreign work should be available somewhere in the country as a matter of national interest. Strikingly, the OSS acquisition endeavor provided a model for these libraries. In a highly unusual arrangement with the War and State Departments, the Library of Congress established its European Mission, whose agents sought all works published in Germany and occupied countries during the war years. Initially conceived as a book purchasing plan, it evolved into an omnivorous, industrial-scale program. Under the authority

of the US occupation government in Germany, it seized materials in research institutes and specialized libraries, helped the military's document
centers screen confiscated works, acquired numerous scientific and technical materials, and collected books with Nazi content and items deemed
to have no intelligence value. In the name of national security and postwar
intellectual leadership, these works were brought to the United States to
build libraries' international holdings.[6]

Beyond these government-backed missions, the war led many individuals
and organizations to seek books and records in war-torn Europe. Soldiers
and civilian officials might pick up books opportunistically for themselves,
but some felt compelled by their war experience and a sense of history to
amass Nazi items for American collections. The Hoover Library aggressively recruited journalists, scholars, refugees, and relief workers to add to
its records of war. Their efforts reveal the gray areas of collecting in a land
under military occupation. The need to preserve their imperiled religious
and cultural heritage led Jewish American leaders and scholars to dedicate
themselves to finding and claiming looted books; they formed an innovative nongovernmental organization, Jewish Cultural Reconstruction, Inc.,
that gained standing as trustee and distributor of these works.[7]

If earlier wars sanctioned the seizure of enemy publications for intelligence, the expansion of American collecting missions at the end of
hostilities had no precedent. "Mission creep" occurred less from long-range
planning and forethought and more as a response to the shifting direction of the war and the growing perception of publications' importance.
Entering the period of occupation, the Allies began to deal with the cultural
destruction and ideological debris of the Third Reich. They confronted the
ubiquity of two types of books—literature with fascist or militaristic content, on the one hand, and looted Jewish books, on the other. In different
ways, these works embodied the Third Reich's vast ideological project.
What should be done with an entire literature believed to have poisoned
the minds of ordinary Germans? How could looted volumes be restored to
the owners who were victims of the regime?

For the American military government, these were complex and only
partly anticipated problems. When it ordered objectionable Nazi books
to be confiscated, gathered in collecting points, and destroyed, it sparked
loud protests from American journalists and librarians, who equated the
American occupiers' deeds to Nazi book burning. At the same time, the very
armed forces that had amassed documents during the war now found displaced libraries and archives hidden in caves, cellars, and castles, including
countless books stolen from Jews in Germany and throughout Europe.
These works were assembled in a depot in Offenbach for preservation,

identification, and ultimate restitution. Disordered, damaged, and in many cases unidentifiable, they posed serious logistical, political, and ethical problems for the military occupation.[8] The disposition of all these books required the collaboration of many in the military government, including librarians, archivists, educators, and communications specialists.

Librarians brought something crucial to these collecting missions: their professional expertise and skills in handling books, periodicals, printed reports, and ephemera, even photographs and music, now put to use in unimaginable circumstances. Title selection, normally a sedate affair of catalogues and dealers, required quick decisions made in bookstores under surveillance, in crumbling buildings, and in caves crammed with volumes. Librarians had only begun to explore the use of microfilm for reproducing publications and increasing access, but it became an indispensable technology when original materials were too difficult to transport. They conserved and organized millions of items in document centers and collecting points. Departing from standard principles of cataloguing, they devised new ways to sort and classify materials instrumentally—to meet the needs of intelligence services and the military occupation. Out of the practices of librarianship, which were often improvised to meet unexpected situations, came new ideas about handling books and information.

The close relationships among librarians, scholars, intelligence, and the military occurred largely in the European theater of war and occupation. Although OSS agents went to India and unoccupied China to find enemy publications, and the Library of Congress placed representatives in postwar Japan, these efforts were limited and must be set in a different history— that of US–Japan relations. Undergirding the collecting missions discussed in this book was a Eurocentric understanding of human civilization. In the interwar years, schools, college courses, libraries, and even radio shows stressed the idea that European cultural heritage was an important component of American national identity.[9] Those who went abroad to acquire books and documents believed they were safeguarding the records of civilization, and some hoped to repair the intellectual ruptures brought about by war. These altruistic aims mixed with an instrumental one: that collecting knowledge furthered American geopolitical power and cultural prestige.

Numerous Americans found their way into collecting and managing books and documents in the war years. Their numbers are difficult to pinpoint because of the tangled web of government offices and military organizations involved in this work. The OSS agency that acquired foreign publications grew from a handful of employees to an organization of nearly two hundred, with many women and émigrés doing the tedious work of classifying, translating, and indexing. G-2, the army's staff organization for intelligence, also became a far-flung operation to gather and analyze enemy reports, archives, and publications. Their work accelerated after the German defeat, even as different branches of the occupation government—Education and Religious Affairs, Information Control, and Monuments, Fine Arts, and Archives—dealt with the problem of books. The Library of Congress was involved in all these agencies and operations. Document centers and collecting points sprang up, where various groups of Americans delved into the growing piles of records and publications. At these places, hundreds of Germans worked as packers, sorters, and clerical workers.

In the foreground of this widespread effort was a smaller set of individuals whose decisions to initiate and carry out a program of mass acquisitions are the focus of this book. Some were public figures, such as Archibald MacLeish, William Donovan, Herbert Hoover, and General Lucius Clay, the occupation governor in Germany. Individuals celebrated for their contributions to knowledge and culture, including sinologist John K. Fairbank, composer Ross Lee Finney, and political philosopher Hannah Arendt, did turns acquiring materials abroad in the war years.

Most participants, however, were relatively obscure individuals, collectors, and keepers of knowledge. They were a more diverse lot than the famed Monuments Men, who tended to be art historians, archaeologists, and museum curators. Many librarians who worked for the OSS came from the New York Public Library, Library of Congress, Harvard, and other research universities. They had often struggled through the Great Depression, working on WPA projects or finding low-wage jobs in libraries, before wartime intelligence gathering beckoned. Joining them were historians, anthropologists, microfilm technicians, and book connoisseurs. Wartime mobilization brought Americans of many backgrounds into uniform, including men with college degrees and foreign language proficiency; some were assigned to intelligence units and trained to gather materials in Europe. Helping to develop occupation policies on books and records were archivists, educational psychologists, and experts on reading and mass communications. Civilian and military men with experience in the National Archives and Library of Congress went to postwar Germany on acquisition missions and operations to denazify and restitute looted books. In the shadows of these official operations lingered journalists, fact-finders, relief workers, and Jewish representatives pursuing collections of books and documents. Jewish Americans and refugees in the military also sought this assignment. Their language skills and experience of Germany joined with a commitment to preserving Jewish knowledge and eradicating the Third Reich. They were involved in documents teams, postwar book acquisitions, and restitution.

This was largely a man's world. The OSS employed many women in Washington to catalog and manage publications, but only one woman went abroad as a field agent: medievalist Adele Kibre, who ran a highly successful operation acquiring and microfilming enemy works in Stockholm. Women's involvement grew slightly after the war. Several female staffers from the OSS and Library of Congress went to occupied Germany, providing clerical support and administering the phase-out of OSS collecting operations. Hannah Arendt and Lucy Dawidowicz, later a distinguished Jewish historian, played important roles in the effort to restitute looted books.

The war challenged these librarians, archivists, scholars, and bibliophiles to turn their knowledge of books and records toward new and unpredictable ends. The immediacy and intensity of their experience tested them psychologically and physically. Whether soldier or civilian, American-born or émigré, these people's lives changed as they engaged in this unusual wartime enterprise. They stepped up to the moment, confronting shifting and perplexing circumstances armed only with vague instructions and few precedents to guide them.

The characteristically prosaic problems of librarianship—selection, identification, classification, conservation, access, and retrieval—raised difficult problems in the war and occupation. Which materials could rightly be seized, and under what conditions? Many library books ended the war damaged by damp and mold, singed by fire, and infested with insects. What efforts should be taken to save them? Germany's defeat left many hungry and scrambling to survive in a ruined economy. With no currency or trade relations, should Americans barter for valuable books and documents with cigarettes and CARE packages? What constituted "legitimate booty," as some collectors called it? Was confiscating and destroying Nazi literature no different from Nazi book burning? Given scarce resources, how much effort might be made to find the victims of looting and return their books?

Decisions on such essential questions were made often without much time for reflection. Several of those engaged in these operations clearly crossed a line, seizing material for private gain or driven by "book lust." Some feared that officials would not do enough to preserve this catastrophic history and endangered culture and took it upon themselves to do so. Beyond such individual choices were collective policies and actions, reached by governments and libraries, that navigated the morality of such acquisitions in wartime and occupation. Those engaged in collecting missions sensed their own role in making history, aware that the future would judge them.

These activities, involving considerable resources and personnel, remained largely unseen by the American public. The OSS and military intelligence considered them secret operations, and the records documenting them were classified for decades. Even after the war, few journalists reported on the Library of Congress Mission—one prominent article appeared in the *New York Times*—although library journals did provide some coverage. On two occasions, public controversy erupted over the handling of enemy works. In 1946, an Allied order to collect and destroy objectionable German literature sparked loud protests from American journalists and librarians, who likened the policy to Nazi book burnings and insisted that the right to read was essential to freedom and democracy. The controversy quickly died down. Two years later, a spotlight shone on the Hoover Library's collecting effort when a dispute erupted over the publication of *The Goebbels Diaries,* the original pages of which had been given as a gift to Herbert Hoover. With the book on track to be a bestseller, the US government investigated whether the diary had been legally acquired and published, or had violated the Trading with the Enemy Act. Yet these were brief episodes of public concern. Even the work to gather and restitute Jewish looted books garnered limited attention beyond the circles of Jewish scholars, religious leaders, and lawyers who had lobbied for authority over the unidentifiable works; by 1952, they had been distributed and absorbed into the nation's library stacks.

American librarians, soldiers, and spies came together in unique conditions in World War II, with its uprooting and destruction of culture, ideological warfare, and state-led mobilization of knowledge. Nevertheless, their collecting missions had lasting effects. They contributed to the tightening web of institutional relationships between the government and the military, on the one hand, and academic and research institutions, on the other. These efforts did not have the impact of government operations that brought German scientists and engineers to the United States or seized German industrial and technical information for use by American business and industry. Yet they must be seen as part of a larger project of intellectual reparations, as historian John Gimbel calls it, all the more powerful for being unacknowledged.[10] The missions gave librarians a new confidence about the importance of research libraries and international collections. Great repositories for research and the dissemination of knowledge in the national interest, they believed, would support American global dominance politically and intellectually. The flood of foreign materials also spurred the development of information science. The acquisition and analysis of "open sources" remained a central concern of national security agencies long after the OSS was dissolved and the CIA was born.

In these ways, wartime mass acquisitions serve as a bridge to developments in the postwar period. Yet, as historians Frank Biess and

Robert Moeller astutely assert, World War II should not be seen merely as an "incubation period of a new Cold War culture." This is especially apparent in the world of books. Although the Library of Congress Mission and Jewish Cultural Reconstruction had high hopes that the books they had amassed would serve history, memory, and cultural heritage, these collections stayed on library shelves and out of public awareness for many years. Only in recent decades have we begun to reckon with this past and address the decisions Americans made about the acquisition of books in World War II.[11]

Today we are experiencing the impact of the digital revolution on the material book, the traditional library, and the control of and access to information. Open source intelligence is not only exploited by national security agencies but has also become a tool of nonstate actors to influence foreign affairs. Libraries and cultural institutions are deliberately targeted in conflict zones, despite the presence of such agencies as UNESCO and a host of international conventions. Illuminating an unusual period when libraries and the military, intelligence and cultural heritage were closely intertwined, *Information Hunters* offers insight into contemporary challenges.

CHAPTER 1

✦

The Country of the Mind Must Also Attack

In the spring and summer of 1941, Archibald MacLeish and William J. Donovan met to discuss the European war and America's future. The men were of like minds as interventionists, convinced that the United States must join the fight. At Donovan's Beekman Place apartment in New York and MacLeish's farm in Conway, Massachusetts, they considered how to persuade the public about the danger ahead but soon veered into a discussion of the government's need for foreign information and what methods might be used to acquire it. Three years later, with American forces fighting around the globe, MacLeish would write Donovan that those talks seemed "farther away now than the first World War." Yet the moment remained vivid. "I still remember those morning meetings on the cool porch in the air of excitement of great things to come."[1] It is doubtless an exaggeration to say that the origins of America's vast intelligence apparatus can be traced to the early conversations of this unlikely pair. Yet it is not so far from the truth.

William J. Donovan was fifty-eight years old at that time. He was a man who had risen from a poor Irish family in Buffalo, New York, to become a decorated war veteran, Wall Street lawyer, and Republican adviser. Hard-charging and charismatic, he had earned his nickname "Wild Bill" on the football field at Columbia University. He headed a battalion of the famed Fighting 69th in France during World War I and returned a colonel with the Medal of Honor. During the 1930s, he frequently traveled overseas, meeting with officials to gauge the European political situation, which he

Figure 1.1. Librarian of Congress Archibald MacLeish meets with William J. Donovan, soon to be Coordinator of Information, 1941. John Phillips, Getty Images (no. 50455332).

came to believe would devolve into a second world war. He was proved right in September 1939, when Germany invaded Poland, and France and Great Britain declared war. Donovan became an informal adviser to President Franklin Roosevelt, to whom he expressed his view that the United States must intervene. In 1940 and 1941 Roosevelt sent him abroad to investigate Great Britain's efforts to fight Germany and how the United States could support them. He also asked Donovan to learn about the British intelligence system and how it might serve as a model for an American agency. British officials gave Donovan a select tour of their secret operations and information gathering methods, and Donovan took the bait. Back home, he presented a radio address broadcast on the three major networks, warning of the danger Germany posed to the world. MacLeish described him as "a soldier returned from a trip through the asbestos curtain and back," drawing an image of catastrophe from the theater, when a stage catches fire and the protective curtain suddenly falls. Although the British would remain strong, Donovan feared the inevitability of Nazi domination, unless the United States stepped in. In that event, an American intelligence agency would be necessary.[2]

Archibald MacLeish's life was unlike Donovan's, yet the two men shared some experiences that led them to a similar view of the war. Nearly ten years younger, MacLeish was born into a world of privilege and letters, his father a wealthy merchant and mother a college professor. He graduated from Yale and was attending Harvard Law School when the United States entered World War I. He volunteered for service, first as an ambulance driver and then in an artillery unit, rising to the rank of captain. After the war, he completed his degree and briefly practiced law, but he abandoned the profession to pursue a literary calling. He and his family moved to Paris to join a circle of expatriate writers and artists in the 1920s. During the Great Depression, MacLeish became well known for his poetry, receiving the Pulitzer Prize in 1932, and for his plays and opinion pieces.[3]

In 1939, Roosevelt unexpectedly tapped MacLeish to become the Librarian of Congress. The library had been led by Herbert Putnam for four decades and needed new direction. At the end of the 1930s, it was in a state of crisis, underfunded and understaffed, with 1.6 million unprocessed items waiting to be catalogued. Although the American Library Association pushed for another professional librarian in the post, Roosevelt wanted a leader with administrative skills who possessed vision and eloquence. FDR confidante and Supreme Court Justice Felix Frankfurter recommended MacLeish, calling him a rare individual who combined "the hard-headed lawyer with the sympathetic imagination of the poet, the independent thinker and the charming 'mixer.'" MacLeish proved to be the president's ideal, moving effortlessly between the worlds of culture and politics. He brought order to the library, modernizing numerous departments into several functional divisions, gaining budget increases, and raising staff salaries. Handsome and compelling, he inspired loyalty and even awe from his employees during his five years as librarian. It was, as one of them put it, like the "brush of a comet." As important, MacLeish brought a new urgency to the work of librarians and libraries. With the growing international crisis, he raised the stakes for books and democracy, calling upon librarians to be not merely custodians of culture but defenders of freedom. Like Donovan, he had perceived the dangers of fascism early and believed in American intervention. As an artist, intellectual, and the nation's leading librarian, he was convinced, as he later put it, that "the country of the mind must also attack."[4]

The meetings between MacLeish and Donovan in 1941 would foster a close relationship between the world of libraries and the intelligence arm of the state. Donovan had absorbed much from his trips to Great Britain; Sir William Stephenson of the Special Operations Executive took it upon himself to guide Donovan's education into secret intelligence. But Donovan's initial proposal for an intelligence agency—sent to Roosevelt six months before America's declaration of war—was largely homegrown. The agency was modeled on a great library, and MacLeish's fingerprints were all over the proposal.

Prior to 1941, there had been no coordinated American intelligence service to track foreign threats. The army and navy had small intelligence units, and the State Department regularly received confidential reports from legations around the world. The FBI had ramped up its domestic counterintelligence efforts. Each agency, however, was oriented toward its own operations and guarded its own specialized knowledge. In June 1941, Donovan proposed a "central enemy intelligence organization" to collect military, technological, economic, political, and psychological information, in order to understand and mobilize against threats to the United States. Although he would later turn to espionage, subversive activity, and code-breaking, his proposed agency initially focused on two operations. One was to use radio broadcasting to counter foreign propaganda and the possibility of "psychological attack against the moral and spiritual defenses of a nation." The main thrust of his proposal, however, centered on open-source intelligence and the prosaic task of gathering and analyzing non-secret material. "Comprehensive, long-range information" was "scattered throughout the various department of our Government," he observed. Donovan recommended bringing those materials together in one central place—the Library of Congress—and recruiting scholars and experts to analyze them. From the first, Donovan had been influenced by MacLeish, who believed that librarians were uniquely qualified to organize, classify, and retrieve information from abroad. Despite pushback from the War and Navy Departments and the FBI, Roosevelt appointed Donovan Coordinator of Information (COI) in July 1941, charging him with developing a full-fledged intelligence capacity in the US government that would become the Office of Strategic Services (OSS).[5]

The two men came together at a fraught moment in world history, and both took its measure. MacLeish headed a venerable institution, founded in 1800 and built upon Thomas Jefferson's library, and he reinvented it in a time of modern war, fought with information as well as armaments. Donovan created a centralized intelligence agency out of whole cloth. The unique qualities of these two men indisputably shaped the wartime Library of Congress and OSS. Yet the meetings in 1941 and "the great things to come" were also a culmination of larger changes taking place in the world of American libraries, academia, and cultural institutions. A new sense of purpose had arisen in the interwar years, characterized by both national ambition and internationalist commitment. New ideas about organizing and accessing information had emerged that challenged the traditional book. The looming destruction of books and culture in the tumult of world affairs could not be ignored. These developments would be yoked to an emergent intelligence and national security apparatus. The result was a novel commitment to open-source collecting as a way to know the enemy.

———— ⁓ ————

American library leaders embraced a wider vision of their work and civic contributions in the wake of World War I. The American Library Association (ALA) had created the Library War Service, which distributed millions of books and magazines to soldiers in training camps and overseas; many of those works became the permanent collection of the American Library in Paris, founded in 1920 as a tribute to US forces. By 1930, librarians and scholars were discussing how to enhance scholarly communication and access to research materials across the country. The American Council of Learned Societies and the Social Science Research Council encouraged efforts to expand and catalog the nation's intellectual resources and expertise, promoting the relevance of the humanities and social sciences to the national interest and international understanding. They created a Joint Committee on Materials for Research, led by historian Robert C. Binkley, which advocated the collection, preservation, and reproduction of printed works and documents, including "fugitive" or ephemeral sources. Librarians had long used master bibliographies and union lists to record holdings across institutions, but now such efforts took on a regional and national dimension. The first edition of the *Union List of Serials*, published in 1927, was an early effort to inventory the periodicals held in the nation's libraries; the Philadelphia Documentation Center started to develop a union catalogue of the works in all the research and academic libraries in its metropolitan area.[6]

The idea that library holdings and disparate collections were national intellectual assets grew during the Great Depression. It was a time of "archival awakening," said Solon Buck, the first Archivist of the United States. The National Archives became a separate agency in 1934 to centralize the record-keeping of the growing federal bureaucracy, and its classical-style building, which housed the Declaration of Independence and the Constitution, was completed in 1937. Although part of the legislative branch, the Library of Congress increasingly served as a national library and cultural institution, and Librarian Herbert Putnam aspired to make it a "bureau of information for the entire country." The federal government backed other efforts to document and preserve national heritage. The Historical Records Survey, one of the lesser known New Deal cultural projects, indexed the holdings of local archives and historical societies across the nation. From 1936 to 1942, it created over two thousand inventories and guides to obscure collections.

Like other WPA programs, it fostered an interest in local and regional history in the service of a distinctive cultural nationalism. The HRS would also provide important training for a new generation of librarians and archivists, including Luther Evans, Paul Vanderbilt, and Sargent Child, who would serve the Library of Congress and government and military agencies in the war years.[7]

The growing attention to records, documents, and collections began to center on the idea of *information*, an important yet ambiguous concept. In one sense of the word, information meant deployable knowledge that might be used for good or ill. The heavy-handed efforts of the Committee on Public Information, or Creel Committee, during World War I led many to think information was propaganda by another name. The rise of mass media at the same time—not only film and radio but also mass circulation newspapers, best-selling books, and advertising—reinforced these concerns. In the 1920s and 1930s, social scientists examined how mass communication media used information to sway public opinion (itself a new conception of the aggregation of citizens) and debated whether this would undermine liberal democracy or provide a positive means for leaders to build support for public goals. Even when not made explicit, these studies had underlying political concerns. In 1936, for example, Douglas Waples and Harold Lasswell—respectively, a sociological investigator of libraries and readers and a prominent political scientist of wartime propaganda—surveyed the foreign holdings of leading American and European research libraries; they believed that Americans' limited access to foreign works, and the information and ideas they contained, reflected and furthered a dangerous nationalism.[8]

Fascism's manipulation of mass media and spectacle and the threat of war provoked new research efforts. In 1939, the Rockefeller Foundation ran a secret seminar to study how to measure public opinion in the emergency and protect Americans from the threat of a fifth column. Communications scholars at Princeton, Columbia, and other universities investigated totalitarian propaganda and foreign broadcasts and considered methods to blunt their impact. Among these projects was the Experimental Division for the Study of Wartime Communications at the Library of Congress. As its director, Lasswell used systematic content analysis to examine radio broadcasts and the press, revealing the strategies used by German propagandists.[9]

Information had a narrower meaning in the world of libraries, best characterized by the term "documentation," an international movement to amass, classify, and circulate the world's knowledge. Although information science is often seen as a post–World War II development, its origins may be traced to the turn of the twentieth century, in the pioneering work of Belgians Paul Otlet and Henri La Fontaine, who founded the International Institute of Bibliography in 1895 (renamed the International Federation for Documentation in 1937). Although information overload seems a chronic human condition, the rapid growth of publications in the late nineteenth and early twentieth centuries produced new anxieties over retrieving and managing them. The advance of scientific and technical research, the expansion of corporate and governmental administration, and the internationalization of knowledge all contributed to the glut. The traditional approach of librarians to bibliography and cataloguing, which treated the book as the physical container of ideas and expression, would not solve the problem. "Documentalists" sought to disassemble that container and extract its content. Their aim was to create large databanks of information in each area of knowledge, through a network of union catalogues, indexes, and microfilm services. Building their collection after World War I, Otlet and La Fontaine called it the Palais Mondial or World Palace (later renamed the Mundaneum), which in ten years grew to fifteen million cards on thousands of topics. With less grandiose ambitions, so-called special libraries serving business, industry, scientific and technical research, and government embraced documentation in the 1920s and 1930s; professional associations, information centers, and exhibitions promoted the movement.[10]

By 1937, a World Congress of Universal Documentation was held in Paris, sponsored by the League of Nations, to consider "the methods and necessities of welding the intellectual resources of this planet into a unified system." Organizers believed that modern developments—from the growth of applied science and business information to global media and mass education—demanded techniques of universal documentation. Beyond the "traditional idea" of printed documents, newer modes of information sharing, such as "the film, the record, the sample and the model," would be crucial for research, education, and the economy. The "world brain," as writer H. G. Wells vividly described it, had a larger political purpose as well. In keeping with the internationalism of the interwar years, Otlet and Wells believed that intellectual cooperation would defeat the forces of nationalism, hatred, and violence. In a time of growing conflict and division, the world brain would advance world peace. The Congress attracted 460 attendees from 45 countries, including a delegation from the United States. After his electrifying speech at the World Congress, Wells promoted this idea on an American lecture tour.[11]

Americans largely ignored the visionary aspects of the European documentation movement, however. Instead, they were captivated by technology, specifically microfilm as a new medium of information storage and retrieval. Boosters touted the miracle of microfilm, the "amazing genii who transport to firesides, office desks and library tables the marvelous miniature images of the world's wisdom." Robert Binkley praised microfilm for enabling humanists and historians to study the contents of rare books and old manuscripts. Watson Davis, a civil engineer and pioneering science popularizer, believed it ensured the most rapid diffusion of current scientific research. Toward that end, Davis created the Bibliofilm Service to distribute agricultural, medical, and census reports from the government. He established the American Documentation Institute in 1937 and hyped the promise of microfilm at the World Congress later that year. The greatest enthusiast was entrepreneur Eugene B. Power, who founded University Microfilms International in 1938, today the information giant ProQuest. He was the first to see the commercial potential for microfilm to serve the research needs of universities, business, and government. Micropublishing—an "edition of one," as Power put it—would produce a niche market of scholars who needed to consult dissertations, sets of data, and specialized reports; it would also be a means of distributing facsimiles of rare books and unique manuscripts around the world.[12]

Microfilm proliferated in the late 1930s, with its promise to be the next big thing in technology. The Historical Records Survey adopted microfilm to reproduce its catalogues; foundations funded large microfilm projects; library schools offered microphotography courses; and a *Journal of Documentary Reproduction* began publication. Library leaders M. Llewellyn Raney and Herman Fussler traveled from the University of Chicago to Paris to demonstrate their microfilm technique, to the acclaim of the documentalist world. "In a few years," Raney predicted, "cameras will be as characteristic in libraries as typewriters." Eugene Power had already placed copy cameras in the Vatican and other European libraries and begun to microfilm the Short-Title Catalogue of early English books at the British Museum, Oxford, and Cambridge. For three months in the summer of 1939, he traveled through Europe hoping to convince librarians and documentalists of the importance of microfilm. He was crossing the Atlantic when Hitler invaded Poland and war was declared. His efforts "were for naught," Power mused. "There would be no easy exchange of scholarly knowledge now."[13] Still, many believed, microfilm was the ultimate answer to the problem of preservation and universal access.

––––––⌒∽––––––

The news from abroad deepened concern about this very problem. The destruction of books, manuscripts, and records punctuates the era, fostering a sense of culture's vulnerability. Few had foreseen the damage caused by aerial bombs and mechanized warfare in World War I. But it was the human-scale destruction of a single library in the earliest days of the war that became an enduring symbol of modern combat's threat to civilization. The University of Leuven in Belgium had been a center of learning for five centuries, renowned for promoting humanism and science. Its library, housed in a seventeenth-century building, was relatively small, but it contained a treasured collection of historic books, incunabula, and manuscripts. After the German army seized Leuven on August 25, 1914, soldiers set the library ablaze using gasoline and inflammable pellets and watched as it burned to the ground. This was not a case of inadvertent damage to civilian property but rather an intentional strike against culture.[14]

The ruin of the Leuven library touched Americans deeply, and an effort to rebuild it began even before the war was over. American architect Whitney Warren designed the new library, and a committee of university leaders, educators, businessmen, and diplomats campaigned for funds. The Carnegie Endowment and the Commission for Relief in Belgium, headed by Herbert Hoover, became major financial contributors, offering over one million dollars. A network of wealthy donors and philanthropic institutions led the effort, but small donations poured in from college students, alumni groups, school children, and individual citizens. Leaders of the campaign viewed the restoration as a symbol of American generosity and idealism, calling it an "American war memorial" to honor US fighting forces. The new library was covered with plaques citing American donors—"names without end all over the building"—and its rededication was intentionally scheduled for July 4, 1928.[15]

The Leuven library remained a potent and festering symbol of national aggression and alliances. Although Americans made the largest contribution to the rebuilding, donations came from France and many other countries. Nor was the rebuilding entirely voluntary: Article 247 of the Treaty of Versailles required Germany to make cultural reparations, transferring rare books and manuscripts from its own collections to the destroyed Belgian library. A controversial incident before the rededication suggests how deeply tensions ran. Warren had planned to place a Latin inscription on a balustrade, "destroyed by Teutonic fury, restored by an American gift," but was blocked by university officials. Fearing the statement would inflame animosity between nations, they replaced the balustrade, which in turn sparked protests from not only Warren but also Belgian students and local citizens, who destroyed the new railings as construction workers looked on approvingly. The officials may have won the battle, but not without another skirmish. At the dedication ceremony, an airplane flew overhead, dropping leaflets with the saying on the gathered dignitaries.[16]

The burning of books in Nazi Germany further underscored the threat to culture. For many Americans, this revealed the true face of the Third Reich. Soon after Hitler's ascension to power, university students staged ceremonial bonfires in May 1933, destroying thousands of books deemed "un-German" because they were written by Jews, Communists, and other enemies of National Socialism. Outraged Americans organized demonstrations in many cities, with over 170,000 protesters marching in Philadelphia, Chicago, and New York City combined. In New York, war veterans, students, Zionist organizations, labor unionists, and city officials paraded from Madison Square to the Battery. The *New York Times* counted "scores of rabbis in long, black robes, bearded denizens of the East Side, dapper young men and women, professional men, and representatives of the literary, artistic, and theatrical worlds." Some marchers held placards, including one featuring "stacks of books [and] a female figure representing Culture and bearing the inscription 'Imperishable.'"[17]

The protesters were, in many ways, ahead of the press in exposing the larger cultural and political danger book burning presented. Although newsmagazines and daily papers condemned the "bibliocaust," as *Time* called it, they often reported the events as mere childishness, a mental instability, or a fever that would pass. American library journals at the time did not even comment. Journalist and writer Walter Lippman was unusual in calling the bonfires a deliberate strategy, "not the work of schoolboys or mobs but of the present German Government." It would take some years for Americans to understand German-Jewish writer Joseph Roth's despairing observation in 1933 that "the European mind is capitulating." Yet the Nazi book burnings took hold in the imagination and fueled antifascist sentiment. Protests occurred intermittently through the 1930s, especially in New York. There, an American Library of Nazi Banned Books opened in Brooklyn, Columbia University students burned orange crates and phone directories in a denunciation of Hitler, and the New School for Social Research displayed books salvaged from the fires.[18]

In the early years of the war, news of cultural destruction and damage to libraries trickled out of Europe. The Leuven library was fated to be a bellwether of cultural atrocity: it had taken fourteen years to rebuild, stood in peace for twelve more, then was destroyed again by the German army in May 1940. The press and radio covered this story, but more evidence came in personal and professional correspondence, through encounters with refugees, and from statements by governments in exile. During the Blitz, British librarians and museum staff wrote their American friends and colleagues, assessing damage to their collections and suggesting precautions. Although many rare books and manuscripts had been sent to safe havens away from urban centers, the destruction of books—in university collections and public libraries—was substantial. "From library after library come dark reports of premises ruined and collections destroyed," stated one article. Incendiary bombs wrecked large portions of the libraries at the British Museum, University of London, King's College, and the Guildhall. An air raid destroyed seventy-five thousand books in the Plymouth public library, including many first editions and irreplaceable works. A librarian in Richmond reported damage with the comment, "to a book-lover, it is heart breaking to see so many books in such a sorry plight, soaked with water or charred by fire." Even the Royal Air Force's bombing of Berlin, which damaged the Prussian State Library on April 10, 1941, did "not create any elation in the minds of any British librarian." Eyewitness reports and photographs underscored both the challenges British librarians faced and their courage.[19]

The onset of the war also choked the international book trade. Naval and economic warfare led Germany to stop direct shipping to the United States, even as Great Britain placed an embargo on German goods. European books and periodicals, including German imprints, continued to reach America, shipped via neutral ports and vessels, but the trade was increasingly slow and unpredictable. The loss of German publications was most acute, as it comprised the bulk of $1.6 million spent on foreign publications in the United States. Librarians strained to find new ways to acquire works from abroad. A Joint Committee on Importations, composed of librarians from several leading research universities and the New York Public Library, formed in October 1939 to address the problem. They were beset with rumors and little reliable information, especially about the degree to which Britain would enforce its embargo. During World War I, American librarians had developed lists of periodicals exempt from seizure, a procedure many found time-consuming and humiliating. They wanted no repeat of that experience. "Under no circumstances should we knuckle to the British," swore Thomas Fleming, a librarian at Columbia University and head of the committee. "Nothing must interfere" with the "continuity of our file of periodicals," New York Public Library director Harry M. Lydenberg insisted to MacLeish in a moment devoid of perspective.[20]

There were larger principles at stake, of course. Americans had a right to read and debate what they read, even German propaganda, the American Library Association asserted; educated citizens could discern truth from lies. "Any interference with free cultural intercourse is harmful, causing injuries which may be irreparable," the ALA wrote Secretary of State Cordell

Hull. As Lydenberg told MacLeish, the government needed only to take a "sane and healthy attitude . . . toward the printed word and the messages it carries."[21] For the British, however, the issue was less the power of propaganda than the need to deny dollars to the enemy. Over the next year, American officials negotiated with their British counterparts to have an inspection point in Bermuda where crates could be opened and publications examined before being forwarded to the United States.

European booksellers continued to ship from ports in Italy and the Netherlands into the spring of 1940, but their wares were increasingly held up. One Italian ship, the *Rex*, sailed from Genoa but was stopped at Gibraltar, where British officials removed two hundred packages of publications bound for American colleges and libraries. By June, with much of Europe under German occupation and Italy declaring war, transatlantic shipping had largely ceased. A route through Siberia was nearly the only channel left to G. E. Stechert, one of the leading foreign book dealers. The problems of importation were "infinitely worse" than in World War I, its New York agent sadly reported. One member of the Joint Committee on Importations rushed to Italy to see about storing consignments of books at the American Academy in Rome and with publisher and exporter Otto Harrassowitz. Yet Harrassowitz turned out to be a controversial choice, because the firm was in Leipzig, the center of the German book trade and a likely bombing target. The entire situation was fraught with uncertainty and confusion, and the committee could only advise libraries to ask German publishers and European agents to stockpile their works in a safe place for the duration of the war.[22] It would be many years before the regular book trade was restored, and during the war and its immediate aftermath, other means of acquisition—largely sponsored by the government—would come to the fore.

By the end of the decade, the crisis in Europe had become a constant presence for many Americans in politics, academia, and cultural institutions. When Germany occupied Czechoslovakia in spring 1939, "as we watched what appeared to be the dissolution of the West," recalled historian Arthur Schlesinger Jr., "we began to understand that this was probably the last time for a considerable period that we could expect to live our own lives." A year later, after Norway and Denmark had fallen, Harry Lydenberg wrote his friend MacLeish, "These last few days make one wonder whether there is anything worth talking about in the way of routine." *So Little Time* was the title John P. Marquand gave his novel about this period of anxious waiting and preparing for an uncertain future. "You could get away from the war for a little while, but not for long, because it was everywhere," a character observed. "It lay behind everything you said or did."[23]

Newly installed as Librarian of Congress in October 1939, MacLeish pondered the news from abroad with the mounting sense that time was running out, as he put it, "not like the sand in a glass, but like the blood in an opened artery." That month, in a speech at the Carnegie Institute in Pittsburgh, he spoke out on the importance of libraries in the contemporary crisis. "We will need to educate people to embrace democratic culture," he told the gathering, "or they will have the 'nonculture,' the obscurantism, the superstition, the brutality, the tyranny" of fascism. The next year, he made a controversial attack on the interwar generation of scholars and writers for their intellectual isolationism. The "irresponsibles," he called them: those who refused to see book burning and the exile of intellectuals as an effort to destroy "the common culture of the West."[24]

In June 1940, writing as the German armies were conquering Western Europe, MacLeish once again considered the role of the librarian, first by contemplating the nature of books. A book exists in two ways, he observed, the physical object "made of certain physical materials in a physical shape," and the "intellectual object made of all materials or of no materials and standing in as many shapes as there are forms and balances and structures in men's minds." If the book is only its material manifestation, then the librarian could simply be a custodian, "a sort of check boy in the parcel room of culture." Perhaps that was once acceptable, but no longer, as "the changes of the time change everything." In Germany, Spain, Russia, and, sadly, in the United States, war was being waged against books as the "records of the human spirit," the physical form of ideas and culture. Librarians must become their advocates and defenders, MacLeish declared; they were now "the counsel for the situation," whose "client is the inherited culture entrusted to [their] care." "The keeping of these records is itself a kind of warfare," he observed. "The keepers, whether they wish so or not, cannot be neutral."[25]

Before the Japanese attack on Pearl Harbor, interventionists and isolationists fiercely debated US involvement in another world war. Librarians were as divided as other Americans. Most supported the Allies but hesitated to see the country enter the war. By September 1940, the American Library Association was encouraging a role for libraries in the national defense. Public libraries began to create information centers and offer programs about defense work and international relations; many started book drives for soldiers, refugees, and prisoners of war. The Library of Congress and New York Public Library, among others, drew up plans to safeguard their most treasured collections and, in the event of war, move them to places deemed safe from air raids. Librarians had long been concerned that their patrons read only to escape into illusory worlds; now they saw an opportunity to lead citizens to engage with serious matters. The ALA's commitment to national defense did not go unopposed. The Progressive Librarians Council warned that growing war hysteria was a danger to democracy. As in World War I, librarians could find themselves the instrument of a war machine, "handing over the tools of culture to forces which are preparing for the destruction of culture," as Walter Rothman, the Hebrew Union College librarian, put it. Perhaps in response, the ALA issued a policy at the end of 1940 that underscored "the essential internationalism of intellectual materials" and called on librarians "to advocate continuing and expanding our cultural relations with all nations in spite of difficulties."[26]

Members of the nation's intellectual and cultural elite—scholars, museum and library directors, and curators—sounded the alarm about the status of cultural objects in the European war. The destruction that had already occurred left few confident that the combatants would observe the principles of protection set out in The Hague Conventions of 1899 and 1907. American cultural leaders began to push for a government policy to shield museums, churches, historic sites, and libraries from destruction by air and ground forces. Their efforts ultimately led Roosevelt to appoint the American Commission for the Protection and Salvage of Artistic and Historic Monuments in War Areas in 1943, headed by Supreme Court Justice Owen J. Roberts, and to the establishment of an army unit known as Monuments, Fine Arts, and Archives, which would carry out a ground-breaking policy of cultural preservation and restitution. Cultural leaders claimed a special role for the United States as rescuer of the European heritage that underpinned the American practice of democratic and humane ideals. This may have been a fabricated past, in which castles and cathedrals heralded Roosevelt's Four Freedoms. But it was compelling nonetheless, as General Dwight D. Eisenhower made clear in the Italian campaign that year when he called upon soldiers to respect the monuments "which by their creation helped and now in their old age illustrate the growth of the civilization which is ours."[27]

Before this program was underway, librarians and scholars had already begun to consider how to preserve European books, manuscripts, and print collections. Robert Binkley's Joint Committee on Materials articulated the urgency—and opportunity—as Europe descended into war. In late 1939, Binkley predicted that "responsibility for the maintenance of the whole tradition of Western culture" would shift to the United States, where libraries would be "keyed to a wholly new and expanded program for American scholarship." Five months later, with the German occupation of Paris imminent, the American Council of Learned Societies held an urgent conference to fix upon a plan "for preserving the records of civilization." Leading figures of American librarianship attended, including Archibald MacLeish, Harry Lydenberg, and Harvard Library director Keyes Metcalf. Also present were experts in microfilm technology and documentation: Paul Vanderbilt and Sargent Child from the Historical Records Survey, and microfilm specialists Watson Davis, Eugene Power, and Ralph Carruthers of the New York Public Library. They believed this was a fateful moment when the nation would take up an unprecedented role: "American scholarship must prepare itself, and is even destined to assume a position of world leadership and must therefore have command of the world sources of scholarship." Such confident assertions built upon the experiences of the preceding decade—librarians' greater involvement with the state, an expanding international reach, and a faith in technology.[28]

The group proposed "a microphotographic expeditionary force" to invade Europe and reproduce every book and manuscript available on the continent. Dissenters scorned the idea as "simply fantastic," a quest for "an impossible completeness." In any case, events outran their ability to turn talk into action, as access to many European countries ceased. Nevertheless, a more achievable objective found support: microfilming materials in the British Museum, Public Records Office, and other British repositories. Eugene Power, who had already paved the way, developed this program with Rockefeller funding. By January 1941, six camera operators were rapidly copying books and manuscripts in a bomb-proof location, and by 1944 they had shot five million frames of microfilm.[29]

The meeting also spurred an early recognition of the need for library cooperation. Studies had shown that the nation's research libraries were uneven and selective in their foreign holdings, depending on institutional needs and scholars' own efforts to build collections. The Library of Congress, "the center of the whole library economy of the nation," would have to lead the way forward, finding a way to distribute and share international resources across the country. "Rugged individualism is as obsolete in the cultural world as it is in the political," Princeton library director Julian Boyd observed. In response, MacLeish established an Experimental Division of Library Cooperation in June 1941 and proposed an array of cooperative microfilm projects, bibliographies, storage, and purchasing arrangements for the war emergency. The idea was controversial, with some Midwestern universities in particular fearing governmental control over library affairs.[30] As foreign materials became increasingly important and scarce, however, these initial efforts would blossom into a robust postwar program of cooperative acquisitions.

⎯⎯⎯ ↢ ⎯⎯⎯

The global conflict spurred American librarians' last-ditch efforts to acquire unusual and threatened materials. They were especially interested in items about the war itself. Many started programs to gather those records, believing them useful for defense mobilization and necessary for future generations. This was the thinking behind the War Documentation Service, created by a consortium of Philadelphia scholars and librarians, to "collect, organize, and make available sources of information regarding the current war." Yale University mounted a special project to acquire not only official reports and government documents but also ephemeral items such as propaganda leaflets, war posters, photographs, radio broadcasts, maps, letters, and diaries. The library wrote alumni, faculty, and American embassies around the world requesting their help. "If it's on paper and if it's about the war send it to the Yale Library," urged historian Sherman Kent, who oversaw the collection. The war coincided with new approaches in historical studies; historians had long recognized the importance of politics and the state, but now they were also interested in the records of everyday life. "How important these apparently trivial things are, and how vital they are to the historian of this war," Kent exclaimed. Initially absorbed by the "business of collecting fragmentary and ephemeral bits of information," he soon joined the OSS and turned his talents to intelligence work.[31]

No institution was more single-minded in acquiring these materials than the Hoover War Library. Herbert Hoover began his war collection when he organized humanitarian relief for European victims of World War I. With long-standing interests in history and collecting, he saw firsthand how ephemeral such records were in devastated nations, where survival overrode most other concerns. Hoover, a Quaker, believed these materials must be preserved if humanity were to understand what led nations to collective violence and war. In 1919 he donated $50,000 to Stanford University, his alma mater, to establish the Hoover War Collection, renamed the Hoover War Library in 1922. Through the interwar years, the library expanded its mission to cover twentieth-century political movements and international affairs. To collect these materials, the Library relied not only on American scholars traveling abroad but also a network of international relief workers and government officials. They had worked with Hoover during and after the Great War and were devoted to the man they called the Chief. "A great many important and valuable materials have come from this cooperation," the Hoover Library director observed.[32]

In 1939, with war threatening, the library scrambled to obtain such records by sending its co-director, German historian Ralph H. Lutz, on a harrowing trip through Europe. Lutz was a longtime associate of Herbert Hoover: as a young officer in World War I, he had been ordered by General John J. Pershing on a special assignment to Paris, where he became a member of Hoover's team of document hunters in 1919. In subsequent years, Lutz made four collecting trips to Europe and built close relationships with a host of academics, book dealers, and organizations in Germany and elsewhere. At age fifty-seven, the scholar returned, hoping to purchase materials and arrange to have them collected and stored until they could be safely shipped.

Lutz received a warm welcome on his arrival in Germany that June. Six months earlier Hitler had awarded him a merit cross of the Order of the German Eagle, one of two Americans to receive this dubious honor in 1938. Officials of the Propaganda Ministry, the Nazi Party Chancellery, and the state libraries pledged their cooperation. Excitedly, Lutz reported an opportunity to buy selections from a major economics library, and he agreed to pay $3000 for them to be held until peace came. It was "our last chance to fill gaps in our German collection," he wrote, "with these materials we will be supreme in the German field." At this time, his political sympathies lay with Germany. He sprinkled his diary with favorable comments about German press coverage and a Goebbels' speech, and reassured German colleagues that the United States would not intervene in a second European war. Although he intended to return to Stanford at the end of the summer, his plans changed abruptly when Germany invaded Poland. Hoover instructed Lutz to stay and organize a network of collecting agents throughout Europe before coming home.[33]

The trip suddenly became a dangerous undertaking. Catching the last passenger train from Munich, Lutz sped to Brussels and Amsterdam. There he tried without success to gain possession of the International Institute of Social History's labor and socialist archives. Lutz returned briefly to Berlin, and then crossed from Germany into Denmark, encountering rough waters and the threat of floating mines on the Baltic Sea. In Copenhagen he visited an archive so well organized that "I could visualize our successors coming over here in the 21st century and filming the confidential documents of this year." He spent an anxious week in Oslo, where the Grand Hotel "seemed to contain at least a dozen belligerent agents," and he received "a number of mysterious house calls purporting to come from Norwegian Professors." Aware of surveillance everywhere, he wrote his father, "If I am able to complete this trip every foreign office in Europe will have a dossier on myself and the [Hoover] Library." While in Oslo, Lutz went to the American embassy for help entering the Soviet Union and Eastern Europe. Consul General Hallett Johnson initially refused, calling it a foolhardy mission, but eventually gave Lutz calling cards introducing him to the Romanian and Hungarian ministries. His next stop was Helsinki, where he arrived the day after many civilians had fled the desolate city, schools had closed, and the university library's treasures had been evacuated.[34]

Lutz pushed on to Leningrad and Moscow, where he toured museums and an agricultural exhibition. He met with Soviet scholars and library officials, promised exchanges with the Hoover Library, and gained pledges from them to send Russian materials. He also sought out Germans living in the USSR for their assistance, including Werner von Tippelskirch, a diplomat at the German embassy and, Lutz remarked in his diary, a "great collector of confidential materials." Tippelskirch greeted him coolly, like "a master of a college fraternity when he learns that one of the brothers has told the password to a stranger," and sent him to his son Walter for military publications.[35]

Riding in a four-berth compartment in a train to Kiev, Lutz found himself bombarded with questions from "real Bolsheviks," Red Army officers, and the secret police. "I was questioned in four languages from the time the train left until 1:30 a.m. and then for hours the next day," he reported. At a meeting with the president and faculty of Kiev University, the grilling went both ways. "We wore out two interpreters," Lutz exclaimed. The Russians wanted to know about US neutrality and American attitudes. One professor requested a copy of Mark Twain's published notebooks, and others asked Lutz to explain his philosophy of history and why he was not a Communist. The exhausting conversations were worth it, for they yielded promises of cooperative exchange and arrangements to put aside materials until the war was over. Lutz's journey continued through Belgrade, Geneva, Paris, Madrid, and many other cities, finally concluding in Rome after six months abroad. He considered collecting a "young man's game," yet the middle-aged professor hustled all over a continent in anguish, convincing scholars, business leaders, and government officials to preserve their records for a library in distant California. He made commitments totaling $70,000 to various agents and dealers during the trip.[36]

That he received any attention at all speaks, perhaps, to a yearning to preserve history, culture, and national identity at a time of great turmoil and uncertainty. His visits may also have rung a note of connection to America, a memory from the last Great War. Yet the American professor was also an object of suspicion when he suddenly turned up at universities and ministries bent on his collecting mission. He feared for his safety as he made border crossings into the Soviet Union, fascist Spain, and elsewhere.

"I ran into all the Secret Services of the belligerents" except the British, he recalled. "I was arrested and searched and treated rough by a great many on all sides." He finally returned home in December 1939.[37]

Another American found herself ineluctably drawn into a collecting mission made urgent by the war. American-born Maria Josepha Meyer—Miss José Meyer, as she was known—had worked on and off at the Library of Congress as a cataloguer when in 1934 she decided to move to Paris. Employed by the publisher Hachette, she also served as the library's part-time European representative. She pursued international exchanges, purchased unusual works, developed microfilm projects, and attended the World Congress of Universal Documentation in 1937. In the summer of 1939, she returned briefly to Washington and asked what she should do in case of war, only to be told that "there would be no war." That assurance quickly proved wrong. Back in Paris, Meyer received a new assignment, to collect official publications, propaganda, maps, music and other documents of the war, no easy matter as France imposed restrictions and suspicion toward foreigners grew. In June 1940, as the German army advanced on Paris, Meyer found she could not leave the city. She had no money, her passport had expired, and she had many possessions—over a dozen cases of books, five trunks, and furniture—that she was loath to leave behind. With the French ministries departed, stores boarded up, and citizens fleeing, "an uncanny silence has descended on an almost deserted city," she anxiously wrote MacLeish. "There is nothing left now but to stick it out." She felt herself cut off and worried she could no longer be useful. The occupation caused constraints on movement, innumerable bureaucratic problems, and a state of fear. The Germans "consistently foment confusion, spread false news, stir up discontent and foster racial, class and political hatred among Frenchmen," she wrote. "The outlook is very dark indeed."[38]

Yet the petite forty-five-year-old American quietly outmaneuvered German authorities to collect materials for the library. Meyer went to small booksellers in remote areas to purchase anti-German and other prohibited works that had been confiscated from the larger bookstores. It was important that "someone on the spot collect diligently and speedily," she observed, before the Gestapo visited the shops to confiscate and destroy such material. In addition to books and newspapers, she acquired German White Books, a map of occupied territory, French resistance literature, and Italian anti-fascist propaganda. She sent the most controversial materials by diplomatic pouch—including resistance handbills and photographs she had taken when the Germans marched into Paris. She stored everything else in Bordeaux, dreading it would be discovered.[39]

Despite the danger, she decided to investigate the impact of the occupation on publishers, booksellers, and libraries, and wrote what were, in essence, intelligence reports on the Nazis' systematic attack on French book culture. She described how Gestapo agents, early in the occupation, had raided all the bookstores and publishing houses. Accompanied by French police, they ordered the owners to collect the prohibited books on the so-called *Liste Bernhard* and hand them over in half an hour. Although the book dealers were not allowed to retain the list, Meyer managed to get a copy from a gendarme she knew, at great risk to them both. He let her keep it overnight, and she had it copied and sent to the Library of Congress by diplomatic pouch. Later, she wrote, "Germans began to ban books more systematically on the basis of publishers' catalogues," and they issued a new list, *Liste Otto*. Principals withdrew schoolbooks, and public libraries purged banned books.[40]

Meyer expressed particular outrage at the activities of book agent Karl Frank, the Harrassowitz representative in Paris. The Library of Congress had used his services for years. Meyer had tried to warn them but did not think it safe to say all she knew about a man she termed the "official Nazi 'Fuehrer' of the French booktrade." His Harrassowitz job had been a cover for spying on book dealers and publishers, especially Jews and German émigrés, she charged. He had prepared the way for the Gestapo raids: "In the first days of the German occupation, before it would have been materially possible to list all the bookshops, the Gestapo agents proceeded in their search and raids with detailed lists containing the fullest and most confidential information on each firm." By October he was managing a "clearing-house for the Franco-German booktrade in Paris," ensuring that "libraries and bookshops [were] flooded with German book catalogs and announcements." She feared he had taken over the Maison du Livre Français, a leading French book exporting agency, and warned American librarians and booksellers that "behind the familiar catalogues, circulars and letterheads, a most odious form of Nazi exploitation operates in the dark."[41]

She gave detailed reports on the organized looting of bookstores, archives and other institutions. The Germans had raided Jewish firms, she told MacLeish, including the Librarie Lipschutz, where "several truckloads of valuable books and autographs were carted away and now the seals are on the doors." Everything in the English bookstore W. H. Smith had been removed, down to the silverware and china in its tearoom, and it had become a "Frontbuchhandlung" or bookstore for German soldiers. Meyer suspected that the Gestapo was preparing the Bibliothèque Nationale for pillage, with the new director Bernard Fay "currying favor with the

German authorities." The reading rooms were "thronged every day with German 'readers,' both in uniform and dressed as civilians, who seem to be Gestapo." She tried to persuade library officials to let her take a set of publications of the French Ministry of Information, but they "feared that the German 'protectors' of the Bibliothèque Nationale would not allow such voluminous material to leave the building."[42] Along with her reports on libraries and the book trade, she transcribed other documents to give Washington a feeling for life under the occupation: a leaflet dropped by British aircraft over occupied France, an open letter from French Catholics to Marshal Pétain, a German circular to booksellers and librarians, a letter from a French journalist about prohibited books, and many more.

MacLeish was moved by this "devoted and extremely energetic representative" and stunned by her reports of the cultural occupation of Paris. He found them so significant—"it goes so near to the heart of the central issue" of the Nazi menace—that he forwarded them to President Roosevelt, with the comment that he had not seen any coverage of the specific threat to books. Indeed, the first general newspaper account in the United States appeared about two weeks later. Meanwhile, Meyer's situation had become increasingly precarious, and she decided to leave Paris in December 1940. The Germans gave her an export permit to take her professional library and personal effects, including her furniture; at the last minute she switched the furniture with the war collection she would have been forbidden to ship. She went on to Lisbon, waited to receive the freight, then booked passage home, arriving in New York in mid-January 1941.[43] MacLeish must have wondered what the United States could accomplish with a band of such librarians.

--------◦◦◦◦--------

Thus, when MacLeish and Donovan began meeting, the ground had been prepared for a new effort to acquire and exploit open-source materials relevant to national security and international affairs. Even as the Coordinator of Information began to imagine far-flung espionage operations, he started with the information sources and research specialists at hand. Donovan recruited academics and experts to the Research and Analysis Branch (R&A) in the summer and autumn of 1941, drawing upon personal networks in Ivy League universities and the government. Those who joined recalled the early days, prior to the American entrance into the war, as a "special time of earnestness and friendliness and comradeship." They started from scratch, ignorant about the enemy, "trying to figure out what it was all about," as Harvard historian William Langer related. Sherman Kent described the R&A beginnings as a "scramble for knowledge," a "mad rush for an enormous amount of factual detail," in order to produce numerous reports that at their best provided useful and broad strategic insight, if not operational information. Whether the beehive of research contributed to winning the war remains an open question. But this pioneering intellectual work—organizing area studies and embracing interdisciplinary approaches—would have an enduring impact on academic scholarship and its connections to national security.[44]

Librarians too felt the impact of the new demands for intelligence. Working with Donovan, MacLeish established the Division of Special Information (DSI), a research unit with a "compiling, editing, synthesizing, and analyzing function," more "bookish" than other war agencies. Pondering how information could best serve the US government, MacLeish had come to believe that libraries had a crucial role "in buttressing spot intelligence with the scholarly element." Only in this way would immediate and irregular information acquire the "necessary depth and weight" to render it meaningful. DSI would root out information wherever it could be found and make it accessible, through reference files, indices, and bibliographies. Its staff would transcribe foreign broadcasts, clip newspapers, hunt for fugitive materials, and scour library shelves. A centralized databank would offer the intelligence agency "not only the relevant, immediately confidential information, but also the wealth of background resulting from a lifetime of study and from access to the accumulated wisdom of other scholars."[45]

MacLeish envisioned the Division of Special Information as a "reserve corps of American intellectuals to support the front-line troops of the Donovan organization." Indeed, its sole client was the Coordinator of Information, and the line between the DSI and R&A quickly blurred, more so because the two groups worked in close proximity in the new Annex Building of the Library of Congress. DSI's administrative head was Ernest Griffith, who directed the Legislative Research Service, a core unit of the Library serving the Congress; William Langer was its research director and soon became R&A chief. Over forty experts joined the DSI by the end of September 1941.[46]

The new intelligence operation generated an immediate problem for librarians to solve: how to organize this storehouse of information and make large quantities of secret material in disparate formats accessible. MacLeish considered traditional cataloguing methods inadequate for this task and wanted a new approach. Yet he did not turn immediately in the logical direction, to a specialist in the documentation movement. Typical of the early build-up of the OSS, "old boy" friendships and judgments often dictated decisions about whom to recruit. During a get-together at his Conway farm, MacLeish told his friend and fellow Yale alumnus Wilmarth

"Lefty" Lewis about his hunt for an expert with imagination and technical library skills. On his drive home, Lewis decided to volunteer for the job. "I gather it is primarily one of cataloguing and filing the material so that it will be immediately accessible to the men who are to use it," he wrote MacLeish. "This is what, to compare small things with great, I have done with my MSS here." Lewis was a wily, voracious collector of everything related to Horace Walpole, the eighteenth-century man of letters, and had turned his home in Farmington, Connecticut, into a singular library of Walpoliana. Drawing upon current business methods, Lewis had devised a complex system of arranging, indexing, and cross-referencing manuscripts and other material not covered by the conventional rules of cataloguing. MacLeish quickly accepted his offer. Lewis chose as his deputy Jesse Shera, a graduate student in library science and information specialist supervising the Census Library Project at the Commerce Department. Together Lewis and Shera created a legendary filing and retrieval system, the Central Information Division of the OSS.[47]

Solving the problem of information management still left the stubborn challenge of acquiring relevant information sources to help win the war. Government agencies and research libraries searched their shelves for books, periodicals, and maps. Even ordinary citizens were asked to mail in photographs and postcards of European cities and coastal scenes that might prove useful to mapmakers. The material poured in, but much of it was uninformative. The collapse of international shipping and high cost of airmail made obtaining timely newspapers, scientific journals, and technical reports from abroad difficult. The Division of Special Information asked traveling scholars to pick up materials and approached foreign legations in Washington for news. They helped when they could. The Norwegian minister, for example, offered to share a long cable he received each day, full of material that "comes out of Norway to Stockholm secretly." In many places, however, no such information was getting out, and the scattershot approach quickly proved useless.[48]

To tackle the problem of foreign acquisition, MacLeish formed a Committee on Materials, to which he appointed Harold Lasswell and William Langer. Its initial approach, before the United States entered the war, reflected the mix of interests within the COI, including domestic security against a fifth column. Opposed to outright censorship, the Committee on Materials nonetheless pressed for measures to counter German propaganda, fearing the potential abuse of the postal service, as well as the use of feature films, newsreels, and even microphotographs to foment fascist sentiments among the American people. It proposed a network of investigators and reading units—"readers of the better-than-average intelligence, education, and imagination"—to scrutinize incoming publications and their recipients. There could be "no objection to the collection by bona fide university libraries of literature of every character," the committee made clear, but a library might be a cover for a subversive propaganda center, and a professor in fact a Nazi proselytizer. These proposals gained little support, because the Federal Bureau of Investigation, Post Office Department, and US Customs Service were already engaged in such work.[49]

The Committee on Materials was also intent on acquiring foreign publications. They discussed preparing press clippings from foreign correspondents and flying "super urgent items" to Washington, but increasingly the focus was on finding ways that the Library of Congress and COI could purchase materials abroad, in Lisbon, Stockholm, "and other places which still provide some freedom of operation." At one meeting with a group of scholars, historian David Rowe explained his plan to go to China for six months to carry out his own research, microfilming newspapers, periodicals, pamphlets, and posters. Inspired by Rowe, the committee thought "this same method of gathering current material could be adapted to our purposes." They initially thought the job could be done with one agent in Europe and one or two to cover Free China.[50]

The attack on Pearl Harbor changed everything, injecting new urgency into the gathering of intelligence. On December 22, 1941, Donovan formally proposed that Roosevelt establish a committee whose purpose would be to acquire foreign newspapers and periodicals for American war agencies. Already a surge in demand for such open-source information had led to "great duplication and great confusion," he noted. The committee would be a clearinghouse for all the war agencies, fielding their requests, and filling them through a network of agents in neutral European cities and elsewhere. The agents would order subscriptions, visit bookstores and newsstands, and when necessary, use secret channels. Microfilm would enable them to reduce the bulk and weight of the works they accumulated, making them easier to transport by diplomatic pouch or in assigned air cargo space. Donovan was emphatic: "The need is urgent in order that we may place our microfilm men abroad."[51] Roosevelt agreed, issuing an executive order that day establishing the Interdepartmental Committee for the Acquisition of Foreign Publications. A motley force of librarians, scholars, microfilm specialists, and collectors would soon be put to the test.

CHAPTER 2

crso

Librarians and Collectors Go to War

No one had a well-defined plan to send microfilm specialists to war when Franklin Roosevelt agreed to William Donovan's urgent request. The Interdepartmental Committee for the Acquisition of Foreign Publications (IDC) was quickly established, but initially struggled to gain traction. Indeed, in its first four months, the new agency failed to obtain a single enemy publication. "Storms were raging about our heads," the committee's executive secretary Frederick G. Kilgour sheepishly observed.[1] Yet over the course of the war, the IDC developed an extensive operation to provide printed sources for intelligence purposes. As bookmen and women became intelligence agents, the ordinary activities of librarianship—acquisition, cataloguing, and reproduction—became fraught with mystery, uncertainty, and even danger.

The IDC was an odd bureaucratic hybrid, seemingly independent and serving a dozen war agencies but understood as an offshoot of the Research and Analysis Branch of the OSS. R&A's chief, Harvard historian William Langer, raided his own institution for scholars and specialists. To head the IDC, he found the twenty-eight-year-old Kilgour in Harvard's Widener Library. After graduating from the university in 1935, Kilgour gave up plans to attend medical school in order to support his mother and grandparents in the Depression, and he took a position as assistant to the library's director. He attended a summer program in library science at Columbia University, through which he met a number of up-and-coming men in the library field. His administrative experience, strong interest in science and technology, and work directing a Harvard project to microfilm foreign newspapers surely attracted Langer.[2]

Kilgour was well suited to lead the wartime acquisition program, yet the start-up proved difficult. Jurisdictional disputes between government agencies over who should control the IDC threatened to derail the fledgling organization. The OSS asserted that IDC's mission—to acquire publications strictly for intelligence purposes—fell within its ambit. The Library of Congress thought IDC's role should extend beyond intelligence to include international acquisitions for its own collections. The State Department, whose legations had long reported on the foreign press, bristled at the OSS encroaching on its affairs. A heated argument broke out in a two-hour meeting of the committee, in which "the main thought in everybody's mind was to grab hold of both the committee's personnel and equipment." The OSS fended off these efforts. Serving numerous wartime agencies, the IDC remained under the command of the Research and Analysis Branch, although tangled lines of authority persisted through the war years.[3]

The IDC faced other challenges. It had to find serviceable microfilm cameras, acquire scarce rolls of celluloid film, and train camera operators. Few people had experience with microphotography before the war. Langer and Kilgour turned to microfilm entrepreneur Eugene Power as an unofficial agent, despite misgivings about his commercial enterprises. Power prepared basic microfilm instructions for the operation abroad, emphasizing the need for uniform and precise procedures, as well as a willingness to experiment when something went wrong, which it often did.[4] The need for security clearances, instruction in intelligence techniques, and visas for foreign travel slowed efforts to send agents overseas.

The most promising path initially was to create a liaison between the OSS and its British counterparts. The British Foreign Office, His Majesty's Stationery Office, and the Ministry of Information (MOI) had well-established methods of collecting foreign newspapers and periodicals for intelligence analysis and propaganda purposes. They agreed to share cabled digests of the European press with the Americans and to cooperate on an Allied microfilm operation led by a private group, the Association of Special Libraries and Information Bureaux (ASLIB). ASLIB had begun an Enemy Periodicals Project in May 1941, funded by the Rockefeller Foundation, to microfilm current scientific and technical periodicals. Now, with US government backing, they expanded this activity to serve British and US intelligence agencies. In April 1942, Power went to London to help get the operation under way, working with ASLIB's Lucia Moholy to set up a studio, which was ultimately housed in the Victoria and Albert Museum. The Foreign Office and Ministry of Information delivered the publications, and camera operators, mainly women, had twenty-four hours to photograph them. At the end of the month, much to everyone's relief, the first 2,100 feet of microfilm arrived in Washington.[5] By late spring 1942, plans were set in motion to send microfilm men—and one woman—to Stockholm, Lisbon, and other neutral cities.

------ ᔕᕉ ------

Adele Kibre was the first of the overseas agents and arguably the most successful. Born in Philadelphia in 1898, Kibre grew up in Los Angeles in a multitalented family. Her mother and stepfather were well-known Hollywood set designers, and among her siblings, Jeff Kibre became a radical labor organizer, Celia married a silent film star and hosted a popular radio show, and Pearl became an eminent historian of the Middle Ages. Although she mixed with the Hollywood set, Adele Kibre's life lay in the world of scholarship. She received her bachelor's and master's degrees from the University of California at Berkeley and taught Latin there. She identified with Roman women who "were clever enough to attract clever men," not modern flappers, who "seem at times to abuse their heads, not use them." She went on to the University of Chicago, where she received a PhD in 1930, writing a dissertation on medieval linguistics. Although talented enough to win a postdoctoral fellowship to the American Academy of Rome, like many women scholars of her time she was unable to pursue an academic career.[6]

Instead, Kibre spent much of the 1930s living in Italy and traveling throughout Europe, doing her own research and making a living by photographing rare manuscripts for two professors at the University of Chicago. At the Vatican Library in 1934, she began to see the potential of microphotography: "I acquired the habit of visiting the photographic studio in order to observe philologists, paleographers, and art historians rapidly filming their research materials with miniature cameras." At first there was no microfilm equipment in the European libraries she visited, so she used Contax and Leica cameras to take pictures. By the late 1930s, the British Museum and a number of large libraries on the continent offered microfilm or photographic facilities.[7]

In addition to her camera skills, Kibre had a flair for gaining access to difficult places. Ed Ainsworth, a gossip columnist for the *Los Angeles Times*, described her efforts to examine an unusually rare manuscript in the Vatican. The attendant, aghast at the request, informed the "beautiful young classical scholar" that "only a certain Cardinal could grant permission." She asked that her card, "Miss Adele Kibre—Hollywood, California," be sent up to him and was immediately admitted. "'So you are from Hollywood!' he cried. 'Come, let's talk.'" After a long discussion of movie stars and the "glamour city of the western world," Kibre received permission to see the manuscript. It was also at the Vatican that she met Eugene Power, who arrived in 1938 to check on the microfilm camera he had installed three years earlier. Impressed with Kibre as a scholar and photographer, Power hired her to do freelance work.[8]

By 1939, rising international tensions blocked her research plans. Forced to cancel trips to Romania and Denmark, she was in the Bavarian State Library in Munich when, she related, "I experienced the outbreak of war and joined in an air raid rehearsal." Soon, many of the valuable manuscripts she needed had been evacuated. The war seemed to track her movements. In the days before the Germans marched into Paris, she took a "hurried trip" to France and "snatched . . . a final glimpse of the Bibliothèque Nationale and its photographic department." She stayed at the Vatican until the beginning of February 1941, and then began the journey back to the United States. "Travelled across desolate tragic France and Spain," she wrote a British friend, "and after considerable excitement and fatigue . . . joined the interminable mob at Lisbon." She had made the trip with seventeen pieces of luggage full of microfilm and photographs of research materials but left her other possessions in Rome. She whiled away the time in Portuguese libraries until gaining passage and returning home in late March.[9]

Kibre found it hard to readjust to American life after twelve years mainly spent abroad. She denounced "America Firsters" and volunteered for the interventionist Fight for Freedom Committee in Chicago. She had secretly tuned in to the BBC in Italy when war broke out and bought a short-wave radio to continue listening. After the attack on Pearl Harbor, she wrote her friend, "at last, all America is awake," and she wanted to join the fight.[10]

Soon she returned to Europe, this time to direct the Anglo-American Microfilm Unit in Stockholm. Precisely how she came to the attention of the OSS is unclear; her personnel file at the National Archives contains only a single sheet of paper. Eugene Power recalled that he had suggested Kibre to Donovan, seeing her as "a real Mata Hari type" who "liked to talk about international intrigue and espionage." She was certainly well known in library and documentation circles and fluent in seven languages. Donovan had intended to send her to Lisbon, but Portuguese authorities denied her a visa. Instead she traveled to London in June 1942, where she received additional microfilm training and met with officials at the British Ministry of Information. Kibre then waited nine weeks in Scotland for the weather to worsen so that her plane could slip into Sweden unnoticed. She finally arrived in Stockholm on August 10.[11]

Of all the IDC units, Kibre's was most closely affiliated with the British intelligence services. In 1940, they had established Press Reading Bureaus (PRB) in Stockholm, Bern, and Istanbul, which provided press clippings and summaries of the important news appearing in European papers. The PRB expanded and systematized a method of information gathering that had long been a consular function and, for the British, an integral part of their imperial intelligence apparatus. The MOI had difficulty transporting publications from Stockholm to London; rather than ship entire newspapers via Vladivostok, which took two months, press digests were sent by cipher cable or diplomatic pouch. The Stockholm Bureau read newspapers from Germany, Scandinavia, Eastern Europe, Russia, and the Netherlands. Initially it focused on news of food shortages and raw materials and forwarded items that could be used in propaganda against the Axis. After diplomat Cecil Parrott was put in charge, the PRB's mission and personnel expanded rapidly, so that by May 1942, it had a staff of fifty press readers, including many émigrés from occupied countries, who were producing press extracts and memos on political, economic, and other information. Parrott hoped to maintain it as an open organization, except for the fact that newspaper subscriptions were ordered under assumed names. However, Britain's wartime spy agency, the Special Operations Executive, wanted press reading to be a cover for covert operations. At the time Adele Kibre arrived in Stockholm, "Parrott House" was increasingly embroiled in conflicts over its proper role, the degree to which it had overstepped its mission to become an intelligence service, and growing doubts that anyone in London actually read its digests.[12]

Whatever the internal British controversy over the PRB, the Ministry of Information saw value in joining the American microfilm unit. Kibre developed a close relationship with the Reading Bureau and with Geoffrey Kirk, a MOI official in London, whose advice and instructions she often followed. The British supplied the publications through their network of subscribers and news dealers, and the Americans brought in microfilm equipment and technical staff. Operating out of the PRB's offices, they created an original master negative of the microfilm for each government, which could be reproduced for the war agencies in London and Washington. "We are making every effort here to start real action as soon as possible," Kibre wrote Kirk soon after her arrival, "there is a colossal amount of material to be microfilmed."[13]

To the frustration of Frederick Kilgour and Allan Evans, the R&A chief in London who handled IDC matters there, Kibre never disclosed the workings of her operation in Stockholm. Kilgour pushed for information. "Do they indulge in any underground work or is everything obtained through ordinary bookstore channels?" he asked. "I wish that sometime you would write me a very garrulous letter describing the set-up in Stockholm and the people with whom you work." He received no reply. Over a year later, he still was "not absolutely certain how the publications are acquired in Stockholm." Communication problems continued for the war's duration. In April 1944, Kilgour tried again. He wondered if "maybe you aren't holding the lid on some problems that must have grown out of the situation" and plaintively asked, "do you suppose that you could write?" Although Kibre thanked him for his "delightful and inspiring letters," she did not keep her "promise to reply as soon as possible."[14]

Believing her to be "retiring and elusive," the IDC men feared that "the thorny problems of personality" would jeopardize the Stockholm operation, and they handled Kibre with a cajoling tone tinged with condescension. "We 'oh' and 'ah' every time your packets come in," Kilgour exclaimed. On one occasion, she acquired a copy of *Industrie-Compass 1943*, a large secret directory of German manufacturers and industries. The German government had restricted access to the volume, which contained "information of value to the enemy and therefore of interest to spies." Kilgour underscored the praise of one U.S. agency: "To get it 'was a real triumph'— your triumph." Microfilm expert Ralph Carruthers, who took over the London IDC station in 1944, remained in awe of the Stockholm agent, and it was only on the momentous occasion of V-E Day that he finally addressed her by her first name.[15]

Kibre clearly wanted it this way. She kept the most meticulous records of any IDC agent in the field, mainly detailed lists of publications she was sending, with rarely a hint of how she had acquired them or reflections about her work. Occasional handwritten notations—such as "!!!" in the margins of a letter from Kilgour anxious that she report her dealings with the British—suggest her disdain for Washington's efforts to manage her. Kibre was careful to maintain the secrecy of her operation, criticizing improperly addressed letters and film shipped without a diplomatic seal, making it vulnerable to Swedish border guards. She warned Evans that further lapses would "arouse unpopularity at the Legation, and at the same time expose our extensive microfilm activities to the Swedes." Having "secured full cooperation of the British reading post," noted one member of the IDC, "she and they work more in the background than similar agents anywhere." Independent, organized, and well connected, she managed her station with quiet efficiency, increasing the staff from two to six, including two scholars she marked as "illegal."[16]

What became apparent, as the first shipments of microfilm arrived, was that Kibre knew what she was doing. "With nothing to guide them but sample runs," the Stockholm unit "never [saw] the finished film, which had to be dispatched undeveloped to London." Nevertheless, the technical quality was excellent, the coverage of the continental press extensive, and her output increased until she was sending microfilm nearly every week. As the OSS London war diary observed, "this was but the beginning of an amazing record of accomplishment."[17]

Kibre received many publications from the British, but she also developed her own channels of acquisition. Some of these were above-board. Kibre made the rounds of local booksellers, contacted sympathetic academics, and entered subscriptions for newspapers and periodicals. She also microfilmed works loaned by several Swedish institutions, including a medical school library, government statistics agency, and the Royal Institute of Technology. Many works were "confidentially borrowed." These included Danish underground publications snuck out of the "Denmark Today" exposition in Stockholm in the summer of 1944, materials from the Yugoslav legation, and a number of periodicals whose export had been forbidden but had escaped the censors. According to Power, she worked with the Norwegian underground, which intercepted mail from Berlin to Oslo and sent it on to Kibre. Contacts in the resistance and clandestine press brought her photographs of air raid destruction in Estonia, the liberation of Copenhagen, and the sabotage of factories and trucks in Denmark. She sent them to William Langer in 1943 with the caption, "Saboteur's comment: 'Sabotage is easy; if caught, we can only lose our heads.'" The OSS pressed her to get permission for the Office of War Information to publish these images to demoralize the enemy. It finally came in 1945 when, as Kibre tersely observed, the saboteur had been killed.[18]

Other acquisitions involved "elaborate operations, together with my British colleagues." She "obtained by indirect methods" a weekly journal from Croatia, in which the upper margins of the first two pages had been "mutilated . . . to remove all trace of identification" of the addressee. She arranged for sensitive technical manuals to be smuggled into Sweden from Germany, along with newspapers and magazines. A notation on an accession sheet indicates that she also received "propaganda from Rolf Hoffman[n], Munich 33, Germany." Hoffmann, a longtime Nazi Party member and Anglophile, had been a leading official in the Foreign Press Service of the Reich Propaganda Ministry, providing information on "cultural subjects" especially for foreign correspondents. Although the details of Kibre's contacts with Hoffmann are unknown, she may have presented herself as sympathetic to the German cause in order to receive his mailings.[19]

Kibre's painstaking methods came under strain as planning for the Allied invasion of Europe intensified. Her carefully composed lists of publications—a "marvel of completeness and order" arranged alphabetically by subject, country of origin, and publications—were now causing delays. These detailed lists arrived after the microfilm, when all that was needed, Carruthers advised, was "a simple contents list, item by item for each roll." "All of us in London are in a hurry for your contents list of material microfilmed," Carruthers wrote, "our people could use a number of the books that have been microfilmed if we only knew on what roll to find them." He commented, "It is absolutely amazing but I have never seen so many people in all my life so anxious to absorb knowledge." Two days after D-Day, he wrote again, "time is of the essence, particularly now that operations have started." Delays meant that publications, especially newspapers, quickly lost their intelligence value. At the same time, it had become increasingly difficult to get materials into and out of Sweden. With tightened export controls and a cut-off in communication with Lisbon, the networks that had funneled publications to Stockholm began to break down. Books from Germany and German-occupied countries were now taking six to twelve months to arrive, and by fall 1944, German technical material had become impossible to obtain.[20]

When the IDC's plans were first made, Lisbon had always been the highest priority for a collecting operation. In the early months of the war, the committee arranged for the American Legation's press office in Portugal to subscribe to German and French periodicals and dispatch the most important. The rising demand from military planners, along with shipping bottlenecks and export restrictions, made it necessary for the IDC to send its own agent to Lisbon to do the same work as Kibre in Stockholm, acquiring publications and capturing them on microfilm. Kilgour tapped a friend, Ralph Carruthers of the New York Public Library, who had mastered the technical minutiae of microphotography. After several false starts— visas were difficult to obtain from the wary Portuguese authorities— Carruthers finally arrived in September 1942. As the workload grew, plans were laid for Reuben Peiss to work with and eventually replace Carruthers. He reached Lisbon the following September. "It has taken about six weeks to get acclimatized, learn the various intricacies of my job, and pick up enough Portuguese to make myself understood in the ordinary, day-to-day transactions," he wrote his former boss at the Harvard Library. Learning to read the language proved easy enough, even with his rusty Latin and French, but pronunciation was a hurdle. Nonetheless, he was enjoying himself. "You will have concluded from the newspapers that life here is not devoid of excitement," he observed drily.[21]

For those in the intelligence business, wartime Lisbon was an exhilarating place to be. Dictator António de Oliveira Salazar had declared Portugal's neutrality, hoping to avoid invasion and keep what was left of its shrunken empire. Sympathetic to fascism but bound by a long-standing treaty with Great Britain, he tacked between the Allies and the Axis. Portugal's neutrality made it the crossroads of Europe and the Americas, a magnet for exiles, diplomats, foreign correspondents, and adventurers. Refugees from occupied countries crowded into Lisbon, enduring long waits for exit visas to England or the Western hemisphere. Cafés, newsstands, and bookstores bustled with newcomers; extravagant parties, dancing salons, and casinos beckoned the wealthy nightly. Not by chance had the city become the travel destination of spies. As one intelligence agent put it, "Lisbon is something like New York on a miniature scale with many visiting firemen passing through every few days." The classic possibilities of urban modernity—anonymity, disguise, the refashioning of identity—were all heightened in wartime Lisbon. Business cards of oil magnates, movie moguls, and consular attachés concealed clandestine lives. Even book buyers might be intelligence agents.[22]

Lisbon had developed its own information economy—an underground market where gossip was traded and rumor bid up. German, British, American, and Japanese agents mingled, listening for intelligence and spreading disinformation. Hearsay was already common currency in a place where press censorship and the secret police prevailed, and the war in Europe stoked the rumor mills. The OSS even sent a memo to its station head in Lisbon about rumormongering, in the upbeat tones of a marketing expert: "In case you have never dabbled in it, the ideal way to spread a rumor is not to tell it in as many places as possible, but to put it in the bonnet of one person whom you know to be a gossip." Agents could also make up their own rumors, as wild as they pleased, except for three forbidden subjects—future military plans, the activities of neutral countries, and the Pope. In the annals of Lisbon spies, none was as legendary as double agent Juan Pujol García, a young Spaniard known as Garbo, who created an entirely fictitious network of agents and served up fabricated reports—based on published maps, travel guides, and a dictionary—to the unsuspecting German agents who had recruited him. It took some time for the suspicious British to believe he was truly working for their side; Graham Greene, who ran the Iberian desk for British intelligence, found in Garbo the inspiration for his 1958 comic novel, *Our Man in Havana*.[23]

At the same time, the risks of exposure were great. British and American agents routinely ran afoul of the Portuguese International Police, who were close to German military intelligence. One of the first shots in the intelligence battle came in 1942, when Abwehr agents revealed Britain's Special Operations Executive and Salazar expelled its chief. Portuguese sympathizers who secretly worked with the British had been subject to an "orgy of arrests, home-searchings, interrogations and so on," wrote Ambassador Ronald Campbell to the Foreign Office. "The matter was assuming the proportions of an international scandal," he commented several weeks later. "Lisbon was humming with it; there was no other topic of conversation." For their part, Abwehr agents concluded that their intelligence work in Portugal, much of which focused on shipping, was highly overrated. They "were not only serviced with planted material—faked by the enemy," one German report observed, but among the Portuguese "a most lucrative information industry was established with the special purpose of fabricating naval information in order to make money."[24]

In this world, Americans were innocents abroad, inexperienced at gathering information and assessing its plausibility and utility, outmatched by the veteran British and German clandestine operations. The first OSS agents lacked training, had no background in military or political affairs, and spoke no Portuguese. In early 1942, one admitted, "No one here, I believe, can help but feel that we are 'behind the eight ball.'" H. Gregory Thomas, assigned to head OSS Lisbon in May 1943, acknowledged that valuable information had been gathered and networks established, but overall the results were poor: "Intelligence was gathered by the sponge system, with little or no attempt at evaluation and only slight regard for security."[25]

This was an understatement. An early OSS agent in Lisbon, Ray Olivera, was a Bureau of Narcotics investigator who, during the Prohibition era, had set up sting operations on swanky speakeasies. Within days of his arrival at the US Embassy, he had managed to outrage the military attaché, the consul general, and the ambassador. It is "incredible that men of common underground police type and background should be sent to the field," stormed Robert Solborg, a legation military attaché with his own troubled ties to OSS. Minister Bert Fish called Olivera a "flatfoot," while British intelligence reports termed him "the gangster." Over the next six months, a pitched battle ensued. Consul General Samuel Wiley accused Olivera of "everything from public drunkenness to consorting with known prostitutes and enemy agents." Olivera shot back that Wiley had "shocked Lisbon society," gambling "like a fool" and appearing in the Estoril casino with a "halfbreed Indian from Florida" whom he introduced as Tu Manchu, a Chinese princess. Wiley defended himself, saying that "his excessive gambling . . . was part of his business [and] his public association with negro women dancers . . . part of his official investigation work." Matters became so fraught that the State Department dispatched George Kennan, then a rising diplomat who had been stationed in Moscow and Berlin, to clean up the intelligence mess.[26]

The sponge system may have led to important and timely intelligence, but it also produced reams of undigested reporting. Solborg kept sending the European command alarming reports about the massing of German armed forces on the Spanish border; these "were utterly fantastic and absolutely worthless," complained an officer, "and were keeping General Eisenhower in a constant state of unnecessary jitters." Agents would report everything they heard, without assessing the quality of the source or plausibility of the information; a nugget of real intelligence might appear in a paragraph, followed by pages of useless gossip. A typical example, written by an agent 423, reported that "one of our men overheard a maid tell a friend over the telephone that she was working for a German lady," who had "made her promise that she would not have any contact with people outside of her house." Pausing for a moment, he concluded, "there may not be anything in this story but pass it on for what it is worth." That phrase, "for what it is worth," was often attached to hearsay several times removed, as if a markdown on cheap goods. This became so much a part of the OSS culture that one wit in the agency wrote a parody of such intelligence reports from the "Office of Soporific Sinecures."[27]

Into the hothouse of Lisbon came those in search of a different kind of information, in the form of the printed word. Salazar's heavy hand did not prevent a brisk business in books, newspapers, and magazines among the polyglot population of the city. Newsstands hawked everything from the *Daily Express* to *Das Reich*, papers from "every major country in Europe except Russia." The city had many booksellers, from the venerable Livraria Bertrand, dating to the eighteenth century, to the newly opened Livraria Portugal, whose owners were sympathetic to the Allied cause. Even stationery stores carried useful works: the Papelaria Fernandes specialized in military subjects, while the Papelaria Pimentel & Casquilho sold engineering books and instruments. Although hamstrung by the censors, customs restrictions, and the shifting political winds, these dealers found ways to import publications and keep their shelves stocked. Lisbon hungered for books and news, and educated Portuguese and travelers alike haunted these places.[28]

Among them were American librarians working for the IDC. They presented themselves to the Portuguese as American officials collecting materials for the Library of Congress and other governmental libraries, "which are naturally interested in preserving the records of the present crisis in our civilization." Trying not to duplicate Kibre's efforts, the Lisbon agents sought publications especially from the southern half of Germany, Czechoslovakia, Poland, Austria, and Hungary, and could count on about seventy newspapers regularly. They openly made the rounds

Figure 2.1. A crowd reading notices at a news agency in Lisbon, 1940. Imperial War Museum (D 1103).

of bookstores and stationery shops and placed subscriptions with news dealers. Sympathetic locals, including scholars, publishers, journalists, and diplomats, also helped, ordering books and newspapers in their own names, as a front for the Americans. The Portuguese did not request money but desired current books and American magazines like *Life* and *Time*. The IDC men would have agreed with an American secret agent who commented, "Some of my most valuable acquaintances in Lisbon have been due to my ability to furnish them with written material otherwise unavailable because of Portuguese censorship."[29]

By 1943 the operation was in full gear. "The publications are rolling in," Ralph Carruthers exulted. "We no sooner begin to see daylight when something else comes along." The sources and flow of publications varied with the war's movements. When the Germans tightened border controls and sources in Switzerland began to shut down, the IDC quickly arranged for a large shipment from a Swiss bookseller to a decoy commercial address in Lisbon. The growing French and Italian resistance spurred the collection of underground publications. The IDC outpost tried to fill urgent requests from Washington war agencies, local embassy staff, and agents outside Lisbon. Kilgour wired for Hungarian newspapers, railroad directories, and prewar Baedekers to aid in military planning. One cable stressed the "great demand for about 250 original daily newspaper issues including duplicates to be obtained with utmost speed." During Operation Torch, the Allied invasion of North Africa, the OSS outpost in Algiers called on Carruthers to send current German newspapers. "It is not likely that we will get them all," he reported, "we will be lucky if we get four out of the lot." In fact, he managed to obtain ten papers by a circuitous route through Tangier that took four days.[30]

After Carruthers was posted to London, Peiss scoured Lisbon and took buying trips into the hinterland. There were still surprising finds, including two hundred volumes on military and technical subjects "nestling in a bookstore." Peiss bought them all. He convinced the Embassy's financial attaché—himself an OSS agent—that security would not be compromised if he walked into the German bookstore in Lisbon and bought overtly. Karl Buchholz, an art dealer and bookseller with Nazi connections, had opened the well-stocked shop in late 1943. "It looks like a gold mine," Peiss wrote Carruthers, commenting that they even displayed books by Stefan Zweig and other Jewish authors. "My impression is that they are eager to make money without worrying too much to whom they sell," but he chose to "drop in occasionally and pick up a few things at a time" so as not to draw attention. He hitched a ride in a Legation car to Porto, Portugal's second largest city, but found little of value and bought only half a dozen books. He turned up a souvenir of sorts, however, which he sent on to Washington— a photograph of a French twenty-franc note with the head of Hitler "neatly inserted in the noose." Increasingly he found it necessary to use "special methods" as requests from Washington and London poured in and acquisitions became more challenging. Through private contacts, Peiss procured a set of maps Carruthers had requested, "a feat which pleased me as much as anything I've done here in Lisbon." He requisitioned special funds, typically used for clandestine operations, to get materials out of countries "by devices which cannot be vouchered in the usual formal manner."[31]

Transporting materials from Lisbon remained difficult. With American censors and customs agents in the dark about IDC operations, crates of books shipped by sea to Washington were sometimes held in port as contraband; Carruthers "received wires from the censors asking what was all that German literature." The most sensitive materials went out by diplomatic pouch to Washington and London. Pan Am Clippers flew every other week from Lisbon to the United States, and the IDC could count on shipping only 165 pounds a month by air. Given the weight and volume of periodicals and newspapers, this was a negligible amount, which made the microfilming operation all the more important, especially for publications that were thought less vital to immediate military objectives. The transportation situation eased by May 1944, when the IDC arranged to ship originals on the

Portuguese airline to Casablanca every Saturday night, where they were transferred to army transport and arrived in Washington on Wednesday. Finally, Peiss wrote, "we have all the plane space we want."[32]

The IDC men were in fierce competition with operatives working for other intelligence services. German and Japanese agents frequented the bookstores and newsstands too, buying up British newspapers and magazines. Foreign agents cultivated locals in shipyards and airfields, who would slip materials from shipments to them. The director of one Portuguese firm, Companhia Suíça de Navegação, got his hands on a number of English technical manuals, which he sent on to Germany. This underground trade was so common, apparently, that a tale circulated about baggage handlers who would move packages of documents directly from one aircraft to another when planes from England and Germany landed. Few printed items from the United States reached Portugal—Carruthers noted that "the newsboys even stop you on the street and ask if you have any American magazines in your hotel room"—but a "ring of smugglers" managed to sneak in American publications for the Germans.[33]

There was also competition from a fellow countryman. Manuel Sanchez, appointed the Library of Congress's representative in the Iberian Peninsula, challenged the IDC agents at every turn. A native of Colombia, Sanchez had earned degrees in engineering and library science, become a US citizen, and worked in American libraries for twelve years before being made a fellow at the Library of Congress in 1941. Two years later, he was on his way to Lisbon to acquire books and periodicals for the LC or "Elsy," as Sanchez fondly called it. Immediately upon arrival, he visited Lisbon's bookstores incognito. "My first impressions here is that there is a mighty good well to be tapped," he wrote. For the first three days, German agents tailed Sanchez, who chose to "sit in the park and go window shopping" until they lost interest in him. He then got down to business, quickly developing an array of contacts among booksellers, officials, and ordinary people. The dashing Sanchez had an abundance of wit and allure, charming the Library's male bosses and female staff, who continually sent their greetings. "Do not get the impression that I have done nothing else but 'book worming,'" he wrote in an early report. "I have seen several shows and movies, native of course, and some portuGAL." Sanchez took particular delight in outwitting the IDC men, "scooping" them in the quest for materials. "About the Carruthers & Peiss incident I am glad you do not object to my using underhand methods," he wrote his boss Verner Clapp at the Library of Congress—he had asked Livraria Portugal confidentially to duplicate the IDC orders—and an amused Clapp wrote back to say, "Keep up the good work!"[34]

The Americans found an ally at Livraria Portugal. Its owner, Pedro de Andrade, had representatives in Paris, Berlin, and Rome, as well as contacts in Hungary and elsewhere. Although he could not obtain many German publications, he sold them hundreds of useful Italian and French books— and then offered some special services. When the Portuguese war ministry sent a set of maps to the Livraria Portugal for repair and binding, Andrade secretly allowed the Americans to microfilm them. His brother Carlos de Andrade even went on buying expeditions to Spain with Sanchez and Peiss, providing cover for them.[35]

Under dictator Francisco Franco, Spain maintained close ties to Germany that made it a desirable yet dangerous destination for the American book buyers. They were followed by the police, shut out of German-language bookstores, and questioned at the border about importing foreign books. Sanchez found that bookstores in Madrid were "not anxious to go out of their way to obtain business," clearly fearful of the secret police. "The first thing most book dealers want to sell me is some edition of Don Quixote," he wrote. "They must think I am Sancho and not Sanchez or that I am a Quixote." As a Portuguese national, Carlos de Andrade attracted less notice and could approach private dealers selling German books. One German *librero*, Rudolph Kadner, refused to sell books for export to the Allies and

Figure 2.2. Livraria Portugal, whose owners aided American efforts to acquire foreign publications during the war, *c.* 1940s.

interrogated Andrade in a "two hour third degree." Andrade told Kadner that a new German bookstore was opening in Lisbon—that much was true—and that Livraria Portugal "had decided to meet the competition by expanding their stock of German books." When Kadner asked how Andrade was going to transport them to Portugal, he answered that there were many ways that the dealer need know nothing about. Pleased with that reply, Kadner swallowed the story, and Andrade left the shop having purchased six hundred books for the Library of Congress.[36]

The book-buying activity in Spain "is proving to be an undercover piece of work," Sanchez joked, so much so that "I am beginning to suspect my own shadow." Indeed, his original mission began to mutate into something closer to secret intelligence. In Spain, a trustworthy dealer helped Sanchez acquire a collection of Communist and separatist works that were forbidden by the state and "obtained through a great deal of secrecy." He secured a vital document that the American military attaché had not seen, nor, apparently, did the Portuguese military possess. "I got it thru a private source which I promised not [to] report and besides I have already forgotten where I got it from," Sanchez wrote elliptically. "I am color blind but they tell me that there [are] certain red marking on it. Those marking are of no great importance. You might say that the[y] are places where new buildings are to be put up. Those buildings might be for any purpose. Oh! You might say that they might be for telephone buildings or anything else you can think of." His source was, in fact, an American who served as the Commercial Director of the Compañía Telefónica Nacional de España.[37]

Sanchez's activities increasingly moved beyond the acquisition of documents. He helped the US embassy's financial attaché in Lisbon find the smuggling ring supplying American publications to the Germans. Later, with the legation's support, he went to northern Spain and Andorra to foster cultural exchange and "make contacts there for French clandestine literature." He met with the anti-Franco and Basque resistance (abertzales), who were working with British and American intelligence operations; they gave him verbal information he was to communicate to a secret contact or organization upon his return. It was important to Sanchez, as it was to the librarians of the IDC, that their work be understood as a "project for the benefit of the war effort . . . not just one of those so called book buying projects."[38]

In September 1943, Sanchez decided to wrap up his purchasing in the Iberian Peninsula, believing he had brought the Library of Congress up to date. "I have purchased good and bad works," he observed. "Our collections in order to render the proper service . . . must of necessity have all." He also had identified the most efficient dealers, and those who could be trusted for forbidden literature. In January 1944 he moved on to Palermo.[39]

The IDC maintained operations in the Iberian Peninsula through most of 1944. A trip to Spain exceeded expectations, yielding important books, high-quality maps, and periodicals of immediate value to the war effort, as well as items of strategic importance. In Lisbon, however, the materials were drying up, with no official German publications and few current periodicals coming in, especially after the Allied bombing of Leipzig and other German cities. Publications "now arrive in mere dribbles," Peiss commented, and the decision was made to close the Lisbon outpost. In late 1944, he left for Bern, Switzerland, to continue this work for the OSS and wartime agencies.[40]

--------- ⌁ ---------

Efforts to acquire open-source intelligence went beyond Europe, and IDC outposts appeared in neutral cities around the world. Collecting efforts in the Middle East were small in scale, with single agents in Istanbul and Cairo working under cover of the embassy and Office of War Information. A substantial IDC mission arose in India, led by librarian Theodore M. Nordbeck and anthropologist David G. Mandelbaum. China continually proved a problem, and a series of men cycled in and out of the station in Chongqing. Harvard sinologist John K. Fairbank first took on the job in 1942 and was followed by Clyde B. Sargeant, a Presbyterian missionary and China historian. Sargeant soon traded collecting publications for special operations, training Korean resistance fighters and rescuing American prisoners of war. Replacing him was George N. Kates, connoisseur of Chinese art and poetry, who had spent the 1930s living in Beijing. He returned to China in 1943 to work for the OSS, but quickly grew frustrated with the work. Herold Wiens, born in China to Mennonites, was an embassy official in Chongqing during the war and made the final push for IDC materials in 1945.[41]

IDC agents found operations in India and China much more difficult than those in Europe. Running water, electricity, telephones, and other services they took for granted at home were unreliable and in short supply. Travel between cities was time consuming and often grueling. IDC men cadged rides on military planes on the dangerous flight over the Himalayas. With space on aircraft and trains limited, George Kates went from Chongqing to Chengdu in a Chinese postal truck, for two days crammed among the mail sacks and other informal passengers. Obtaining publications from Japan and occupied China was especially difficult, the supply lines long, hazardous, and shifting.[42]

The organization of the book trade also impeded their efforts. The Indian publishing industry was highly decentralized, which left them unable to rely on any single book dealer. On a buying expedition in Bombay in July 1945, Sergeant Wayne M. Hartwell started with large bookstores and then checked smaller outlets and secondhand shops. Unable to find helpful clerks or inventory lists, he ended up "snooping" the book stocks on his own and discovering materials through "methodical shelf checking." When Fairbank tried to place orders for Chinese magazines, he learned this was an established "racket" in which dealers never delivered the issues to the unsuspecting subscriber.[43]

Like their European counterparts, these agents sought the help of local librarians, scholars, and officials, but had limited success tapping into the dense network of pre-existing relationships in universities and government agencies. Fairbank tried to link his acquisition work to a nascent effort in cultural diplomacy, run by the State Department, in which American scientific and technical reports were reproduced on microfilm for Chinese universities. He hoped to "get results through the cultural relations microfilm business, which is selling like hotcakes with free maple sugar." The agents in China and India repeatedly pressed Washington to send recent American publications and presentation copies they might exchange with people they encountered. Book talk and gifts helped satisfy the hunger for knowledge and intellectual community, and even conferred prestige on the recipients; they also helped mitigate the Americans' sense that their mission was exploitative. Their pleas went unheard. Although Kilgour "realize[d] that some of you are embarrassed by not being able to do little favors," he repeatedly denied requests for exchange materials.[44]

In China, the IDC men found that the closer their relationships with local governments and universities grew, the less satisfying were the publications they received. "Unless one leaves the beaten track, one now spends one's days in an atmosphere more American than a few years ago," Kates observed about his travels through North China. He had acquired a mimeographed scientific journal that featured articles which the State Department's microfilm service had earlier distributed: "Its materials are only a Chinese reflection of what has originally come [from] us." Chinese academics had taken to using stencils and mimeograph machines to compose what Kates called "informal publications," which were common but ephemeral and hard to obtain.[45]

The IDC tried to enlist Americans already in China, such as John Lossing Buck, an agricultural economist at the University of Nanking (and Pearl Buck's former husband), who ran a statistical and fact-gathering organization. Although Buck signed on, it soon became apparent he was more interested in selling subscriptions to his statistical service than in acquiring publications for the IDC. The most impressive ally was neither a book buyer nor an academic but an Iowa-born Catholic bishop, Thomas M. Megan, who had been Prefect of Xinxiang since 1936. On his own initiative, Megan established a supply route for publications from occupied China to Xi'an, working with Nationalist Chinese guerilla forces and the Chinese Military Affairs Commission, and spending his own funds. Indeed, he was considered the only "effective and continuous channel" for obtaining newspapers, magazines, and books from Japan and occupied China, as well as battle order information and documents for military intelligence. These were often dangerous operations. At one point, Japanese soldiers pursued Megan's couriers. "Fearing that they would be caught, they threw away their bundles," although one managed to reclaim his and deliver it to the IDC. In spring of 1945, Megan proposed adding nine more agents to expand his secret operation into Taiwan, Beijing, and Shijiazhuang.[46]

Although the IDC worked closely with its British counterparts in Europe, its representatives in India became embroiled in the politics of empire, exposing fractures in the Anglo-American "special relationship" during the war. British officials tried to block the Americans from acquiring publications about India, especially those produced by nationalist organizations. Robert I. Crane became a target of both British and American officials for his anticolonial views. Born in India of missionary parents, Crane worked in the State Department's Division of Cultural Relations during the war, providing free reference libraries to Indian universities. His outspoken views supporting Indian independence drew concern, but his wealth of contacts among Indian scholars, publishers, and book dealers made him an ideal IDC agent, and he was appointed in 1945. Despite being told to shun Indian politics, he could not resist. He acquired highly sensitive National Congress Party planning documents whose existence, outpost chief Theodore Nordbeck warned, "should not be revealed to the British." Crane crossed the line when he wrote a secret report for the State Department, which made William Donovan "absolutely hit the ceiling." Kilgour ordered Crane "to keep *miles* away from this kind of business." Now OSS counterintelligence, known as X-2, began to monitor Crane's movements and questioned Nordbeck about a "Bombay incident" involving Crane. Nordbeck defended his agent: "Whenever we purchase books here we stress the fact that we are serving [the Library of Congress], and avoid references to OSS or other government agencies." The X-2 man pressed further: "Do you have to buy any books here anyhow?" Nordbeck acidly protested to Kilgour: "I could answer 'No' and . . . let Bob sit on his fann[y] in New Delhi guzzling gin and lime juice all day, but presumably that is not what IDC sent him to do." In the Indian political climate, even the seemingly innocent act of buying books for a library generated suspicion of darker motives.[47]

---------᠃᠕᠉---------

What was the value of these acquisitions? In the shadow world of intelligence, the printed word was clarifying, or so it seemed. The materiality of publications made them measurable—number of books shipped and microfilm reels shot. Scientific periodicals, technical manuals, and industrial directories directly from Axis and occupied countries were studied closely for evidence of enemy troop strength, new weaponry, and economic production. Even trivial items could prove meaningful: society pages might reveal the location of a regiment, and gossip columns "provide clues to scandals which a secret agent could exploit." The disposition among the well-educated to favor printed over spoken words made such sources seem more reliable. In Lisbon, with its rich diet of rumor and speculation, OSS chief H. Gregory Thomas relished the Legation's press digests and observed, "many leads I find can be derived here from the local press which I of course read daily." Even the clandestine Secret Intelligence Branch, which sought human informants, found that "intelligence material from the foreign newspapers is of great value."[48] War agencies in Washington also considered these materials useful. But there was more to this perception than the simple act of reading texts. The librarians of the IDC transformed the familiar forms of books and serials into the genre of intelligence.

This transformation was spurred by the very success of the IDC outposts in Stockholm, Lisbon, and elsewhere. In six months, the operation "attained large proportions," Langer wrote Donovan in July 1942. They had placed six operatives abroad, their microfilm units were in high demand, and most important, European newspapers and scientific publications were rolling into Washington. By the end of that year, microfilm with 137,000 pages of publications had arrived from abroad, and 1.2 million pages had been duplicated and distributed to twenty-six agencies, which found nuggets of useful intelligence in open sources. More than half of the IDC's acquisitions arrived on microfilm shot at the foreign outposts; in March 1943, that figure had risen to 90 percent. The microfilm weighed only a fraction of the original publications. "A pound of microfilm will bring 130 newspapers," Kilgour commented.[49]

Even as the IDC began to fulfill its mission, however, complaints poured in from the agencies it served. Many users disparaged the poor quality of the microfilm. Technicians in the field examined test batches, but the film rolls themselves were developed in Washington or London. Not everyone produced the crisp, high-contrast images photographed by Adele Kibre's skillful operator in Stockholm. "John K. Fairbank's results are cinematically useless," Kilgour groaned. "They look as though filmed in a rainstorm." Silver emulsion film was scarce under wartime restrictions, so the IDC experimented with substitutes; they tried an inexpensive new process called Ozaphane but the images were frequently illegible. Microfilm readers were in short supply too, and those who used them disliked reading on the screen. Everyone wanted positive prints, but this was very costly. The time lag in receiving publications was another problem. Bureaucratic snafus— delayed visas, transportation hitches, slow payments to suppliers—meant that important newspapers often took as long as two or three months to arrive.[50]

The greatest drawback, however, was the sheer quantity and randomness of the microfilm. The overseas units shot film quickly, with little time and few personnel to select and organize the material. Except in Stockholm, where Kibre sent detailed content lists, reels with newspapers might simply be labeled by country and scientific publications listed only by name. They "photograph scattered issues of a great quantity of publications," complained Jesse Shera, deputy chief of the OSS's Central Information Division, "with the result that not only are the files incomplete, but the volume of film now being received greatly exceeds the ability of our staff to digest it." Shera started a checklist of items on each film roll, but that was not enough. The backlog was such that Library of Congress staff could only determine whether IDC had a certain publication on a particular reel by telephoning them. Nor did readers have a way to know what particular issue or volume might contain the information they sought. John L. Riheldaffer of the Office of Naval Intelligence concisely stated the problem. "There is a great mass of information which would be of value to the various sections of ONI," he observed, but "we find that the time necessary for proper perusal is so great that it would require a special section for this purpose alone."[51] The bounty had become a curse.

This problem demanded a shift in the IDC's understanding of itself and its mission. Kilgour had quickly embraced the idea of IDC as "a service agency supplying unprocessed intelligence to the Army, Navy, and War agencies," as he described it to Donovan in August 1942, drawing a sharp distinction between its operations and general library acquisitions work. Even so, in the first months after his arrival in Washington, Kilgour recalled, he "was still thinking of the job from the library point of view and not too much from the point of view of the information in publications."[52] As librarians, the IDC staff were oriented to bound books and periodicals, properly catalogued or indexed by author, title, and subject. Traditionally, responsibility for discovering the contents of publications rested with the reader. The initial conception of the Interdepartmental Committee, in fact, was that civilian and military officials would request the foreign publication they needed, and the agents abroad would find it for them. Microfilm was simply a different format for supplying these works, enhancing their reproducibility but not changing the protocols of accessing content.

As the organization developed its overseas channels and a Washington clientele, Kilgour came to understand that *information*, not the publications themselves, was the IDC's product. To produce information, they needed to extract useful knowledge from the journals and books that contained them and make it identifiable to officials with many different interests. How should information be organized to guide users to exactly what they required, or to information they did not yet know they needed? Ultimately, they decided on a tiered system of access. Kilgour's staff polled wartime agencies, asking them to provide categories and keywords, and then created a subject index of newspapers and periodicals tailored to their needs. This was, in effect, a giant press reading service. The Subject Index Section of IDC began its work in August 1943 and initially issued weekly indices. The index quickly became a daily publication, and within six months, three hundred copies were being regularly distributed to forty government agencies. By March 1945 there were 170,000 subject cards in the index file. Given the vast quantities of material, they could not cover all newspapers, and they omitted foreign journals of medicine and chemistry, which were already indexed. Instead, they focused on items pertaining to economics, aviation, the military, physical sciences, and noteworthy individuals. After identifying items of interest in the index, users could request an abstract and even a full-text translation. The IDC produced précis of about 4 percent of the indexed items and were able to translate forty-two languages, sixteen of them swiftly. This new function led to the rapid growth of the agency, which hired a small army of translators and indexers, including many émigrés and women. The staff more than doubled from 1944 to 1945, reaching a high of 183.[53]

Using these techniques, the IDC converted the discrete periodical or book into units of intelligence. In their material form, the IDC's intelligence reports came to resemble those produced by the OSS through interrogations and informants: each report included the extraction of nuggets of information from a text, reformatted with the source of information, brief abstract, and the use of a numbering system for filing. For the Washington-based librarians at IDC, the line between open-source and human intelligence became blurred and the information interchangeable.

Thus, as Kilgour put it, the IDC changed "from an acquisition group to an active producer of intelligence."[54]

---cᐱᗐ---

Far from Washington, the IDC agents in the field also redefined their work. They had been explicitly ordered not to go beyond their charge and only to acquire publications needed for the war effort. What Kilgour called "extracurricular" activities were forbidden—no secret intelligence work, espionage, or collaboration with the covert divisions of OSS, beyond microfilming materials for them. "IDC Field Representatives are to do only IDC work," Kilgour commanded. "Political, economic, cultural, and any other kind of reporting for anybody else is out." They were even told to ignore notes slipped into the pages of books, which might contain pleas for help or offers of information. Security and discretion were necessary. Carruthers, for example, did not hire Portuguese technicians to help with the microfilm operation. But none of the IDC agents received code names or numbers to protect their identity, because acquisitions work did not require such precautions. When Peiss traveled to Madrid and Barcelona to buy military publications, he went openly. Clearing his trip, an OSS official commented that "his passport includes the fact that he represents [the IDC], and will purchase what he wants through the established book dealers."[55]

Yet in the field, these librarians found it difficult to toe the line separating their work from secret intelligence. The military and financial attachés in the embassy, engaged in clandestine work, sought out their microfilm equipment and expertise. Copying photographs of Axis agents and confidential reports "temporarily borrowed" from Portuguese government offices proved to be exciting work. "All this is hot stuff!" exclaimed Carruthers, and his group worked long hours to meet the demand. It proved impossible to fence off the IDC from other operations. The slippage was apparent when Carruthers tried to excuse the disarray in the IDC financial accounts: "The newspaper work we were doing was so closely tied up with other projects being done through our agents" that he failed to keep the payments separate. By 1944, James Wood, an intelligence agent under cover as the embassy's financial attaché, made more and more requests for assistance. In addition to microfilming, Peiss translated German documents for him, selected materials, and even went on a trip into the field. The requests kept him in the office late into the night. He wrote Carruthers, "By this time I am staggering around as if I had been going the round of the night clubs, with none of the resultant exhilaration."[56]

The immediate needs of American intelligence operations merged with
a desire to do something more than acquire books and produce microfilm.
The IDC men began to report their impressions of public opinion: the word
on the street. Some of this was thoughtful information about Portuguese
perceptions of the United States, which might be useful in assessing foreign policy and devising propaganda campaigns. Carruthers reported, for
example, that the Americans had failed to put out a positive account of
their bombing raids. "The Germans and Vichy come out immediately with
their version," he noted. "From the news as printed in Portuguese papers
one gets the idea that we Americans are doing nothing but killing women
and children." In spring 1944, as the Allies put greater pressure on Spain
and Portugal not to trade with the Germans, Peiss commented that the
Portuguese press had censored the story and "there is a kind of tenseness
in the air—i.e. the apparent readiness of Gt. Britain and the U.S. to get
tough," along with a worsening economic situation, tightened rationing,
and growing fears of violence.[57]

Much that was dutifully reported as intelligence, however, was merely
the idle chatter of cafés, bars, and dinner parties. The wife of a Portuguese
diplomat in Paris confided at a dinner that "Paris designers are out-doing
themselves" but "collaborationists are being cleaned out one by one"; a bar-
tender had heard from a friend in the Portuguese legation in Berlin that the
average German wanted to stop the war. Everyday life in Lisbon held the
possibility that valuable information lay just beneath the surface. One day
the IDC men and a member of the Financial Attaché's staff went to see the
film *Baron Munchausen*, which had received widespread publicity in Lisbon.
Nazi propaganda minister Joseph Goebbels had commissioned it to sur-
pass *The Wizard of Oz*, both as a fantasy story and for its use of a new color
process. They went, Carruthers explained, "somewhat dubious about the
propriety of going to see a German movie but consoling ourselves with the
idea that we might pick up something useful." There was little intelligence
to be had, beyond Carruthers's expert opinion that the color was "damn
good, but not perfect."[58]

At one point, rumormongering got Carruthers into trouble. He had
been ordered to Madrid to buy books and look into setting up an outpost.
When OSS Lisbon chief H. Gregory Thomas heard this, he sent an urgent
cable to stop him. Thomas himself was engaged in a delicate negotiation in
Spain with the American ambassador, Carleton Hayes, who opposed the
OSS presence there. "The situation here is too precarious for Carruthers, as
he lacks proper security sense," wired Thomas, using his code name Argus.
"We do not care to have him here." When he later heard how gravely his
message had been taken, he clarified his position. Carruthers's error was

not a serious breach of security but simply involved gossiping to friends, "which was not of a nature to prove seriously embarrassing to us here in Lisbon" but might have been harmful in the "extremely tense situation" in Madrid. Once he had been warned against loose talk, there were no further problems. It was probably with some relief that Carruthers could report at the end of 1943, "Portugal is very quiet at the moment. No rumors."[59]

It is hard to trace unauthorized and secret activity, but it seems that some IDC field agents in Europe crossed the line between collecting publications and clandestine work. According to family stories, Adele Kibre on several occasions took a fishing boat from the Swedish coast and slipped into occupied France; she likely worked with her brother Bert, an experienced photographer who had joined the army and who, working from England, aided in the reconnaissance of the French coast during planning for the Normandy landing. OSS records provide no substantiation, but there were gaps of several weeks to a month's duration in 1943 and 1944 when Kibre sent Washington no packages or airgrams. That might have reflected simply the ups and downs of her collecting efforts, but it is possible these were times she left Stockholm on other missions. Reuben Peiss also engaged in clandestine intelligence activities, moving from collecting to covert operations, although like other OSS agents, he had acquired the habit of secrecy and maintained "silence as to the confidential sides" even after the war, as a colleague recalled. One story about him suggests his ease with the shadow world. In spring 1944 he received a cable instructing him to plan a transfer from Lisbon to Bern; although the transfer was to take place after Allied forces had opened the French-Swiss frontier, he understood it to be an immediate order. He secured a fake passport and visa and began to arrange a flight to Stuttgart on a German plane—a dangerous, even foolhardy scheme—when the OSS chief in Lisbon stopped him.[60]

The IDC/Far East went further, allowing some of its agents to combine acquisitions work with human intelligence. The OSS in East and South Asia was a "very loosely knit organization" throughout much of the war, Theodore Nordbeck commented, without the sharper functional divisions in Europe. In addition, tensions with British intelligence and military authorities impeded the kind of Allied collaboration that occurred elsewhere. The result seems to have been operations in which the distinct and separate role of IDC was not maintained, due to conditions on the ground as well as the disposition of the agents themselves. As Nordbeck observed, "Things are a lot different out here from anything I had conceived in Washington."[61]

The OSS gave John K. Fairbank permission not only to acquire books but also to work as an intelligence operative and analyst, using the code name Gauss. He found book agents and the cultural relations program useful but quickly learned that he needed to use covert techniques to gain Japanese materials. He felt hampered by the machinations of the American and Chinese "cloaks and daggers": US naval intelligence, led by Colonel Milton Miles, closely cooperated with the Chinese intelligence service, headed by Dai Li, a ruthless leader in the Nationalist government. Dai Li called the shots, and Miles told Fairbank to take orders from him. As a result, Fairbank had had little success. "I have so far tried to avoid the whole pussy-foot business and stayed indoors at night," wrote Fairbank in 1942. "But in the end, no Jap things are likely to turn up unless we see the hush people among the Chinese here; I have means of doing it and shall do so if our team can't get results pretty soon." Meanwhile, Fairbank's "dual status" caused "confusion and undue suspicion" in Washington when his letters for one boss landed on the desk of another. His professorial cover was blown when the *Shanghai Evening Post and Mercury*'s gossip column reported that Fairbank was in Chongqing for the OSS and the IDC. Still, being a bookman could be an excellent disguise, permitting contacts that, as Langer put it, "might get the rest of us into trouble." When Kates held talks with a Formosan leader, for example, he could innocently assert he was "simply following his business of collecting publications."[62]

Some chafed under the confines of their assignment as book buyers in the field, insisting that acquiring publications could not be isolated from the rest of intelligence gathering. Like Fairbank, anthropologist David G. Mandelbaum had been sent to India wearing two hats. "The microfilm which we have sent you is only a token of the materials available here," he wrote. "There is a great range of sources which we have not begun to exploit," from the Burmese government's newspaper collection to the Engineer Corps of India's records. "It is precisely my intelligence work which opens up these leads," he observed. After four months, he concluded that "there is a great deal more intelligence available than ever appears in published documents." Personal contacts and extensive interviews akin to fieldwork—what Mandelbaum called "perambulating research" and Fairbank called "local knowledge"—yielded surprising results. As he prepared an intelligence report on Maymyo, Burma, Mandelbaum found that "the ex-prisoners knew a great deal that they had never been asked for previously. There were photographs which had never been completely interpreted, there were officers who knew important aspects of the target from personal experience." He proposed using such information not for the broad background reports R&A typically produced, but for "specific and contemporary studies." The value of this information could be seen in the reactions of their users, he said: one official's "eyes lit up, he couldn't read the document fast enough," while another report "brought a chortle of glee from one American Colonel who had been looking for just such information."[63]

George Kates offered the most thorough critique of the acquisition program. "Much of this general plan for omnivorous and utopian book gathering, I feel I ought to say, is on paper; and has no great bearing on the winning of the war," he wrote his chief. He was using every means possible to secure relevant publications, but he had come to believe that "some of the most vital information that this organization can gather is *not* in printed form, nor does it seem likely that it will become so." People simply could not write in conditions of economic hardship and wartime destruction. "Many of them are primarily occupied in find[ing] their daily food and in many cases it is not prudent for them to speak out their minds in print," he observed. He planned to annotate the materials to help Washington-based readers understand them.[64]

From their headquarters in Washington to outposts around the world, these bookmen and women found that the conventions of the printed word ran up against evolving conceptions of intelligence. Among those who needed to manage information flows, printed texts were reconceived as bundles of usable information that could be pieced together and analyzed for hidden knowledge and larger patterns. The IDC reworked techniques of librarianship to organize this intelligence and make it accessible to war agencies. For the agents in the field, the familiar practices of acquisition were reconceived when applied to intelligence gathering. In contrast to their colleagues at headquarters, the complexity and murkiness of what could be known—and the limitations of printed sources—came home to them. In both cases, the seeming stability of the printed word turned into a liability that required interventions—texts disaggregated and classified as intelligence, on the one hand, their contextualization through human sources, on the other. These operations gave open-source intelligence more value, if not necessarily more veracity. As George Kates put it, "No matter how full and perfect may be our coverage, it will never reflect the true condition of affairs, as we see them living here on the ground."[65]

What difference, then, did such large-scale acquisition of foreign publications make to the war effort? In his budget requests, Frederick Kilgour highlighted many examples of intelligence that came "almost entirely or completely from foreign publications." These included information on the reorganization of German industry, armaments and munitions production, natural resource extraction, labor mobilization, and military communication systems. Among the gleanings from open sources were data about mining activity in German-occupied Europe, the recruitment of

French men into the Waffen SS, and evacuation measures taken in Berlin because of the air war. Publications provided otherwise unavailable information about Poland, Czechoslovakia, France, and Belgium, he observed in 1943, and "small local newspapers are the only sources from which the effects of rationing, housing shortages, the closing of industries, etc., can be obtained." In interviews long after the war, Kilgour emphasized how the IDC had secured scientific periodicals with important information on German rocketry and the atomic bomb. Assessing the impact of the intelligence culled from open sources remains difficult, perhaps impossible. These sources contributed substantially to OSS reports on the enemy's economy, politics, fighting capacity, and morale, which were useful to wartime and postwar strategic planners. The Office of Naval Intelligence and other war agencies believed German publications in particular "provided intelligence material not as readily available through other means."[66] Yet these open-source works were not sufficiently timely or informative to guide military operations or tactics. The IDC's impact may lie less in the intelligence it produced than in the information methods it developed. Experimenting with microfilm technology and addressing problems of information management and access made the IDC's war work a significant episode in the development of information science.

CHAPTER 3

⟡

The Wild Scramble for Documents

In the days before the liberation of Paris, fifteen teams known as T-Forces—over eighteen hundred men representing twenty-eight intelligence agencies—assembled in the Twelfth Army Group. Carrying lists of targets, maps, and photographs, their mission was to find enemy personnel and gather the documents of war. The path into Paris was not smooth. Although feted by French civilians in the daytime, they traveled in darkness, fearing pockets of German resistance. Commanding the operation, Colonel Harold Lyon later remarked, "It is questionable whether the chances taken, without combat troops to protect the Force, were justified." They reached Paris on the night of its liberation, August 25, 1944. Saul Padover, an OSS officer attached to a documents team, described the thrill of this moment, when "the world seemed to have gone off its hinges." Driving around blocked roads and past smashed barricades, the T-Forces came into the city, where "people were cheering us madly, throwing flowers at us, yelling," the Free French Forces shot guns in the air, and everyone sang "The Marseillaise." After two days of celebration, the OSS men went to work. They searched for useful intelligence materials but mainly arrived at their targets too late, Padover wrote. "Everywhere we entered we found that whatever the Germans had not carried off the French had already requisitioned." In his official report, Lyon presented a different timeline and outcome: his teams rushed to their targets immediately but got "ahead of the staff organization." After eleven days of operation, the "documents collected became an insurmountable pile."[1]

An enormous collecting effort occurred during the final stages of the war. Intelligence gathering and assessment took on increased importance as the Allies advanced on the continent after D-Day. In anticipation of Germany's defeat, demand grew for materials to aid planners of the Allied occupation, provide evidence of war crimes, offer intelligence about the Japanese and Pacific theater, and reveal Soviet postwar intentions. A special mission known as Alsos searched for intelligence on German nuclear and weapons projects. At the end of the war, Project Paperclip famously tracked down scientists who had worked on atomic physics, rocketry, and other top-secret research. FIAT (Field Intelligence Agency Technical) units sought German patents and technical reports that could be used by American industry. Those well-known programs were only the tip of the iceberg in a far-reaching effort to acquire documents and information.[2]

The librarians, academics, and information specialists involved in the acquisition of open-source intelligence for the OSS now became members of T-Force collecting teams, attached to the military. In the process, their mission was transformed. In the early days of the OSS, their focus had been on periodicals, books, directories, and manuals useful for intelligence analysis, and their method was largely to haunt bookstores, order subscriptions, and develop personal contacts. Now they were part of a military operation, signified by their wearing uniforms and operating within the system of army billeting, mess facilities, transport, and passes. They fitted themselves into documents teams with a high degree of resourcefulness and expertise, relishing an enhanced role as intelligence agents. At the same time, their sense of identity as bookmen and ongoing contacts with the learned community back home focused their attention on the book trade and its fate in the war years. They conducted POW interrogations to learn about the destruction of libraries, bombing of publishing houses, and removal of endangered collections. Then, when by happenstance so many of these relocated collections were found hidden in caves, mines, and castles in the American zone of occupation, their mission became one of mass acquisitions, even of materials with few intelligence-related uses. If their work at times raised ethical questions, their mission to conclude the war and secure knowledge that would facilitate reconstruction on American terms overcame such concerns. The compulsive logic of collection—its expanding reach and scope, its opportunistic quality, its diffuse purposes—extended to books, periodicals, and even whole libraries.

———∞———

The value of enemy documents to the war effort only became apparent during the Italian campaign in 1943. Planning the invasion of Rome, the British created the first Intelligence Assault Force, which entered the Eternal City hours after it had been taken by Allied troops, secured buildings and offices, and gathered records, documents, and equipment over ten days. This action "paid huge intelligence dividends," it was generally agreed, and led to a full-scale effort to acquire and exploit such materials after D-Day. A joint British-American umbrella group, the Combined Intelligence Objectives Subcommittee (CIOS), oversaw these operations. CIOS sought to balance competing intelligence needs and priorities among the jostling agencies to prevent any single group from gaining control over materials.[3]

The use of rapid-strike documents teams, the T-Forces, became a key feature of military planning for the invasion of the Continent and defeat of Germany. The teams were made up of army personnel, whose skills ranged from bomb clearing and truck driving to interrogations and translation, along with experts in particular disciplines or types of material. They received priority target lists vetted by CIOS and operated within military intelligence units, known as G-2, in specific army groups and the Supreme Headquarters Allied Expeditionary Force (SHAEF). In its original conception, T-Forces would enter newly captured or liberated territory steps behind combat troops. Operating even under enemy fire, they would secure buildings, post guards, disarm booby traps, and quickly examine and seize the "cream of intelligence material" before moving on.[4]

Quickly, however, "T-Force" became a broad term for the numerous investigating teams that arrived days, even weeks, after an army had advanced. As the OSS official Allan Evans explained, T-Force had "rapidly become generalized to mean any group sent out under military auspices to collect documents in military areas." Indeed, T-Forces went beyond document hunting. They might be a "combat operational force, a team of specialist investigators, a complex organization for selecting objects or recruiting personnel, or a combination of any of these." Some were ordered to secure technical and industrial machinery, laboratories, and military equipment, and to interview and detain individuals with knowledge about them. Documents teams, the most common type of T-Force, acquired governmental records, Nazi Party archives, scientific and technical reports, business papers, periodicals, books, maps, and films, exceeding the original mandate of intelligence gathering. Technical experts, economic warfare specialists, army engineers, civil affairs officers, and counterintelligence agents participated on these teams, seeking documents in their own fields. Competition among them was a growing problem.[5]

The OSS viewed T-Forces as a welcome opportunity to gather intelligence of a more long-term and strategic nature, as well as to make the case for the agency's postwar survival. The agency pushed the military to add OSS agents to documents operations and allow them to create their own T-Force. With the Allied invasion underway, their anticipated "cross-country run" as they followed the armies into Germany often stumbled. Military commanders were suspicious of Donovan's agents, who roamed freely and removed whatever they found, maneuvering outside channels. They often arrived without orders at military bases and talked themselves onto teams, or operated "on their own, using 'T' Force only as a supply base." At the same time, the agents found themselves utterly reliant on the army for food, billets, and transport so as not be "encumbered with the many problems of daily living," as one put it. Many on Research & Analysis (R&A) teams preferred the more glamorous work of reporting and analyzing and neglected to gather documents. Just as troubling, they often arrived too late to pursue their collecting mission, the military teams having already picked over the materials. They would need to get there more quickly, wrote one OSS official. "Otherwise unit G-2s, Army T-Forces and SHAEF T-Force Outposts, not to mention souvenir hunters, manage to do a thorough job on the most obvious sources of information." At the same time, the OSS provided important information for tactical decisions that was unavailable elsewhere. Much of it came from R&A, a Third Army G-2 report stated, including a "Bember's Baedaker, German Zone Handbooks, publications and documentations on German cities, roads and bridges, [and] criteria for identification of anti-Nazis in Germany."[6]

The turn toward document collecting in war zones enhanced the role of the IDC, whose agents had valuable library skills and fluency in European languages. By summer 1944, the committee's customary activities— bibliography, acquisition, and microfilm—had given way to target research and planning for a presence on OSS and army documents teams. As an R&A report noted, "the Inter-departmental Committee has been completely identified with the T-Force since its inception." Specialists in open-source intelligence, they were able to assess and manage the massive amounts of materials T-Forces found. IDC would continue to acquire scientific and technical volumes, as well as publications for immediate intelligence and military use. But their collecting aims expanded in this period as war planners turned to postwar objectives, including the denazification of Germany, war crimes prosecutions, and managing relations with the Soviet Union. The IDC also itched to know what had happened to Europe's book world in the wake of war.[7]

Allied intelligence services and civil affairs officers too were interested in that question. They wanted to know about German universities, museums, and libraries. They discussed how to disinfect German communications media from fascist ideas, denazify educational institutions, and rebuild the press and publishing industry when the war was over. British interrogators even questioned two POWs familiar with publishing before the war, who told them about the impact of Nazi control, Allied air raids, and paper restrictions, and provided thumbnail sketches of important figures in the industry.[8]

However, it was Max Loeb, a private in the US Army and German-Jewish émigré, who grasped the value of interviewing friendly prisoners of war knowledgeable about libraries, publishing, and the book trade. Loeb was twenty-five when he fled Nazi Germany with his wife in 1937. He had worked as a journalist in Frankfurt, but once in New York he established himself as a book dealer on Madison Avenue. MacLoeb Books sold works on European history, the military, and aviation, specialized periodicals, and even satires of the Nazi regime; among his clients was the Hoover Library. Not yet a citizen, he enlisted in the army in 1943 and completed basic infantry training. His fluent German and civilian experience as a reporter on European commercial and political matters led him to be tapped for military intelligence. At Camp Ritchie, Maryland, and the American School Center in Shrivenham, England, he received special training in combat intelligence and the interrogation of German prisoners of war. He was then attached to the IDC Division of the OSS in London.[9]

Working on his own, Loeb interviewed nearly three hundred individuals at POW camps in Great Britain from November 1944 to April 1945. He focused his efforts on the status and location of book collections, publishing houses, libraries, and archives in Germany and German-occupied territory. From these interviews, he compiled lists of targets for T-Forces, "presented as raw material to make them available quickly," which indicated where publications and documents might be located in Germany. These included publishers, wholesalers, and book dealers in Berlin and Leipzig, as well as libraries and archives secreted in hiding places. This was a significant shift in direction for the bookmen, whose traditional work of bibliography was now defined in terms of military targets.[10]

Loeb's reports revealed more than the state of the Continental book world. What at first seemed marginal to the main thrust of intelligence work yielded nuggets that excited the interest of military officers, specialized intelligence teams, and OSS Chief William Donovan himself. "Maxie hit the jack-pot yesterday," Frederick Kilgour commented when the British War Cabinet requested his reports. Marveling at Loeb's interrogation skills, Chandler Morse, head of the R&A branch in Europe, observed, "from the outset, it became apparent that he was obtaining . . . information on personalities, relocation of government and party headquarters, and industrial targets far beyond the scope of his immediate interest." Loeb produced a number of special reports related to politics, medicine, and counterintelligence.[11] His innovative approach further entangled the acquisition of publications with the methods and purposes of intelligence.

Loeb interviewed German prisoners of war deemed "friendly" and willing to relate what they had seen and heard in Germany. His reports stated the prisoners' military ranks and civilian occupations, with brief assessments of their reliability: "very accurate and seems to be a sincere collaborator although he is somewhat too eager to please"; "seems to be a sincere Anti-Nazi"; "formerly a convinced Nazi; now somewhat of an opportunist." Some provided the names and addresses of people in Germany, such as anti-Nazi Catholics, who knew about the removal of books. One even guaranteed the "political integrity" of his bride, a librarian at the Prussian State Library, who he promised would provide accurate information when the Allies arrived in Berlin. Before the war, these men had been publishers, journalists, academics, administrators, priests, and students. Now they opened a window on the wartime fate of German library collections, archival records, book stocks, and printing presses.[12]

The POWs described the toll of Allied bombing raids and enabled American and British officials to fill in their sketchy knowledge of the geography of cultural destruction and dislocation. In Kassel, one POW reported, four libraries and museums had been destroyed. In Berlin, the Technische Hochschule and a wing of the Prussian State Library were severely damaged. Leipzig, one of the great centers of European publishing and printing for centuries, was particularly hit hard. One prisoner "was in Leipzig after the large attacks in 1943," reported Loeb. "He observed personally large damage inflicted on the building of the 'Deutsche Buecherei' (German National Library)." According to another, 90 percent of the publishing industry in Leipzig was gone: "Printing establishments, stores of paper, and books have been nearly all destroyed."[13]

The Nazi regime had anticipated the air attacks and laid plans to safeguard library collections and archives, evacuating the most valuable from urban areas. Beginning in 1941, a secret unit in the Ministry of Propaganda had been organized for this purpose. The POWs gave quite similar descriptions of the work of this unit. Collection squads of police, party officials, archivists, and civilian specialists gathered the material and took them to collecting points, where they were examined and sorted. "No receipts are given, and the owners are told they have to trust the archivists," explained a prisoner whose father had had ten boxes of records removed.[14] Lower priority items often stayed in place, but treasured collections and important archives were packed in specially made crates, then transported to hiding places in small towns and the countryside. To hold the volume of books and archives, cellars were dug or expanded, mines seized, and tunnels carved into mountains. Party officials requisitioned monasteries, castles, and private estates for storage.

The relocation effort reached across Germany. Loeb interviewed Joseph Blanck, former manager of a printing plant in Württemberg, who had heard from two sources that in September 1942, "careful plans were made to organize the evacuation of the most important parts of the collections, libraries and archives of Stuttgart and other large cities of Wuerttemberg." The curator of the Landesmuseum oversaw the work, and each organization received detailed evacuation orders. In the provincial capital Sigmaringen, a number of large cellars had been prepared for storage. Blanck gave the precise location, saying "the heavy steel and wood doors can be seen from the street." Two POWs explained to Loeb that despite the destruction in Berlin two million books from the Prussian State Library and University of Berlin, along with government records, had been carefully packed and moved in army trucks to "a score of little villages of no strategic importance." Another confirmed that portions of these collections had been placed in a former quarry near Frankfurt and shelters in the Harz Mountains. Rolf Ehlers, who had been a young judge in Trier, described an elaborate series of tunnels built by army engineers in the hills of the Mosel River. He also noted that "non-essential" archives and libraries had been sent to a concentration camp for British POWs in Bad Godesberg, a decision based on the conviction that the camp would not be bombed.[15]

This was a complex choreography of relocation, based on competing assessments of priorities for protection. In some cases, the libraries of private collectors, small museums, and monasteries were confiscated to free up space for more valuable material; as one informant said, "The SS had requisitioned the buildings, which were used for storage purposes." Castles, outlying estates, and monasteries were deemed safer than large central institutions more easily targeted by Allied bombers. Interestingly, several POWs described how German nobles resisted demands that they accommodate evacuees or Nazi Party offices by opening their homes to relocated museum and library collections. Although the party sought to stop this practice, these aristocrats had organized themselves into a "vigorous movement, spread only amongst trusted friends," preferring to provide storage space for the protection of cultural heritage than to have displaced persons or party officials on their premises.[16]

The German special unit assigned to shield books and archives was overwhelmed by the mass bombing attacks, and, according to Loeb's informants, by mid-1943 local officials, library directors, and other citizens were stepping in to provide protection. Directors of the University of Berlin Library, Prussian State Library, Kaiser Wilhelm Institute, and similar research centers developed an unofficial system of safeguarding books and archives that had not been evacuated, entrusting them to librarians, faculty, and administrators to store at home. When bombing demolished much of central Hanover, medieval cellars under a destroyed church were reinforced, and the remains of the city library and provincial art museum's collections stored there. Loeb carefully noted the informant's directions: "The cellars can be reached thru two large and easily worked iron gates in the market place."[17]

Loeb gleaned information about artworks, manuscripts, and rare books, treasures that had been systematically looted during the German occupation of western and central European countries. This subject was of growing interest to US officials, and an Art Looting Investigation Unit of the OSS had been authorized in November 1944. Loeb interviewed several POWs who told him about the status of these collections. Max Pohl, a "special consultant" for the Kunstschutz, the German art protection unit in northern France, had "intimate knowledge of the looting of museums and libraries" and provided a list of collections that had been removed. Other prisoners offered useful information: A student knew of confiscated treasures from France and the Netherlands, originally sent to the Dusseldorf art museum but later dispersed to castles, monasteries, and a stalactite cave when the danger of bombing increased; he had assisted his father install telephone lines between the hideaways and gave Loeb the exact locations. A journalist whom Loeb must have known in Germany told him about a storehouse filled with "large quantities of stolen art collections, libraries, and archives from nearly all the larger cities of Poland and Russia." Loeb also reported on Nazi efforts to assemble vast collections of Jewish books and records. A Catholic priest said that "the confiscated libraries of nearly all Jewish communities in Austria" had been gathered in the University of Vienna's Oriental Institute, while another prisoner described the looted library holdings at the Institute for Research on the Jewish Question in Frankfurt.[18]

Loeb's informants offered a glimpse into the behavior and attitudes of private citizens as the German home front deteriorated. They resented the extravagant facilities made for the storage of things, not the protection of people. A large tunnel built near Koblenz to secure government records, party archives, and even the stocks of large textile and shoe companies "caused much ill-feeling among the population," observed one POW, "since the construction of shelters in Koblenz proper has been neglected." In Munich, another commented, the first items to be moved were Nazi Party property, "which gave the signal for a flight of the civilian population and for a scramble to safeguard all valuable possessions." Many wanted to hold on to a world of books and culture, and at times they united to protect these materials in advance of any state directives. Loeb heard from one man how "civilian alarm at the sudden erection of large bunkers all over Nuremberg in 1940 was the signal for a general removal of stocks of libraries, archives and bookstores to villages in the neighborhood. . . . private homes, farms and barns were used." In contrast, after the bombing of the National-Bibliothek in Berlin, "there was much looting of the building." A POW and former journalist stated, "The black market trade in the library's books became so large between January and March 1944 that the police had to publish an official warning against the purchase of such publications."[19]

German publishers and bookstores struggled to serve readers in these years. One POW, Carl George Babus, offered a detailed description of the book trade in Munich. With limited paper stocks and printing facilities destroyed, many small publishers were forced to give their equipment and supplies to the larger houses. Those permitted to stay in business struggled to find alternative facilities when their buildings were demolished. J. F. Lehmann, publisher of medical periodicals and Nazi books, moved the firm's staff, paper stocks, and books from Munich to an outlying town, where he operated out of restaurants and small hotels. In early 1944, all the bookstores except the official Nazi Party dealers were ordered to give 20 percent of their stock to libraries. Later, said Babus, the authorities instated a rationing system "to avoid another rush on the bookstores by people with money to spend, such as that of Christmas 1943." Shops could sell two books per customer and had to close four days a week. "Store windows were forced to display (although they could not sell) the best available books to impress the many foreigners still in Muenchen at that time," he observed. "Particularly valuable books were after this sold 'under the counter' at black market prices." When he was captured, Babus had been running a Front Bookstore (Frontbuchhandlung) in Normandy, which sold mainly propagandistic books to the German occupiers. The buyers asked for "anything which is not connected with the war," especially children's books. They "were always ready to pay with coffee and butter for such 'treasures,'" he recalled.[20]

Loeb's interrogations not only produced information about the location of materials sought by intelligence agencies, they had painted a rare, even poignant portrait of the devastated book world in wartime Germany. In October 1944, Loeb completed his first target list in anticipation of the assault on Germany. Meanwhile, his colleagues in the OSS had gone to Paris in search of publications.

An OSS contingent crossed the channel soon after the liberation of Paris, combing the city and its environs for documents and publications. "Action was hasty," observed Allan Evans, as the T-Force raced to find materials ahead of the "advancing hordes" of other agencies. The team quickly examined one hundred official targets in Paris, including a number already visited by army intelligence. Fortunately, "documents of general or strategic interest . . . were mostly left behind for us to clean up," noted Dwight Baker, who headed the Paris R&A T-Force.[21]

In fact, they were astonished at the finds. "We have been going great guns," wrote Baker after a few weeks on the job. "I have been jeeping to all corners of Paris and to all kinds of targets." He noted, "we have had wonderful hauls especially in German documents and published materials of the last four years." These included "maps, correspondence, inventories, personnel files, secret military and non-military orders, yearbooks, and business directories, films, current periodicals in German, French, Japanese, and Russian, and so on." Among the first targets were a wholesale book firm of the German Labor Front, subsidiaries of German banks, commercial and industrial firms, and a Front Bookstore warehouse fifty miles from Brussels. After the initial targets were exhausted, they searched French broadcast studios, newsrooms, and hotels that had housed German agencies. Baker also served as a liaison with military intelligence's G-2 Documents Section, which had set up a large depot in SHAEF's Versailles headquarters. The OSS team raked through that material as well. By the end of November, the Paris personnel were complaining about being "understaffed and overworked." But as Lieutenant Edward Tenenbaum wryly observed, "They all seemed enthusiastic about the opportunities for exhausting themselves in coping with the mountains of material they had managed to collect."[22]

The IDC agents in Paris did not neglect the kind of work it had done in the outposts. They subscribed to French newspapers, systematically visited bookstores, placed orders with publishers, and contacted academics, government officials, and business leaders. Books came from former German distribution agencies and the German bookstore Rive Gauche, and they discovered "approximately 500 hitherto unavailable titles" at W. H. Smith, the British bookseller that had become "the largest retail distributor of German material during the occupation." Publishers Dunod, Presses Universitaires, and Hachette Livre were significant sources of materials, and Hachette offered a staff of searchers to help the IDC find books. They reproduced German publications at the Bibliothèque Nationale and had their own microfilm lab to copy materials of the German occupation, the Vichy regime, and the French resistance.[23]

At the same time, much of their labor departed from the earlier patterns of IDC, as new recruit Ross Lee Finney discovered. Finney was a recognized modern composer and music professor at Smith College, but in spring 1944, he left rural Massachusetts to join the OSS. As a student of Nadia Boulanger in the 1920s, he had come to know Paris well, and, encouraged by his friends Archibald MacLeish and Wilmarth Lewis, he decided to return, this time to help win the war. "The job is nebulous—of necessity, I understand why, now," he wrote his wife, and "considerably different than what I had expected to be doing." The niceties of bookshops and libraries had gone by the boards. He now used "slightly different methods of acquiring foreign publications than I or anyone in Northampton would use." He entered targets and confiscated large quantities of materials. "I requisitioned a 2 ½ ton truck today," Finney wrote. "I needed a convoy of them, actually." He learned how to interrogate informants and follow suspicious people. "I find I'm pretty good at sniffing down an alley and tracing things," he wrote. "I enjoy it and it seems instinctive to me." On Thanksgiving Day of 1944, he made "the best catch of all the time I've been in Paris." He had been investigating industrial targets for French and German technical publications, following up leads provided by French scholars, when at one firm he found a huge cache of French patent abstracts concerning rockets and jet propulsion. Overcoming his earlier caution and insecurity, Finney had turned into an intelligence agent.[24]

Finney especially loved work in the field, "to really get the job done I came over to do, so I go out in my old clothes and do the dirty work—and as a result have the time of my life doing it." Like other OSS civilians, he was required to wear a uniform when on a mission, and this gave him the feeling of authority and legitimacy the policy intended. A tall man, he knew his appearance in battle dress made an impression on others. "Everyone seems aware of my size," he exclaimed. Most important were the ties he developed with the enlisted men he worked with. Their acceptance meant everything to the composer. "I like these guys, I like to shake hands with them and feel this enthusiasm in what I am up to."[25]

He grew close to one in particular, Stanley (Ladislas) Rubint, "really the most brilliant boy in our outfit—even if he is only a GI." Rubint took a winding path to document gathering for the Allies. Born in Budapest in 1921, he was a student at the University of Madrid at the outbreak of the Spanish Civil War. He served as a medic on the Republican side, working with Edward K. Barsky, a prominent American surgeon and antifascist activist. With Barsky's sponsorship, Rubint emigrated to the United States in 1938, was a medical student for a time, and worked at an export firm in New York. In 1943 he enlisted in the US Army as a private and became a naturalized citizen. Fluent in many languages, Rubint was assigned to the IDC and became a key T-Force member from mid-September 1944 to VE Day, "on continual field assignment" in operations "which extended across the entire line of the armies." During this time, he examined over sixteen hundred targets in France and Germany.[26]

The most exhilarating—and frightening—time came during a two-week trip to the south of France. Finney and Rubint traveled in a command car with a trailer, carried guns (just for show, Finney assured his wife), and passed the time "in stitches of laughter" as their driver regaled them with stories of his love-making prowess. Arriving in a small town nestled in a mountain valley, they were the first Americans to appear since the liberation. "All the people crowded around the car eager to talk, eager to give us wine, eager to see our things, eager for cigarettes, francs, and eager for our gasoline." In Grenoble, Marseille, and Nice, they collected and microfilmed provincial newspapers and looked into the political scene. They met with representatives of the Left, including Étiennette Gallois, who had edited underground and Communist newspapers in Toulouse and gave them substantial materials. The trip yielded much useful information, such as German counter-espionage intelligence, code names, and military orders. Despite continual reassurances to his wife, however, the journey nearly turned deadly in Nice when Finney stepped on a landmine and was hit by shrapnel. He came out of the ordeal without lasting damage, although the wound continued to bother him months later. "My luck in the whole affair is something I don't like to talk about," he wrote his wife. "I can understand how guys feel about religion over here."[27]

The IDC met in Paris in late November 1944 for a week, bringing together the newer recruits, such as Finney and Rubint, and the older hands, including Frederick Kilgour, Ralph Carruthers, and Reuben Peiss. Only Adele Kibre did not attend, due to concerns she would not be permitted back into Stockholm. The days were filled with meetings and nonstop conversation between those who had spent months, even years, abroad, and the Washington-based Kilgour. They discussed the relationship between Washington and the outposts, their participation on T-forces, finances, and observance of copyright rules. Looming over the visit was a recognition that the end of the European war was in sight and their mission would necessarily change. Kilgour now gave orders for the "last collection drive in Europe." Most of all, they shared their experiences and impressions, as men whose once-cloistered lives had given way to a world of action and intrigue.[28]

At night the "visiting firemen" repaired to Finney's rooms, with its piano and homey touches, and continued to talk business over Cointreau and cigars. "We harangued until about ten," Finney wrote. "Then we decided to go out to a little French café around the corner and talked over a cognac." To the men who had been in distant outposts, Paris was a wonder. Eating real meals, taking in shows, and strolling the streets, they marveled at the beauty and insouciance of the city. "It is funny to see the reactions of these people," Finney observed. "They fell for this place." In a letter home, Reuben Peiss contrasted "gray and grim" London, "worn out by the long ordeal," to Paris, which he found "enchanting" and "absolutely beautiful." It "seems outwardly untouched by the war, yet people who knew it before say the old *joie de vivre* is missing," he commented, but "the women of Paris are still chic (and how!)." The IDC gathering also heightened the meaning of their work in their eyes. Said Finney, "The visit of the gang has meant a *very* great deal to me. It has given me more direction in my work, made me realize more its importance. . . . It is something to feel that what you are doing is contributive and interesting and even a little glamorous."[29]

By early 1945 the Paris IDC had settled into a routine. "Scouting through the bookstores," they acquired French works and continued to discover surprising quantities of German books, because Parisians "come in to sell them their personal copies." They continued to sort through the materials gathered by earlier collecting teams; the G-2 Document Center had "cellars literally full" of books. To find new sources of information, Finney made personal contacts with publishers, scientific and medical institutes, and government officials. He also took advantage of his growing musical reputation in Paris: invited to society dinners and salons, he would inevitably play the guitar and sing the American folksongs of his Minnesota boyhood. "The guitar is certainly an ice breaker," and his songs—"unusual, a little primitive"—moved French listeners. He and his Russian contacts played into the night, which eased a negotiation with the Soviet Embassy to get copies of "a formidable collection of pre-war Russian material, most of which ha[d] never appeared in the United States."[30]

As he began to look forward to the end of his OSS assignment, Finney reflected on his mission. He wrote his wife, "Now and then I have wondered how I was helping the war effort in collecting French materials and then it has dawned on me that I was helping the peace effort and in the long run that would mean a hell of a lot." He was convinced that France would be a leading force in western Europe after the war. "Nobody will know that I have done it," he mused, but many people would need and use the material he had gathered. This, he believed, would be the legacy of his intelligence service.[31]

For policymakers, collecting and managing enemy documents became a pressing matter as Allied troops advanced in France and Belgium during the second half of 1944. "Everyone [is] getting archive-conscious," a British intelligence officer observed, but the disorganized performance of T-Forces in Strasbourg and other places worried Allied commanders and planners. "There is complete chaos at present owing to uncoordinated exploitation," he said, raising the specter of a "wild scramble for documents."[32] The sheer quantity of the captured materials was nearly overwhelming, hindering efforts to control, catalogue, and use them.

No one had fully anticipated the thorny logistics of document collecting. T-Forces operated in dangerous working conditions, often without electricity, on sites that might have sustained bombing or other damage. There were ongoing problems with transportation and storage facilities; as one report put it, "Arrangements for the retention and evacuation of material were extremely fluid." The situation on the ground called for a great deal of improvisation. In small towns, T-Force commanders unexpectedly found themselves dealing with hungry and frightened local residents before civil affairs officers arrived. The T-Force "represented the United States," said one leader of a team. Although the citizenry "had never seen or talked with an American soldier or officer," he continued, "they looked to the officer in charge of the team for direction, assistance, and support in such different matters as food and politics." He was expected to respond, and "failure to do so was not understood."[33]

Finding targets and selecting materials challenged documents teams. German documents and archives had been moved, often more than once, in an effort to protect them from bombing or ground troops, and target lists were often incomplete, inaccurate, or out of date; in some cases, they had not even been distributed. In one city, the T-Force had a target list but no maps, so they used an old prewar map found in a police station and a telephone directory to chart the sites to investigate. The best targets were usually the largest and most diverse in terms of materials, but they were hard to screen under time pressure. "It must be emphasized that documents collection is not a 'clean' job," an intelligence report stated, "conditions in target buildings do not normally favor examination and analysis on the spot from a specialist point of view."[34]

Document collecting was a massive undertaking, involving many military and civilian agencies. Substantial jurisdictional disputes arose over who would control and process enemy records, in what location, and for what uses. A conflict raged between those who would protect archives and those who would exploit them. The G-2 Documents Section insisted on precedence over captured materials and complete freedom to remove and use them for military intelligence. The Allied military headquarters wanted everything important sent to London or Washington immediately. A "vast library frozen on the Continent," a British Air Ministry official complained, would be of no use to the campaign for victory.[35]

The army's Civil Affairs Division, known as G-5, pushed back, arguing that records be preserved in place. Their job was to plan for military government and administer the occupation, and they would need the enemy's administrative archives in order to govern Germany after the war. This view was reinforced by the Control Council for Germany, which oversaw policy planning for the postwar period. The Monuments, Fine Arts, and Archives Section (MFAA), part of G-5, spoke for historical and contemporary archives as foundations of a nation's cultural heritage and necessary for its reconstruction. Such records also undergirded human rights: in a time of dislocation and destruction, archives enabled people to establish citizenship, claim property, and even discover the fate of family members. But the tensions were not resolved, and as military archivist Sherrod East put it years later, "cooperation and understanding between the G-2 and the G-5 left much to be desired."[36]

As secretary of the British Public Records Office and an MFAA adviser, Hilary Jenkinson took the lead in making the case for archival protection. Jenkinson was legendary in the archive world, having served a similar function during World War I and written the definitive text on archives administration. Under his guidance, MFAA created a general list of German archives and instructions for documents teams on how to handle them safely in the field. Believing in maintaining the holistic integrity of archives, Jenkinson argued they remain in situ to assure unbroken custody. Intelligence operatives "should certainly *not* be 'free to collect what documents they require,'" an exasperated Jenkinson replied to one proposal. Trying to balance immediate and long-term needs, he urged "preservation before exploitation, and in interest of exploiters."[37]

At times the debates sounded like a seminar in archives theory. A British "working party" under the Director of Military Intelligence debated the nature of documents, archives, and information—a term used only by the Americans—and the relationship among them. Removing documents from archives piecemeal (or even shuffling their order) pulled them out of context and broke up collections without thought to future use. One official observed that "every Archive is related to others in the same accumulation and derives some, often a large part, of its significance from the place in which, or the persons by whom, it was preserved." While this made sense from an archival standpoint, it did not comport with the realities of war-torn areas. There materials had already been relocated in often haphazard ways, combat endangered repositories, and a limited post-conflict civil affairs presence made archives vulnerable to looting.[38]

Military leaders determined to gain greater control over the collecting teams, establish more orderly procedures, and create centralized repositories for materials. They reorganized the T-Force Sub-Division in February 1945 to coordinate "all Allied investigators of intelligence targets in occupied or liberated countries in Europe" and to prevent the duplication of efforts. The Sixth Army Group's G-2 devised a "specialist camp," which would house arriving investigators, process their orders, and arrange transportation, as well as a "target service" to prepare dossiers. They tried to prevent the inadvertent destruction of materials by troops, which might not consider enemy documents a valuable source of intelligence. They drilled into soldiers the message: "Every paper is a document. All documents go to G-2."[39]

Nevertheless, the directives were interpreted very differently by the various armies, as C. H. Noton, head of the British Enemy Publications Committee, found when he toured them in June 1945. The Seventh Army command decided to centralize its huge caches of records, while Third Army documents teams left the records they found "in situ with guards where possible or necessary." The Ninth Army had a center called Camp Dentine, in which the "emphasis is on pulling all documents in and exploiting immediately irrespective of any long-term interest." Noton was disturbed that "important questions of siting, storing, removal and setting up of records are frequently made at the lowest level of Officers." Indeed, looking back on the latter phase of the war, Jenkinson detailed an archival mess in which documents had disappeared or been dispersed because there was "no single system of control."[40]

Policymakers did not address the question of what to do with books and other publications that had been scooped up by T-Forces and taken to document centers. These rarely provided timely intelligence for military operations, so G-2 saw them more as bycatch in its nets. Remarkably, the MFAA gave little attention to printed culture, except rare works and important library collections. Books were "always left out" of the discussion of archives, one individual commented.[41]

Thus, the IDC became the primary channel for captured books and periodicals almost by default. The London office received sacks of publications unwanted by the joint Military Intelligence Research Section (MIRS) and microfilmed "unique and operational books and good files of serials" the military wanted to retain. "The G-2 (Docts)-MIRS channel has been functioning almost too well," wrote Kilgour, "publications have been flooding in from Paris." Although still on the lookout for intelligence materials, they increasingly selected publications relevant to American postwar objectives and scientific and technical research.[42]

However, a new directive in February 1945 opened the door to acquisitions far beyond the committee's earlier mandate: "IDC will also survey the areas of penetration for the purpose of evaluating bookstores, libraries of all kinds and any other collection of publications in order to facilitate at a later date a more thorough exploitation." Now based in Paris, Ralph Carruthers had difficulty understanding the scope of the new orders, which on a practical level asked the field agents to acquire multiple copies of foreign publications for US government libraries. Did they want "duplicates to the nth degree regardless of cost," Carruthers asked, even if the works were already in Washington? Would there be funds to purchase such large quantities, or would the army simply allow them to requisition what they wanted? "IDC may very easily and unwittingly corner the market" in foreign publications, he warned, hampering the efforts of other libraries after the war. "My inclination is to get the stuff while the getting is good," he told Kilgour, "but I cannot quite forget that I was once a Librarian." Kilgour had no qualms. No one knew why the IDC continued to collect when the war was almost over, he wrote in a cheery outpost letter, but "in the meantime pretty nearly everything obtainable in Western Europe is being obtained it seems."[43]

When the Allies took Strasbourg, crossed the Rhine, secured Cologne, and pushed eastward, they found distinct landscapes of destruction, flight, and preservation, which shaped their collecting practices. T-Forces seized opportunities when they could, trying to follow a pragmatic ethics in situations that were often difficult to assess. In November 1944, Germans hurriedly evacuated Strasbourg, leaving behind half-eaten meals and secret papers they were unable to burn in time. At the Gauhaus, a large complex of Nazi agencies, "the Germans were completely caught off balance," G-2 reported. "The tape in the telecrypter machines was still running when elements of 'T' Force entered the Gestapo building." One month later, Lieutenant George W. Overton led an OSS documents team into Strasbourg, with the city under martial law, early curfew, and constant patrols. The military had supposedly posted guards at the Gauhaus, but the OSS team found it in complete disarray, "filled with papers, books, pictures, movies, and odd files and photograph albums, all heaped on the floors or in overturned cabinets." A parade of people had trooped through the building. The French Forces of the Interior celebrated the German defeat by "wrecking things [and] smashing pictures of Hitler"; billeted American infantrymen kept warm by burning documents in the fireplaces; French civilians wandered in, looking for usable goods and paper to light fires. And then there were the "countless agencies normally attached to a regular T-Force" which had "more or less gone wild." Each one had "bagged material for itself in the 'first come, first served' manner," said Overton's colleague Lewis Allbee. "As a result, most of the targets here have already been pretty well combed and even ransacked in some cases."[44]

That still left plenty of material. The OSS T-Force took out four tons and sequestered another two, a "gold-mine" of books, maps, and other items. Among their most valuable finds was a Nazi Party membership list for the area, with notes on each member's loyalty, and the files of a German engineering company, containing maps and information about Russian railways in Ukraine. Overton's greatest realization was that "the collection of documents is a bulk job—a matter of how many 2½-ton trucks you can take out—and not a job of looking through a library catalogue, which we somehow used to think in Washington."[45]

Conditions were far worse in Cologne, as another OSS T-Force reported when it entered the city four days after the Allies captured it. They witnessed extraordinary destruction: although the cathedral towers still stood, three-quarters of the central city had been destroyed. There were thirty thousand casualties from the final raid. "The list of names alone covered six pages of newsprint," their report commented. "The city had a very peculiar odor of death." The devastation disturbed the OSS men deeply. Stanley Rubint, veteran of the brutal Spanish Civil War, remarked that "the city of Cologne is the sorriest sight I have run across yet in any war." They went from site to site on their target list, only to discover all but one had been destroyed. "There is nothing left to buy and nobody to buy from," Rubint observed. Lieutenant Leonard J. Hankin, who led this detachment, "felt no qualms about going into rubble which used to be such stores and removing any items of value." They requested Coleman lamps, candles, and flashlights, because most of the extant documents had been discovered in unlit sub-basements.[46]

Despite their first impressions, they sent back to Paris "a tremendous mass of material," most of it—twenty-eight bags—a "magnificent fulfillment of IDC's assignments." They had arrived at the moment when the military had secured the city but before civil affairs officers and the rear echelons had appeared: "It is during this period that the lid is literally off and almost anything goes." They were allowed to remove whatever they wanted from bookstores and libraries, and their "richest haul came from the University itself." Hankin felt compelled to explain their actions. "The point might easily be made that in forwarding this material our function is merely that of shipping agents and, more seriously, that in evacuating these documents from centers where R/A and other scholars are apt to look for and expect them in the future we may be doing a disservice," he acknowledged. However, the poor condition of the university library put the materials at severe risk, and the T-Force had decided this justified removal "in the absence of specific directives to the contrary." Military government would not permit local archives or historical collections to be removed, but "they are without personnel to protect the contents of the libraries, archives, etc."[47]

The team moved on to Bonn, where the university library had been destroyed by fire in October 1944, and collections moved to cellars in and around the city. Military government was already in place, Hankin noted, so "the period of the snatch is therefore past." They would have to use formal requisitions or reproduce material on microfilm, both of which were time consuming. Items from "going concerns" could be requisitioned as material "required for military operations," with the owner "later recompensed by the German government." Although inclined in this direction, the team faltered when faced with the collections belonging to the university library; instead Hankin explained to the cooperative head librarian the kinds of publications they were interested in and asked him to gather them for later retrieval. Later, they went to a bookstore that carried periodicals and maps they were looking for. "Having neither the required form nor (in the presence of a large number of interested German civilians) the inclination to just seize the stuff and stalk off," Hankin wrote, "we paid about 140 marks for the lot." Yet he drew the line at one publication, *Nauticus 1944*, an annual review of German maritime interests that included a strong dose of Nazi propaganda. When he refused to pay for it and advised the clerk to "dispose of the others," she "promptly proceeded to take all the copies off the shelf and gave them to me." The preface of the book, touting National Socialism, had already been cut out of each volume.[48]

Although there were rules governing some of these situations, often decisions were made in the moment. When a given city or territory had just been seized by American troops and before makeshift order was imposed, T-Forces believed they had the greatest latitude. They were answerable to military leadership, not local populations. If military leaders gave permission or looked the other way, T-Forces felt little hesitation in taking material freely. This was, in fact, built into the conception of T-Force, whose mission was to safeguard material, examine it, and remove what was valuable. Teams learned quickly that delay meant destruction, and their instinct was to seize documents—company files, governmental archives,

Nazi Party records, and the like—because of their uniqueness, perishability, and potential for intelligence analysis.

With the arrival of civil affairs officers in defeated German cities and the beginning of an occupation government, official policies took on greater weight. "While the war was in progress it was often possible to exploit targets at one's own convenience," observed Captain Lloyd Black, of the OSS Map Division. "Now, since people have returned to their homes and offices, it is usually necessary to find authorities in charge and/or custodians with innumerable keys." By June, Woodrow Borah, a Latin American specialist, saw "the end of the earlier period of discovery of large deserted business files and free removal of materials" from abandoned industrial plants and corporations. Ironically, the presence of military government often did little to protect records from perishing. When Borah's team returned to sites they had earlier secured, they often found the collections had been destroyed. In one case, they found the export records of a Junkers motor plant hidden in huts and left them in "perfect shape," only to find three weeks later that American troops billeted there had "systematically wrecked, torn, and scattered them."[49]

It was standard practice to requisition books and serials from publishers, and the American occupiers expected cooperation. Rubint's team went to Stuttgart and found that Ferdinand Enke Verlag's stocks had survived; the owner and employees were compliant, he reported, and they took one copy of every book published since 1939. This seems to have been effected as a private arrangement, as "Stuttgart was still under French control and difficulties would have arisen had we disclosed our mission to the French authorities." At the same time, some Germans began to assess when they could assert their property rights and push back against such demands. By early June, Max Loeb wrote, "some publishers start[ed] to refuse to supply books, claiming that Military Government ha[d] prohibited" them from doing so. Loeb said enigmatically that he "was still able to overcome the difficulty"—whether through persuasion or force is unclear—but "it looks as if the easy time, where we could just requisition without difficulties, is over."[50]

———⚬⚬———

The war against Germany ended on May 8, 1945, but the work of collecting had only begun. Led by Captain Black, two OSS teams set out from Paris to Wiesbaden, where G-2 had installed its headquarters and a document center. One team, attached to the Sixth Army Group, then took a southern route to Stuttgart and Munich. The other was attached to the Twelfth Army Group. It went north, into Thuringia and Saxony, and spent ten

days in Leipzig, with the express purpose of "looking into German private
and learned publishing which centered in the Leipzig printers and book
wholesalers."[51]

Arriving in Wiesbaden, the Northern team checked into the "specialist
camp," which already had facilities to handle the numerous visitors—four
hundred to five hundred daily—who flooded in to examine target reports
and pursue information. The group included Max Loeb and Woodrow Borah,
who went to look at targets in Frankfurt am Main while Black obtained official approval and passes for their trip. This was an area Loeb knew intimately, as he had lived in Frankfurt for some years. He kept running into
"old friends of mine . . . 12 of them, a lot of fun"—a surprise, perhaps, for
someone who had fled Nazi Germany. But his energies were focused on
inspecting the scientific, technical, and medical libraries of businesses and
research institutes, none of which had been touched by earlier T-Forces. At
the main library of the I. G. Farben company, where the US military was
establishing a base of operations, he found thirty thousand books, German
chemical periodicals, and a patent library. "This neighborhood is just plain
full with IDC-targets of greatest importance," he reported. Black had even
given him a jeep to collect as much as possible, but he was unnerved by the
enormity of the task. There were "so many tempting targets," he wrote,
that "even after a good and successful day," when he seized one thousand
books and runs of twelve periodicals, he felt "uneasy, because there is still
so much undone."[52]

They arrived in Leipzig on May 17. Although many printing presses
and book stocks had been destroyed, the team tracked down a number
of the publishers and book wholesalers on Loeb's list, with results "especially gratifying to IDC." At the Deutsche Bücherei, the national de-
posit library, they found bibliographies of new books and a secret list of
banned books, which they arranged to microfilm. They purchased many
volumes, requisitioned others from bookstores and publishing houses,
and removed books from the Chamber of Commerce library. There were
other triumphs. "The IDC lads have made some remarkable discoveries
of unpublished manuscripts in Leipzig," OSS official Harold Deutsch reported, over one hundred works on scientific, political, and economic
topics, which publishers had been unable to issue during the war. The
Leipzig firms had tried to concentrate on politically neutral works,
"restrict[ing] themselves to technical books as much as possible during
the Nazi years," a T-Force member learned. "The bulk of propaganda
and Nazi pseudo-scientific material came out in special government-
sponsored institutes and publishing houses in Berlin, Stuttgart, and
Munich."[53]

University libraries still functioned in Leipzig and other places, and the T-Force respected the integrity of academic collections. They used library catalogues to compile lists of new titles, then tried to find them at book wholesalers. University collections in the service of Nazi ideology were another story: "The library of the Institut fuer Rassenkunde [Institute for Racial Science] was all in the building, and that we felt fair game," wrote Borah. Business and freestanding technical libraries were often seized, when they had not been placed off limits by military police. Loeb found the library of the optical firm Zeiss in Jena unharmed but guarded by a tank company, and he was not allowed to remove it. When he discovered another scientific library stored in a restaurant, he could only have it moved to a safer location in a leather factory and guarded.[54]

As the investigators delved further, they uncovered vast quantities of books and other publications in surprising locations. The Stassfurt salt mines contained two hundred carloads of materials; the Berlin University library had been found in a coalmine near Vacha; nineteenth-century historical archives were hidden in an I. G. Farben potash mine. The salt-potash mine at Ransbach—where gold and art treasures had been stored—also yielded up a large portion of the Prussian State Library, two million volumes in disarray, piled up in tunnels, and no card catalogue in sight. Tragically, a fire had burned for several months in the Ransbach mine

Figure 3.1. Piles of books from the Prussian State Library stacked in the Ransbach salt mine near Heimboldshausen, 1946. Library of Congress (LC-DIG-ds-07886).

(possibly set by refugees trying to keep warm) when the OSS team came to inspect it in July 1945. The library "is in the process of gradual destruction from fumes, smoke, and dampness," they reported, and asked that the information be conveyed to the Library of Congress. The unexpected discovery of vast hidden deposits of archives and libraries in Saxony and Thuringia spurred another mass collecting push. Harold Deutsch wrote William Langer, "Again and again the team working in that region came across collections of such size that it had no hope . . . of either transporting the collections entirely or of making appropriate selections on the spot."[55]

To add to the challenge, Leipzig and the surrounding area was set to become part of the Soviet zone of occupation on July 1, 1945. After the Allied bombing in 1943, publishers and libraries had sent their remaining holdings to castles and small villages in eastern and southern Saxony, occupied by the Red Army at the war's end. Parts of the Deutsche Bücherei were stored in ten castles in this zone. Also behind Russian lines were large stocks of books and periodicals purchased on account by American libraries, stored near Meinersdorf. Hampered by a lack of transportation, the poor physical conditions of the targets, and a looming deadline, the T-Force hurried to move books and periodicals collected by Loeb from scientific publishers, microfilm an extensive index of wartime German periodicals, and photograph the manuscripts and unbound sheets of unpublished scientific books. In early June, they "got only a fraction of the haul that might otherwise have been possible," Borah commented, but that amounted to two tons of material. Additional personnel were sent to support the effort, including Reuben Peiss as a technical adviser, who determined what to take or reproduce before Americans had to relinquish the area. They removed another four truckloads, acquired through requisition and purchase, not by "the straight snitch."[56]

"All work on this project was shadowed by the imminent Russian occupation," wrote Peiss, and "the core of the problem is to choose those targets which can most productively be exploited quickly." His team had been working in the Stassfurt mines when they heard the British had been given forty-eight hours to leave, with American troops soon to follow. The mines "are piled high with cases of documents. These stand in salt chambers completely unlighted, so that it is necessary to flash miners' lamps on each document in order to identify it." He weighed whether mass appropriation or careful selection made more sense: "With regards to archives and other documents, the process of identification . . . takes a prodigious amount of time. Removing the whole archive, on the other hand, may well involve us in the transportation of very old records which have relatively little value strategically (or even historically) as compared with targets located in other places." In contrast, the Zeiss plant library at Jena was a well-defined target. Although Peiss and Loeb arrived without the needed passes, Loeb had already contacted a captain he knew, who let them examine the library. It contained periodicals on optics, electronics, and similar subjects, as well as medical, military, and legal titles. Peiss drew up a list of titles to be microfilmed, "which are not yet well represented in our holdings and a few of which I had never heard."[57]

With Woodrow Borah, Peiss inspected the library of a German foreign policy research institute (Institut für Aussenpolitische Forschung) in a manor on a hill in Sondershausen and interviewed the librarian in charge, a Dr. Stoepel. She provided a sketch of the library's history. The Hamburg-based institute had been especially interested in the West, had subscribed to leading foreign newspapers, and kept an extensive clipping file. Its director had been forced out when the Nazis came to power and the institute moved to Berlin in 1937, where it had become associated with Nazi propagandistic work. It continued to receive newspapers from the western hemisphere until US entry into the war, and it obtained the European press until April 1944 "through the Foreign Office and the Gestapo, which acquired them in Lisbon." Institute members were sworn to secrecy about what they had read in the foreign press. In September 1943, most of the library, with its clipping files, was evacuated to Sondershausen. Peiss recommended that everything in the German language be removed, about half the holdings, "along with such material as might not be expected to be already in our hands," about ten to fifteen thousand volumes, "skim[ming] the cream of the collection while leaving the watery bulk to the Russians."[58]

In July 1945, Frederick Kilgour and the European IDC agents met in Paris for the last time, to plan the liquidation of this wartime agency. Reuben Peiss and Ralph Carruthers finally met Adele Kibre, whose Stockholm outpost had closed not long after the British Press Reading Bureau ceased operation. Coincidentally Eugene Power was also in the City of Light, arriving after trips to London and Frankfurt to discuss microfilming captured German documents. He ran into Kibre, and the next day, Bastille Day, they "walked all over the city as the Parisians toasted the holiday, their liberation from the Nazis, and the end of the war, all in one enormous blowout."[59]

For months the Washington office of IDC had been deluged with shipments, with packages filling the basement bookshelves. Over the summer of 1945, they continued to arrive. Seventy crates of publications went to the Army Medical Library, the Library of Congress, and the Alien Property Custodian, which reproduced scientific and technical serials for the American business and academic communities. Legal publications and Nazi documents were sent to the Office of the Chief of Counsel, in preparation for the war crimes tribunals. Eighty more crates went into storage, ultimately for the Library of Congress.[60] But this did not mark the end of mass acquisition projects or the presence of collectors in the world of postwar reconstruction.

The scramble for documents—and the sweeping up of books and other materials not directly relevant to winning the war—brought librarians and collectors further into the structure and culture of the military. T-Forces had a propulsive logic of their own and, for the most part, those who served on them took the mission on its own terms. Yet, even in moments of victory, there was occasionally an underlying awareness, even defensiveness, of a line potentially crossed. It is apparent in the phrase "period of the snatch": these same actions, done by individual soldiers or civilians, might be a criminal offense. None of the Americans went on the record in the way a British T-Force soldier did when he recalled long after the war, "I was a member of an official looting party." Yet the ethical quandary was apparent, at least to some. In split seconds choices and imperatives were weighed: the moral injunction against looting and the opportunity to get away with it, the rights of the victor and his qualms in the presence of the vanquished. In Strasbourg, Stanley Rubint found the bookstores closed, but even if they were open, he questioned their "right to requisition the books left behind." Nor could Leonard Hankin in Bonn bring himself to seize the merchandise, when the appraising eyes of German bystanders witnessed his encounter with a bookseller. Americans distinguished their values and behavior from the plundering of Nazi Germany and the "trophy loot" of the Soviet Union.[61] They did, in fact, respect important boundaries, for example, cordoning off university and public research libraries. Through the work of Monuments officers, they rescued and restituted millions of artworks, books, and treasures that constitute European cultural heritage. Yet in this phase of the war the overall American acquisition mission, in its scale and scope, was a particular form of trophy taking, in which knowledge about technical matters, scientific advances, and state secrets were the spoils of war.

CHAPTER 4

✿

Acquisitions on a Grand Scale

In the summer of 1945, Luther Evans, Archibald MacLeish's second-in-command and newly appointed successor, met with leaders in the library field and officials in the State and War Departments to develop a "blanket buying effort," or, as he put it, "mass-acquisitions" for the postwar world. With the international book trade shattered, the Library of Congress proposed to procure foreign works wherever "the ordinary means of commerce were inadequate." Its agents would go to Europe and, with the US government's logistical and political support, purchase three copies of every wartime publication. Evans was a cautious man, and only reluctantly did he recommend "the facilities of the Government be used in this way." He appreciated the enormous challenge for the military in newly liberated and conquered areas devastated by battle, where hungry populations, broken economies, and political disarray required immediate attention. Yet, he wrote the secretary of state, "The national interest, both in times of war and in times of peace, is intimately affected by the holdings of the large research libraries." This, he averred, was "a deep conviction based upon daily experience." Privately Evans worried that he had gone out on a limb.[1]

From this proposal emerged a unique collecting effort, the Library of Congress Mission to Europe (LCM), which in its short existence acquired 1.5 million books, periodicals, and other materials for the Library of Congress and numerous research libraries. The LCM would help transform the sentiments Evans put forth hesitantly into a forthright assertion of the American library's importance in national and world affairs. The Library of Congress had not been ready for the "test of wartime demand," he told his professional staff soon after the mission had been established. Now it must aim at "control of the total body of recorded knowledge that was deemed . . . necessary or advisable for the best interests of this country."[2] International collections, and a national will to collect en masse, would transform the nation's repositories of knowledge into sites of American intellectual and cultural leadership in the postwar world.

⸻ ✃ ⸻

During the war, research libraries tried desperately to acquire what foreign publications they could, seeking the help of loyal colleagues, students, and alumni to send books and other printed material from war zones. Classicist Mason Hammond took time from his duties as a Monuments officer in Italy to gather such materials for Harvard; Elmer Sitkin, a Stanford student and embassy code clerk in Moscow, collected Russian items at his own expense for the Hoover Library. Sheer interest in books and the threat of cultural ruin spurred librarians in the armed forces. "What will grieve me will be the scenes of destruction not only of monuments but records and books," Charles Dornbusch wrote from a troop ship en route to Europe. He sent items back to his employer, the New York Public Library. "Did you receive that single issue of a German Wehrmacht paper?" he asked. "With a bit of blarney and credentials, one could pick up a deal of important material in Europe." His colleague Stanley Pillsbury, based in China, combed the bookstores for works on typography and bookmaking, as well as children's literature. "There is so much of interest from the book and printman's point of view," he observed, that he accumulated far more than he could transport.[3] These individual contributions were welcome but could not make up for the shutdown of commerce.

At first, an influx of European Jewish refugees in the book trade helped these libraries work around wartime difficulties. Centered in New York City, they specialized in the secondhand book market and resourcefully found ways to secure books for elite libraries. The librarians' appreciation was sometimes tinged with antisemitic distaste. They had always welcomed the "older and better-established book-sellers . . . as brothers and colleagues," but felt sullied by the exiles' "sharper sense of the book-trade business, and business for profit," a Harvard College librarian observed. Nevertheless, these dealers made it possible for Harvard to achieve a degree of stability in their orders, with those of 1942–1943 about the same as two years earlier. By the next year, however, even the émigrés were unable to procure European books.[4]

Only the Library of Congress, with its national mission and government backing, managed to maintain an active program of acquisitions throughout the war. It benefited from its relationship to the OSS, gaining one hundred thousand original items and countless pieces on micro-film produced by the IDC. Adele Kibre collected works for the Library of Congress, in addition to her duties overseeing the Anglo-American mi-crofilm operation in Stockholm. Outlining her orders, Frederick Kilgour mused, "I, personally, would feel somewhat like a goop walking into Brentano's, picking up one copy of everything in sight, and saying, 'I want to buy these.' But this is what the Library of Congress wants you to do." The library had sent its own agent, Manuel Sanchez, to Spain and Portugal, and he went on to acquire aggressively in Algeria, Italy, and France. In Italy, he purchased over forty-four thousand items and received nearly twenty-nine thousand as gifts. "Sanchez sent back to the United States more important publications . . . than any other American book collector in a similar period of time," Reuben Peiss observed, "and this under difficult, and often dangerous, conditions."[5]

Library leaders had suspected the weakness of their international collections before the war. In an often-cited 1936 study, Douglas Waples and Harold Lasswell had shown that even the top academic libraries failed to acquire foreign books systematically or comprehensively. The large war-time demand for these publications made this an acute problem. In early 1942, research librarians wondered whether microfilm or photo-offset printing might be used to reproduce foreign materials, although some expressed qualms about doing so without copyright, "especially when we are looking toward a future world order with higher ethical standards than now prevail." A government agency, the Alien Property Custodian, stepped in with a secret republication program in 1943. In an unusual interpreta-tion of its mandate to seize and administer enemy property, it asserted the power to grant or "vest" copyright of enemy scientific and technical publications for the duration of the war. The APC selected journals and books secretly obtained by the IDC in such fields as physics, optics, and organic chemistry. It issued licenses to commercial publishers to reprint these works and distributed them to about nine hundred subscribers engaged in the war effort; half were in business and industry, and one-third in universities and scientific research. By the war's end, the APC had reproduced over one hundred periodical titles and licensed nearly seven hundred books. Yet the publications were often out of date, and there were long periods when the IDC sent nothing at all. On several occasions, the Alien Property Custodian considered expanding the scope of the program beyond "war-urgent" periodicals to include those in the humanities and social sciences, but ultimately the American Library Association rejected this suggestion. Only Eugene Power saw commercial potential, proposing a cooperative microfilm project to make reproductions widely available.[6] These wartime efforts did serve research institutions but were limited in scope.

Holding out hope for the rapid restoration of the international book trade, librarians fretted over the situation of European booksellers and publishing centers. In 1940, many American libraries had arranged for dealers to store their purchases and stock standing orders for the duration. Now, with the Allied push to victory, they awaited word of the fate of their longtime European associates. They reached out to government officials, from the State Department to the Office of War Information, to no avail. "We know little, practically nothing, except what we learn from the newspapers," commented Harry Lydenberg, who at this time headed the ALA's International Office.[7]

News finally began to surface after the liberation of Belgium and France. Dealers had taken great risks to obtain periodical subscriptions and continuations for their American clientele. Martinius Nijhoff, a major book exporter in The Hague, had saved enough material to fill 200 to 250 cases, "practically everything up to September 1944, when we became completely isolated," including a nearly complete file of the Dutch underground press. Tragically, three members of his staff had been murdered by Germans and a printing plant robbed. Otto Hafner, in charge of the Paris office of G. E. Stechert, secretly purchased periodicals for American colleges, storing them in rooms he rented throughout the city. He was briefly jailed when the police caught a friend publishing a clandestine newspaper that had been kept in the same place as the Stechert materials. Hafner reported that their stocks in Paris were mainly safe, but there could be no direct dealings for some time. With the shortage of paper, new books were scarce and went out of print quickly. One French publisher suggested using GIs as intermediaries to send books to the States and deliver payment in person. No one knew for certain about German publishers and agents. Based on newspaper reports of Leipzig and Berlin, most American librarians believed that German periodicals for the war years had been destroyed.[8]

Americans were eager to get into the European theater with their own agents. "It is of first importance to have representatives of American libraries get a chance to pick up what there is left," Harvard library director Keyes Metcalf insisted. This was not a genteel world, as librarians well knew. They worried about a repetition of the aftermath of World War I, when American institutions bought up private German collections cheaply, preying on impoverished professors. One ALA leader was "astonished at the avidity" of those seeking to acquire books in Europe, while Eugene Power found his clients "almost frantic" for reproductions of continental material. The Association of Research Libraries even formed a Committee on Postwar Competition in Book Purchases, which surveyed its members in fall 1944 and found many scheming to send buyers abroad. One library might "get ahead, gobble up the market, and let the rest trail along as well as they could," Lydenberg feared. At one point Metcalf erupted—"Has the Hoover Library been able to jump the gun on the rest of us?"—when he heard a rumor that an agent of the former president had arrived in Paris. Believing that "too many libraries are already buying on the black market," he grew ever more agitated as the war came to an end.[9]

To avoid such skirmishes, library leaders considered sending one or more agents to Europe to represent the interests of American research libraries as a whole. The idea of cooperative acquisitions had been batted around for some time. In fall 1942, Archibald MacLeish had met with his Librarian's Consultants at Wilmarth Lewis's home in Farmington, Connecticut. In what came to be known as the Farmington Plan, they proposed to divide responsibility among American libraries for acquiring materials in particular subject areas, assuring that at least one copy of every book published worldwide would be available in the United States. MacLeish estimated that at least twenty million research titles were not available domestically. These were not only esoteric works but those "indispensable to victory for the forces of freedom." At the same time, cooperative acquisitions might alleviate the concern that libraries would soon become too large and unwieldy for users. With collections expected to double every two decades, MacLeish worried about "thralldom to sheer masses of books" and believed in user-oriented services to supply "the book that each needs at the time he needs it." A national division of responsibility for specific subjects—"inclusiveness through cooperation," Metcalf described it—would serve this goal.[10]

The end of the war seemed the perfect time to initiate such a plan. Shortly after VE day, Metcalf proposed a European library mission to Secretary of State Edward Stettinius, arguing that the lack of foreign publications had hindered the war effort; a government-sponsored mission would avoid "unnecessary competitive ransacking and the wild rush of commercial and library buyers." The program was presented as a corollary to the effort of American institutions to rebuild devastated European libraries and restore intellectual relations. However, the State and War Departments gave only a slow and halting response to an idea they must have perceived as a low priority.[11]

By June 1945, however, there was new urgency to the matter of books in Europe. The Library of Congress started to receive word of the army's seizure of vast caches of material. Felix Reichmann—émigré bookman, former OSS agent, and now an Information Control officer in Heidelberg—eagerly contacted Luther Evans. "We confiscate every day great quantities of books," especially Nazi literature, he wrote. "It is most likely that I [can] get hold of books which you do not have." Evans scribbled a note on the letter, "Here's a hot trail—let's bear down fast." Evans heard from Sargent Child, an old colleague from their days in the Historical Records Survey, who had gone to Germany as a Monuments, Fine Arts, and Archives adviser. Child informed him of talks among military officials about the possibility of removing scientific and technical libraries from Germany. "The amount and value of the material *can't* be overestimated," Child exclaimed, "you can't afford to miss this boat." The army had hauled in governmental records, scientific research, historical archives, collections looted from occupied countries, and countless items with Nazi content, from scholarly works to popular fiction and textbooks. There were about three hundred thousand censorship withholdings as well. The military's intelligence staff, charged with handling these materials, had begun to wonder whether many books and pamphlets not needed by government agencies would be of interest to American libraries as a historical record. OSS officer and scholar Harold Deutsch, who had worked closely with the IDC on its collecting mission, approached Evans about making such an arrangement.[12]

The decision to establish the Library of Congress Mission to Europe (LCM) came rapidly that summer. Luther Evans gained approval for the book acquisition program from the War and State Departments, which stipulated that purchasing would be on behalf of all research libraries. A cooperative plan would divide the works according to scholarly fields and distribute them to libraries across the United States. The mission's agents would retrieve any prewar orders that had been stored by European dealers. The army agreed to provide transportation, storage, and shipping facilities. The program would continue until regular commercial channels reopened. "This all seems to be a wholesale deal," Lydenberg commented, with items "handled in bulk," payment in "so many pieces or pounds or other units," and no returns.[13]

The arrangement was designed to address the needs of both the military and the library world. For the libraries, the revival of German publishing and the book trade lay in an uncertain future; in the meantime, materials published in the war years were in danger of disappearing. As a government agency, the Library of Congress had energetically contributed to the war effort; now, in the wake of the Allied victory, it envisioned a strengthened international role. University libraries also recognized an opportunity to build their European collections and agreed to a plan of cooperation rather than competition. To the Cabinet secretaries, Evans had proposed a high-minded program to serve the national interest, but his tone changed when he wrote Yale library director James Babb about the deal. "I have placed orders for three copies of practically everything issued in the war years . . . and have agents running around over the place trying to round up the material," he said. "I've got the Army lined up to bring in a few hundred tons of liberated material without cost. You will get a nice cut on that, too, for a share of the administrative cost of distribution."[14]

To the military, the Library of Congress Mission was a "peculiar operation," and not all officials were on board. According to one general, intelligence officials had initially favored a "first come, first served" policy, but many army officers disdained the presence of any civilians, thinking them a hindrance and distraction. Nor did theater commanders see their mission as one of preserving records and artifacts that did not have a military use. Major James Horan, Coordinator of War Department Libraries, pushed back against the plan. "The Army will not trot around from house to house, shop to shop, warehouse to warehouse" to serve librarians, Lydenberg quoted him as saying.[15]

There were two good reasons to support the library mission, however. By summer of 1945, books and library materials in the European theater had become a target of private interests. That June Reuben Peiss stopped one officer removing books from Leipzig, but arrived too late to prevent "an American Army officer with energy, imagination, and lack of discretion" from looting the Nazi Party publisher Eher Verlag and shipping many packages to American colleges. General Lucius Clay, then Eisenhower's deputy, had begun to grumble about fielding requests from commercial firms, including a US chemical company that wanted the complete bound files of German scientific journals. Concerns grew that book collectors would arrive willy-nilly in Europe, and a free-for-all would follow. As one intelligence officer commented, some months after the Library of Congress plan had been put into effect, "so far as the Theater is concerned, one book buying mission is all we can handle."[16]

Just as important, military leaders were increasingly stymied by the scale of the captured German materials already in their possession and growing daily. Investigative teams continued to uncover new targets through the summer. Many deposits had been left in place, or stored in German churches and towns, and there was growing pressure to remove them. At times officials made hasty decisions about their fate. One colonel, Sargent Child reported, had "released 11 train loads of books to the Russians with practically no screening." The army did not have the personnel to sort, assess, and classify these materials, and the LCM offered expertise for this work of librarianship, which prompted military commanders and intelligence officials to favor the proposal. The War Department therefore agreed to make the Library of Congress the "implementing agency for the collection of documents and publications of non-military interest in Germany." These included surplus volumes and duplicates of periodicals, as well as "one-copy materials on industrial, technological, and scientific subjects." The LC's representatives would have "semi-military status"—wearing uniforms, carrying orders, eating in mess halls, assigned to billets—and gain full access to the military's document centers. "The Army has developed a very considerable sense of responsibility for the captured documents," Luther Evans told Hoover Library director H. H. Fisher, "and machinery is starting to move whereby valuable documents will be preserved and routed through channels."[17]

In conceiving this project, the Library of Congress turned to the Interdepartmental Committee for the Acquisition of Foreign Publications as a model and as a source of experienced personnel. The agency was winding down, but its staff was still in Europe. Frederick Kilgour suggested using these agents for the new mission; after all, they had done similar work secretly during the war. In Paris to plan his organization's dissolution, he raised this possibility with two IDC field representatives, James Glennen and Reuben Peiss, and in August 1945, they were reassigned to the Library of Congress while retaining their IDC affiliation. Glennen was stationed in Paris to work in France and Belgium but remained on the sidelines. The real action was in Germany, and Peiss was named head of the mission there. Adept at maneuvering within and around military protocols, both men had already acquired large collections of publications and documents. For Peiss, this was a "natural transition from IDC to L.C." Luther Evans was not so sure: he had only a dim understanding of conditions in Europe and had put the mission in the hands of a young librarian no one at the Library of Congress could personally vouch for.[18]

--------⚬⚬--------

In its first months, the Library of Congress Mission in Germany was largely a one-man show. Peiss worked his way through a military bureaucracy that operated "like a Rube Goldberg contraption," arranging for the basic needs of the LCM, including housing, storage facilities, and transportation. The mission was attached to the intelligence documents section (G-2 Docs) of the US Forces European Theater (USFET), commanded by Colonel Frederick Gronich. Gronich provided a large warehouse in a former I. G. Farben factory, with railroad sidings, office space, and a sizable crew of German civilians and POWs to gather, sort, and crate boxes for shipment. It was located in Fechenheim, a short jeep ride to the massive

USFET headquarters in Frankfurt am Main, also in a Farben complex. Peiss hammered out rules for acquiring and shipping publications through military channels. General Walter Bedell Smith, Eisenhower's chief of staff, gave him the green light, affirming he would "be very glad to do anything I can to help the Library of Congress."[19]

The original aim was a book-buying mission, including the assignment to retrieve publications ordered and stored in Leipzig before the war. Peiss moved quickly to ferret out bibliographical information and hidden book stocks, and he retained dealers to purchase wartime and postwar imprints. He sought three copies of all works published from 1940 to 1945—even earlier if the subject were the physical or social sciences, the law, politics, or statistical works—and anything related to Nazism since 1933. He hired Dr. Hans Broermann, of the publisher Duncker & Humblot, to be the Library of Congress's purchasing agent, with instructions to buy copies of significant books and journals. But the library mission was transformed by the military's T-Forces and documents teams. "Purchased books at the moment are a small problem and we must work on the other angle," Peiss explained to Verner Clapp, director of the LC's Acquisitions Department and his primary contact. "The major share of our acquisitions will be through the G-2 Documents Control Section."[20]

Document centers had sprung up in Berlin and the American zone for the tons of records and publications the military confiscated at the end of the war and continued to find months later. Each center was an archival beehive, with intelligence agents, military groups, government officials, and a bewildering array of civilians swarming over the materials. Items earmarked as having strategic, operational, scientific, or technical value were retained, but voluminous quantities were set aside. Sargent Child feared for their fate and begged the "G-2 Docs boys" to save them. Colonel Gronich's reply—they would not destroy anything valuable, only "stuff that nobody wanted"—was hardly reassuring. Peiss also emphasized the value of these works. They "may well be the only copies which will remain in existence," he reminded intelligence officers, and should be preserved for libraries and posterity. He urged them to delay until the Library of Congress Mission had the opportunity to screen the materials.[21]

The work was overwhelming. In a transatlantic teletype conference with Clapp, Peiss admitted, "I'm a little tired, and a bit discouraged, but otherwise all right." He traveled constantly, shuttling between Frankfurt, Berlin, and other German cities, with trips to London and Paris as well. "You know there's an awful lot to do here," he said, "I've got about 20 balls in the air at one time." When Major Horan complimented the "swell job" he was doing, Peiss replied wryly, "I'm not getting very much done yet except finding out what is to be done." Operating in the makeshift and wrecked environment of postwar Germany posed continual challenges, and "you don't live a normal life, you see." For all the press of work and a flulike illness he could not shake, Peiss embraced the task. "It sounds as if you are doing fine," Clapp astutely observed, "and it sounds somehow as if you're having a good time also."[22]

The mission immediately needed more personnel, and Peiss turned to Max Loeb. Loeb had remained in the OSS in Germany, and when that agency was dissolved, he was assigned to its successor, the US Army's Strategic Services Unit. He continued his target investigations, locating and reporting on libraries and collections of documents for the IDC, the Chief Counsel for the Nuremberg war crimes trials, and other agencies. Although not yet officially attached to the Library of Congress, he was already working on its behalf by late August 1945. That fall, he made frequent trips to northern Bavaria, where he identified and confiscated numerous libraries of Nazi organizations and government agencies, as well as small collections of Jewish and Russian materials looted by the Nazis. He also travelled to Vienna, where he arranged to buy wartime publications and pressured the city's cultural office to let him take three hundred confiscated libraries. Loeb had a knack for cutting through red tape, scrounging for trucks and gasoline, and in the early days, even removing materials without explicit clearance.[23]

A few other men already in Europe, with ties to intelligence, books, and documents, joined the LCM. Peiss eagerly sought Jacob Zuckerman, his "British IDC counterpart," whom he had come to know well in Lisbon. Of German-Jewish background, Zuckerman had escaped from Germany in 1933; trained as a lawyer and fluent in eight languages, he served during the war as a press analyst for the British Embassy in Portugal, "attempting to detect leakages of secret information through the German press." He accepted the offer to work for the LCM and returned to Germany in January 1946, stunned by the turns in his life, which he likened to a dream or film. He changed from a "harmless civilian into a uniformed equal," lived in lavish accommodations, and saw the "master race" become servile laborers. Zuckerman's assignment was to direct the mission's activities in Berlin, which included negotiating with the quadripartite authorities and achieving an agreement to retrieve publications in the Soviet zone of occupation. "I am totally shocked by the scale of the responsibility that is entrusted to me and the great trust placed in me," he wrote his wife.[24]

Also joining the Library of Congress Mission was Douwe Stuurman. A Rhodes Scholar and English professor before the war, Stuurman had been drafted into the army as an ordinary GI, assigned to the Sixty-Third Infantry

Division. He worked on a T-Force at the Third Army Intelligence Center, investigating targets and screening captured enemy materials in the Munich area, from the end of the war through the fall of 1945. Bored by the job and increasingly concerned that valuable items were being lost, he talked his commanding officer, Major Dudley Digges, into letting him search for material on his own. Digges even gave him a truck and warehouse space with shelving. Stuurman took off, ultimately gathering over one hundred thousand books and pamphlets of the Nazi regime. Sargent Child spoke in awe of his achievement: "He has run from Vienna to Nürnberg like a brilliant open field runner – he has gained access to cellars, attics, storerooms – thru the help and cooperation of German and Austrian scholars – and by playing no tricks with them so that they learned to trust him – has come up with the beacon." Stuurman claimed to be only an amateur collector, having "the time of my life."[25] He transferred to the LCM in November 1945.

Despite the addition of new staff, Peiss pushed the Library of Congress to send a team from home. Although the mission had made progress, with six freight car loads already sent back and much more to come, it was "racing against time and the whittling-down of occupation forces." He needed library professionals—fluent in German and able to tolerate demanding physical conditions—to organize and oversee the recording, evacuation, transport, and storage of books and to advise the document centers. "We are losing golden opportunities because I cannot get personnel in this theater," he fretted. "There are a hundred and one things to do and people to see and I simply cannot be everywhere at once." He wanted "three or four live-wires" but no prima donnas: those in the field had already had "distressing experiences with people who came over with high-falutin' notions of their abilities and assignment and were far from adaptable."[26] Ultimately, this split—between those who had served in army units or the OSS during the war, and those who had not—would shape both the actions and perceptions of the LCM in the course of its work.

After many delays, the promised reinforcements finally arrived in Frankfurt on a dark, freezing morning in January 1946. Of the seven "missionaries," three were staff members of the Library of Congress, two had served in the IDC, and one in the Office of Censorship. The most distinguished was Harry Miller Lydenberg, a leading light in the library world and seventy years old when he set sail for Germany. He planned to strengthen ties between the mission and the military, assess the book situation in Germany, and help rebuild international relations among libraries shattered by the war. "Mr. Lydenberg is too old a man and too high an echelon to put into the work of collecting," Clapp cautioned Peiss, but for the Library of Congress, he provided cover in a risky operation: "We need an

Figure 4.1. Reuben Peiss (center) and the Library of Congress European Mission at OMGUS Headquarters in Frankfurt, 1946. Library of Congress (Mss. Div., LCM Records, box 29).

elder statesman to inspire confidence in the whole business." Lydenberg's folksy manner and old-fashioned courtesy overlay a sharp and capacious intelligence. He brought a buoyant sensibility to the mission, believing in the restoration of Germany's intellectual life and the possibilities of renewed cultural exchange. He also offered strong backing for the mission's work, whose spirit "has been most commendably and thrillingly directed toward the whole library scene the country over," he wrote in typically embellished style, such that "future generations of scholars and librarians will thank LC for making this possible."[27]

Two other librarians stood out among the group. David Clift had been the IDC's second-in-command in Washington during the war and was known for his administrative know-how and steady hand. He had recently been appointed assistant librarian at Yale when he was asked to join the mission. He and Peiss were friends from their shared OSS experiences, and Peiss awaited his arrival eagerly. Clift's job was to coordinate day-to-day operations, and he took charge for several months that spring when Peiss became ill and returned home to recuperate.

Richard Hill was Clift's opposite number temperamentally, but he played an important role in the LCM as well. A member of the reference staff of the LC's Music Division and editor of the Music Library Association's journal *Notes*, he was, as a colleague later described him, "reference librarian *extraordinaire* to the music lovers and musicologists of the world." He also might have found a calling in intelligence work. During the war, he surveyed the newspaper *Deutsche Allgemeine Zeitung*, tracing patterns of concert reviews, the presence or absence of certain theaters in the news, last-minutes changes in operas, and notices to ticketholders about refunds. From this information, he drew conclusions about the timing, location, and extent of bomb damage in Berlin during the initial phase of Allied air attacks. He published "Concert Life in Berlin: Season 1943-44" in *Notes*, and later remarked that the War Department had requested copies. Beyond serving the overall aims of the LCM, his job was to acquire music books, scores, and recordings of the wartime period. Unlike Clift and Peiss, who had acquired the habit of discretion and discipline from their OSS days, Hill impulsively made his own path while in Europe.[28]

Like so many American visitors to Germany, the newcomers tried to absorb what they saw: scarred houses, bare shops, rubble-strewn streets with barely space for a car to pass, old men picking up cigarette butts from the street. They watched people navigate the wreckage in their daily pursuits and wondered about the mask of obsequiousness among the defeated. Lydenberg was struck that "destruction and desolation greet you in almost any city of size or importance," yet "life is busy, crowds bustle around, trolleys are . . . packed." In a letter to his wife, Clift commented upon Frankfurters' makeshift attire—worn-out clothes and poor shoes, sometimes topped with stove-pipe or opera hats. They contrasted these scenes to the high living of the conquerors in Frankfurt, who occupied the modern, undamaged I. G. Farben administrative buildings, where they dined at the Kasino, attended movies and theater, and found barbers, tailors, and other services.[29]

A mission "powwow" in early February 1946, with everyone gathered in Frankfurt, underscored the challenges and uncertainties of the task ahead. The Office of Military Government, United States (OMGUS) was a complicated bureaucracy and, as Clift observed, "one really needs a great deal of snafu tolerance in this place." There were no clear answers to basic questions about who controlled various collections, how to pay dealers, and what procedures for selection and transport should be followed. Even the authority of the LCM to operate was not always acknowledged by the military brass. "Much G-2 material [is] never sorted or examined," Stuurman observed, "stuff [is] disappearing."[30]

Soon the LCM was in full swing. The newcomers fanned out, "chasing publications" in jeeps, trucks, and trains throughout the American zone. "Targets are turning up all the time," Clift reported. They initiated relationships with the British and French and made overtures to the

Russians over publications stored in their zone. Their warehouse was humming, with truckloads of books arriving daily and crates loaded onto railcars for shipment abroad. Berlin became their most active base of operations, with Jacob Zuckerman in charge, assisted by Richard Hill and Lothar Nachman, overseeing a workforce of German librarians, book dealers, clerks, drivers, and laborers. Hill irreverently described the daily routine: "The constant conferences with OMGUS, the finding and clearing of 'Targets' (G-2's euphemism for places we can loot), planning work for the forty Germans we employ here in Berlin and seeing that they are all kept busy." They worked until midnight most nights. "We go out together when we go out, but generally we stay home together," said Hill, "the three of us live in each other's pockets."[31]

————⌀————

Now at full strength, the LCM's first task was to approach German booksellers and publishers to buy books and periodicals of the war years. In postwar Germany, this was no easy task. The publishing industry had been entirely shut down at the end of the war, as booksellers and publishers underwent denazification and relicensing, a slow process in the American zone of occupation. Many lost their inventory in bombing raids or had evacuated it to sites that were no longer accessible. Berlin book dealer Otto Enslin, for example, had stored works for medical libraries in Boston and Cleveland, but his "whole establishment had been completely demolished by bombing," wrote Peiss, "this I saw with my own eyes." He estimated that 75 percent of book stocks had been destroyed. Yet even those whose inventory was safe proved reluctant to sell to the LCM. At the February gathering, Loeb observed that books were disappearing from the shelves, and he feared publishers were simply putting them away or selling on the black market. "Our purchasing [will] be a complete flop," he worried.[32]

Some booksellers tried to hide past Nazi affiliation or put up resistance to American inquiries. In one case, the New York Academy of Medicine had placed books on order before the war with a Berlin dealer named Robert Müller, who specialized in medical and scientific publications. A "notorious Nazi," he sold his stock to another bookseller in the British sector after the collapse of Germany. Müller was there when Jacob Zuckerman went into the bookshop looking for items to purchase and saw a set of books on dentistry. Told they were not for sale, Zuckerman pressed the issue, at which point Müller responded testily, "We are in the British Sector. We do not have to sell you the books, and we do not have to answer your questions." Zuckerman reported the encounter, and the British authorities arrested

Müller, who admitted he had the New York Academy books, already paid for, hidden in a storehouse.[33]

The uncertainty about payment and an unstable currency also played into booksellers' reluctance. This was, in fact, a concern of the LCM as well, which for months was unable to access funds deposited by the Library of Congress to pay its book dealers. Berlin agent Hans Broermann used his own funds, "pawned his furniture and owe[d] money to many of his friends," but the LC could not find a way to pay his invoices. "All in all, we are beginning somewhat to feel as though the sheriff is hot on our trail," David Clift, the mission's second-in-command, grumbled. Books purchased by the LCM, among the first exports from Germany after the war, were entangled in the evolving American policy toward German economic reconstruction. The military government wanted tight financial controls in Germany, and the Trading with the Enemy Act remained in effect; the Library of Congress could not buy with German marks, only American dollars. The idea that books were unique or distinctive goods did not persuade the occupation authorities. Import/export control insisted on clearing all government purchases, Harry Lydenberg complained, "no matter whether it is for calcium carbonate in shipload lots or leather by the ton or books by the hundred."[34]

Despite these problems, many publishers tried to renew the relationships of the prewar years. F. A. Brockhaus, a venerable Leipzig publisher, had done business with the Library of Congress for decades; as the war intensified, he made his last shipment to the United States in June 1941, through the American embassy in Lisbon. Nazi authorities shut the firm down in the fall of 1943 and bombing raids at the end of the year destroyed much of its machinery, stock, and records. "After two years' work I have succeeded in building up a small printing and binding establishment, literally out of the ruins of the old plant," Brockhaus told Lydenberg. "You can certainly imagine how much we have been missing the exchange of ideas with other countries during the terrible years which lie now behind us." This was likely the case, but Brockhaus also prudently hid some of his book stocks outside Leipzig, waiting for more favorable terms of trade. The ambivalence of booksellers, when encountering the American purchasing mission, had other sources, too. Thomas P. Fleming, a latecomer to the mission, found little available in the British zone. He observed, "what remains of importance is being jealously guarded by the booksellers who take some pride in their own national libraries and who wish to see their destroyed collections replaced."[35]

Richard Hill, during his sojourn with the mission, provided a running commentary on the challenges of acquiring one particular type of publication, German music books and scores. Hill estimated that fifteen thousand published pieces of music had been issued in Germany and Austria in the war years, but none of it had been acquired by the IDC or swept up by T-Forces. Nor were they readily available from publishers or in music stores. Hill especially wanted an original edition of Norbert Schultze's "Lili Marleen," but it was nowhere to be found. Music publishing had been concentrated in Leipzig, now in the Soviet zone, and firms were skittish. Few music publishers even responded to the LCM's requests for information. None would admit to having Nazi music books or compositions, claiming to have turned in such objectionable materials already or destroyed them when the Russians entered the city. At the same time, music publishers had found ways to protect their stocks, especially shielding rare or high-quality editions. One told Hill that he had nothing to offer officially but various employees had purchased copies they might be persuaded to sell, although at five or six times their original price. "It's really very scarce, and one has to do a lot of persuading to get a publisher to sell any of his stock," Hill observed.[36]

Feeling the urgency of the situation, Hill tried different means of persuasion. He asked two friends in high places—Russian-born composer Nicolas Nabokov and British music officer Eric Clarke, both with OMGUS's Information Control Division—to help him work around the bureaucratic obstacles. "Naturally, every cultured person here is glad to do what they can to get stuff for the Library of Congress," Hill commented, but being on a first-name basis with these top officials gave him vital access. He hired German music agents to make personal contacts with publishers and dealers, but they were undependable. He suggested the Library of Congress send books to exchange, to no avail. Like most Americans in occupied Germany, Hill ultimately turned to cigarettes, the most reliable form of currency. After haggling with the publisher's employees over price, he bartered two cartons of cigarettes for the items he wanted. He implored his colleagues at the LC's Music Division to send extra cartons. "Most of the Mission's purchases are made at pre-war prices, but this is only when the publisher has plenty of copies in stock," he told them. "I simply can't afford to get some of the rarer items for the Library except with cigarette-marks."[37]

Another time Hill went too far working around military procedures when he tried to help Jewish émigré Walter Hinrichsen, whose family owned the noted music publisher C. F. Peters in Leipzig. Walter and his brother Max had escaped to New York and London respectively when Hitler came to power; their father and other siblings were murdered in the Holocaust. Walter Hinrichsen became a US citizen, served in the army, and was an officer in the occupation government, working under Nicolas Nabokov. At the end of the war, his detachment had briefly occupied Leipzig, and Hinrichsen took the occasion to post large "off limit" posters on his publishing house, which remained hanging months later. Nevertheless, he feared Russian authorities would soon merge all the Leipzig publishers into a single state-run house, and he searched for a way to remove his book stocks and send them to the United States. Hill was sympathetic, seeing a moral justification in Hinrichsen's claims as a victim of Nazism and an American soldier, "trying to save something out of the wreck of his family and firm." He proposed an illegal scheme to get around occupation policies prohibiting private business activity. "Although you have instructed me to work through channels, I'm sure the problem can best be solved outside of them," he rationalized to his superiors at the Library of Congress. They quickly quashed Hill's initiative.[38]

How to handle individual collectors with private libraries proved an even more complicated problem. They came forward with books and collections to sell. When refused American dollars, they asked for German marks (in one case 90,000 RM for a private mathematical library), cigarettes, or food.[39] Some wanted to present books as gifts, with expectations of assistance or favorable treatment from the Americans. They believed deeply in the value of their books and libraries, treasures carefully preserved amidst the devastation.

These encounters sometimes invoked prewar connections, a sense of intellectual community and international exchange nurtured not only in academia but also in the book world. Some nostalgically reminded their American friends and contacts of those earlier times. Dr. Alfred Hildebrandt, for example, was a pioneering balloonist, collector of aeronautical literature, and member of an international circle of aviation experts and writers since 1893. He had been involved with the Wright Brothers, welcomed to the White House, and in 1932 sold part of his collection to the Library of Congress. During the war, he was forced to evacuate from his Berlin home and leave his collection behind, which remarkably was left intact. In September 1945 he offered a gift of his books and other materials to the Library of Congress Mission, with the hope that this would enable his return to Berlin. Five months later, William F. Heimlich, head of US military intelligence in Berlin, moved thirteen sacks of Hildebrandt's books—including some he had not intended to give—from the British sector into Lydenberg's possession and ultimately to the Library of Congress.[40]

Negotiations over private libraries often dragged on for months. Dr. Ludwig Mach, elderly son of the famed physicist and philosopher Ernst Mach, was himself a physicist, inventor, and community doctor who owned a scientific library of several thousand volumes. Beginning in August 1945, several intelligence agents reported on strange experiments he conducted in his backyard, his expertise in microfilming, and his valuable scientific equipment. The library contained much of historical interest, and more than one American investigator suggested it be acquired. Mach wanted compensation, however, hoping to move himself and his library to the United States, or to receive a guaranteed pension from the American government. When the matter was referred to the LCM, Reuben Peiss noted the "slightly crackpot (or senescent) air of plaint and persecution" in Mach's story, but sent Douwe Stuurman to negotiate with him. Like Mach, other collectors hoped for transit out of the Soviet zone or sponsorship to the United States. The LCM rebuffed these requests and urged American libraries not to help individual Germans emigrate because of their collections. When it came to private collectors, Peiss observed, "The whole business is so confused by passion, prejudice and technical difficulties."[41]

———— ✺ ————

Beyond its book-buying program, the Library of Congress Mission faced the challenge of securing German books and periodicals stored in the Soviet zone of occupation. Before the war, the Joint Committee on Importations had frantically arranged with Leipzig book agent Otto Harrassowitz to stockpile German publications for American research libraries. They waited years for news, until word finally came of the dealer's fate. "I have seen and talked with Harrassowitz!" Peiss breathlessly wrote Keyes Metcalf in June 1945. Separately, he and Albert Gerould, a librarian and intelligence officer, had entered Leipzig to learn from Otto and his son Hans, now manager of the firm, what had happened during the war.[42]

Leipzig's book trade had sustained great losses, with at least half of the most important firms destroyed or seriously damaged. In the publishing quarter, Peiss observed, "one can stand on a street and look out over acres of devastated buildings, ground down to rubble or standing like shattered skeletons." Harrassowitz's two large warehouses, holding one million volumes, were completely destroyed, and the company reduced to two floors of a building, with Hans operating out of an apartment. When American troops took the city in April 1945, according to one story that made the rounds, "Harrassowitz had three flunkies standing at the front door, announcing in loud voices that all Harvard's material was being safely held. The first three American officers to arrive were Yale men, and upon hearing this said, 'You go to hell! We're from Yale.'" In fact, the military government quickly issued orders to protect the firm from being seized for billets or offices, noting it was "acting as Library agent to the main USA-Libraries and is holding great quantities of books and periodicals." These were worth approximately $250,000.[43]

Hans Harrassowitz had continued to buy for American libraries through the war, especially journals and serial publications. "Experiences of the first world-war had guided me in collecting this material," he later stated, "and it had been the ambition of the whole firm to gather continuations in good shape and without any lacunae." This became increasingly difficult, as war-time restrictions on publishing grew and his own funds ran low, but he had been remarkably successful. The news was not entirely good, however. Like others in the book trade, Harrassowitz decided to move these stockpiles to safety in the outskirts of Leipzig. The American materials were in six small towns, five of which were under Russian control, including one across the border in Poland. Before the Soviets took over, T-Forces had removed truckloads of materials, including copies of books from Leipzig publishers, but they were unable to rescue the stashes for American libraries.[44]

The LCM made a concerted effort to get these materials beginning in early 1946 but faced numerous snags and delays. More than six months into the occupation, Harrassowitz was having trouble rounding up and transporting the stored books from the hinterlands. Railroads were not functioning well, and the political situation made Poland inaccessible. Nor had the firm informed the Soviet occupation authorities about the American books, and, Sargent Child reported, it was "getting jittery because of [their] constant probings." In March, the LCM decided to tell the Russians about the stored materials, only to learn a month later that Hans Harrassowitz had not declared one hundred boxes he wanted to keep hidden. The situation was a delicate one for Harrassowitz, which, unlike many other German publishers at that time, hoped to remain in Leipzig under Soviet authority and still maintain its long-standing relationship with American libraries. "The only way I'll feel safe is to play the game with all cards on the table, face up," observed Harry Lydenberg, closely involved in the early rounds of negotiation. "That, however, will be dangerous, even suicidal . . . for Hans Harrassowitz and the firm."[45]

The Leipzig venture posed acute political and economic problems. Like OMGUS, the Soviet occupation authority controlled the publishing industry in its zone and had been careful about establishing the loyalty of publishers and issuing licenses to them. It had good reason to be wary of American intentions in Leipzig. In the period before the Americans transferred authority to the Russians, Information Control personnel, led by Douglas Waples and Helmut Lehmann-Haupt, helped a number of publishers move their operations to Wiesbaden in the US zone. The problem of interzonal trade and import-export controls remained unresolved. Direct payment and delivery from German firms was impossible, prohibited by the Trading with the Enemy Act. Nor could crates of books be shipped directly from the

Soviet zone to the United States. The materials would have to go via regular Frankfurt channels, sent "as if it were an export from the American Zone." Also under negotiation was the purchase price: the books had originally been purchased in prewar marks, but Russian authorities wanted payment in American dollars, so they haggled over the conversion rate, finally settling on a thirty-cent mark.[46]

After several months requesting permission, Lydenberg and Clift took the first LCM trip to Leipzig in early April 1946, where they met with twenty publishers and dealers, along with Soviet officials, in order to work out logistics. The Germans decided that Harrassowitz would act for all the publishers holding books for American libraries. Not long after, American and Soviet occupation officials met in Berlin to negotiate the terms. These were "quite uncharted steps under difficult conditions in an occupied country," LCM member Joseph Groesbeck observed, and "required policy-making at a high level by two great governments."[47] It took another four months before the problems were resolved and the LCM returned to Leipzig.

After the Soviets received payment of over $106,000, a convoy of four trucks finally left Berlin on August 13 to pick up the first shipment of stored publications. The fifteen men in the group included Peiss, Zuckerman, various American and Soviet liaisons, and a number of GIs. The trip was uneventful—they were waved through Russian checkpoints— except for an encounter with an "Autobahn Girl" by the road, crying out "my darling" in hopes of getting them to stop. They arrived that afternoon and Harrassowitz's employees loaded the boxes onto the trucks. Their Soviet guide arranged for them to stay at the Fürstenhof, the city's best hotel, where they ate an elaborate dinner served "in the grand style." Peiss stressed the cordiality of the Russians, the lack of surveillance, and his increasingly frank talks with the Russian liaison—a tankman who had been seriously injured in the war—about books, art, and their two countries. Parked nearby, the trucks attracted a crowd of curious Leipzigers. Everyone stared at them, "almost as if we were visitors from Mars." They returned to Berlin the next day, loaded the materials onto railroad cars, and sent them to Frankfurt and finally across the Atlantic. "Lydenberg operation successful," Peiss playfully wired Clift, now at Yale, "patient expects to leave hospital Monday."[48]

Peiss and Zuckerman went back to Leipzig in late September, this time to buy books published in the war years. There was little available, and some publishers did not bother to meet them, perhaps calculating the cost of cooperating with Americans in the new political environment. The Soviet authorities had put the Leipzig firms to work publishing Russian political literature and textbooks and had just begun to permit them to print German books. One publisher who saw them was Max Niemeyer, who reported his stock was low because a British intelligence team appropriated his publications the previous year, including periodicals intended for American libraries. He had never been paid, even though "one of the Britishers remarked that they would not just take the stuff without payment, 'as the Russians do.'" On this trip, the Americans went to the movies and a concert, with performers and audience in formal dress. It all had an "air of 'normalcy,'" Peiss commented, "one would never have thought that Leipzig had been through a war and was enduring an occupation." Yet their presence on the streets caused rumors to fly. "What an effect you have had here!" one Leipzig publisher remarked to Zuckerman before they left. "From three separate sources I have heard that the Americans are going to reoccupy Leipzig and that a preparatory commission has been inspecting the city!"[49]

The LCM's triumph in Leipzig stirred the deep-rooted internationalism of these librarians abroad, their hopes for "the future, an intellectual Germany that is an intimate member of the international world of scholarship." Yet already the cultural Cold War was setting in. Even as the Harrassowitz negotiations were underway, German librarians and book dealers in the American zone, supported by the Information Control Division, proposed a West German competitor to the established Deutsche Bücherei in Leipzig, in which all German publishers had traditionally deposited their works. Moreover, they were eyeing the cache of one million books of the former Prussian State Library, moved from Berlin to Marburg at the end of the war, which some wanted to make the "nucleus of a new national library." Members of the LCM criticized these moves toward cultural schism. If "we take steps which are motivated by pessimism and which emphasize the differences and the barriers between the zones, then we work toward increasing disunity, not only culturally, but politically as well," Peiss explained. A latecomer to the mission, Scott Adams from the National Library of Medicine, pointed out that Information Control had also barred the sale of publications from the Soviet zone and Soviet sector of Berlin. All of these moves, he warned, tended "to compartmentalize Germany's intellectual life, to widen an existing cultural gap, to further international distrust, and to work against the objectives of the Potsdam agreement."[50]

—⟨∽⟩—

Whatever the success of the book-buying program and the Leipzig operation, ultimately it was the ongoing confiscation of documents and published materials that had the greatest impact on the American library world. The initial agreement with the War Department had the LCM screening items brought into document centers and selecting among those not required by the military. No one had foreseen the vast scale of confiscation or what the seizure of so much material would mean for the LCM or American libraries. Long after the early finds, collections of books and documents continued to turn up in cellars, caves, and castles. Interrogations often revealed hidden libraries, and individuals with a Nazi affiliation or on an automatic arrest list would have their libraries seized. The "rule of three"—acquiring three copies of every work published in the war years—was the LCM's initial mandate, but the logic of collecting led to mission creep. With the Library of Congress's assent, works of the entire Nazi period came under their purview. Moreover, as Verner Clapp explained, "the alliance with the Army has had the effect of bringing in certain books of a still older vintage."[51]

Peiss, Loeb, and Stuurman—all men involved in the OSS or documents teams during the war—embraced mass acquisition. They collected widely and immediately, with minimal sorting and assessment on the ground. They were not working with "want lists," which required librarians to prioritize the most valuable acquisitions. Their wartime experiences made them fear the evanescence of the printed word and, feeling the press of time and lack of personnel, their tendency was to seize first and let the accumulation be sorted out later, in the United States. Yet their commitment to a universal collection of German imprints went beyond the practical matter of operating in a devastated country under military government. A philosophical conviction, perhaps even a psychological need, drove these men, propelled by a desire to document the world-changing events they had just lived through.

Peiss encouraged all LCM representatives to collect the record of Nazism abundantly. Not only had the Allies banned these publications, as part of the policy of denazification, but American libraries had only limited holdings on a subject of great historical import. "We should get as many copies as possible since what we acquire will be the only remaining record of that work," he directed. Even when the British Enemy Publications Committee informed the LCM not to bother collecting duplicates for them, he suggested, "We should still help ourselves liberally to material which might some time prove useful for international exchange." The British "may change their minds several years from now," he added. His view of what items might be worthwhile was all-encompassing. Stopping in Lisbon on his way back to the United States, he asked the American ambassador to give the Library of Congress its impounded German publications, not only works of science, politics, and history but also propaganda. "It must be kept in mind," he observed, "that even those publications often classed as 'junk' by both scholars and laymen have great value for the large research library which is interested in preserving the record of a culture."[52]

The confiscation practices of the military government brought in many materials—archives, documents, photographs, and ephemera—that were not, strictly, published. Did these fall within the mission's mandate? There were also libraries that mixed Nazi-era publications, looted works, and legitimately purchased volumes. Behind the sheer numbers of targets inspected and collections confiscated lay the political and ethical ambiguities complicating the LCM's work.

The handling of the Rehse Collection reveals the twisting path of collection, preservation, and confiscation involved in American mass acquisitions. F. J. M. (Friedrich Josef Maria) Rehse, a photographer and art publisher based in Munich, started a private archive during World War I, acquiring photographs, newspaper clippings, posters, and other ephemera, with a particular interest in propaganda from the right and left. A driven and wily collector, Rehse visited Adolf Hitler as early as 1921 to ask for documents on National Socialism; before requesting posters from the Communist Party, he put on a red armband with a forged party stamp. Financially strapped in 1928, he decided to sell the collection. The Hoover War Library expressed interest, as did libraries in Berlin, Leipzig, and Moscow, but the Nazi Party decided to purchase it and install Rehse as its director. To protect the collection during the war, he broke it up and hid it all over the Munich area.[53]

Even before the LCM had started operations, American bookmen wondered about the notorious Rehse Collection. "A member of our staff has suggested that we ought to find out [its] whereabouts," Keyes Metcalf wrote from Harvard. "He says this was the best, and for a long time the only, collection of the early publications of the 'voelkische' movement, including Nazism." If it were discovered, Metcalf wanted to know its condition and whether it was for sale. Rehse came up repeatedly in teletype conversations with the Library of Congress, too. "We have been on the trail of this collection for several months . . . it is now being held by an army intelligence unit," Peiss stated in September 1945. This was, in fact, one of Douwe Stuurman's great discoveries when he was investigating sites in Freising and Munich, and he continued to be responsible for it after he joined the LCM. The collection had been plundered not long after the war, and it was "in very bad shape," Peiss noted. "Stuurman has a number of Germans cleaning it up and so on, putting it together again." However, this was only a portion of what was better described as a set of special collections. Rehse was "one of those inveterate collectors who will collect almost anything," and in addition to political materials, he amassed everything from cabalistic lore, found in Heidelberg, to pornography, which

Figure 4.2. Don Travis of the Library of Congress Mission examines vestiges of the Rehse Collection in a sub-basement of the Bürgerbräu in Munich, 1946. Library of Congress (LC-DIG-ds-07878).

had disappeared. "Looters [seem] to have a nose for this kind of material," Peiss drily commented.[54]

The operations in Bavaria went far beyond the Rehse Collection. Peiss insisted that Stuurman's men had conducted "a selective operation on the vast masses of material . . . they never simply packed up collections wholesale and sent them out." Indeed, some materials were clearly part of non-Nazi German cultural heritage and were turned over to the Monuments, Fine Arts, and Archives unit for restitution, and even—against procedure—directly to the Bavarian Cultural Ministry, ultimately for reconstructed German libraries. But much of the material fell under the LCM's purview, and Peiss urged a broad interpretation of their mandate. He told Stuurman of the LC's "increasing emphasis" on collecting as much as possible, even if they ended up using items as gifts to rebuild libraries or, for that matter, throwing them out: "We want duplicates and we want them in mass."[55]

Stuurman prepared four freight cars of material for shipment in February 1946, paying out of pocket for labor and hiring a German moving agency, both against regulations. He marveled at their finds—political pamphlets, Jewish literature, Nazi periodicals, newspapers "of all political colorings, illegal and 'auslandsdeutsche' newspapers too," recordings of Nazi speeches, millions of newspaper clippings "reflecting the Nazis in the world press," and 50,000 posters. He described it as "undoubtedly the world's biggest and best collection, made largely by the world's biggest and best collectors, the Nazis and Rehse." Nor was Stuurman done. The property control office assured him that "the period of confiscation is not yet necessarily over and that good veins may still be worked." Several years later, Stuurman justified the collection of "unbound and even unprinted documentary material," which was outside the LCM's initial charge and a challenge for the Library of Congress to process. "There was a deep conviction as well as a definite theory behind the collecting of the Mission," he wrote, "born of a first-hand acquaintance with the materials in the field." Published works, he argued, offered less insight into the history of Nazism than Nazi Party archives, police records, newspapers, and ephemera, including "thousands of hideous poems dedicated to Hitler."[56]

From his perspective as a music librarian, Richard S. Hill questioned this approach. "I can see perfectly clearly that quantity is of the essence," he observed, especially with respect to confiscated materials, but it was "absolutely essential that at least *some* emphasis be placed on quality." He wondered whether the "average American librarian, who has not had to struggle with conditions over here," would protest receiving "three definitive tomes and fifteen decidedly mediocre ones as his share of the spoils." He wrote Clift more pointedly, "I'm all for getting lots of copies of even such cheesy items as the hundreds of Nazi song books that were published. But I just don't see any point in going over the dam on standard junk just because it happens to have been published between 1939 and 1945."[57]

The others found it hard to tamp down their fascination with Nazi collections, even when they had to go through ethical contortions to make the case for their seizure. The LCM as a rule "scrupulously avoided removing documents from private houses" but wanted an exception made in the case of two elite Nazis, Reichsführer-SS Heinrich Himmler and publisher Max Amann. Their private libraries contained numerous presentation copies, books in mint condition, and in Himmler's library, works with inscriptions of bibliographical and psychological interest. They represented "a kind of monument to Nazism which we believe Military Government desires to eradicate"—and, left unsaid, the LCM desired to preserve. Richard Hill coveted a collection of 1920s experimental films made by UFA, the famed German motion picture studio that had come under Nazi control. "It could be considered as a record of an important new art form, and thus definitely archival—and untouchable," he reasoned, acknowledging the films should therefore be turned over to the MFAA and eventually returned to a German cultural institution. But he could not quite let go. "These films never belonged—properly speaking—to the German people in the same way that a library or museum belonged to them," he suggested, "it is probable that a loop-hole could be found in this history for seizing them." Even Paul Vanderbilt, the LC's photography librarian and a Monuments Man, was tempted. He was wary of the mass acquisition program, fearing that important cultural heritage would be removed from Germany. Yet his qualms dissolved when he laid eyes on a vast collection of several million disarranged images, found in a Berlin restroom and containing a mix of photographs, many with Nazi and militaristic themes, but many without. Vanderbilt sought Peiss's help in justifying their removal. "This stuff *might* be legitimate booty, available as an LC accession," he suggested. "It seems to me commercial property and not a national cultural resource." He looked for any Nazi angle, knowing he was "stretching a point" to find a reason for the photographs to be seized. Ultimately, Himmler and Amann's books came to the United States, but the line was drawn at the film and photograph collections; the objectionable images in the latter were removed and the rest approved for use by German newspapers.[58]

The number of items collected—"acquisitions grand scale," Luther Evans called it—far exceeded expectations. In the LCM's two active years, in addition to its book purchases, the Library of Congress received 141 collections of materials from Nazi Party units, officials, and military organizations, an estimated two million items. (Many of these were ultimately transferred to other research libraries under the Cooperative Acquisitions Project.) These were large quantities even for the Library of Congress to absorb. The vast inflow of confiscated materials had subsumed the original book-buying mission, presenting itself both as a logistical problem and, to some, a political and ethical concern. Luther Evans went on record that "the Mission will not engage in activities of 'liberation' on its own." Even before the LCM began, Verner Clapp had directed the library staff to segregate books with stamps from legitimate German academic and cultural institutions, for their ultimate return. The following April, he raised the possibility of hiring an expert to document the background and provenance of the acquired material and "the legitimacy of our possession of them."[59] He asked questions about the methods used to evacuate material from targets: Were they indiscriminate? Did the LCM get clearances for everything removed? Behind such questions was a larger one, had the mission engaged in theft or looting?

There was one clear case of an LCM member deliberately crossing the line: Max Loeb. He had used his military rank and the Library of Congress' name to acquire books he then sold in his New York bookstore. In one instance, he approached Berlin bookseller Hans Reich about purchasing a set of scientific imprints for the library. At the same time, he sent an urgent telegram to Peiss stating—falsely—that the bookseller was a former SS man in hiding, which led to his arrest and confiscation of the volumes. Months later, Peiss pieced together what had happened. "It now appears that this deal was one of Loeb's brainstorms," he concluded. "He got the information from Reich and sent me the telegram, told Reich at the same time to pro-tect his stuff, and then after we had taken it away, said 'so sorry.'" Similar shady dealings occurred in Vienna. "We fully trusted Mr. Loeb who came from the Headquarters of the American Military Government in Frankfurt, and therefor[e] for us was one of our liberators," two book dealers stated. "We did not find anything wrong in it when Mr. Loeb bought pretty large quantities of books, and paid for these first purchases in cash in the cur-rency of our country." When Loeb returned in 1946, having left the army, he ordered a substantial number of books but paid only a fraction of the bill. Now, the dealers complained that their own standing as reputable businesses had been called into question, "blamed [for] crediting an unre-liable and dishonest customer [for] such an amount of goods." In Austria, where every dollar needed to go to economic reconstruction, it was urgent that the debt be paid. Loeb's book business was built on such deceptions. "One thing is sure," wrote a rare book dealer to Luther Evans, "Mr. Loeb brought from Germany *hundreds* of books and . . . listed them in several mimeographed lists and sold them to libraries."[60]

Loeb's dodges were openly discussed by members of the LCM. "Maxie, the One and Only," Clift and Lydenberg called him. Peiss alone wavered, the bonds of wartime friendship, forged in their service together in the IDC and T-Forces, outweighing his scruples. He pondered Loeb's request that a number of packages be shipped to New York, which "seem to go con-siderably beyond personal purchases." "On strict moral grounds" the LC could not allow one person to profit when it has "been fighting for impar-tiality in the collection and distribution of German books." Still, he turned a blind eye and arranged for shipment, "without further inquiry as to what is in the packages." Months later, his successor Mortimer Taube, Assistant Director of the LC's Acquisitions Department, discovered more packages addressed to Loeb, with multiple copies of titles clearly intended for re-sale. Taube threatened to inform the inspector general of the US Army, but then, worried that the LCM's reputation would be tarnished, he did nothing. Clipped to Taube's letter was a note: "Contrary to all policy con-cerning mission—perhaps should be taken from file."[61]

The American librarians and others engaged in cultural missions made a sharp distinction between acquisition for a personal library and that for commercial gain. They were bibliophiles and frequently tempted. As Taube observed, members of the mission bought "articles for themselves at ad-vantageous prices." A few volumes lifted from a target or collection were usually considered to fall within the category of "legitimate booty" and were simply mailed home without question. The number and scope of these removals is unknown, but they were commonplace and mainly unacknowledged in occupied Germany.[62]

Larger questions had been raised about the mission's activities as a whole, operating under the weight of the military's confiscation program. Peiss answered them at length. "Eight or nine out of every ten confiscated volumes that find their way into the Library of Congress will have been collected and shipped by *Army* document teams," he reminded LC officials. These teams had usually made a preliminary evaluation about them before calling in the LCM, whose role was more "to confirm a decision or a desire to dispose of these materials." As of May 1946, they had "screened several million volumes, of which several hundred thousand have been turned over for research library use."[63]

Recognizing they may have made some mistakes, Peiss was "convinced of the moral cleanliness of the operation as a whole." He insisted that neither military documents teams nor the Library of Congress Mission had intentionally confiscated materials essential to the restoration of German cultural institutions or intellectual life. Beyond the chaotic early months of the book mission, procedures for getting clearances had been established and followed. The LCM tried to segregate materials from "bona-fide non-Nazi and non-military sources." This was not always easy, because of the mingling of explicitly Nazi research centers with legitimate academic libraries, as well as the Nazi takeover and redirection of preexisting collections. He acknowledged that there had been tensions with the Monuments Men, who looked with suspicion on the LCM, believing mass acquisition for American libraries was fundamentally at odds with the aims of cultural reconstruction. Nevertheless, some of the hostility eased as the two groups worked with each other. The LCM had discovered or been offered many collections that fell outside its mandate and turned them over to the MFAA. Numerous books looted from German-occupied countries, including several hundred thousand volumes the LCM rescued in Berlin, went to the MFAA for restitution. "Our Mission will do no looting, but on the contrary will do everything in its power to aid in the legitimate restoration of German cultural life and particularly of German libraries," Peiss averred. "One day we are going to face accusations and we may find we have made unwise decisions on a few specific issues, but I think we shall continue to have a clear conscience."[64] Over the years, questions and accusations did come, in requests from German individuals and institutions to return items, from American librarians stuck with quantities of second-rate Nazi fiction, and in the 1990s, in public inquiries over Holocaust assets.

By fall 1946, the Library of Congress Mission's work was largely over. Peiss left Germany, praising General Clay for supporting "a unique and sometimes troublesome venture," and thanking Evans and Clapp for being willing to back "a dark horse all the way to the final wire." He handed over the reins to Mortimer Taube, whose job was to liquidate the mission. Taube shuttered the operations in Vienna and Munich, closed out transactions in the British and French zones, and settled bills with their German agent; a skeletal staff was left in Berlin for another six months.[65]

Taube saw the LCM through the eyes of a civilian and Washington bureaucrat and was dismayed to find an operation that had played fast and loose to achieve its ends. Scant recordkeeping, shifty accounts, office no-shows, personal jaunts at the LC's expense, high salaries, and inflated civil service classifications: Taube blasted the mission's day-to-day operations and its sense of entitlement. Even the lowliest staff member "bumped Colonels out of lower berths," Taube grumbled. How would he explain the irregularities? Sourly he acknowledged the LCM's legendary feat—it had "got the books" through audacity, daring, and know-how—even as he surveyed the mess he would have to clean up. Janet Emerson, the mission's secretary and an object of Taube's particular scorn, offered a different perspective. "At the beginning so little was known as to what the real work of the Library of Congress Mission would be," she stated in her final report. It had thrown together "so many types of men" in "difficult 'prima donna' conditions." Each had his own project, yet they pursued the mission in collaboration—and to great effect.[66]

In the end, they had gathered far more than anyone had anticipated. The Library of Congress gained extraordinary holdings of German and other European publications from the interwar period to the early postwar years. Unique Nazi pamphlets, posters, photographs, and ephemera poured into the library. According to Richard Hill's estimate, 50 percent to 75 percent of the wartime music publications of Germany and Austria had been acquired. Through the Cooperative Acquisitions Project, over 588,000 items were distributed to 113 academic and research libraries. Mass acquisitions to build foreign collections, proposed tentatively as a matter of American national interest at the end of the war, had been a success. However, the LCM's efforts to renew earlier commitments to internationalism and cultural exchange proved more difficult. Harry Lydenberg pushed to restore older institutions and practices—a central book repository, interlibrary exchange, and a bibliography for all of Germany—but this was impossible without unification. "The point at which politics and scholarship cross," as Reuben Peiss put it, produced a different kind of intellectual internationalism with the United States at the helm.[67]

CHAPTER 5

✧✦✧

Fugitive Records of War

The alliance between the Library of Congress and the military controlled access to publications in occupied Germany, even as it produced a bounty for American collections. It quieted the clamor of research libraries to send their own agents to hunt for books—all except one. The Hoover Institution and Library on War, Revolution, and Peace, its official name in 1946, pursued an independent and aggressive collecting policy in the immediate aftermath of the war. Where Harvard, Yale, Columbia, and other universities accepted their reliance on a government-led program, the Hoover Library went its own way, with a resourceful and cunning team of administrators and collectors. The unique influence and reach of the former president enabled a private institution to operate where others were barred. Herbert Hoover's collectors journeyed through devastated Europe, leveraging his deep relationships and making their own ties to civilians and military authorities. Even when the Hoover Library won an authorized spot on the Library of Congress Mission, it continued to work in the shadows of the occupation government.

The American public knew little about the collecting missions undertaken by the US military and research libraries, beyond an occasional newspaper article. The light of publicity shone in early 1948, however, with news that Doubleday would publish the diaries of Joseph Goebbels, the powerful propaganda minister under Hitler. Journalist Louis Lochner had translated and edited more than seven thousand pages of typescript entries to produce the "inside story of Nazi officialdom." The *New York Times* dramatically reported that the diaries had been "tossed about unrecognized and unwanted" in Berlin, rejected by the Russians, entered an American document center, and then were "lost in a welter of unclassified papers," until sharp-eyed publisher Frank E. Mason found them and brought them to the United States. This was a compelling account but nearly all of it was untrue. As word of the book spread, government officials began to question how the diary had been acquired and slated for publication. They launched an investigation, which revealed a tangled web of stories and explanations. Yet one important fact stood out: the Hoover Library was behind this acquisition. The release of the Goebbels diary raised thorny legal and ethical questions. As the leftwing newspaper *PM*—no friend of Hoover—asked, "What right has an individual American citizen during Allied occupation to obtain possession of documents of such obvious historic interest as Goebbels' diaries and bring them to this country?"[1]

The Goebbels diary was the tip of the iceberg, one acquisition in a large-scale collecting mission largely hidden from view. Unlike the LCM, with its official mandate, the Hoover Library drew upon an overlapping informal network of collectors, war correspondents, intelligence agents, and visiting experts who made their way to postwar Germany. They knew how to ferret out information and had a keen eye for the records of war Hoover sought. In the rubble economy of a defeated nation, they found a gray market where information and documents could be traded for food and favor. Engaging in complex encounters between victors and vanquished, they worked to fulfill Hoover's vision.

———cハっ———

In June 1941, Herbert Hoover proudly presided over the dedication of the Hoover Tower, looming over Stanford's campus, far from the nation's eastern elite. Despite conflicts with the Stanford administration and faculty over the Library's independence and politics, his vision of the collection as the foundation of an institute for research and policy analysis was coming to fruition. "Its records stand as a challenge to those who promote war," serving the cause of freedom, peace, and security, he declared. The American entry into World War II only deepened this conviction, and he pressed the library to aggressively acquire wartime documents, especially "fugitive and ephemeral material." After D-Day, he sought official permission to allow his agents into European war zones but was refused. Nevertheless, the library's new director, H. H. Fisher, along with Perrin Galpin, head of Hoover's Belgian-American Educational Foundation (BAEF), planned a full-scale offensive. They hoped to locate the network of book dealers, government officials, professors, journalists, and "honorary curators" who had channeled materials to the library in the interwar years. Stanford historian Ralph Lutz had made arrangements with many of them in 1939, but as Galpin remarked, "no one knows what's happened to the people who were to make the collections or to the materials."[2]

Hoover's old compatriots began to resurface with the liberation of France and Belgium. Louis Chevrillon, the Paris-based representative for Belgian relief since 1915, sadly reported his failure to acquire many records of the occupation and resistance: "All through France, documents, newspaper collections, archives of Vichy have been destroyed in large quantities for fear of police investigations." His colleagues in Belgium, Jacques van der Belen and Lea Swaelus-Godenne, had more success. They had gathered documents during the German occupation and stored them in cellars; despite their concern about bombing and the theft of a few packages, this material survived the war. With the liberation, they advertised in newspapers and on radio, asking the public to donate issues of the clandestine press and other wartime materials. Among those who answered the call was a janitor in Brussels. During the occupation, he had found work at a Nazi propaganda agency. As the Allies neared the city, his German employer ordered him to burn the archives and posted an SS guard to ensure it would be done. When the guard took shelter during air raids, the janitor snatched what records he could and hid them in his living room. He sold these to Swaelus-Godenne for $200. "The C.R.B. life is regaining activity here in Brussels," exclaimed Belen. "I shall take personally this Hoover War L. business in and make it a go. Count on me!"[3]

Beyond these Hoover loyalists, library officials tried to enlist the help of humanitarian agencies and European-American cultural organizations. They asked the United Nations Relief and Rehabilitation Administration if their agents would collect the documents produced in their relief work. No historical training was required, Fisher assured the UNRRA librarian, only "some time indoctrinating the field workers to make them realize that while they are making history they must also record it." They convinced the head of an UNRRA delegation to Poland to acquire materials, but the trip fell through. They even tried to get the names and addresses of former exchange students in Poland, hoping to offer them jobs as collectors. Stephen Mizwa, head of the Kosciuszko Foundation, mordantly replied to this request. A list of such students "would not do anybody any good," he observed, for they were "scattered in foreign countries, some are in German concentration camps, some enjoying the Russian hospitality in the far-off Siberia, and not a few are beyond the worries of this earth's affairs." "Warsaw's addresses," he added, "have been somewhat disarranged."[4]

Hoover Library officials tried other ways to gain documents of Poland's history of Nazi and Soviet occupation and resistance movements in one of the war's worst "bloodlands." They approached émigré leaders who might have access to refugee communities and governments in exile. One was Jan Karski, a heroic member of the Polish resistance. Karski brought the first eyewitness account of the Holocaust to Franklin Roosevelt in 1943, and his extraordinary 1944 memoir *Story of a Secret State* was a bestseller. In it he described the "conspiratorial apparatus" of his work in the underground, including collecting and preserving an archive hidden in a Warsaw restaurant. "Known to every Pole," Karski became a paid agent of the Hoover Library, using his many contacts to secure Polish records in the United States and abroad.[5]

Polish exiles had collected materials assiduously since the fall of 1939 and published indictments of Germany based on documentary evidence, such as *The Black Book of Poland*. Acquiring such records was important, Karski observed, "when so many individuals, governments, political organizations will try to falsify the circumstances and the picture of the war." He traveled to London in early 1946, where he discovered that Polish institutions endured "as a policy, symbol, formal continuity—but, unfortunately, they do not exist in the form of buildings, staff, offices." He approached people in the exile community who wanted to sell their collections before returning home, and he began to collect personal accounts and memoirs of ordinary Poles, "very simple people, soldiers, peasants, workers, children, etc." In a strange incident, he was arrested for smuggling gold currency out of England. Although the problem was quickly patched up, his collecting expedition continued to pose difficulties. Hoover's men feared becoming too entangled with the owners of these collections, who often asked for subsidies or help emigrating. The political status of Poland had changed rapidly, too, with the United States recognizing the Communist-backed government in July 1945. Library officials did not want to appear to take a position, and Karski needed to act with discretion. To their surprise, he succeeded beyond their expectations. Karski "is getting letters from all over the world which are the result of the work which he started," one commented, and significant Polish materials had come in: from photostats of the underground press to first-person testimonies of Poles who had been deported to Russia in 1939 and 1940.[6]

Like the Library of Congress, the Hoover Library tried to place its own agents in Europe in the final stages of the war. Only one found his way there: Merrill T. Spalding, a Russian historian at Stanford "devoted to the Chief and the Library" since their days in the Belgium relief campaign. He had traveled to North Africa and Spain in the summer of 1944 to collect materials, and by fall was looking for a way into the heart of Europe. He thought about using his connections in the OSS but backed off when warned that some might "think that the job of collecting materials for the Hoover Library was merely a 'cover' for some secret OSS assignment." Somehow he secured permission from Eisenhower's command to visit the European theater and travel to Aachen, where he arrived in early 1945. This was the first German city to be occupied by American troops, and even after three months, the situation was unstable. Spalding offered his services to the civil affairs officer in charge, who "seemed glad to meet a book-hunting civilian" and asked him to carry out a job for him. Doing so did not win him any special treatment, however. Unlike prewar days, when he could leave instructions with a host of book dealers, now he "couldn't buy a single volume." The army had frozen books and documents in place, and its T-Forces had swept in. "I am not at all enthusiastic about . . . rushing into 'occupied' countries and trying to grab 'fugitive' materials," he wrote. "There has been plenty of such rushing and grabbing in both Italy and Germany, but most of it has been done by Army units which have a very definite—and sometimes a temporarily exclusive—priority." Gaining permission to examine materials in a document center, he nevertheless had to compete with government agencies "greedy for all kinds of political, economic, social and military literature," and fight "the confusion, the delays, the lack of adequate communications, and all the other difficulties which total war has bequeathed to the Europe of 1945." The official documents teams had transportation, funds, clerical help, and government authority, while Spalding spent much of his time trying to cut red tape. "I sometimes feel like a person armed with a bow and arrow going out to fight a fleet of modern tanks," he gloomily concluded. "Reconnoitering trips are not sufficient . . . some sort of systematic campaign will have to be waged."[7]

◦◦

Although combat ended in May 1945, the situation in Germany remained chaotic through the summer and fall, as the Allies faced staggering challenges to supply the basic necessities of life and govern the defeated population and the displaced persons within its boundaries. It was not until July 1 that Allied forces were repositioned to their respective zones of occupation, determined at the Yalta Conference five months earlier. On that date, Soviet officials finally permitted US and British troops to enter Berlin, which had been divided into sectors under the London Protocol of 1944. Among the first to arrive was intelligence officer William Heimlich, who recalled the "desperate summer of 1945" and "the total inadequacy of our preparations psychologically, intellectually, and even physically, for the occupation of a great modern city." Allied bombing had destroyed Berlin's homes, industry, and infrastructure; Russian soldiers had brutally raped thousands of German women; hospitals were overcrowded, with little medicine available; the population was hungry and traumatized. Adding to the small numbers of German Jewish survivors were growing numbers of refugees and ethnic German expellees from Poland and other countries to the east.[8]

How to collect in a devastated and occupied country, without official sanction or a legitimate commercial trade, tested the Hoover Library as a private institution and the representatives it sent abroad. Civilians needed authorization to travel to Germany and necessarily relied on the military for transportation, meals, and lodging. Despite the logistical challenges, numerous government officials, experts, investigators, and reporters journeyed to postwar Germany, especially Berlin, to gather information, survey conditions, and chronicle "year zero," the beginning of a new post-Nazi era. Among them were political scientist John Brown Mason, sent by the War Department as an interrogator, and Frank E. Mason (no relation), appointed by a press syndicate to report on defeated Germany. Both men also had a private assignment, to procure publications and documents for the Hoover Library.

John Brown Mason arrived in Germany in July 1945 with a group of American scholars appointed by the War Department's Historical Branch to question former German leaders about non-military aspects of the Nazi regime. Born to American parents in Germany, Mason moved to the United States as a young man, earned a PhD, and became an expert on the Nazi legal system. He developed ties to the Hoover Library during the war, when he directed a program at Stanford that trained civilian personnel to work in military government. The job with the historical commission was not arduous, and he received permission to scout materials for the Hoover Library as he carried out his duties. He even carried a letter of introduction from Eisenhower that helped open doors. "We are definitely in the big league now," he bragged. Mason used his credentials to visit book dealers, private libraries, and army document centers, acquiring what he could and arranging for shipments when conditions improved. Hoover Library director H. H. Fisher later remarked, "Mason's activities, when not illegal, were at least irregular." Hoover fretted that he was not aggressive enough, too willing to work within the dictates of the US Army and Library of Congress. He should not have worried: as librarian and Berlin intelligence officer Albert Gerould reported to the LC, Mason was "looting the place for the Hoover War Library."[9]

Frank E. Mason arrived in Berlin soon thereafter, ostensibly to write syndicated articles on the occupation for the North American Newspaper Alliance. He had been an intelligence officer during World War I and went on to a career in print journalism, radio broadcasting, and public relations. Mason was attentive to his journalistic duties, but he had gone to Germany at Hoover's behest and with funding from Jeremiah Milbank, a conservative philanthropist and Hoover associate. His press credentials enabled him to follow leads for caches of documents and books, including inside the Soviet sector. Mason immediately contacted Louis P. Lochner, a renowned foreign correspondent and long-serving bureau chief for the Associated Press in Berlin, who had returned to Europe in 1945 to report on the war and its aftermath. Mason and Lochner identified with each other as old hands in the news game. Part of a large press corps covering the big story of the American occupation, they scorned the complacency of many American journalists who lived comfortably in the "press camp" and parroted the military government's line. Horrified by black-market corruption, the mass rapes of German women, and the "hopeless shuffling of starvation," they wanted to know the angles and underside of the occupation. Mason also met up with William Heimlich, a friend from their student days at Ohio State University and later as colleagues at NBC. Heimlich had worked in wartime military intelligence and when Mason arrived, he held a key position as Assistant Chief of Staff in the Army's G-2 operations in Berlin. The two men were "constant companions" during Mason's three-month trip.[10]

Figure 5.1. Frank Mason (right) with Louis Lochner and jeep driver, Berlin, 1945. Herbert Hoover Presidential Library (31-fem-b05-f06).

Intelligence agents and journalists mingled in postwar Berlin, their work often barely distinguishable. Reporters approached officers for leads and lingered around the document centers, hoping for sensational information about the Nazi regime. At that time, intelligence services were a "strange hodge-podge," with information gathering and analysis involving not only G-2, but also agents from the navy, air corps, Information Control, and the OSS before it disbanded. Foreign correspondents often helped intelligence services, noted Heimlich, by tracking down criminal activity or uncovering problems in military government, and some agents returned the favor. He may have had Mason and Lochner in mind when he made these comments: the three men frequently shared tips and helped each other collect documents and other materials.[11]

Their first encounter involved the records of the Reich Party Press House for the "provinz press," a place where provincial German reporters sent to Berlin could go to research and write their stories. Lochner told Mason he had learned of it from a former employee of the Associated Press, Willy Brandt, a photographer and picture editor. Brandt had apparently safeguarded the Berlin bureau's records during the war, and after the German collapse, set up a new office to replace the bombed-out one. He had discovered the press house material and posted an "off limits" sign to preserve it. Lochner and Mason visited the building, intact amidst the rubble. Books, files, propaganda manuals, and a newspaper morgue lay in disarray on the floor. Mason ecstatically wrote his wife. "This one *haul* I found today through Louis Lochner is better than my wildest dreams, and I am sure the Chief will be pleased." Russian investigators, more interested in Nazi Party records and political affairs, had not seized or destroyed them. Sergeant Szajko Frydman, a Russian interpreter at the Allied governing council—and himself a relentless collector of Jewish material—told Mason that the Russians were "a pretty disorganized bunch" but not when it came to records. Fearing their return, Mason scrambled to remove the press house cache, but logistical and bureaucratic roadblocks stood in his way.[12]

Heimlich came to the rescue. Giving verbal orders, he arranged for two "turn-around" trucks that supplied Berlin from the American zone, had the materials packed and loaded on them, declared they had no intelligence value, and secured transit clearances with US and British authorities. "The whole procedure of my getting them down here is highly irregular from the point of view of military regulations," Mason explained to Hoover. At one point, the shipment was stopped when Mason could not produce the proper documents. A counterintelligence officer looked Mason over, saw an "American in a blue serge suit," and asked why he was "getting out of the correspondent field and mixing in the Library without specific authority from Washington." As a civilian journalist, his press pass gave him considerable freedom of movement but no right to remove such materials. With Heimlich and other military officers as allies, however, Mason could work around the regulations of the occupation government, maintaining his "amateur standing as a document hunter." The orders finally came through—aided again by Heimlich—and the shipment went on to Paris, Bordeaux, and finally Palo Alto.[13]

The entangled web of friendship and good turns extended to Brandt, who had steered the men to the documents. Lochner wanted to assist his former colleague, who could not be rehired by the Associated Press unless cleared of Nazi affiliation. Mason "arranged for Brandt to take a roll of pictures of Bill Heimlich for later political purposes"—Heimlich hoped to run for office—with the understanding that "Bill will clear Brandt by CIC." However, the Counter Intelligence Corps' investigation found that Brandt had done photo work for the Waffen SS and a "completely Nazified" picture agency during the war; at first the Information Control Division refused to relicense him, but eventually he was permitted to return to the AP. In the meantime, Mason hired Brandt to collect documents for the Hoover Library.[14]

Such transactional relationships and informal bonds enabled people to navigate the constraints of life in an occupied city. They offered something for everyone: news for the reporters wanting to write the big story; intelligence for occupation officials struggling to impose order and handle a new geopolitical reality; favor and legitimacy for Germans making their way in the post-Nazi world. And one item of exchange was, remarkably, archives, documents, pamphlets, and newsletters, the fugitive material captured for a powerful patron—a former president of the United States.

———⁂———

Although he did not hesitate to use subterfuge to send collectors abroad, Hoover wanted an authorized team of agents combing through Europe for the library. Those who had managed to get onto the Continent early did not think they could go it alone. Merrill Spalding urged an alliance with the Library of Congress, even if it seemed "a rather unholy one"; in Italy he had encountered Manuel Sanchez, who had been energetically collecting for over a year, and decided to make some arrangements with him. John Brown Mason arrived in Germany at the very time that the Library of Congress was negotiating a foothold in Europe. He wrote Luther Evans about the possibilities of collecting confiscated books and documents and made an arrangement with Berlin book agent Hans Broermann to purchase for both libraries. Evans even authorized $50,000 for Mason to buy materials, as a hedge in case the Library of Congress Mission fell through. In fall 1945, with the Mission underway, Evans invited Stanford University to join the cooperative acquisition program among American research libraries, and informed Herbert Hoover about European items already being forwarded to the Hoover Library.[15]

Evans believed he had come on board, but Hoover relentlessly pushed for a separate mission. "We have made great sacrifices to create an institution of national service, the only one in the United States," the former president emphasized. "It is in the national interest that it should be built up to fully cover the present war." The War Department demurred, fearing "uncoordinated and competitive activities" and insisting that "a properly representative, but integrated, mission" would best serve American libraries and the military. It had heard complaints about John Brown Mason and wanted no more than one collecting mission to deal with. Yet in Germany, some military officers resisted the Library of Congress Mission and quietly gave assistance to Mason and the Hoover Library.[16]

In February 1946, matters came to a head. The LCM had ramped up with the arrival of the team of librarians from Washington, but it faced questions about its legal authority to purchase and ship publications. One obdurate occupation official thought the mission violated the Trading with the Enemy Act. Even as that problem was being ironed out, officials from Stanford, the Library of Congress, and the American Library Association held a summit meeting, where they struck a compromise agreement to permit the Hoover Library to place its own representatives in Germany. At this very time, President Truman asked Herbert Hoover to head a Famine Emergency Committee to assess and report on the worsening European food situation. Over the winter of 1946, American officials increasingly feared that hunger and disease would undercut nascent reconstruction efforts. To Hoover, long praised for his food relief efforts in World War I but spurned during the Great Depression, this assignment also involved a degree of political rehabilitation. On the eve of his well-publicized trip, however, Secretary of War Robert Patterson rejected the library agreement. The LCM had balked at the number and autonomy of the Hoover Library agents who would go to Europe. Hoover angrily wrote Patterson that he had learned this "astonishing news" just as he was about to depart.[17]

The setback did not deter him. Hoover chose a group of specialists on food and humanitarian relief for the journey abroad. These included businessman Maurice Pate, a Red Cross official during the war and later a founder of UNICEF; diplomat Hugh S. Gibson, who had worked with Hoover organizing European relief efforts after World War I; and Dennis Fitzgerald, an agricultural economist with the Department of Agriculture.

Identified in the press as "regional food experts," John Brown Mason and Charles Delzell also joined the trip, as did Frank Mason, ostensibly to help coordinate and publicize the committee's work. A confidential memo called it a "happy coincidence" that "several of the relief experts on this mission were also Hoover Library experts," but in fact they were along only to hunt for books and documents. The two Masons were old hands at this game, but the inexperienced Delzell—a Stanford graduate student and former army criminal investigator—was reminded to "say little about the Library collecting business because this is a food mission you are going on."[18]

Hoover was seventy-one when he led this food mission, traveling to over twenty-five countries in fifty-seven days. He surveyed famine conditions and campaigned for food relief in person and on radio. His dramatic speeches painted a stark picture of hunger stalking the people of the world, and he called on Americans to conserve food and donate it to those abroad. The expedition had the trappings of a celebrity tour, especially in Europe— "a traveling circus," one of the Chief's men called it. Hoover's return stirred many Europeans who remembered his World War I humanitarian aid, the rebuilding of the University of Leuven library, and other acts of philanthropy. They often expressed their gratitude by offering presentation copies of books and rare manuscripts.[19]

In the shadows of the Hoover food mission, the collectors tried to secure materials for the library. In Berlin, they were often thwarted by the military government, which stage-managed Hoover's entourage and refused it free rein. "The most striking thing about our visit," Hugh Gibson commented in his diary, "is the superb job of insulation that has been done on us." Hoover, accompanied by Mason and Galpin, did spend a morning touring the Allied Document Center, which held the voluminous archives of the German Foreign Office. He tried to use his influence to acquire several important diplomatic agreements but was rebuffed.[20]

The LCM worked strenuously to block Hoover from leaving his collectors in Germany, as he had hoped. Unable to contain his animus toward the ex-president, whom he privately called a "mountain of hypocrisy," Reuben Peiss warned that Mason may have been barred but "there will be other 'food experts' acting as scavengers." Mason and Delzell moved on to friendlier territory. In Austria, General Mark Clark, commander of US occupation forces, allowed Mason "to continue *sub rosa* with [his] full knowledge." Delzell traveled to Italy and Spain, where he secured records of the German Cultural Institute, a "center of Nazi propaganda"; the *Christian Science Monitor* reported on his big catch, noting "the method of obtaining the underground documents is a library secret."[21]

Finally, in June 1946, the warring parties reached an agreement. The Hoover Library would appoint one official representative to the LCM, who would concentrate on personal papers and documents, not books, and would be answerable to the LCM's chief. "The Hoover mission is out as an entity," Peiss told his colleagues, "but they will probably attach a saboteur to our staff." Hoover personally asked Lochner to serve, and he joined the LCM in Germany from August to October, carrying detailed want lists with him. After his departure, Daniel Lerner took over as the Hoover Library representative from November 1946 to March 1947. The twenty-nine-year-old Lerner was formerly an officer in General Robert McClure's Psychological Warfare Division (PWD), a propaganda and intelligence agency that studied enemy morale and used mass communications to undermine it. He was writing a dissertation on "sykewar," as he called it, and eager to return to Europe to collect materials for his own work. Lerner's interests and the Hoover Library's proved a perfect match.[22] Lerner joined the mission as it was closing out its operations, its staff reduced to only one of the original representatives. While observing the niceties of cooperation, Lochner and Lerner pursued Hoover's goals with a singleness of purpose.

Hemmed in by the LCM, which had already acquired extensively throughout Germany, Lochner decided to "burrow around in places where the Mission did not get." He concluded after a ten-day trip to Berlin, "there is all sorts of material floating around or hidden, of which one learns the more, the longer one is here." He called on military officers he knew, counting on their friendship as he explained the Hoover Library's devotion to documenting the war. Although intelligence items remained restricted—including the Foreign Office records Hoover coveted during his visit to Berlin—some officials saw little harm in offering duplicates or even originals. One intelligence officer informed Lochner there were enough documents in the War Department "to keep the staff there busy for TWO HUNDRED years"; he turned over a truckload of phonograph records, news clippings, and reports. Frank Mason's friend William Heimlich supplied Lochner with many items, including a portion of Goebbels's diary from 1925, on "'permanent lend-lease' to the Hoover Library." Even Deputy Military Governor Lucius Clay contributed confidential minutes of the Allied Control Authority, "to be handed privately to Mr. Hoover."[23]

Lochner believed his true strength as a collector lay in his acquaintance with Germans in all walks of life, going back to his prewar days as a journalist. "I don't know how receptive my contacts will be to the idea of giving up their personal papers," he wrote Hoover. "But I am thinking all the time of people who might have valuable 'inside' stories laid down in their diaries or memoirs." One of these was a seamstress named Frieda Schmidt, whose diaries contained "information of a homey nature regarding how morale went up and down in a typical little German village." Lochner visited her, finding a "simple woman of the people," with a "flair for writing that is quite unusual." Schmidt had kept a diary since 1932 about the Nazi years, hiding the volumes under an asbestos pad in her stove. She gave them to the Hoover Library.[24]

Lochner's letters hint at the complex feelings of those he approached about parting with cultural patrimony. One evening, he met with the editor of a Stuttgart newspaper, who gave his support "enthusiastically, as he was completely 'sold' on the world mission of the Hoover Library"; earlier that day he had visited a former judge, who upon reflection decided to retain his collection for the rebuilding of German libraries that had suffered such widespread destruction. More than any of his encounters, Lochner's visit to Hanna Kiep underscores the wrenching choices under fascism that led to the creation and preservation of documents. She was the widow of Otto Kiep, a German diplomat, who had met Hoover during his presidency; Lochner knew him later when he headed the Reich Press office. Kiep had been arrested and executed in 1944 for participating in the July 20 plot to kill Hitler. While imprisoned, he wrote letters, poems, a memoir for his children, and "stenographic notes on his imprisonment and torture." A warden with considerable courage had preserved these for Hanna Kiep—"notes which she cannot read as she does not [know] stenography and which must first be pasted together since the warden had to go through the motions of tearing them up." Lochner told Hoover that she "feels she is too close to the murder of her husband to give these papers up" but promised to contact him. He hoped she would eventually allow the Hoover Library to photostat these "human documents," but that did not come to pass.[25]

When Daniel Lerner stepped in as the library's agent, doors to American military sources opened that were previously closed. Lerner had achieved some renown during the war as editor of an innovative weekly intelligence report; he had been "a member of General McClure's teams and hence 'belongs,'" Lochner commented. When Lerner visited his old unit, a general welcomed him with access to the Psychological Warfare Division files, and Lerner spent three days in the documents room. "Though many of the treasures have been pilfered privately, the largest number still remain," he noted. He secured many items of wartime propaganda, including radio scripts broadcast to the enemy and a file of captured German documents.[26]

Lerner embodied the close ties between intelligence and collecting in the postwar period. As a psychological warfare expert, he had learned interviewing techniques and emotional appeals that proved useful to a collector. He embraced the persona of a clandestine agent whose secret operation took the form of gathering historical records. Describing a frustrating trip to the US Legation in Bern, he spun a tongue-in-cheek tale of intrigue and derring-do. After a fruitless meeting with American Ambassador Leland Harrison, who refused to release wartime materials, he visited some libraries and private collectors, and then "went back to the cloak-and-dagger section of the Legation to see Hazeltine, an OSS character. . . . He is still playing hush-hush, with overclassified reports and double-locked file cabinets, and it was clear that an honest collector couldn't make a living there." Lerner retreated, and "with a swish of my black cape I leapt across the parapet to the 'press and culture' section." There he charmed attaché Mildred Allport, who praised him for his "magnificent" wartime intelligence reports, "read avidly by all members of the Legation," and offered him some Balkan materials.[27]

Lerner's knowledge of the Left—gained as a student in New York and in psychological warfare—gave him an entrée with Communists, socialists, trade unionists, and former resistance members, whose records he sought for the Hoover Library. He met with Benedict Kautsky, the son of Marxist philosopher Karl Kautsky, and Walter Nelz, a leading Trotskyist before the war and archivist of the Swiss Social Archives. Both men had been imprisoned during the war, Kautsky in a concentration camp. Lerner bonded with the men as they caught up with news of American Communism and its leaders. "I never thought my acquaintanceship with Burnham, Cannon, Shachtman would stand me in such good stead in so many places," he joked. Lerner pursued a large private collection of a Monsieur Ranc, whose activities traversed leftwing international politics from the 1910s to the 1940s, including the Zimmerwald group of neutral socialists, the Communist Party, Trotsky, the independent Spanish Communist Party POUM, and the French resistance. "The collection documents this biography," Lerner marveled. "Everywhere that he participated, Ranc has kept a meticulous file of leaflets, brochures, newspapers, periodicals."[28]

In the midst of fascism's threat and war's devastation, these collectors had created archives as an act of defiance and political resistance, of memory making and memory keeping. The documents were often deeply personal, signifying choices made and risks taken; preserving them, despite grave danger, also meant saving themselves. As an intelligence agent, Lerner could not find a trace of Rote Kappelle (Red Orchestra), a clandestine group that had engaged in anti-Nazi subversion. Its Berlin leaders surfaced after the war, and he tried to negotiate with them for their records but found they were nervous about turning over their files to capitalistic Americans. "Every original is regarded as 'Heiligtum' [sacrosanct] by one or another of their members," Lerner wrote. He planned to invite them to

Christmas dinner to ease "their grinding distrust of American institutions" but would not offer compensation. "These men are radical idealists and would have been genuinely hurt if I had put the transaction on any sort of a business footing."[29]

Transactions did happen frequently, however. Sometimes they occurred on the black market, where cigarettes were the currency for everything from cameras and war souvenirs to documents and information. Willy Brandt, for example, got a rare copy of the last Nazi newspaper issued in Berlin from a journalist who asked to be paid in cigarettes. "Whenever you are able to offer things like cigaret[te]s or foodstuff[s]," he explained, "people are much more inclined to give up their treasures." Hoover's men usually used their PX ration cards and ordered food parcels for potential donors and helpers. "Food means everything," Lochner exclaimed. "Happy to say I have thus far not had to BUY anything. I did it all with food or requests for CARE packages!"[30]

The Cooperative for American Remittances to Europe (CARE) was a humanitarian effort of American welfare, religious, and labor agencies in 1945 to respond to the problem of widespread hunger after the war. Providing emergency relief, CARE packages contained the surplus rations of American soldiers; over time, these were replaced with items more appropriate for families in need. CARE was a large-scale operation organized along a business model of assistance, based on Hoover's post–World War I food programs. Yet it personalized relief, an unusual feature that received much praise. Donors could specify the recipients of food aid: for ten dollars, a forty-nine-pound package of meat, grains, butter, and sweets would be delivered to European relatives and friends, marked with the name of the benefactor.[31]

For the Hoover agents, CARE packages turned a transaction between victor and vanquished into an act of benevolence and friendship. Lochner could not offer money to Frieda Schmidt for her diaries. Suggesting they might eventually be published, he agreed that she would retain copyright and he would pay the cost of a typist. However fanciful that hope, he alleviated an immediate need by sending a CARE package each month for a year. "At this she nearly wept for joy," Lochner wrote Hoover. Lerner also found a CARE package or PX rations made a "friend for life." On one occasion he received a substantial acquisition promised John Brown Mason when one of Hoover's old friends, a colonel "ready to do-or-die for old H/L," distributed eleven CARE packages to those holding the materials.[32]

Lochner provided other forms of assistance, too, mediating between Germans and the occupation government, as he did for his AP colleague Willy Brandt and others who had fallen under suspicion for Nazi ties. One was Gerhard Kramer, deputy director of Seehaus, a radio listening post that intercepted broadcasts from around the world for intelligence and propaganda purposes, similar to the BBC's efforts on behalf of the Allies. The military government had arrested him, but Lochner insisted Kramer was an anti-Nazi and helped free him from custody. In gratitude, Kramer presented eight bound volumes of international radio transcriptions broadcast on a single day, October 21, 1944, when the Allies captured Aachen. Like the LCM, the Hoover agents drew a line when Germans asked for help to emigrate to the United States. Lerner judged he should not "implicate the H/L in these difficult and dangerous human relations."[33]

Taking the measure of the occupation, Lochner and Lerner used their know-how to work within and around the military government, search out information, and succor needy Germans, in order to "separate [them] from their libraries." They were official members of the LCM, cooperated with it, and acquired many items under its authority. Lochner even penned a flattering press release on its activities. Yet they had few qualms about overstepping or violating the library agreement. Upon his departure to the United States, Lochner announced he was taking with him records of the Lithuanian legation in Berlin, correspondence between Ribbentrop and Hitler, and eyewitness accounts of German expellees from Eastern Europe—all without official clearance. "Now, letters and brief exposes of this kind are quite messy to handle, and can easily get lost in the shuffle when thousands of bulky things such as books are handled at the same time," he rationalized. "It therefore seemed wisest to me to take material of this kind right into my travel bag and carry it to New York and Washington personally." The Library of Congress and War Department objected to his "unauthorized removal of intelligence materials from the field," but were unsuccessful in calling him to account. Lerner too gathered "loads of material" without the knowledge of the remaining LCM agent.[34]

The two men found the work of collecting endless yet gripping. "I only wish the days had 36 hours!" Lochner exclaimed after six weeks on the job. "Although I work from early till late, I always feel as though I were only skimming the surface." Lerner confirmed the sentiment: "There is so much material to be had, so many leads to be followed." After his unproductive trip to Bern, he traveled on to Vienna, where he found an abundance of materials, a "megalomaniac's dream." He included a handwritten note in his official account, "I want to report the feeling that when one has had such a lucky week as this, one loves this work and finds it worth all the pain of weeks less glorious."[35]

———⚬———

Through these means, the Hoover Library built significant collections on Germany, fascism, and World War II—the only private institution that succeeded in penetrating war zones and military occupation, sometimes in an official capacity, other times surreptitiously. The Hoover Library's acquisition of the Goebbels diary—or rather, over seven thousand pages of this voluminous work—was not out of the ordinary and likely would have occurred without notice. Joseph Goebbels had kept a daily diary from October 1923 to April 1945, a few weeks before he committed suicide, and different portions turned up in the immediate postwar period. Counterintelligence agents found one part in a pile of trash, while an army captain discovered a leather-bound diary from the mid-1920s. Microprinted glass plates of the diary, buried near Potsdam, were unearthed by French and Russian officers, with most of them taken to the Soviet Union. The portion acquired by Hoover, comprising the years 1942–1943, had been found in fall 1946.[36]

The publication of the diary brought this acquisition under government scrutiny. The Alien Property Custodian, which seized German assets in the United States, had the unusual power to assume the copyright of literary and other works by enemy authors. Now the APC began to examine the military and legal issues involved with the diary's publication. Was the diary subject to military government regulations and if so, had it been acquired and brought to the United States illegally? Those regulations required screening Nazi-era documents so that material useful to the American occupation would be retained. Private American citizens had no right to take enemy documents or other property without authorization. Soldiers may have seized war booty and "souvenirs" with impunity in the chaotic days after the war, but circumstances had changed. Publication rights were also in question: Who held legal title to the physical pages of the diary? Did the diary's content belong to Goebbels's heirs under a common law copyright? Or did the US government possess title, under the APC's right to "vest" German enemy works? The Justice Department sent a team of investigators—George Elkan, Hermine Herta Meyer, and Frank Korf—to Berlin in February 1948 to begin to answer these questions.[37]

Over the course of many years, Hoover's men offered different accounts of how they acquired the Goebbels diary, from descriptions in the published book and press interviews at the time to oral histories recorded long after the fact. The Justice Department investigation and contemporaneous private correspondence likely provide the best body of evidence for ascertaining what occurred, although the full truth of the matter may never be known. All parties—American and German—tried to cast their actions in the best light. Yet the differing stories are themselves worthwhile, revealing the informal connections, chance encounters, resourcefulness, and opportunistic moves that made it possible for the Hoover Library to collect documents in the occupation.

Attention focused immediately on William Heimlich as the individual who had obtained the diary pages. Interviewed by the Justice Department investigators on February 18, 1948, Heimlich said that a "German acquaintance" had telephoned in December 1946 or January 1947 to say that papers from Goebbels's Propaganda Ministry had been sent to a pulping mill. When he went to investigate, his "attention was called to a pile of ordinary typewriter paper, about three feet high," which he thought might have been copies of Goebbels's diaries. He asked whether Soviet officials had screened them and was assured this was the case. He then brought them to his office, where a secretary sorted them. Questioned about this statement, however, his story began to change: In one version, a man named Breier had taken the documents to his house and given them to Heimlich, who offered him a few cigarettes; another had Heimlich at the Propaganda Ministry site itself, with the Russian guard "induced to 'look the other way'" for a carton of cigarettes. The interrogators pushed him, wondering how an ordinary German worker would have gotten Heimlich's private phone number. "Wouldn't you think it slightly surprising that a common laborer would know that these documents were important?" asked Frank Korf. "We had trouble determining the importance of [the] documents ourselves." Heimlich deflected the questions. The acquisition was "a very casual thing," Heimlich said. "I have had many Germans approach me wanting to sell paintings, books, manuscripts."[38]

The investigators then questioned Robert Breier and several other Germans, who presented a different set of facts. They painted a more detailed picture of the way that casual trade in documents might figure into the encounters and living strategies of Germans during the occupation. In their final report assessing all the evidence, the investigators gave credence to the Germans' testimony, observing that they had not had time to consult with each other, yet their stories were consistent, in contrast to the shifting versions Heimlich gave.[39]

The Germans all agreed that Breier had found the documents. Breier was an elderly junk dealer who bought and sold waste paper and rags, until his license had been cancelled by Nazi authorities; after the war, he received a new license from the US military government and began to call on his old customers. In October 1946, he went to the site of the former Reich Ministry of Transportation, in the Soviet sector of Berlin. He bought a load of paper that had been stored in the cellar; no Russian had been present. When he brought these materials to a paper-reprocessing mill, he saw a number of heavy sheets, which had typing on one side and were blank on the other, and he thought they might be salvaged as writing paper. He separated them and took them with him. He brought sample sheets to a café to show Erwin Richter, a friend or acquaintance. Richter was the manager of a brewery, and his brother-in-law Paul Hermann worked as a foreman there; the two men examined the sheets with great interest. The papers were unusual: typed with a large and distinctive font, the sort used by Nazi officials, they offered detailed information not known to the general public. "We read things that were not in the newspapers, and that, of course, surprised us," explained Richter. Concluding they were loose pages of Goebbels's diaries, Richter went on, "I said to myself as a businessman that these might turn out to be a very profitable business."[40]

The three men debated what to do with them, deciding the best course of action would be to offer them to the American authorities. One of Richter's employees, George Kapp, had a daughter Alice whose American boyfriend, Harry H. Janssen, served in the military government under Heimlich. According to Alice, it was Janssen who showed a few pages of the diary to Heimlich. She accompanied the two Americans when they went to Richter's apartment to see the whole set that November. When the question of compensation came up, Heimlich warned Richter he could just have the military police seize the papers. Richter denied any interest in profiting from the papers, but "they were merely interested in seeing these papers 'in the right hands.'" As the investigators put it, the German men "insisted that they did not intend 'to sell' them" but they did expect a reward. Heimlich gave them about five cartons of cigarettes, which they split among themselves. This was a substantial payment; Breier had wanted cash as his portion, and his carton sold for one thousand marks.[41]

The investigators then turned to the disposition of the diary after Heimlich took possession. Heimlich insisted to them and in later testimonies that he had respected the chain of command, reporting the find to G-2 military intelligence, the Berlin Document Center, the Office of the Political Advisor, and the Counter Intelligence Corps. No one was interested. He tried to contact the LCM but was unsuccessful. The diary pages "sat there for nearly 3 months in my office gathering dust," he observed, and "anybody who might remotely have an interest was shown these pages." He admitted to the investigators, however, "that all his reports were made informally by telephone, or orally from person to person" and had not been put in writing. Moreover, at the time he received the diary pages he was no longer head of military intelligence in Berlin sector, which might have justified his retention of the document; although he often represented himself as an intelligence officer, he had transferred to the Political Affairs Branch of the military government as a civilian in September 1946.[42]

Heimlich had not kept the diary secret, and scuttlebutt "went around among Army document circles in Berlin shortly after the documents were discovered." But neither the Justice Department team nor a later FBI investigation found anyone to corroborate Heimlich's claim that he had done due diligence. Hans Helm, then chief of the Berlin Document Center, emphatically denied that Heimlich had contacted him: "Owing to the 'hot' nature of such documents compared to the many tons of less important documents we handled, such an offer would have received my earnest attention." His assistant Captain Francis Saur concurred. The Reich Propaganda Ministry was a "priority target of first importance," and documents officers were constantly looking for archival material for use in war crimes trials. "I would have strenuously objected to the turning over of Goebbels' diary to any outsider," he stated.[43]

Heimlich had not asked permission before presenting the Goebbels diary to President Hoover, who had returned to Berlin in February 1947 on a second food mission. Traveling with him were Heimlich's friends Frank Mason and Louis Lochner. Heimlich had met Hoover during his first trip to Berlin a year earlier in an unforgettable encounter: Heimlich in bed with the flu, Hoover "walking up and down the room," talking with him for two hours about postwar Berlin. Now he joined Hoover's group at their Berlin guest house for meals and conversation. Two days before the food mission's departure, Heimlich arrived for lunch. He "brought a number of bundles of papers for the Library containing the diaries of Dr. Goebbels," Hoover's colleague Hugh Gibson noted in his diary, "the bundles look too bulky for diaries but anything coming from the little doctor should be interesting." Heimlich was one of many who made such offerings to Hoover. "The house is filling up with undigested documents brought in by government offices, officers and civilians, and by Germans who seem bent on swamping Louis [Lochner] under files, bundles, and binders," Gibson wrote. "I did not attach much importance to the matter, it being only another 'item' among many millions in the War Library," Hoover later stated. "I was so engaged in the mission that I forgot all about it."[44]

Heimlich viewed the Hoover Library as a legitimate repository for these documents. After all, the government had accredited its representative to work with the mission of the Library of Congress. He recounted the assistance he had given both libraries when he had served as an intelligence officer from summer 1945 to fall 1946. "In the early days of Berlin there were truckloads of such documents given to [the Hoover Library]," he said, "I remember having furnished three trucks of documents to go all the way to Paris," which were approved by his superior officer—Frank Mason's Reich Press haul. Heimlich had also been instrumental in working out arrangements for the LCM to go to Leipzig, in the Russian zone, to retrieve books. "The Hoover party is only a private agency, is it not?" the investigators reminded Heimlich, who replied, "Is it? If I get an order from General Eisenhower that the Hoover Library should be given all possible information even with respect to classified material?" That was not an order Eisenhower had given, of course. "A General cannot change the status of a library," one of the investigators retorted.[45]

Heimlich also distinguished between documents that required official handling through the military chain of command and those that were war booty. "This manuscript I looked on as something which had been thrown away by an ally and was . . . a legal war trophy just like picking up a rifle off the battle field," he explained to Frank Mason. "Thousands of books, cameras, arms, furniture and God knows what have been sent with the consent of the U.S. Army." He made the same point to the investigators: "I consider the finding of the papers to have been an event of the war," he told them. "I do not think we looked at such things at all as government property, more like trophies." They pushed back: "At that time still?" Heimlich replied, "Yes, in 1945." They reminded him: "You got those papers late in 1946." Germany was no longer a war zone and the occupation had become routinized. Heimlich acknowledged, "we were beyond the days of arbitrary action."[46] This distinction was continually erased in the various press reports, oral histories, and private letters describing the acquisition of the diary.

In February 1948, the Alien Property Custodian challenged Doubleday about its right to publish the work. The publishing house, in turn, sought answers from Frank Mason. At the time of Hoover's 1947 food mission, Mason was sole owner of Fireside Press, a small publishing house that specialized in anti-Communist books. That May, Mason approached Louis Lochner about editing the diary for publication. Through the summer and early fall, Lochner translated the work, selected excerpts, and prepared annotations and an introduction. Mason arranged a book contract with Doubleday, a large commercial publisher able to market the work widely; not coincidentally, one of its executives was Hugh Gibson, a familiar presence in Hoover's circle. The book had all the makings of a blockbuster, until the APC threw a wrench into the works when it insisted that royalties be put into escrow until it concluded its investigation. Mason wanted to refuse, but Doubleday contemplated delaying publication.

In an effort to reassure Doubleday, Mason borrowed a recording device, attached it to his phone, and then made a transatlantic call to Heimlich. It was February 18, 1948, the very day Heimlich had been questioned by the Justice Department team. The two men declared their innocence as they got their stories straight. Mason told him that the royalties for the book were going to be large, a remarkable development, he reminded Heimlich, because the disarranged diary sheets "didn't look like anything when we got it—a bunch of communiqués." They confirmed to each other that no one had expected to profit from the diary, and Heimlich had given no remuneration to the German who had found them. That was a fundamental question for the APC in determining whether the two men had violated the Trading with the Enemy Act.[47]

Whatever their avowals to each other, payments and profits had been on their minds from the start. Heimlich must have raised the matter of the commercial value of the diary with Mason, if not directly with Hoover. The day after Hoover accepted the diary, he wrote Heimlich a letter assuring him of "full property rights for publication during the lifetime of the copyright." Nor was this the first time Heimlich had thought of publishing documents. Months earlier, he had discussed the possibility with Lochner and decided to offer several diaries to the Hoover Library as a loan rather than an outright gift, to retain the option of publishing them. By this time, American publishers were deluged with German "diaries, documents, and manuscripts purporting to tell 'the real truth'" of the Nazi era, as one journalist observed.[48] Mason, Lochner, and Heimlich seized their opportunity with the diary of a notorious Nazi leader.

Heimlich's actions the day Mason called suggest his concern that the story would not hold up: he sent German police officers to Breier's apartment to summon him to Heimlich's office. Breier told investigators that this was, in fact, the first time the two had met. Heimlich wanted to talk about the diary pages. When the junk dealer asked why this should be his concern, Heimlich said there was no reason, but prompted him, "you remember, you received cigarettes"—and gave him another dozen before he left.[49]

Nevertheless, Doubleday felt sufficiently reassured by Mason's telephone transcript that they went ahead with the publication. They agreed to the APC's terms, placing royalties in escrow as the case continued, and printed a notice in the book stating the APC had granted permission to publish the diary but did not rule on its authenticity or the accuracy of the translations. When *The Goebbels Diaries* appeared in April 1948, it sold briskly and garnered significant publicity, with newspapers running excerpts and reviews, and the Book-of-the-Month Club adding its imprimatur.

Reviewers had different reactions to the diary itself. Reading the book was "a repulsive experience," said critic Orville Prescott. "It makes one's skin crawl as if it were coated with a foul scum." In contrast, a *Los Angeles Times* reviewer called it "a bore." "Goebbels was a tenth-rater by any civilized cultural standard," he went on, "these jottings . . . show him as cheap, vulgar, indecent, and criminal." Whatever the quality of the text, however, many saw the book's relevance to current events in Europe. Goebbels was a master propagandist "worth several armies," wrote renowned OSS agent Allen Dulles. "He set a pattern which Moscow is using effectively in the cold war." The diaries "show how a whole people can be deceived, cozened, and betrayed by a fanatical minority into national suicide," a *New York Times* editorial agreed. "It would be well for the whole Western world to heed and understand their import."[50]

Meanwhile, what had begun as a routine investigation turned into a pitched battle. The Alien Property Custodian had "an atom bomb with the fuse already ignited," opined an FBI official, "all the persons interested in this particular matter cannot be satisfied." Finally, the APC issued its decision. The diaries had never been properly cleared for removal from Germany. As an official record of a Nazi leader, the pages should have been seized by military occupation authorities or turned over to them; as enemy property, they fell within the purview of the APC. The agency rejected the argument that *The Goebbels Diary* was "an American book by American journalists," as Lochner later put it. It issued a vesting order in April 1949, claiming literary property rights in the book, as it had done with over one hundred thousand enemy works, including unpublished ones. Royalties from the book would go to American prisoners of war and civilian internees under the War Claims Act of 1948. In making its decision, the APC explicitly absolved President Hoover of any wrongdoing, concluding he had "acted in utmost good faith," and it permitted the original diary pages to remain in the Hoover Library. Unable to retain royalties, Doubleday backed away from promoting the book and tried to remainder it; when it did not sell, the publisher pulped thirty thousand copies.[51]

Hoover and his men believed the furor was politically motivated, fanned by leftist publications like *PM*, residual New Dealers, and Soviet sympathizers. The APC office "is full of ex-adherents of Henry Morgenthau and Harry Hopkins," railed Hoover, who also blamed the Library of Congress, which had tried to block his representatives from collecting in postwar Europe. Mason perceived an organized Communist effort, entailing a "public warning to the entire book industry of the power of Red Forces." He believed Heimlich's staunch anti-Communism contributed to his being hounded by the Justice Department. Already a fierce Cold Warrior, Heimlich had become head of Radio in the American Sector (RIAS) in 1948, turning it toward more propagandistic broadcasting in the months before the Soviet blockade and Berlin Airlift.[52]

Lochner and Mason did not let go of the issue. They attempted to recover over $130,000 in royalties in a lawsuit in 1950 and filed a complaint against Harold I. Baynton, former acting chief of the APC, whom President Truman nominated to be assistant attorney general. During the Senate Judiciary Committee hearings on the nomination, Lochner testified against Baynton, accusing him of intentionally derailing the book. Baynton stood his ground, stating that one could not acquire literary rights by paying for a manuscript with cigarettes or taking property that had been thrown away. Looking back on the episode nearly three decades later, Mason saw a trail of misfortune: the negative publicity and loss of royalties, to be sure, but also personal calamity. Hugh Gibson had fallen seriously ill, which his wife blamed on the strains over the book, Lochner suffered a heart attack, Mason had a nervous breakdown, and Heimlich had to defend his reputation and career. "The Goebbels Diaries are bad luck," Mason concluded. "Everyone who handled them had that experience."[53]

Heimlich, Mason, and Lochner thought the Goebbels diaries would serve historical understanding and prove personally lucrative, but that dream withered when the APC reacted forcefully to the book's publication. Yet this episode obscures the effectiveness of the Hoover collecting mission and the driven agents who worked their way across postwar Europe on behalf of the library. In Germany under military occupation, this was a shadow world of collecting. It drew upon the same sources of intelligence, web of connections, and recompense of cigarettes and food that enabled Americans and Germans to operate outside military government's rules and channels. Their work hastened the large-scale collecting efforts that saw the Hoover Library more than double its prewar holding in the first five years after the war. Begun as a collection documenting World War I and its founder's humanitarian efforts, the specialized library pushed itself into national prominence and international influence as a center for the study of twentieth-century global politics, war, diplomacy, and societies. Hoover understood the present as contemporary history and, unlike many private collectors, sought materials with "research value," not "museum value."[54] Collecting fugitive records from around the world before they vanished, housing them in the United States, the Hoover Library became a repository and intellectual center for the new confrontations of the Cold War.

ᴄᴋᴏ

Book Burning—American Style

Even as American libraries expanded their collections through relationships with the military, the American occupation government faced its own problem of mass acquisitions. The Allies had agreed to purge Nazism from German society and culture, including its book world. The military confiscated countless volumes, sequestering and even destroying them. "The circulation of Nazi and militaristic books has been prohibited since the arrival of the Army in Germany," General Dwight D. Eisenhower observed. Bookstores and publishers had been forced to surrender these works to military authorities. Many objectionable volumes had been swept up in the mass collecting of information and publications undertaken by US Army intelligence, the OSS, and the Library of Congress Mission. Over time, this became a remarkable operation to make an entire body of published works inaccessible and unreadable. In this effort, government officials recruited communications experts, social scientists, and progressive educators, who applied their homegrown experience and research to the unsettled and alien conditions of Germany. Librarians, too, were deeply involved.[1]

What had seemed a matter internal to the occupation government became the subject of American public uproar when on May 13, 1946, the Allies signed Order No. 4, on the "Confiscation of Literature and Material of a Nazi and Militarist Nature." It prohibited works that promoted Nazism, fascism, militarism, racism, *völkisch* ideas, anti-democratic views, and civil disorder. It required schools, universities, and public libraries, as well as booksellers and publishers, to remove these works from their shelves and deliver them to Allied authorities; they would then be "placed at the disposal of the Military Zone commanders for destruction." American officials must have assumed that Order No. 4, as an extension of earlier policies, would attract little notice when they announced it in Berlin that day. Instead, reporters clamored for explanation and demanded a second briefing. In a hastily organized press conference that night, Vivian Cox, an ex-WAC and low-level assistant in the Armed Forces Division, was called in to address the skeptical crowd. She told them that a single passage could condemn a book and "billions" of volumes might be seized. "Was the order different in principle from Nazi book burnings?" they asked. "No, not in Miss Cox's opinion," reported *Time*. This was a front-page story: Americans were burning books.[2]

The ensuing tumult at home was brief but pointed. Newspapers, librarians, scholars, and some politicians castigated the occupation authorities for the atrocity of book destruction as "contrary to democratic principles."[3] How could a policy that smacked of Nazism lead the German people to embrace liberal democracy? And just as important, what did it say about American ideals in the aftermath of the war? Separating these questions, the occupation government perceived books and reading to be a danger to the future of Germany, even as it affirmed Americans' right to read. Its mass acquisitions policy resolved the contradiction by preserving some of these works for research and study while it endeavored to destroy the rest. Not fully evident to American authorities or journalists was how much the practices of confiscation had taken on a logic of their own prior to the announcement of Order No. 4.

———⚭———

In April 1945, with the collapse of Nazi Germany imminent, the Joint Chiefs of Staff issued JCS directive 1067, which established a strict framework for the American occupation. It ordered "the elimination of Nazism and German militarism in all their forms," to "prevent Germany from ever again becoming a threat to the peace of the world." The Potsdam Agreement in early August ratified this goal among the Allies specifically with respect to education. These documents set out the guiding principles of demilitarization, denazification, and democratization for postwar reconstruction. Nevertheless, the policy was never clear-cut, and behind it lay many tangled decisions over the fate of books among the Four Powers and within the American military government itself. There were numerous practical and philosophical challenges in executing the principles of occupation and reconstruction, manifested in the handling of Nazi and militaristic literature. What would it take to transform the defeated nation from tyranny to democracy? As Feliks Gross, a Polish émigré and sociologist involved in educational reconstruction, put it, "under what conditions do the character and ideals of a nation change?" That question might have applied as well to the Americans: How would they navigate the contradictions of being a "democratic occupier," using coercive and repressive means to achieve democratic ends? There were no easy answers where books were concerned.[4]

American and British experts began to tackle the problem of how to deal with German publications as early as 1943. Books fell under the purview of different military and civilian governmental agencies that sometimes worked at cross purposes. Educational materials were handled separately from publishing and the book trade, with libraries falling somewhat in both camps. Adding to the difficulties, the larger policy for postwar German reconstruction shifted in the final year of the war, toward the hardline position of Treasury Secretary Henry Morgenthau. Although his plan to turn Germany into a weak, rural state did not prevail, his view of the enemy as innately militaristic and nationalistic had a strong impact on denazification and media policy.

The policy toward German textbooks emerged in the collaboration of two groups in wartime London, the informal Working Party on German Re-Education, led by Oxford scholar E. R. Dodds, and the Education and Religious Affairs (ERA) section of the German Country Unit, which planned the military occupation. Captain John W. Taylor, an education researcher and expert on German schools, supervised the ERA's efforts for the Americans; collaborating with him was Grayson Kefauver, Dean of Education at Stanford University and a State Department consultant on educational reconstruction. Later, Taylor would recruit his own mentor, Richard Thomas Alexander, a leader in progressive education. Initially operating in ignorance of each other, the ERA and Dodds's Working Party began to coordinate efforts in May 1944. While recognizing the need to purge Nazi ideology, Taylor and Kefauver at first articulated a positive vision of education to support democratic and humanitarian values, paying homage to the Four Freedoms. Seemingly unaware of the shifting political winds in Washington, the ERA imagined a reconstructed Germany that would be like the Weimar Republic. After their first handbook was criticized "for being too 'soft' in its policy toward the Germans," they stiffened their approach to denazification.[5]

The policy called for the elimination of all schoolbooks that had indoctrinated youths with the malign tenets of Nazism and militarism. Few changes had been made to textbooks in the early years of Hitler's regime, except for the inclusion of new prefaces and introductions touting National Socialism, which could be excised or pasted over. By 1937, however, Nazi ideology permeated students' daily lessons: physics books applied "scientific principles to war uses, biology and nursing texts had long chapters on racialist theories, while algebra texts were filled with examples and problems based upon the use of artillery, the throwing of hand grenades, the movement of military convoys, and so on." History and geography had been rewritten to highlight the losses caused by the Versailles Treaty; Latin readers glorified strong leaders and individual sacrifice to the state. Allied education planners wanted such textbooks impounded and replaced. They decided initially to reproduce Weimar-era texts as a stopgap measure and planned to publish new works authored by non-Nazi German educators.[6]

If there was agreement on the role of books in children's education, the question of reading matter for adults was more contentious. Although the Education and Religious Affairs experts weighed in, the responsibility for the postwar book trade lay with the military's Psychological Warfare Division. Its chief, General Robert McClure, had made the PWD into a powerful army unit, with a large staff and independent operations. At the end of the war, it became the Information Control Division (ICD), charged with the denazification of German media, including radio, film, and the press, as well as publishing houses, bookstores, and commercial lending libraries.[7] The direct line from psychological warfare to information control—and the influence of ICD in the early phases of the occupation—was critical in shaping American policy toward Nazi publications.

On its face, the military government's perspective was simple: Nazi books were akin to a virus or infestation that required quarantine and elimination. If this seemed self-evident to many, underlying this view was an array of social science research. To a remarkable degree, the American military developed its media policy by seeking the counsel of psychologists, public opinion researchers, sociologists, and German émigré intellectuals. For decades, communications experts had warned of the power of media to influence a mass audience. Some had specifically investigated state control and media indoctrination in totalitarian countries, while others considered how Americans could fend off such influences and build morale through effective propaganda. Émigré social theorists, such as Franz Neumann and Herbert Marcuse, also shaped perceptions of Germans' psychological state under Nazism and reinforced the need for thorough cultural change. The OSS even interviewed Thomas Mann and other prominent German writers, who thought that "Nazi education and literature must be stamped out," yet "placed little confidence in teaching democracy from books." Although contradictory, their suggestions leaned toward using the methods of totalitarian propaganda and indoctrination in the service of democratic values. "We had much advice from those who professed to know the so-called German mind," commented General Lucius Clay sardonically, "if it did exist, we never found it." Nevertheless, transforming the "Nazi mind," as it was often called—and thus the German reader—became a problem of postwar reconstruction.[8]

Few communications scholars paid attention to books and reading, however. Douglas Waples was the rare specialist and a key figure in the postwar book confiscation policy. Waples had developed quantitative approaches to the study of reading as a social process in the 1930s. In an era of widely circulated magazines, bestsellers, adult literacy programs, and public libraries, he saw books as the one form of mass communication that uniquely fostered freedom of expression. Readers exercised more choice than radio listeners or moviegoers, Waples argued, controlling the experience by turning the pages and stopping to contemplate or reread. Initially hopeful that books would foster an educated citizenry, the Great Depression and rise of Nazism darkened his view. Increasingly he saw how print spurred partisanship and mass mobilization, and he came to doubt readers' abilities to resist spurious and manipulative texts. Yet by 1942 he was again questioning the "widespread and hysterical notion that propaganda is omnipotent," and like other communications researchers at this time, suggested that media effects were limited, shaped by people's predispositions and selective perceptions.[9]

Waples himself became a propagandist during the war, conducting counter-subversion and morale operations known as "black propaganda." In 1944, he joined the Psychological Warfare Division as chief of its Publications Branch, a position he continued to hold in its successor, Information Control, where he was responsible for restarting the book and magazine trade. At the end of the war, Waples proposed a sweeping policy that required publishers and book dealers to destroy objectionable materials or turn them over to military authorities, who would decide their fate; he encouraged pulping these works to produce paper needed for the renewal of the publishing industry. At the time, his supervisors rejected his plan as too extreme—"let's not get into this," a higher-up scrawled on the proposal—but it foreshadowed the terms of Order No. 4.[10]

Many experts and military planners believed books had a profound effect on German intellectual life and public opinion. Book sales per capita were substantially higher in Germany than in the United States. The book had "more lasting effects than the newspaper and radio," claimed a field manual for publications officers, likely drafted by Waples; it appealed to educated upper- and middle-class readers who influenced social attitudes and was "about the only medium by which issues of fundamental importance can be presented effectively to the German mind." Books had been "one of the main instruments for the spread of Nazism," British Colonel R. J.

Percival insisted, all the more so because Germans were passive readers, "well trained to believe implicitly what they read, unlike Anglo-Americans who are much more critical."[11] Although postwar publications and older humanistic works would help inculcate democratic values, the objectionable materials of the Nazi era remained dangerous.

These judgments, influenced by the psychological and social scientific approach of the postwar planners, were based on only partial knowledge of the German book situation. From intelligence reports like Max Loeb's interviews of prisoners of war, they knew that National Socialists had placed strict controls on book publication, content, and distribution. Many independent publishing houses had been closed or incorporated into the party apparatus, while party-controlled publishers such as Eher Verlag "flooded the market with literature, much of which was written for purposes of indoctrination." The planners were less aware that Germans in the "media dictatorship" could still read a range of works until the war began, as historian Jan-Pieter Barbian has found; they tended to be uninterested in ideological tracts and wanted to read light entertainment. Sizable shifts in German publishing also occurred in the war years, as a new mass market of frontline soldiers came to dominate the book trade. Publishers and dealers rushed to produce mysteries, romantic fiction, and adventure stories—all suffused with Nazi ideology—to entertain the troops. With state subsidies and paper allotments diverted to these "field post" editions, books for domestic readers dwindled in the final stages of the war, and bookstore shelves were often empty.[12]

Not everyone agreed that banning books with Nazi or militaristic content was the solution, and they questioned the psychological and political impact of such a policy. An unnamed official argued that the experience of defeat had exposed Nazi propaganda for what it was. "To any but the impressionable juvenile mind, 'objectionable' literature in print has been largely if not wholly debunked by the catastrophe which the war has brought upon the German race," he wrote. "From a psychological point of view," he mused, "it might be a good thing to *require* every German adult to re-read *Mein Kampf* and its derivative literature following our occupation!" Others recognized the attraction of the forbidden: Would Germans resurrect and reread works that otherwise would have gathered dust? They discussed previous instances of book prohibition, including efforts to restrict pornographic literature in England and the United States. Above all, they wanted to avoid accusations that the Allied policy was a "repetition in reverse" of Nazi practices of book burnings.[13]

The American and British policy toward books evolved in the final stage of active fighting and the early months of the occupation in Germany. As the Allied armies advanced and captured individual towns and localities, military commanders secured all media of communication and shut down libraries, bookstores, and schools. Under Military Government Law No. 191, Information Control prohibited book publishers, retailers, and commercial lending libraries from selling or distributing objectionable publications. Sequestering and surrendering these publications was the initial step in the program to denazify, license, and reopen the German book trade and print media. In June 1945, Information Control issued instructions specifying categories of banned works, focusing on Nazi propaganda and militaristic literature but extending the prohibition explicitly to include writings that promoted nationalism, racism, or public disorder. Some exceptions were allowed, particularly in scientific books, where prefaces or objectionable sections might be excised so that they could continue to be used. In the schools at this time, Education and Religious Affairs instructed principals to put all teaching materials reflecting a Nazi or militaristic perspective under lock and key.[14]

Public libraries and universities were initially seen in a different light. The *Handbook for Military Government*, issued in December 1944, had ruled that books in these libraries "not be removed, impounded, or destroyed." Education and Religious Affairs in particular favored unrestricted access to any library material, drawing a distinction between adult reading and required school textbooks. Through the spring, however, the policy hardened. Local army commanders closed libraries and ordered librarians to halt the circulation of objectionable works, although this effort was haphazard. New guidelines hammered out in June made clear that public libraries were to be brought into line with publishers and booksellers. They required that all forbidden materials be removed from open shelves and placed in secure rooms, available only with the express permission of the military government. Staff members filled out *Fragebogen*, detailed questionnaires intended to reveal Nazi affiliation or beliefs. Library directors were required to sign a certificate stating, "I fully understand that it is my responsibility to see that the library is completely denazified." Applications to reopen a library certified that "no ardent Nazi will be employed" and no literature circulated that supported Nazi doctrines, militarism, or discrimination on the basis of race, nationality, creed or political opinion. Once approved, military government officers had the authority to reopen non-commercial libraries. Similar rules applied to university libraries. Academic librarians segregated objectionable volumes in rooms that could be used only by authorized researchers. Into the fall of 1945, these materials were largely works by prominent Nazi authors or those with explicit militaristic ideology, such as Clausewitz's *On War* or biographies of Bismarck.[15]

Removing Nazi literature from German homes proved to be a red line. Although a committee drafted a directive to this effect, it aroused strong opposition in the US Control Council. To accomplish this goal, one general objected, they would need not only a vast *index expurgatorius* of "tens of thousands of titles" but also armies of inspectors to search every home and bookshelf. "The ease with which printed matter can be concealed is obvious," he said. Even more than these practical matters, however, the Control Council balked at an action reminiscent of Nazi book burning: American public opinion would be outraged, and Germans would perceive this as a hypocritical and punitive measure. Even the Nazis had not gone on house-to-house searches for banned books. A counterproposal recommended a publicity campaign to encourage Germans to voluntarily give up their Nazi books as "an act of personal cleansing or expiation" that would convert tainted works into paper pulp and new reading matter. This idea was repeatedly raised, especially by the British, as an alternative to coercive measures.[16]

Officials also debated which materials to ban, and whether to require a blacklist of specific titles or a blanket prohibition. Douglas Waples suggested proscribing all works published in Germany since 1939, every publication of the Nazi Party and its precursors since 1918, and all war literature since 1914. The Americans and British decided against such extreme measures, especially the blacklist, concerned not to raise the hackles of civilians back home. Even if they could compile a complete blacklist—which seemed an impossible task—they also feared it would inadvertently stimulate public curiosity about these books and give renewed life to Nazi ideas. Their Soviet counterparts had no such qualms. In their view, what made a work fascist was readily determined on an ideological basis, and they compiled a 526-page catalogue of volumes forbidden in the Soviet zone. Although secretly consulting this tome, the American Information Control Division released only an "illustrative list," twenty-eight pages in length, that identified types of works to be eliminated, such as war novellas, youth training manuals, and texts on racial superiority and colonial expansion. It would be up to German librarians, scholars, and public officials, as active readers cleared of National Socialist affiliation, to deliberate and remove objectionable literature. Tying the goal of political democracy to individual psychological transformations, and hoping to distance themselves from Nazi book purges, the American occupiers required Germans to take responsibility for their own denazification. At the same time, the policy ran the risk of arbitrary implementation. As one critic observed, permitting multiple interpretations of what it meant, for instance, to "glorify war" could produce incoherent results.[17]

For German citizens required to interpret and execute the Allied policy, tendentious literature was not an abstraction, but part of the material book world in which they lived. Through the Nazi era, books were burdened with political symbolism, and this remained true during the Allied occupation. Eliminating objectionable books communicated obedience or acquiescence to the occupiers. Like the "cleansing" of the successful *Fragebogen* or the removal of militaristic monuments, book purging was a performance of denazification.[18]

Wuppertal, a small city in western Germany, offers an example. Libraries there had been a refuge during the war, especially after air raids closed its theaters and concert halls. Bombing attacks demolished many books, about one-quarter of library holdings; thirteen thousand prized volumes placed in an air raid shelter for safety were destroyed by "an explosion caused by [a] looting mob." The city in ruins, its citizens homeless and hungry, Wuppertal surrendered to the Americans in April 1945. Immediately the army commander began to execute denazification directives, arresting Nazi personnel, removing Nazi signs from streets and buildings, and ordering the press, schools, and libraries closed. A mere five weeks after the surrender, the mayor's office submitted a progress report touting the libraries' compliance with the denazification order. They had reopened reading rooms on weekdays, and lending would commence once Nazi books had been eliminated. The main town library, the report remarked with some irony, possessed "a certain amount of literature prohibited by the Nazis which can take the place of the now confiscated books."[19]

Germans scrambled to fulfill the order to remove objectionable materials in libraries, schools, municipal offices, factories, and technical firms. Poet Stephen Spender observed this behavior throughout the British zone, where he had been sent to oversee the denazification of libraries in 1945. In many cases, "Germans had automatically set about purging their libraries on the day of their towns being occupied by the Allies, if not before." Those "closest to the Nazi policy were the quickest to understand and interpret our aims in the most far-reaching way," having already gone through the purging of Jewish and socialist writers. "Please don't trouble, Mr. Spender," a librarian in Aachen told him. "We understand exactly what you want, and there is no difficulty whatever about carrying out your instructions." Rumors even spread that the military government had ordered communities to destroy their Nazi books by public bonfires, leading Eisenhower himself to intervene.[20]

Not all bookstores and libraries acted with the dispatch of those in Wuppertal. In forty-eight hours in July, Americans held a series of surprise raids codenamed Operation Tallyho, in which soldiers swept through cities and towns to round up potentially subversive individuals, munitions, and contraband, including some Nazi literature in plain sight. The next month, a spot check of libraries in a number of cities revealed little consistency in the removal of Nazi books. In Nuremberg, libraries had suffered severe damage but "a sincere effort [was] being made to de-Nazify public libraries." A library committee in Heidelberg had "cleansed" the main branch, with seven hundred to eight hundred books removed and locked in an attic. In contrast, Regensburg showed "no evidence of

Figure 6.1. Tallyho operations involved surprise searches for unauthorized items, including forbidden books. In November 1945, a GI in Bremen checked a bookcase for banned publications. National Archives at College Park, Still Picture Branch (111-SC-225395).

the De-Nazification of libraries." Chronically understaffed, with a make-shift "W.P.A. atmosphere," the Education and Religious Affairs Division had great difficulty supervising library purges even as it undertook the mass production of new textbooks.[21]

German librarians and textbook committees sometimes struggled to make the choices the Allied occupiers had put in their hands. A conversation with a young librarian in Cologne, reported by sociologist and psychological warfare officer Edward Hartshorne, is revealing. She was committed to purging Nazi literature but "wanted to know how much of genuine German values they would be allowed to keep." Hartshorne suggested this was "something she and her fellow librarians would have to work out since it would be a difficult task to define what was 'genuinely German' but at the same time neither militaristic or Nazi." He went on: "It would certainly be in the best interests of Cologne libraries as a group if they could regard the rules under which they would have to work as more an expression of their own attitude than simply commands from a higher power." A zonal textbook committee in Lübbecke uneasily identified objectionable works they nonetheless deemed worthwhile. They divided schoolbooks into three categories: "Purely Nazi books of no value," "unobjectionable books," and "Nazi influenced books which, however, had a value from their information or scientific contents." The latter were forbidden to students but could be placed in a special section for reference by teachers. "A certain number of Nazi books were needed in order to work against the Nazi spirit," the committee reported. A scientific librarian in Düsseldorf considered it "extremely difficult to disentangle the Nazi from the non-Nazi works in various learned periodicals," with their "strange mix of articles of real learning and valueless propaganda." Just as he had preserved Jewish volumes, so he believed these books should survive, for the historical record and as a weapon against the resurgence of Nazism.[22]

Stephen Spender reflected deeply on the ironies and apparent futility of the Allied confiscation policy of 1945. He could not decide if he approved of a plan that made the Allies seem like Nazis and could not prevent Germans from keeping or getting objectionable books. These purges were largely "window dressing," he commented. "All it amounted to was taking some Nazi books off the shelves and putting them somewhere else." The literature itself was mind-numbing, and reading it seemed like ingesting a drug. "It would take three or four months even to read through this great mass of unread propaganda," a German librarian told Spender, surveying the stacks he had been told to screen. Still, Spender concluded, "Nazi propaganda was a conscious and deliberate decision." When he read from Goebbels's diary or an Ernst Jünger novel glorifying Hitler, he could not help but think of the nameless Nazi victims he had seen at a Wuppertal burial site. "One opens a book and reads a page like this in a public library in Germany . . . with somewhat the same emotion as one stumbles on a mass grave," he wrote. "The day of triumph is here identical with the day of downfall, the day of shamelessness with the day of shame and disgrace."[23] Word and deed were inseparable. Was this not a compelling reason for the destruction of Nazi and militaristic works?

In October 1945, Marshal Georgy Zhukov, the Soviet representative to the Allied Control Council, proposed to toughen the policy on Nazi and militaristic publications. He would extend confiscations to public libraries and private collections, widen the categories of prohibited materials, use blacklists of specific titles, and mandate the destruction of these books. He had already taken these steps in the Soviet zone—called by journalists the "Zhukov action"—and, with French backing, wanted them applied to all of Germany. Months of debate and numerous drafts followed, with reports and responses from the quadripartite military and political directorates, as well as committees on information control and education. A much-revised version would eventually become Order No. 4.

The military directorate, including its American representative, embraced Zhukov's hard line. "The way to root out naziism was to root it out," an ERA official characterized its position. The directorate wanted to eliminate forever the possibility of renewed German warmongering, and understood Order No. 4 as a demilitarization order, akin to the ban on war memorials, military or paramilitary athletic organizations, and Germans wearing military uniforms. Objectionable books, whether field manuals or fiction for soldiers, fostered German aggression and should be destroyed, with harsh punishment meted out to those who failed to turn them in.[24]

American civil officials, however, raised sharp questions about the Russian proposal. Robert Murphy, the US political advisor in Germany, warned against a sweeping policy of confiscation and destruction, believing it impossible to enforce, "psychologically unsound," and likely to produce a backlash. Secretary of State James Byrnes agreed, concerned "lest a program for suppression of allegedly noxious printed material lead to grave abuses reminiscent of Nazi book burnings and similar acts of violence to the intellect." Throughout, British representatives argued most vociferously against the proposal, especially the problem of creating and enforcing blacklists. They continued to prefer voluntary book drives to rid shelves of Nazi books.[25]

The Americans never fully discussed or reconciled their disagreements, and the order seemed to drift among different branches of the US military government in Germany. The Political Affairs office wrote the paper outlining the American position but did not seek a consensus with Information Control and Education and Religious Affairs. Some officers privately expressed qualms, but neither division objected forcefully or raised concerns about public opinion at home. Poor communication and a failure to take responsibility took its toll, yielding a weak US response. There were "numerous false starts," concluded one postmortem, "the staff action was badly bungled."[26]

In the final negotiations on Order No. 4, American and British officials argued against the blanket suppression of objectionable works, especially the inclusion of personal libraries, saying such a policy contradicted democratic ideals and looked too much like Nazi book burning. A Soviet representative denied this comparison. "There was nothing in common between the classical works which the Nazis destroyed and Nazi books which [propagated] militarist ideas and hatred toward humanity," he insisted. If a guiding purpose of the occupation was to eliminate German militarism and Nazism, "to allow Germans to keep Nazi literature in their homes in no way contributed toward the fulfillment of this task." However acute these remarks, the Anglo-American Allies could not accept their logic and drew the line at blacklists and purges of private libraries and homes. They conceded, however, to the order's proviso that objectionable books be confiscated from public libraries and destroyed. They also accepted new guidelines expanding the categories of objectionable works beyond the earlier Information Control regulations of June 1945. Zone commanders would continue to have a degree of discretion, which they hoped would soften the policy's severity.[27]

While blocking the most extreme measures, American officials did not resist the policy's overall goals. Indeed, even as the proposal worked its way through the labyrinth of committees in the winter and spring of 1946, they intensified efforts to eradicate objectionable books. A new "drive to cleanse bookshops, book stores and lending libraries of material including militaristic, nationalistic, or racist ideas" gathered steam in February and March. Booksellers had already sequestered these works, but now they were collected and pulped for paper stock, which was in short supply. In the Munich area, soldiers seized thirty tons of book dealers' stocks in February alone. Within the Information Control Division, some expressed alarm that these new operations would draw the notice of an influential journalist such as

Dorothy Thompson, who would condemn "their resemblance to Nazi book-burns." She had earlier questioned a re-education program that included banning militaristic books in precisely these terms. ICD instructed their personnel to play a supervisory role but let German employees handle the "selection, segregation, handling, trucking and pulping" of books. Although the policy was not a secret, Americans were to be as invisible as possible in its execution.[28] Indeed, reporters took little interest in these operations. Only with the public announcement of Order No. 4 did the press erupt.

———✢———

The assault on books had been a particularly resonant symbol during the war, shaping popular understanding of fascism and the reasons for US mobilization. "Books cannot be killed by fire," President Roosevelt declared on a famous wartime poster. Poet Stephen Vincent Benét's 1942 radio play, *They Burned the Books*, became part of a repertoire of remembrance and protest, rebroadcast on the radio and performed by local theater troupes, schools, and clubs during the war. Publishers, booksellers, librarians, and the Office of War Information all promoted the freedom to write and read as a core American value and universal right. On the tenth anniversary of the Nazi book burning, nearly two hundred libraries and bookstores showcased displays of banned books and publicity materials from the Council on Books in Wartime. In Hartford, Connecticut, librarians even came up with the ambitious idea to run the library as if it were in an occupied country for the day, but they did not have the staff to pull it off.[29]

Book burning touched something deep in many Americans. It was a response that went beyond library events and staged protests to a consideration of the larger meaning of the war for humankind. "During these ten years the dim-out for all European civilization has been inexorably proceeding," remarked a librarian introducing a broadcast of Benet's play. "We are bound too closely to European culture for its tragedy not to affect our own." Journalist Alfred Kantorowicz called Nazi book burnings "one of their greatest crimes against humanity," while First Lady Eleanor Roosevelt termed the regime's suppression of knowledge a means of enslaving the German population. By the end of the war, Americans had come to believe that books "are symbols of freedom." At the same time, they had become an instrumental means of waging war—epitomized in the slogan "books are weapons in the war of ideas," and, more pithily, in the radio show *Books are Bullets*.[30]

Now, one year after victory in Europe, days after the thirteenth anniversary of the book burnings, Americans suddenly learned that the Allies were following in the Nazis' footsteps. Journalists wondered how Americans could have accepted this agreement and blamed Russian and French pressure in the quadripartite negotiations. "It appeared to surprise and trouble American political, propaganda and education authorities in Berlin," one reporter commented. "It seems plain, however, that the Americans were just as openly a party to the order." Journalists and editorial pages railed against the use of Nazi methods. These would be "bigger and better book burnings," the *Wall Street Journal* warned, including many works of history, philosophy, and economics. Pointing out the vague guidelines of the order, the *Baltimore Sun* questioned how zonal military commanders, "henceforth known as literary and art critics," would make decisions about what to preserve or destroy. Reports speculated that everything from Clausewitz and Karl Marx to Tom Paine and the Bible could be banned. Mixing its metaphors, the *Christian Century* thought the order would lead to a witch hunt, drive Nazi literature underground, and make book "bootlegging a national cult."[31]

American librarians also responded vigorously. Increasingly over the 1930s and through the war years, many had come to see themselves as guarantors of free speech and democratic debate. The American Library Association fired off telegrams to the president and the secretaries of war and state to condemn the order. Although Librarian of Congress Luther Evans did not go on the record, he privately urged the head of the ALA, Carl Milam, to encourage librarians to write their members of Congress. As Milam characterized Evans's views, only "loud howls in Congress" would "blast the United States and the Allied governments in Germany out of the present position." Librarians across the country opposed the order to confiscate and destroy Nazi books. The United States had fought the war "to stamp out the *practice* of these perverse systems," wrote Bangor librarian L. Felix Ranlett to Senator Owen Brewster of Maine, "but the book destruction method, wherever tried in the past, has always strengthened rather than destroyed the idea against which it was directed." The preservation of the historical record was vital for future generations to understand the horrors of this era and avoid them in the future.[32]

Behind the argument that democracy required the free and robust exchange of ideas lay certain assumptions about the role of books and reading in the rise of National Socialism in Germany. During the war, Americans had been told that Nazi propaganda, promulgated by an all-powerful state media, held sway over the German people. In the wake of Order No. 4, some Americans continued to hold the view that Nazi books remained toxic to a defeated people "still full of Nazi poison." A combat veteran criticized the *Chicago Tribune*'s campaign against the order, saying that he and his fellow soldiers had seen the "beautifully bound volumes filled with the vicious lies of Hitler, Rosenberg, and Ludendorff" and "wondered at the time whether they would be allowed to remain and poison the minds of future genera-tions of Germans." The newspaper felt obliged to reply. "There is nothing sacred in the physical aspect of a book," and ideas live even when books are destroyed. "By descending to Hitler's level . . . we merely confess to the German people our inability, or disinclination, to defend and advance the ideals of international morality and human decency."[33]

Some wondered how much reading itself determined the German em-brace of Nazism. Journalist J. Emlyn Williams expressed doubt that Hitler's *Mein Kampf* or Alfred Rosenberg's *The Myth of the Twentieth Century* had done so. "Despite the fact that the Nazi ideology struck deeply into the German social pattern," he commented, "it would nevertheless be inac-curate to give more importance to the written 'philosophy' of National Socialism than it actually deserves." In contrast, librarians and scholars believed deeply in the power of reading and wrote President Truman that the only way to eradicate Nazi ideas was to "expose them to the light of reason and to offset them by literature and reading matter which enables people to see their falsity and depravity."[34] Citizens were necessarily readers, who had the literacy and ability to assess content and sift truth from propaganda, yet only the conditions of freedom and democracy would create and support such readers. In response to Order No. 4, American public opinion, as articulated in these protests, thought postwar German readers would behave like Americans—or as Americans should, in a free marketplace of books and ideas.

For the military, this was a public relations disaster. Harvard Library director Keyes Metcalf warned the War Department that the controversy would "raise high emotions" and "could easily get out of hand." US officials responded awkwardly to the protests. Deputy Military Governor Lucius Clay insisted that the order involved no change in the army's year-long policy of seizing Nazi publications, except that it now included libraries. A sample list of unacceptable books had been created by "prominent German bookmen," he said, "there can be no argument about their out-and-out Nazi flavor." The order focused on the content of books, not their authors or publishers. Nor would there be "ceremonial book burning," no public spectacle, only pulping, an industrial process handled by German firms out of sight, which would serve a genuine need for paper basic to the revival of the book trade. LCM representative Harry Lydenberg made the same distinction to colleagues at home. "Over there everyone—or at least the people we came in contact with—realized that the Nazi burnings . . . were symbolic rather than wholesale," he commented. "The new effort was in-tended to clear out this harmful propaganda stock."[35]

Whether this was a distinction without a difference, military officials understood the need to perform a delicate balancing act as an occupying force and as representatives of the American people. "We are faced with an exceedingly complex task in dealing with Nazi propaganda," Secretary of War Robert Patterson replied to a protest from John Haynes Holmes of the American Civil Liberties Union. He reminded Holmes that Germany remained "an enemy country under military occupation . . . subject to many controls which are not entirely consistent with the civil liberties enjoyed by American citizens." It was "inconceivable," he said, "that we should permit schools, libraries and other public institutions . . . to function as publicly-supported propaganda centers for the doctrines which carried the Nazi party to the depths of crime and depravity and brought the catastrophe of the last war." In an open society, an Information Control officer explained, "the good would in due course drive out the bad," but that was not yet possible in the "psychological setting" of postwar Germany. General Clay explicated the many ways that civil liberties were inconsistent with military occupation, with its responsibility to ensure that Nazism and militarism cease. He lost patience with complaints about the removal of books that kept alive these toxic views. As he put it bluntly, "Should we hang a Goering and let his works go merrily along?"[36]

The firestorm over Order No. 4 forced the military government to retreat, seeking to minimize the damage through implementation directives, as yet unwritten. The Library of Congress Mission offered a way out of their problem. "As bookmen in the theater, we are concerned about the sensational press reporting of ACC Order No. 4," Reuben Peiss and Harry Lydenberg told the top generals in Berlin. To counter the charge of book burning, they proposed that a given number of each objectionable title be retained as record copies, for the use of US government agencies, American research libraries, international bodies such as the United Nations, and ultimately German universities and institutes when democracy had been established. Clay embraced the plan, and after further debate, the Allied Control Council agreed to this modification.[37]

The new policy gave the LCM an official supervisory role in the execution of Order No. 4, screening confiscated books, selecting copies for research, and releasing the rest to pulping mills. It would assure "the total destruction of no title" and preserve the historical record of Nazism, observed LCM member Scott Adams. "This operation in no sense constituted an eradication of Nazi literature." Yet by putting itself in the middle of the operation, it had turned the traditional work of librarians—selection, classification, access—toward the ends of Order No. 4. Thus, ironically,

American librarians became integral to the machinery of book suppression and destruction.[38]

Like the military government, the LCM also felt the heat of disapproval from across the Atlantic. "Is it safe to say that General Clay has given assurance that in no case will holdings of research libraries be raped in such a campaign?" asked Verner Clapp, their agitated boss. Peiss insisted that the American press had sensationalized and distorted what really happened in the theater of occupation. "Actually the practice of the military authorities has been reasoned, enlightened, and in no sense undemocratic," he replied. "They should be commended rather than reproved." Despite these assurances, Clapp continued to worry about the nation's leading library purging books. "Our only excuse for engaging in [the] Order No. 4 . . . project is to get material." Was any of it valuable? "If not," he said, "be coy about participation until a judgment can be formed." Clapp had good reason to be wary. Although some of the early confiscated materials included significant legal publications, official documents and limited editions, later acquisitions, seized from lending libraries and 'people's libraries,' added little.[39]

In the summer of 1946, the three parties involved in executing Order No. 4—the Library of Congress Mission, Information Control, and Education and Religious Affairs—worked out procedures for implementation. This would be an "operation of fantastic magnitude," Peiss commented, to create, in effect, a "master library of Nazi literature." Public libraries, universities, and schools, as well as the commercial book trade, faced a two-month deadline to turn over objectionable books to military commanders or transport them to assembly points. German state ministries and local officials set up one hundred of these collecting centers in schools and warehouses to receive the volumes. Announcements on the radio and in newspapers also urged Germans to purge their private libraries voluntarily. ERA oversaw the collecting points for popular literature, while ICD managed the more valuable stocks of publishers and booksellers. The LCM screened and catalogued the books, removing up to 150 copies of each item for libraries and government agencies; its mandate included all German imprints from 1939 to 1946 and books with a Nazi perspective since 1933. The Monuments, Fine Arts, and Archives section took "all non-propaganda or pre-Nazi books . . . whether or not they bear stamps of Nazi organizations," setting them aside for the reconstruction of devastated German libraries, or if looted, for restitution. German research libraries could apply for an exemption to make Nazi literature available to legitimate scholars and investigators, while law firms, courts, newspapers, and hospitals received permission to retain materials needed in their work. "The notorious

Order No. 4 has had practically all of its teeth pulled," one LCM member exclaimed. "In fact, one wonders now what there will be left to pulp."[40]

Although not a ceremonial book burning, Order No. 4 added to the performance of denazification, a cleansing of the taint of Nazism and enactment of the idea that Germans had to undertake their own rehabilitation. Detailed instructions for non-commercial libraries in Bavaria—including church, school, technical, factory, university, and public libraries—explained that, as it was the "policy of having the German people learn democracy and its ideals by practicing it and shouldering its responsibilities," they would be "responsible for screening their own non-commercial libraries." Barred from selecting volumes based on publication dates, a list of banned books, or other "mechanical or arbitrary screening," they were to be critical readers, assessing each work for its tendency to promote National Socialism, racism, or *völkish* ideas.[41]

Despite these plans, the actual implementation of the order was chaotic. The American occupation staff was reduced in the midst of this vast operation, so there was little oversight or coordination of the German civilians in charge of the collecting centers. Many booksellers and libraries had already purged their shelves, but a number of small towns and remote communities had not. In some cases, large state and city libraries were still unable to retrieve the collections moved to safekeeping during the war. And some paid only lip service to the military government's order. Asked to submit inventories of Nazi works in their university, one rector presented a brief list of "100 strikingly Nazi and militaristic books." Another gave examples from departmental libraries but noted disingenuously that for scholars in many disciplines, "characteristic Nazi propaganda was mostly unknown to them."[42]

By the end of 1946, the collecting effort was only partially completed. The lack of clear principles of selection, Scott Adams noted, resulted in "many weird interpretations of tendenz and militaristic literature" and "over a hundred inadequately housed stockpiles of dubious value to anyone." Adams thought the collections were "75 percent junk," filled with cheap Nazi novels and schoolbooks. The ultimate purpose of the operation, he came to believe, was less to eradicate Nazism than to produce paper, using "tons of surplus publications for which no cultural or political need was indicated." Two military government investigators, inspecting fifteen collecting points in the American zone in early 1947, found that little had been done to implement Order No. 4 except for the amassing of books. They described a typical visit: "The director's first act was to rummage through the collection and hand us a copy of *Mein Kampf*, hoping thereby to dissuade us from further perusal."[43]

The decentralization of governing authority, mandated by the Potsdam Agreement, contributed to the uneven execution of the order. A few collecting centers were well organized. In Greater Hesse, for example, the German Education Ministry inventoried one million volumes, and five universities and several town libraries received permission to retain their collections in secure rooms. Many centers were in disarray, however, with books stacked and unsorted, no inventories, or inaccurate lists of holdings; they had also been "visited innumerable times and culled over by unauthorized Americans seeking souvenirs and collector's items." In Württemberg-Baden, lack of transportation hindered efforts to centralize the materials gathered in numerous small assembly points. The situation in Bavaria was even more confused. There were twenty-three scattered warehouses at paper mills, where inclement weather and theft had taken their toll. American officials did not know how many collections had been surrendered. Amidst the piles of books were scores of military objects such as flags and helmets, which people had decided to hand in for good measure.[44]

The LCM's mandate to screen all books slowed the operation to a crawl. "This work has been dragging for a long time," an Education and Religious Affairs official complained to Don Travis, the one remaining member of the original operation. In 1947, he and twenty-six German employees in Berlin tried to compile a master file of objectionable books, clear out the "junk," and retain only important works. Many collecting points had still not submitted inventories, and the mission's catalogue differed substantially from the Soviet blacklist. By May, the other zones had completed their work and concern grew that Nazi publications were appearing on the black market. "The other three powers complied with the law with greater dispatch than did the United States," Douglas Waples observed. "We feared the newsmen." Two months later the mission ceased operations and turned over its catalogue of twenty thousand titles and the remaining collection to the occupation government.[45]

The cumbersome procedures also slowed the American effort to reconstruct German libraries and schools through the late 1940s. Joseph (Tony) Horne, a Monuments Man inspecting archives and libraries, described the situation in 1946: "Everywhere the problems are the same. Libraries closed because no one has gotten around to denazifying them, [and] when denazified nearly all the material for young people is gone. One library lost 95 percent of its books." A German official in one town told him, "First the Nazis removed what they didn't like, now you remove what you don't like and we have nothing left."[46] Two years later, many libraries still lacked heat and their collections remained depleted. The situation was little better in the schools. "From the smallest one-room rural school to the university there is a universal dearth of textbooks and workbooks," declared a group of visiting educators. A study of children's books showed how much more needed to be done. "In some classrooms, particularly in the primary grades, the only book is in the hands of the teacher, who copies short lessons on the blackboard for the pupils to learn 'by heart,'" reading specialist Bernice Leary reported. "In other rooms, one may find partial or even complete 'sets' of prewar readers, all badly mutilated by the deletion of objectionable content." Students still used textbooks with militaristic content, including a fourth-grade reader "liberally sprinkled with pictures of marching German soldiers bespattered with blood"; remarkably, it was a reprint of a pre-Nazi textbook that the United States had issued as a stopgap two years earlier. In 1947, nine German textbook writing centers were established in the American zone, and American organizations began to ship English-language publications to German academic libraries and schools. As ERA officer Richard Thomas Alexander commented, however, "they represent[ed] only a drop in the bucket."[47]

--------⚬⚬--------

For all the uproar when Order No. 4 was first announced, attention dwindled as the book purges went on. Only one journalist, Hal Foust of the *Chicago Tribune*, followed up to report that despite earlier news articles, no books had been burned and no items of merit condemned. The diminished interest may have had many reasons, as breaking domestic and international news, especially the Cold War, claimed the front pages. Still, the short-lived yet disproportionate response to the order is striking. Interestingly, little of the original coverage actually addressed the German book collections themselves or the challenge of democratization. Rather, the outrage directed at US authorities dwelled most anxiously on what book purges said about the future of American freedom and democracy in the postwar world. The emphatic protests pushed back against Americans' experience of the war, when state power had been inserted into all aspects of daily life including, crucially, Americans' consumption of information produced by an expansive state and growing mass media. Ironically the promotion of a "right to read"—against the evil of book burning and fascism—had been part of this very propaganda and mobilization campaign. The tensions between Americans' belief in liberal democracy and the mounting presence of a leviathan state—felt in the New Deal and deepening during the war—did not disappear when the war ended. But in 1946, they erupted at a safe distance, focused on an occupation government in the enemy's land.[48]

Only one editorial confronted the assumptions about reading and American ideals underlying the controversy over Order No. 4. The *Pittsburgh Courier*, a leading African American weekly, agreed with other newspapers that the order contradicted American principles of free expression. But, the *Courier* pointedly declared, Americans should "do at HOME what we are doing abroad." If bigoted literature was unacceptable, "there would be MOUNTAINS of books, preaching racism and the inferiority of Negroes, eligible for the fire. Indeed we should have to EMPTY a large number of our libraries if we burned all books written in an anti-democratic spirit." Although the editorial ultimately concluded that the destruction of books anywhere was wrong, it made its larger point. The faith that the "right and moral idea needed only a hearing" had not defeated white supremacy and racial prejudice.[49] Indeed, those beliefs, deeply embedded in American institutions, had poisoned the hearts and minds of most white Americans, with no program of re-education and reconstruction to cure them.

The stockpiles of Nazi works amassed by the Library of Congress Mission, as it turned out, garnered little public interest. It had collected numerous copies, imagining a great demand from government agencies, learned societies, and international organizations. Although UNESCO asked for twenty copies of all the works, few other agencies followed suit. Rather, the Library of Congress and American universities received the windfall of German publications—about two million—from Order No. 4 and the larger confiscation practices of which it was a part.[50]

The distribution of the books occurred through the Cooperative Acquisitions Project that Archibald MacLeish and other research librarians had proposed in 1942. They had assumed that foreign acquisitions would be purchased and involve a degree of selection. Instead, as shipments from the Library of Congress began to arrive at colleges and universities in 1947, librarians staggered under the volume, dismayed by the quantities of cheap Nazi fiction and blatant propaganda. Although 113 libraries signed up for the program, half dropped out by the end, unwilling to pay for useless and inappropriate books. Complaints poured in about class number 188, the catch-all for popular fiction. College librarians and German professors disdained these works as "beyond the pale even if literature were defined in the broadest terms." The Library of Congress ended up giving refunds to the remaining institutions if more than three-quarters of their takings fell into this category. Although Harvard, Yale, and other leading libraries found much that was useful, they expressed relief when the project ended in 1948. Having received 111 cases of materials, the Yale library director said, "It has been a terrible job to assimilate all the material."[51]

The appearance of these books in American libraries made a distant policy of confiscation tangible, and some research librarians had second thoughts about their participation. Rudolf Hirsch was one. The son of an antiquarian bookdealer in Munich, Hirsch emigrated in 1933 to the United States, where he became the quintessential scholar-librarian. In 1944, he went to London to help develop the policy on the removal of Nazi books and had even drafted a directive on pulping these materials. Three years later, as a librarian at the University of Pennsylvania, Hirsch felt uneasy about being the beneficiary of this policy. In library staff meetings, he reported that some shipments had good materials, but others were "all 'junk,' 95% being classification 188." He worried about whether to accept books "containing the stamp of old, established German libraries, in spite of the superseding LC duplicate marking," which indicated the US Army had screened and transferred them to the LCM for distribution. He returned several volumes, stating it was "against our policy to add to our library items with uncancelled library stamps, even if those libraries are in enemy countries."[52]

Penn library director Charles David supported Hirsch, even forming a committee of research librarians to question the American government's policy on confiscated German books. Joining him was Julian Boyd, director of the Princeton library and one of the initiators of the Farmington Plan. Although nothing came of their objections in the end, their correspondence captures some of the tensions over the fate of Nazi books. Boyd believed the army's actions were undemocratic, violated rights of free inquiry, and were illegal under international law, which condemned the seizure of private property. Order No. 4 was a "travesty of the Bill of Rights," he declared, and librarians would feel "shame in the future if we do not now publicly take a stand." He identified the connection between American foreign policy and domestic politics: "This issue is part and parcel of the fight against censorship and compulsory loyalty that we librarians must make with the forces now rampant in this country." At this time, books were being banned in schools and locked in library cases, sexual content expurgated, leftwing perspectives suppressed, and self-censorship applied by publishers, editors, and writers—all pervasive practices of the Cold War period. Boyd wrote in 1948, when the American Library Association spoke out against the House Un-American Activities Committee and other censorship efforts, and strengthened the Library Bill of Rights.[53]

The Library of Congress defended itself and the military's actions. Some mistakes had been made, officials admitted, particularly when it came to "twice confiscated" works, in which the Allies seized collections of Nazi organizations only to discover that they contained Jewish-owned volumes, libraries of pre-Nazi trade unions, or cultural items of an earlier era. These would be returned. Overall, however, they viewed the handling of books in the American occupation as scrupulous and exceptional. "Libraries have always been considered spoils of war," Reuben Peiss observed. "This is the first time in history that careful measures have been effectively taken to protect legitimate cultural institutions." Boyd was not convinced: "We seized books in Germany not because it was the good or the right thing to do but simply because we had the power to do it."[54]

Order No. 4 was quickly forgotten, as were the quantities of Nazi literature that had arrived on American shores. In the long run, these books were integrated into the general collections of research libraries, often located in off-site storage, recognizable only by their "Library of Congress duplicate" stamp or a handwritten classmark, used mainly by scholars if at all. Despite Rudolf Hirsch's consternation, at the University of Pennsylvania they became Collection 1100C, containing many "items of such minor value" that they were "catalogued as one group, with brief cataloguing for author cards, one subject card, and a special number," a method that insured they would be difficult to identify. One lot of Nazi books ended up in the barn of ERA officer Richard Thomas Alexander, who, while executing Order No. 4, had gathered a number of volumes to ship home. "My dad wanted a set," recalled his son. "I never was quite sure why but he had a set sent to our place over there in North Carolina and I had to put them in the barn—took up half of the hayloft." There the books sat for years, and when the elderly Alexander tried to give them away, no one wanted them.[55]

In the immediacy of the occupation, however, American soldiers and information experts felt the physical presence of these books in German life and their malign influence. Whether justifying the Third Reich's expansionism and racial policies, indoctrinating the young, or serving as entertainment, these works were weapons in an ideological war. As such, they had to be disarmed—removed from the public and destroyed. Yet such measures provoked their own anxieties among Americans, over the meaning of books in a democracy, and how to preserve the record of past abuses and crimes without providing inspiration for the future. Collaborating with librarians and scholars, the military's enormous effort to identify and collect these volumes sent most to pulping mills, but a sizable number came to the United States. They would be joined by another group of publications—looted books—whose existence further challenged the military.

CHAPTER 7

✧

Not a Library, but a Large Depot of Loot

In the final months of the war, American troops found millions of books looted by the Third Reich and hidden in mineshafts, caves, and remote villages. Nazi pillaging campaigns had seized the libraries of Jewish individuals and institutions in Germany and German-occupied countries, as well as Masonic collections, leftwing publications, and archives. The army's Monuments, Fine Arts, and Archives (MFAA) section set up a temporary collecting point for these materials in the Rothschild Library in Frankfurt am Main and then requisitioned a large warehouse for these operations across the river in Offenbach. Often understood as sites of Jewish cultural preservation, the Rothschild and Offenbach collecting points were, in fact, military installations. Occupation officials, archivists, librarians, Jewish scholars, and restitution officers from France, Belgium, and elsewhere joined together in the practical challenges of dealing with millions of books in locales that defied description. There were no neat stacks, orderly collections, and catalogues. "This was no library in any sense of the term," Jewish American scholar Koppel Pinson described the Rothschild Library to his colleagues back home. "Most of the materials were in packing cases. Cheap editions of prayer books or Bibles lay side by side with priceless incunabula and manuscripts." When Captain Seymour Pomrenze arrived at the Offenbach Archival Depot (OAD) to take charge, he later recalled, his first impression was one of chaos: "As I stood before a seemingly endless sea of crates and books, I thought what a horrible mess!"[1]

Even more than the problem of Nazi publications, the discovery of these looted and displaced books tested the American occupation government.

Gathering, conserving, and identifying them posed intractable difficulties on a daily basis, even as military and civilian authorities faced intense domestic and international pressures over the looted Jewish books. Pomrenze, his successors, and the many experts who came to the collecting points found that these works required innovative methods of librarianship, designed to rapidly manage and redistribute the disarrayed and damaged volumes. For the Americans, endangered and orphaned books also generated new understandings of the meaning of book collections, and different ways of thinking about ownership, restitution, and cultural heritage.[2]

The decision to save and restitute looted books grew from an earlier American pledge to preserve European cultural heritage in wartime. Persistent lobbying by museum curators and scholars led to this unusual war aim in 1943, when President Roosevelt established a federal body, the American Commission for the Protection and Salvage of Artistic and Historic Monuments in War Areas, chaired by Supreme Court Justice Owen J. Roberts. Serving as a liaison between the military and the world of arts and letters, the Roberts Commission developed guidelines for wartime cultural preservation. Scholars created lists of European churches, museums, and historic buildings to be avoided by ground forces and drew maps to guide bomber pilots away from significant cultural sites. They wrote manuals on how to repair buildings and rescue damaged objects and contributed to the numerous "soldier's guides" that informed troops about respecting the places they had conquered. Some of these experts became the core of the MFAA section of the US forces in Europe. It worked closely with its British counterparts during the Italian campaign, the liberation of France and the Netherlands, the defeat of Germany, and throughout the period of military occupation.[3]

Like civilians in the war, culture itself had been on a forced march, uprooted, disoriented, and in disarray. As the Allies rapidly advanced into Germany in the final months of the war, soldiers uncovered vast deposits of looted art, books, furniture, and other cultural property. These were the riches of France, Belgium, Poland, and other occupied countries, and the stolen treasures of Jews within and outside Germany. In early April 1945, the Third Army discovered gold reserves and masterpieces in the Merkers mine, a find so remarkable that Eisenhower himself toured the site. By July, the MFAA had learned of over eight hundred sites in the American zone where art, libraries, and archives had been stored. Many more caches would continue to be discovered long into the American occupation.[4]

Against a tidal wave of destruction, the Monuments Men resourcefully intervened, preventing the ruin of historic sites and rescuing art and culture. Although there were never enough personnel for the job, they shored up roofs and walls, moved works away from damp and mold, and posted guards to prevent opportunistic looting. At the end of the war, the MFAA quickly turned to the restitution of looted cultural treasures. It created a patchwork of temporary collecting points in undamaged public buildings and commercial facilities to house the materials found in hidden deposits; these gave way to several Central Collecting Points where artworks were identified and their repatriation arranged.

For the Monuments Men, libraries and archives were secondary to fine arts and cultural monuments. At the Roberts Commission, only Archibald MacLeish spoke up for the needs of libraries. In July 1944, he noted, no archivists and only one librarian served in the European and Mediterranean theaters of war, and no effort had been made to locate looted library collections. The situation was not much better the following April, as the army rapidly advanced. With only two archivists on duty—including one unable to handle "the rigors of frontline living" and who had to be removed—there was a "desperate need for records experts." No one addressed the lack of librarians in the MFAA.[5]

A few days after discovery of the Merkers mine, a Third Army unit went to Hungen, a small town about thirty miles from Frankfurt, where it found innumerable Jewish books, rare manuscripts, Torah scrolls, and other sacred objects—the living heritage of Jewish culture in Europe. These were the spoils of a program of organized pillage led by Dr. Alfred Rosenberg, Hitler's chief ideologist and head of the Einsatzstab Reichsleiter Rosenberg (ERR), one of several major looting organizations in Nazi Germany. The ERR had plundered prominent national collections in occupied countries and confiscated libraries in Jewish homes, synagogues, and cultural institutions within and outside Germany. In addition to the Jewish collections were vast press files used for articles and propaganda, numerous photographs, and archival materials.

In light of the Holocaust, the Nazi preservation of Jewish books came as a shock. This was "one of the great and ironical paradoxes of human history," explained Jerome Michael, a Jewish American scholar lobbying the military for the restitution of these works. "At the same time that the Nazis were exterminating the Jews of Europe they were carefully and methodically collecting and preserving Jewish religious and cultural objects and employing them as a means to Jewish annihilation." Indeed, these materials became part of the Institute for Research on the Jewish Question (Institut zur Erforschung der Judenfrage), which was to be part of an elite Nazi university, the Hohe Schule der NSDAP. Its library in Frankfurt contained prominent Jewish collections looted from occupied France, the Netherlands, and Eastern Europe, stocks of Jewish bookstores, and the Rothschild family libraries; by April 1943, it held about 550,000 volumes. In a glowing press release, the Hohe Schule vowed it would be "*the* library for the Jewish question not only for Europe but for the world."[6]

Allied bombing raids put an end to that promise. While some of the collection remained in Frankfurt throughout the war, Rosenberg's institute moved much of the plunder to safer locations in and around Hungen, depositing books and artifacts in a late Renaissance castle, a bank vault, the tax office, a church choir loft, brickyard sheds, and several cellars. In the building of a singing society, the US Army found collections from Amsterdam, Salonica, Lodz, Kiev, Minsk, and Norway. The Hungen deposits were initially classified as a military intelligence target and placed off limits. The MFAA inspected samples of the materials in late June 1945. They "do not appear to be of immediate intelligence value," Mason Hammond reported, but "they include historical materials of great importance."[7]

Monuments officers learned of the looted books still in the Frankfurt building of Rosenberg's institute from Jewish American soldiers who, on their own time, searched for vestiges of Jewish life in the rubble of the city. Joseph Gutmann, a German-Jewish refugee (and later an eminent art historian), was drafted into the army and stationed in London. Assigned the job of reading captured German mail, he found flyers and press releases about the institute's disturbing collections. When he arrived in occupied Germany as a member of the US Strategic Bombing Survey, he "immediately checked a Frankfurt telephone directory" and, with a colleague, "jumped into a jeep and sped off to locate the Institute." The building had been destroyed, but they found fragments of Hebrew manuscripts on the ground and then a small opening marking an emergency exit, which led to cellars and tunnels. "I couldn't believe what I saw," Gutmann later recalled, "hundreds of crates neatly stacked in several rows lined the basement walls." They contained over one hundred thousand volumes looted from leading Jewish libraries. As the local MFAA officer, Lieutenant Julius Buchman began an inspection, assisted by Sergeant Abraham Aaroni, a former high school Hebrew teacher assigned to aid the surviving Jewish communities in Frankfurt and Wiesbaden.[8]

MFAA officials scrambled to find a structure to serve as a collecting point for these endangered books. They requisitioned the Rothschild Library or Palais, as it was also known; formerly the residence of Baron Mayer Carl Rothschild and his family, it became a public library in the late 1800s and came under municipal control in the 1920s. Once stately and elegant, it

Figure 7.1. US Army Chaplain Samuel Blinder examines looted Torahs in the cellar of Alfred Rosenberg's Institute for Research on the Jewish Question, Frankfurt, 1945. National Archives at College Park, Still Picture Branch (111-SC-209154).

was in disrepair and too small to contain the estimated 1.5 million items found in Frankfurt and Hungen. "Undamaged buildings do not exist of the type desired," fretted Hammond, who knew Rothschild would have to be a stopgap measure.[9]

Unlike the Offenbach Archival Depot, whose leaders wrote extensive reports, took photographs, and ensured its historical legacy, documentation of the Rothschild Library Collecting Point is sparse. When acknowledged at all, Rothschild appears as an awkward first step in the American program of book restitution. Nevertheless, it served as the primary collecting point for looted books for six months, until the end of 1945. Despite severe material and logistical problems and only sporadic attention from the military, its history marks a significant if precarious early effort to preserve, sort, and identify the looted books.

———— ⌘ ————

The head of the Rothschild Library Collecting Point, Glenn H. Goodman, stumbled into the job. Born in 1911 into a Protestant family of steelworkers and farmers in Ohio, Goodman aspired to the world of German high culture.

Figure 7.2. Rothschild Library, showing bomb damage and ongoing repairs, early 1946. National Archives at College Park, Still Picture Branch (239-SFM-242).

After graduating from college in 1934, he traveled abroad to study at the University of Heidelberg. There he met Felicitas Daniel, a Hungarian born of ethnic German parents, whom he married in 1937. After a brief stay in the United States, they returned to Germany in 1938, where he taught English literature and she worked as a translator. Unable to leave when the war broke out, Goodman spent the war years in concentration camps for English-speaking enemy aliens, barely subsisting in brutal conditions. Finally liberated by the Allies and deemed a displaced person, he reunited with Felicitas in Tübingen and did clerical work for the French military government there. Goodman wanted to return home with his growing family, now with two children and a third on the way. On July 4, 1945, a friendly soldier gave him a ride to Frankfurt, and the next day he joined a throng of supplicants in the American military government compound. Intrigued by the directory listing for the MFAA, Goodman waited hours until called in by Lieutenant Buchman. Assigned the task of handling the ERR collections, Buchman was at his wit's end. "What do you know about books?" Buchman asked, handing him three rare volumes to identify. Goodman answered, confident of two and bluffing on the third, but Buchman was satisfied, telling him to report to the Rothschild Library. "Whether I was to be a mere book carrier, a librarian, or a library director, I didn't know," Goodman recalled. He quickly learned he was an amateur "assigned to a job that nobody else wanted."[10]

Arriving at the building, he met an anxious German librarian Luise Weiss, whom the Frankfurt City Library had sent to work at Rothschild. Looking around, she had found nothing on the shelves and asked Goodman where the books were. Before long, truck after truck arrived, and a quickly assembled crew of German workers unloaded crates stored in the Rosenberg institute's cellars a few miles away. Soon books filled every corner of the building: 1,400 boxes containing 130,000 volumes as well as ceremonial objects had been transferred in nine days. Goodman realized the futility of shelving these volumes—the quantity and disorder were too great—and to Weiss's horror, he ordered many of the stacks removed and began to group boxes on the floor according to their labels or markings. The task ahead was overwhelming. Goodman had never been in a warehouse, let alone manage workers, and suddenly he had to make consequential decisions. "The truth is, I had no pattern to follow," he commented. The MFAA gave him trucks, gasoline, and laborers, but offered little advice or supervision. Buchman told him, in the parlance of the day, "it's your baby, you've got to rock it."[11]

In the days and weeks after he arrived at the Rothschild Library Collecting Point, Goodman assembled a staff, including Germans he knew from before the war, and began to devise a work process to prepare the way for restitution. The number of librarians and manual laborers quickly grew to sixty. The building itself needed repair: bomb-damaged windows were replaced, walls replastered, and the heating and electrical systems fixed. An architect inspected its structural integrity under the weight of heavy books. A civilian security force policed the building around the clock. Torah scrolls and manuscripts were placed in a special room, with the most valuable items locked in a safe. Meanwhile local laborers cleared of Nazi Party affiliation unpacked crates and roughly sorted volumes. Many books needed first aid. Employees cleaned books of dirt and mold, and interlaced sheets of paper between the pages of books to absorb moisture. Thousands of volumes infested with bookworms and pests went to the Frankfurt city hospital, where a disinfection unit fumigated them. Beyond conservation, workers at Rothschild focused on sorting and repacking collections, initially grouping crates and boxes according to names or markings. Sixty-four libraries had been identified by the end of July 1945. The rough sorting process continued through October. Although too few in number, a specialized staff of Frankfurt librarians, German scholars, and Hebrew experts started to examine and identify individual books, manuscripts, and loose documents.[12]

As the Rothschild Collecting Point began processing its holdings, the MFAA had growing concerns about the vast deposits still at Hungen. In July, these remained under guard as an intelligence target, for the time frozen in place. Goodman and a small group from Rothschild went to the site to survey their extent and condition. Many were in damaged buildings or exposed to the elements; everything had to be moved before fall rains and vermin caused further deterioration.[13]

Beyond Hungen, the MFAA knew that other caches of books were secreted in the American zone and sought information about them. After Buchman placed a notice in the army newspaper *Stars and Stripes*, he was deluged with phone calls, letters, and postcards from soldiers and local residents. "It seemed that every church and castle basement was filled with material," Goodman noted. Large deposits continued to be found. In August, following reports in the *Frankfurter Presse,* Goodman and Dutch restitution officer Major Dirk Graswinkel drove to Hirzenhain, north-east of Frankfurt, where they located eight carloads of looted books on Freemasonry, totaling over half a million.[14]

A new building was needed for these books, and the military requisitioned a fireproof warehouse in Offenbach, across the Main River from Frankfurt, to house them. Originally owned by the I. G. Farben conglomerate, it was an "ugly five-story reinforced concrete loft building," as long as a city block, relief worker Lucy Dawidowicz (née Schildkret) recalled. It had substantial space for storing and processing vast quantities of books.[15] German workers removed the Farben supplies, repaired the windows, and constructed stacks. Truck loading platforms and railroad sidings flanked the ends of the building, and there was anchorage for barges along the river, steps from the plant. It became the Offenbach Archival Depot.

Goodman and ten German workers moved to Hungen to crate and evac-uate the ERR books, a process that took several months. Although some collections were neatly organized on shelves and in boxes, many loose books—"mice eaten, torn and damp"—had been thrown willy-nilly into rooms and cellars. They retrieved disorganized card files and catalogues, and even found a torn sheet of paper in a wastebasket with part of the ERR's coding system for boxes. In a brickyard were large crates of books high on a scaffold, stacked on platforms with wooden floors. When workers scrambled to the top, they found the Bibliotheca Rosenthaliana, a famed Jewish cultural collection that had been looted from the University of Amsterdam. Getting a truck with a crane into the brickyard, with its soft dirt surface, proved a challenge, solved by a local German who had been a streetcar engineer. Still, it took a week to lower the boxes and transport them to Offenbach.[16]

While workers emptied Hungen of its holdings, operations at Rothschild and Offenbach slowed, and longstanding problems came to the fore. "Much valuable work has been done," stated one report, but there were many troubling signs. With eighty-six workers now split among three sites, the staff was too small for the work of salvage and identification. In contrast, fifteen hundred Germans worked in the Ministerial Collecting Center, with thirteen hundred tons of books and documents. Goodman had little leverage as a civilian and the workload exhausted him. Buchman fell ill, and the MFAA officers who replaced him already had full-time duties. By mid-December, both collecting points had reached a state of paralysis. Rothschild was filled with books, many of them deteriorating, and the building constantly needed repair. At Offenbach, two million books were stored and guarded, but the lack of reliable electricity, transportation, and coal supplies prohibited other activity. Since June 1945, not a single book had been restituted.[17]

While the military government faltered, some had ideas about what to do with the books. Buchman proposed that the MFAA reproduce the valuable volumes on microfilm, to distribute at no cost to libraries and research centers; the suggestion, he later noted, "received no response." The idea may have come from Karl Feldmüller, a German publisher and microphotographer. He had arrived in the early days of Rothschild with a private car and gasoline and offered to drive Goodman to inspect libraries in the area. He was then hired to operate a microfilm unit at the collecting point. It is unclear whether the Americans knew he had published works of Nazi propaganda during the war, which should have barred him from employment. As the problems at Rothschild mounted, Feldmüller proposed taking over the entire operation, including "trusteeship [of] the material." Criticizing the inefficiency of a large staff that had "come together accidentally and [was] paid by the City," he offered to establish a private firm run like a factory. It would sort the books, microfilm their title pages, and compile them into catalogues, not for the purpose of restitution but for scholars to purchase reproductions. "The unusually rich material assembled in the Collecting Point" could "serve as a source of information about all Jewish questions now and in [the] future," he wrote. Remarkably, this was a proposal to reproduce Rosenberg's institute. Feldmüller's push for this impossible plan was a measure of the malaise at the collecting points.[18]

Visitors also came to Rothschild's doors, in search of their stolen cultural patrimony. Restitution officers from France and the Netherlands pressured the Americans to release identified collections of books looted from their countries. The French were particularly insistent, claiming all books in the French language as their own. Goodman and Buchman consistently deflected these requests to military higher-ups, who themselves awaited directives from Allied authorities. Restitution was a complex issue among the Allies. Although the 1943 Inter-Allied Declaration Against Acts of Dispossession had asserted the right to restitute all looted property, it limited itself to earlier principles of restitution to the country of origin, not to individuals or nongovernmental groups. After the war, the Four Powers argued over restitution and reparations, as well as implementation and enforcement. Within the American government too there was little agreement on how to proceed.[19]

A key challenge to the military government—and to the collecting points—was the persistent yet tangled claims of Jews for the ERR's looted works. During the war, several groups arose in Great Britain, the United States, and Palestine to document Nazi looting and rescue Jewish heritage. In 1943 British scholar Cecil Roth called attention to the "systematic depredation" of Jewish libraries, museums, and archives in Europe: the Nazis were "among the few persons in the world to-day who take Jewish scholarship seriously," in a "violent . . . perversion of the truth, in a manner to suit their malice." Roth formed a committee for the restoration of European Jewish culture, sent out questionnaires about the fate of Jewish institutions, and proposed that collections be removed from Germany. "The rescue of Jewish books from piratical hands" was a religious duty, he observed.[20] In the United States, various Jewish scholars, religious leaders, and organizations vied for influence, including the World Jewish Congress and an inter-seminary group led by Abraham Neumann, president of Dropsie College. Bringing together many interested parties was the Commission on European Jewish Cultural Reconstruction. Eminent Jewish historian Salo Baron served as its chair and hired Hannah Arendt to direct its research arm. In 1944 the commission produced the *Tentative List of Cultural Treasures in Axis-Occupied Countries*, a noteworthy guide to looted and endangered Jewish materials, based on information gleaned from newspapers, welfare agencies, and government reports, as well as letters from Jewish servicemen and army chaplains.[21]

Press reports in spring 1945 prompted Hebrew University president Judah Magnes to approach the American Consul General in Jerusalem about how to lay claim to the newly discovered Jewish cultural treasures. Magnes believed Hebrew University was the proper repository and trustee as a "requirement of historic justice." They had been stolen from institutions and communities that had themselves been destroyed and "were the property and are the concern of Jews with little reference to Germany or any specific country." Magnes asked whether "it might be possible to exclude them from the complicated question of reparations and restitution." That would have been a sharp departure from contemporary understandings of restitution to nation-states and the rights of individual claimants. Although Magnes backed off somewhat from this broad position, he believed Hebrew University should shelter the unidentifiable works. "Large section of the Jewish World have expressed their agreement with our request," he wrote Judge Simon Rifkind, Eisenhower's adviser on Jewish Affairs, in November, 1945. "Depositing and using these books here would contribute to the development of Jewish learning and the revival of Jewish culture and religion."[22]

Jewish American groups had other ideas, with many arguing that unidentified books be sent to the United States. Theodor Gaster, Hebraica librarian at the Library of Congress and a founding member of the Commission on European Jewish Cultural Reconstruction, thought this a matter of US national interest. Influenced, perhaps, by the LC's Cooperative Acquisitions Project, he suggested putting the books in the "hands of an impartial government agency" as the only way to stem "chaotic cut-throat competition" among Jewish institutions. He dismissed Magnes's claims for the Hebrew University, observing that it was not the "national library of the Jews, since there is no such thing as a Jewish state in Palestine," but "merely a Palestinian Jewish institution, no whit different from any corresponding institution here."[23]

These arguments would rage for many months among Jewish organizations, libraries, and policymakers at the highest levels of government, but they also played out on the ground in Frankfurt. Jews came to the Rothschild Library, asking to borrow religious volumes for the small surviving community in the city. On one occasion, an American officer barged in, intent upon taking books to a Jewish displaced persons (DP) camp, only to be fended off by librarian Luise Weiss. With the military government's approval, the staff loaned Torahs and other spiritual objects for Yom Kippur and Rosh Hashanah services, and sympathetic librarians slipped books to individual supplicants.[24]

Koppel Pinson's request for a loan of twenty-five thousand Hebrew and Yiddish books was another matter. Pinson, a Jewish American professor of history, went to Germany in September 1945 as a representative of the American Jewish Joint Distribution Committee (JDC), an international relief agency founded in World War I. Pinson directed educational and cultural programs in DP camps, working to renew communal life among Jewish survivors and refugees. He struggled against the "stern realities of military occupation," only to report after a frustrating two months, "we have done practically nothing." The DP camps desperately needed books for libraries, schools, and religious observance; American Jews had donated many volumes but they did not meet the demand. Pinson visited the

Rothschild Library for the first time in late November and was inspired by the sight. "I never in my life felt such reverence, such humility and such personal inadequacy as I stepped into the rooms and saw the shelves lined with books, tables covered with priceless treasures and the careful hands that are now trying to make good the damage done," he wrote Arendt. He understood that "there is the conflict between the urge to satisfy the craving hunger of the Jews in the camps," and "the responsibility we owe to world Jewry to see to it that proper disposition is made of all this material." Nevertheless, here were the books Jewish DPs needed, and Pinson asked Judge Rifkind to intercede with the military government.[25]

This request may have seemed a simple humanitarian act, but, as Pinson knew, looming over the decision was the charged political and ethical question of restitution. General Lucius Clay, the deputy military governor, initially rejected the request, wanting to "freeze" the collection until a policy was decided. Rifkind then proposed a committee of experts to select only books that were not rare, valuable, or identifiable property. He reminded Clay of the dire needs of Jews in the DP centers. "To prevent the use of these books, at a time when there are no practicable alternatives, out of deference to possible claims and out of regard to administrative complications," Rifkind suggested, "is to attach greater significance to the less rather than the most important considerations."[26]

As Clay reviewed the decision, Pinson and his staff went to Rothschild, picking books from the shelves and piling them up for packing. Checking these lots, Goodman found numerous works with identifying marks, including many from private libraries. The ensuing conflict in the stacks presaged some of the long-term problems with the identification of looted books. Pinson "claimed that 'ownership' should be established *only* by a bookplate, rubber stamp, or other device actually bearing the name of the library," while Goodman countered that "*any* way of identifying ownership should be held valid, including manuscript marks, methods of numbering, symbols, etc." Taking Goodman's side and sharply protesting the JDC loan, Monuments adviser Paul Vanderbilt explained that these methods were "common in library practice and become known only to personnel who work constantly with the material." Pinson pressed on, at least for a time. Clay reversed himself and approved the loan but wanted stringent safeguards on book identification and selection. In so doing, he laid bare the crisis of the collecting points: no one was fully qualified or prepared to screen these books. "The whole thing blew up in the face of the MFAA people," Seymour Pomrenze commented. "For a month practically nothing was done since nobody could come and inspect the books and declare them to be within the category intended by General Clay to be loaned."[27]

Figure 7.3. Koppel Pinson with coworkers at the Rothschild Library, 1945. Koppel S. Pinson Collection, Magnes Collection of Jewish Art and Life, University of California, Berkeley.

In late December, the military government decided to halt regular operations at Rothschild and Offenbach, leaving only a skeleton crew to unload boxes and do emergency salvage. The suspension lasted two months. Numerous officials came to inspect, but no one seemed capable of a solution, beyond a decision to close Rothschild permanently and shift all work to Offenbach. What had gone wrong? The lack of military leadership, a limited staff, conflicts within the occupation government, and the enormity of a challenge nearly beyond comprehension all played a role. Pomrenze observed that the officers in charge "partly neglected to do their duty in properly safeguarding the materials and partly were bewildered by this mass of books in all European languages most of which they could not read." Goodman "did the best he could" but, as an American civilian and DP, "he could not get the army to co-operate."[28]

The problems ran deeper than this. As art restitution progressed rapidly and the army demobilized, the MFAA began to wind down its operations. With fewer personnel, long-standing tensions flared over the collecting points. The museum and art specialists were military officers, part of a chain of command. Archivists such as Sargent Child and Paul Vanderbilt were civilians sent to postwar Germany as technical advisers. "Their ability to do anything depends on their understanding of army channels and the convincing way in which they serve as Josephs to Pharaohs," Pomrenze observed. The MFAA was "tied up in a setup which may have been excellent in March 1945 but [was] completely outdated" nine months later. Moreover, many of the remaining Monuments Men seemed more interested in reviving German cultural life—putting on art exhibits, reopening libraries, and sponsoring concerts—than solving the problems of collecting points straining under the weight of looted books.[29]

Indeed, for the MFAA, books were a different species. Their experience lay in the fine arts, where catalogues, provenance records, art historical knowledge, and evidence from the works themselves typically made identification possible and often rapid. It is no wonder they gave priority to the notable collections of rare books and manuscripts stolen from France and the Netherlands, which were quickly identified and repacked to await shipment. The vast majority of books, however, were not comparable to art objects or cultural treasures. They came from institutional libraries and individual collections, looted from many countries, written in many languages—including a majority in Hebrew—and often without library stamps or bookplates. In the absence of catalogues with classification numbers or other finding aids, the MFAA wanted the Rothschild Library staff to speed up operations by simply examining the markings on boxes and assuming they correctly indicated the origins of the items within. In that way, libraries could quickly be "segregated according to value, origin, and ownership," necessary steps toward restitution. As Goodman later observed, the Monuments Men "judged success by the number of books we had packed and sent back."[30]

Goodman thought, however, that identification "was the very nature of our task" and objected to this streamlined procedure. He pointed out that Rosenberg's Institute for Research on the Jewish Question had rushed to evacuate its holdings, hastily packing boxes and throwing loose volumes into trucks. Labels on boxes did not always match the contents. Although some of the collections were readily identifiable, others required closer examination and expert knowledge, including study by Hebrew specialists. Seeking a greater degree of accuracy than the MFAA demanded, Goodman had the staff open boxes and make short author-title lists of their contents, one of which went back in the box before being resealed, the other into the collecting point's records. "There exists no shortcut which is reliable," he asserted. This painstaking work, in which only about three hundred books were processed daily, contributed to the growing paralysis at Rothschild. Goodman estimated that with a proper staff and good working conditions, the work could be completed in two to two and a half years. Military inspectors complained it would take more like twenty years to inventory the collection and require a trained staff "equivalent to that of a major national library."[31]

In an acute analysis of the situation in February 1946, with Rothschild closed and Offenbach operations suspended, Lieutenant Albert A. Mavrinac observed that the books housed at Offenbach were a unique problem for the military government. Neither the wartime policy on restitution, which required "expatriate cultural material be repatriated with the least possible delay," nor the policy on archives, which required textual records be frozen in place, applied to the case of books. Calling Offenbach a *collecting point*, the term used for art restitution, conjured a museum-like space that produced "exact inventories, photographic processing, and research into questions of ownership or origin." Given the vast numbers of looted books and their poor condition, Offenbach would never fit that description. Instead, Mavrinac reimagined Offenbach as a *depot* that would use the techniques of warehousing: workers would sort books "by job lot," grouping the "immediately identifiable" materials by nation, crating them, and immediately shipping them home. Mavrinac wanted an experienced military officer in charge, someone who knew how to solve problems "by tenacity and, where justified, intrigue," as the best leaders did in the American zone. It was "not absolutely essential that this individual should be a librarian, bibliographer, or archivist," just someone with a "lively appreciation" of books and "a pragmatic outlook." A man well-versed in Hebrew would be even better.[32]

———— ༠ঌ০ ————

The job was made for Seymour Pomrenze. Born in Ukraine in 1916, he emigrated to Chicago as a boy with his mother and brother, after his father's death in the 1919 pogroms. He worked toward a PhD in history at the University of Chicago and, needing an income, found employment at the National Archives in 1939. He joined the army when the war began and served in the China-Burma-India theater, including a stint doing

Figure 7.4. Crates of books at the Offenbach Archival Depot, 1946. National Archives at College Park, Still Picture Branch (260-PHOAD-II-18).

intelligence work for the Office of Strategic Services. He went to Germany in December 1945, asked by Archivist of the United States Solon Buck to conduct a survey of German archives in the American zone. An observant Jew fluent in Hebrew, Pomrenze initially was tapped to help screen the books selected for the loan to the Joint Distribution Committee. By mid-February, Rifkind and the MFAA had decided he was the right man to direct Offenbach: a command officer who could organize on-the-ground operations, manage complicated institutional challenges, and have cultural sensitivity and credibility with the different claimants, especially those representing Jewish communities. Pomrenze later remembered the assignment as providential, but at the time he objected that he was an "archives man," not a "storage and warehousing officer," only to have his objections overruled. "This is one of the nastiest assignments I have ever had," he wrote Oliver Holmes, a colleague at the National Archives, but he hoped it would "be one of the most soul-satisfying when I clean the place up." "Mind you," he added, "it is a library problem and do not let the name Archival Depot fool you."[33]

Arriving during a February blizzard, Pomrenze swept into Offenbach determined to move swiftly, following the blueprint drawn by Mavrinic. He hired German workers to sort, move, pack, and store books, quickly

Figure 7.5. Seymour Pomrenze with two French restitution officers, Offenbach Archival Depot, 1946. National Archives at College Park, Still Picture Branch (260-PHOAD-I).

increasing the number of personnel from 12 to 167, and operating the plant on two shifts. Soon after he took over, he addressed the workforce. With Goodman translating, he underscored the favorable terms of their jobs, including "less working time and higher wages than other workers in similar organizations." They received a noonday meal at a military dining facility (later a lunchroom in the OAD) and were even permitted to take food home to their families—a boon when Germans lived on limited calories and meager income. In return, they would do a full day's labor, not discuss politics, and take nothing from the depot. Police patrolled the building and guards stood sentry around the clock. Employees were examined, even strip-searched, for stolen books and equipment, and a locked room secured the rare manuscripts and religious pieces. Pomrenze had already investigated missing articles and was prepared to arrest the perpetrators. "In the future I won't speak about such things but will act," he warned, "you know what that means." The workers were required to complete *Fragebogen* questionnaires and be clear of Nazi affiliation. Pomrenze kept his distance from the German workers, treating them fairly but brusquely. It was left to Goodman, staying on as deputy director, to handle the staff and supervise daily procedures.[34]

Pomrenze ran Offenbach for two months, and in that time turned it into a well-functioning unit. "Only Pomrenze has really had this matter in hand," commented MFAA adviser Paul Vanderbilt, present since the early Rothschild days and worried about the fate of the books. "That something over here is important is no sign that anyone is going to look after it." Despite the ongoing operations, Pomrenze wanted to return home. His successor, Isaac Bencowitz, also proved an adept administrator. Born in Russia in 1896 and emigrating to the United States in 1913, Bencowitz was a chemical engineer, who held a PhD from the University of Chicago and worked at the Texas Gulf Sulphur Company for many years. A veteran of two world wars, he was fifty years old when he took over the OAD in late April 1946. His scientific background, toughness, and fluency in Eastern European languages impressed Pomrenze. The two men created a set of procedures and relationships, within the OAD and without, that removed the earlier uncertainty and gave substance to the American commitment to restitute looted books.[35]

For all that high-level policymaking and international politics swirled around Offenbach, at its core lay a large-scale book processing plant. Pomrenze and Bencowitz embraced the techniques of industrial work, designing a production process to handle the hodgepodge of boxes, cases, and loose items brought into the OAD. Restitution, the ultimate goal, dictated how the work would be done. Pomrenze focused initially on the task of sorting. Workers opened closed boxes to assess quickly the nature of their contents, dividing identifiable, unidentifiable, and semi-identifiable materials. Items with legible ownership marks, bookplates, or signatures were readily sorted by country of origin; often these were famous libraries known to have been looted by the ERR, such as the Domus Spinoza in The Hague and the Rosenthaliana collection. Similar to MFAA's procedure for art restitution, these items were placed in "national rooms," or in this case cubicles, where restitution officers from France, the Netherlands, and other countries could identify provenance and arrange for their return. Many of these materials had already been identified and crated at the Rothschild

Collecting Point. In March 1946, the first full month under Pomrenze's command, five freight cars filled with looted books departed for France and 371 cases went by barge to the Netherlands. But, Pomrenze made clear, the majority of items were not "segregated in neat piles and available for restitution as separate library collections," and nothing had been done about the semi-identifiable materials.[36]

Isaac Bencowitz devised a way to sort those items, using what he termed a "mechanical" method, striking in its simplicity and ingenuity. Thousands of books in the OAD had stamps, bookplates, and markings in Hebrew, Yiddish, Russian, and Polish, languages the German personnel could not read. For a time Bencowitz worked side by side with the sorters, and he found that some markings appeared so frequently that he remembered them and could sort quickly. He realized that workers only needed to recognize the iconography of the stamp or bookplate, not the book's author or title, to identify it. He had photographs taken of the stamps and *ex libris* and assigned a number to each—eventually over five hundred different *ex libris* and four thousand library marks, 2,277 of them from Eastern Europe. Sorters memorized a small number of stamps and when they found one as they went through the piles of books, they put it in the properly numbered

Figure 7.6. Restitution officer Dirk Graswinkel and OAD Deputy Director Glenn Goodman in front of a barge returning looted books to the Netherlands, 1946. National Archives at College Park, Still Picture Branch (260-PHOAD-I).

box. "It was a very elementary technique," Pomrenze recalled, "but it showed the genius of Bencowitz." They completed a preliminary sorting by the end of April 1946. At that point, Bencowitz instituted a permanent sorting process, in which books were taken to the top floor, distributed by conveyor belts and hand carts to different departments, sorted, and then sent to a packing room or storeroom on the second floor. By June, workers were completing the last stages of sorting, including an examination of handwritten marks and names. They separated unidentified books by language and divided German books into two classifications, Jewish culture and general knowledge.[37]

This sorting method was effective but not perfect. Under the pressure of time, workers undoubtedly misrecognized stamps or placed them in the wrong bins. Dust, dirt, and mold from storage in damp cellars made book stamps hard to decipher; some works had been intentionally damaged or defaced. Moreover, because books travel and change hands, the markings Offenbach workers saw may have identified earlier owners, not those from whom the books were looted. Among the bookplates were some from collections in the western hemisphere, books that must have been purchased or received as gifts by people in Germany or occupied countries

Figure 7.7. General sorting room at the Offenbach Archival Depot, where books were quickly classified using book stamps and *ex libris*. National Archives at College Park, Still Picture Branch (260-PHOAD-II-19).

whose own libraries could not be determined. Books without stamps, bookplates, or handwritten names might still have detectible markings, as Goodman had pointed out earlier to Pinson. Indeed, the category of "unidentifiable" held many such books, as would later be apparent.

Relying on recognition of stamps and bookplates also opened a space for intentional inaccuracy and misdirection. This seems to have occurred with works returned to the Yiddish Scientific Institute (YIVO). Founded in Vilna, Poland (now Vilnius, Lithuania) in 1925, YIVO fled to New York in 1940 but could not prevent the ERR from seizing much of its library and archives. Many of these materials were later found at OAD. Preparing them for shipment in 1947, the staff checked the contents of crates packed the previous year and found many non-YIVO volumes among them. The head of the World Jewish Congress claimed Pomrenze had "put labels on books allegedly belonging to the Yivo which really had not been theirs." Lucy Dawidowicz, representing the JDC at the depot, believed her predecessor Koppel Pinson had diverted many books intended for the DP camps to YIVO. She commented that "too much has disappeared on the way for the loss to be accidental." She also possessed a YIVO book stamp Bencowitz had fabricated in order to establish provenance for these books. Although the extent of such actions cannot be known, clearly identification and sorting may have been deployed for unsanctioned ends.[38]

Curiously the mechanical method also solved a problem the OAD might not have had, if it had employed Jewish and Eastern European displaced persons. Many of them would have been able to read book titles, owners' marks, and inscriptions as a matter of course, and the elaborate photographic apparatus and sorting procedure would have been unnecessary. Yet in April 1946, with a workforce of 172, only three DPs worked at the OAD. By way of contrast, the International Tracing Service, an agency that located victims of Nazi persecution and wartime refugees, did employ Jewish DPs. There may have been security concerns: Pomrenze noted how easily a worker or visitor could slip a volume out of the depot, and perhaps he and Bencowitz feared these tangible objects would prove a greater temptation to Jewish DPs than non-Jewish Germans.[39]

Instead, Jewish scholars came to the OAD to work with the books. They included Maurice Liber, the learned chief rabbi of France, and eminent scholar Gershom Scholem, who traveled from Hebrew University. Some settled in for long stints. Koppel Pinson and military chaplain Isaiah Rackovsky, who volunteered his free time to identify loose documents, were such frequent visitors that their work areas were named after them. These men authorized themselves as advocates and consultants on Jewish book matters. Strikingly, within days of becoming director, Bencowitz froze out

Goodman, who had interacted most closely with the German workforce. When he resigned in protest, Bencowitz appointed a Jewish American corporal, Rouben Sami, as his second in command.[40] Through 1946, Jews held considerable administrative and intellectual power at Offenbach.

The military government and Jewish groups usually characterized Offenbach Archival Depot as a "Jewish Collecting Center," as one archivist called it. The ERR loot found early in Frankfurt led to the assumption they were "dealing with a large antisemitic library consisting primarily of Hebrew and [Y]iddish books." However, OAD housed a mix of diverse materials. The Hungen deposits contained books from Communist organizations, Catholic churches, Masonic lodges, and even Rotary Clubs, along with archival materials, Torah scrolls, Russian slides, and phonograph records. Nor were all the books at Offenbach looted. Over seven hundred thousand volumes from the Prussian State Library, wrapped in waterproof packages, were discovered in a Frankfurt railyard and brought to Offenbach. Returned to Berlin in April 1946, they often are counted in the totals for books restituted at Offenbach, inflating their number. The ERR's "working library"—about eight thousand books with Nazi content that had been purchased or whose owners were unidentifiable—fell under the denazification order banning such publications and were transferred to the Library of Congress Mission, which shipped them to the United States. "The vast quantity of books and documents concentrated here was far from exclusively Jewish in origin," stated an OAD survey, and "the ramifications of ownership far greater than anticipated." Pomrenze and Bencowitz convinced the military government to expand Offenbach's mandate as the sole archival depot in the US zone for all books and printed material that required sorting and restitution.[41]

Still, the Americans continued to find caches of Jewish books. In Berlin, the LCM salvaged approximately 425,000 volumes looted by the Gestapo, which, like the ERR, had created a Jewish library for the ideological and propaganda arm of the Reich Main Security Office (Reichssicherheitshauptamt, or RSHA). These had been stored in the basements of a former synagogue and Freemason's lodge, and many were water-soaked and in poor condition. The Red Army had removed books of Russian origin from this site during its conquest of Berlin, but when the Americans occupied the US sector, they did little to secure the materials or take responsibility for them. Jacob Zuckerman, the LCM's Berlin chief, visited the RSHA building in February 1946 and discovered a librarian "sorting out books which she intended to take over for her library, although all these books showed clearly the names of the former Jewish owners." An American lieutenant had given permission to choose books to rebuild local libraries; 120,000 volumes had been sent to the Prussian State Library. Zuckerman feared many had vanished and "probably found their way to the Black Market." He called in Berlin intelligence chief William Heimlich and the MFAA, which stopped these activities and decided to transfer the volumes to Offenbach. When the Monuments officers could not manage the logistics, the LCM offered its assistance, eventually providing one thousand boxes, twenty ten-ton trucks, and German labor. Transportation was scarce, so Zuckerman sent the trucks when he could, with the first arriving at Offenbach in early May.[42]

The OAD needed an influx of books to keep it in business, and despite this seeming bounty of materials, the flood tide had turned. "We are hard up for books, believe it or not," Bencowitz wrote Zuckerman, asking him to speed up the delivery. In an overhaul of military government assignments that June, Bencowitz feared he would be sent to a security job and only permitted to direct Offenbach on the side. Although fending off that threat, he knew the situation was changing. He told Pomrenze, "The work in the Depot is simplified and there are not as many books coming in." He saw less and less of Pinson and Rackovsky, who had been stalwart visitors. The number of German personnel was cut in half over the summer, down to eighty-eight in September. By October, Bencowitz wrote up contingency plans for retaining essential workers and prepared to leave the OAD himself the next month. He had several recommendations for his replacement: he would need to be tactful with restitution officers and "resist enormous pressures of conflicting interests"; take initiative with security and personnel, noting the "Germans [were] unreliable"; and most important, gather the books still hidden in deposits around the American zone. Bencowitz stepped down in November and went on a three-week "temporary duty assignment" to Palestine; he returned briefly to run the OAD at the end of December and finally returned to the States after the New Year.[43]

After Bencowitz's departure, Theodore A. Heinrich, the Monuments Man in charge of Hesse, temporarily added Offenbach to his responsibilities, although the new job took a back seat to his major commitment, the art collecting point at Wiesbaden. An American-born Protestant, he also brought a different tone to the depot, notably throwing an elaborate Christmas party for the German employees and their children, with decorations, a Santa Claus, ice cream, and gifts for each, "having hoarded my rations for many months." In January 1947, Joseph (Tony) Horne, a wartime photographer and MFAA adviser, was appointed the new director. "Very tall, thin, lanky, and blond, he was the only American there," Lucy Dawidowicz recalled. At the time he took over, OAD operated with only forty-one workers; there was no coal to heat the plant and little material coming in or going out. Not even a year had passed since Pomrenze had roused Offenbach into endeavor and purpose, and already it had reverted to a state of inertia.[44]

There would be one more burst of activity, as Horne renewed the mission to round up deposits of looted books hidden away in outlying places in the American zone. On a snowy day in February, he and Heinrich took a road trip to the village of Reichelsheim, where, Heinrich wrote, "we picked up the local policeman to escort us on the last lap to our destination, a lofty castle." There, five thousand books had been deposited in the tower, "ostensibly the property of Heidelberg University, but every last *one* of them stolen from three French universities." In summer 1947, Horne focused on Bavaria, uncovering numerous collections and a "library of 'entartete' books" from the Reich Institute for the History of the New Germany, many with their *ex libris* removed. "I have been dashing madly in all directions at once, locating and gathering in outstanding lots of material which were still lying about in repositories," he commented. His efforts paid off. He announced a "flood of material coming into the Depot," including twenty freight cars loaded with books and archives from Bavaria. Horne and his team brought in nearly 475,000 items by the end of 1947, for a total of over nine hundred thousand in the Depot.[45]

Slowly workers whittled this number down using the now-familiar process of sorting and identification, but experts no longer streamed in to help with the task. On one memorable occasion, Dr. Ernst Grumach, a Jewish-German scholar whom the Gestapo had ordered to build its library of looted Jewish works, arrived at the OAD. He gave Horne a lesson in identification, pointing out types of binding, fly-leaf papers, dates of rebinding, and penciled notations. But Grumach also recognized ownership marks from memory. He had personal knowledge of many families in the *ex libris* files and their tragic fate. "Certain ex-libris are very old, the families had vanished during the period of the Third Reich," he told Horne, and he "did not feel that any large percentage of known owners would be found." Nevertheless, he examined a number of valuable works in French, Latin, and Hebrew, and in half a day had tentatively identified 5 percent of them.[46]

Horne's one regular was Lucy Dawidowicz, JDC representative and an American-born Jewish historian. Not long after Horne became director, she came to the depot to choose five thousand books for DP camps, the remainder of the loan promised a year earlier to Pinson. At the same time, she searched for materials looted from YIVO, where she had worked as a researcher in Vilna and later as assistant to founder Max Weinreich in New York. Opening volume after volume, she immediately recognized the institute's unique numbering style on periodicals, its double perforated labels with accession numbers, and Weinreich's name and handwriting. Horne entreated her to stay, as "it had become quite clear that previous sortings of the books had been quite inadequate." She continued at Offenbach for four months. "My job is very dreary," she wrote, describing how a German boy would "bring piles of books" to a table where she sat and sorted them into categories. By the end of May 1947, she had examined over 162,000 Hebrew and Yiddish works, half of them previously considered un-identifiable. She identified nearly 33,000 of them.[47]

Offenbach carried on after Dawidowicz's departure with Horne in charge, a dearth of personnel, and only two yeshiva-trained DPs employed part time to identify Hebrew and Yiddish materials. By the end of 1948, the Depot had handled 3.2 million publications. There were still more than 367,000 items awaiting a decision about their fate.[48]

———— ❧ ————

Looming over the work of collecting, identification, and the outflow of materials at Offenbach remained the question of Jewish cultural property. As the OAD began restituting looted books in earnest, Jewish groups stepped up pressure on the American government for the unidentifiable and orphaned volumes. The barrage was such that Koppel Pinson, now a liaison officer to Seymour Pomrenze, urged them to back off. "You must understand that what we are dealing with is not a library in any sense of the term, but a large depot of loot," he wrote Judah Magnes; the US Army faced a "tremendous job" simply collecting and organizing the materials. Pinson bluntly told Salo Baron that he was doing "all the hard work and all the dirty work while our great leaders of Jewry send telegrams from their offices or come on inspection tours of three to five days." He added, "all the troubles they cause come right into my lap." Pomrenze too complained that the Jewish agencies needed to stop sending "people who are merely 'ts' dakah ta-zeel mi-mawes' representatives," that is, self-serving do-gooders. "These people come, expect to be entertained, waste good gas, oil and food and do nothing—report and make speeches," and harm the Jewish cause.[49]

Complicated political questions hampered a resolution. Accepted policy provided for restitution only to recognized states, not to non-state actors. As Pinson observed to Magnes, Palestine was not "a country from which no part of this collection has come and which, unfortunately, is not recognized as possessing any legal claims to restitution in proceedings." Although the Four Powers approved some general principles about the disposition of cultural objects, no binding agreement had been reached. Soviet and French demands for reparations—in-kind compensation for war damage—muddied the issue of cultural restitution. At the same time, the Americans grew resistant to claims from Poland, the Baltic States, and other Eastern European countries where the Soviet Union now dominated governance. Making a unilateral exception for Palestine might trigger further demands from the USSR for works originating in Eastern Europe and Russian-occupied Germany. German and Austrian Jews also pressed for a decision about the "internal restitution" of works looted from their communities. All these issues needed resolution.[50]

Pinson's letter took nearly two months to reach Magnes, but he replied immediately, making a case based on a Zionist cultural vision. The materials at Offenbach were not merely books or property to be handled legalistically, but were the "spiritual goods which German Jewry has left behind." Like the "living human beings who have escaped from Nazi persecution," the books must find their true home in Palestine. "As anxious as we are to build up our Library," he wrote, "we are much more anxious that the Jews of the world should recognize that it is our duty to establish our spiritual and moral claim to be in the direct line of succession to the Jewish culture and scholarship of European Jewry."[51]

Interestingly, some proposed keeping all the orphaned books together, creating a collection whose meaning rested in their forced displacement and rescue. Jean Thomas at UNESCO and Danish librarians proposed a European Jewish library and international research center in Copenhagen. No Jewish group embraced this proposal. Despite their ongoing disputes, they agreed that these books belonged to the Jewish people and began to cooperate on a plan for a representative Jewish body to serve as their trustee.[52]

Spearheading this effort, the Commission for European Jewish Cultural Reconstruction, with other organizations, proposed an international committee representing Jewish libraries to make decisions about the un-identifiable materials, including those that had originated in Germany. Although they expected the materials to be distributed worldwide, they definitively turned away from Europe and toward the United States and Palestine. "Europe is no longer and, it is very unlikely that it can again become, a center of Jewish spiritual and cultural activity," Jerome Michael, acting chair of the commission, wrote the State Department. The books by far "exceed the religious and cultural needs" of the "ghost communities" of European Jews, he argued. Although there would be tribunals to adjudicate individual claims, their proposal was less an idea of restitution and closer to a concept of collective restoration. As Librarian of Congress Luther Evans described it, the decisions would be made "less from the point of view of specific property rights than from the point of view of the cultural value of the material to the Jewish people."[53]

This proposal and others generated heated discussion among American government agencies at home and abroad, and a reluctance to take the lead on such a politically charged issue. "The decision on who gets this indeterminate stuff is hot," Paul Vanderbilt wrote Evans. "The MFA and A doesn't want any part of it." The Monuments Men would be disbanding soon and the "solution might take years." He agreed with Pomrenze, who had embraced the idea of a representative body and suggested the materials be moved to the United States, as "the best place for them while clarification takes place," using the military channels already established by the LCM. Having seen the earlier entropy at Rothschild, Vanderbilt worried: "Will anyone actually list all this material, or circularize anything, or even look it over again item by item, as Pomrenze's crew [is] doing? When it is suggested that the material be divided between nations, I wonder just on what basis—mere bulk?" Although initially interested in the unidentifiable material, Library of Congress officials tiptoed around the issue. "It's going to be as difficult to settle that problem as it is to settle the Palestine immigration problem," Reuben Peiss said in a teletype conversation from Germany with his boss. "There are so many points of view, all of them very strong, and most of them one-sided, that it's going to be an awful headache." The Library of Congress finally backed away, refusing to serve even as a temporary repository for these works; in this decision, LC officials took a lesson from the firestorm of controversy when several hundred looted paintings, rescued by the Monuments Men, were sent from Germany to the National Gallery of Art, supposedly for their protection.[54]

In a flurry of cables and memos to the War Department, General Clay repeatedly resisted the proposals from Jewish advocates on both procedural and substantive grounds. "We deal only with governments" and "are not free [to] effect unilateral changes," he declared. Moreover, the rules of restitution of articles looted in occupied countries were clear. The country of origin had a well-established claim to them. An international agency would have to be accorded a higher level of authority, "acceptable to Allied Control Authority and generally to world opinion," to overrule it. That might be necessary for Jewish cultural property, he conceded, but only the Four Powers could decide that. Clay also objected to the proposal to seize Jewish items from German cultural institutions, however they had been acquired, which, he thought, would violate The Hague Convention of 1907 and lead to a "cultural rape of Germany." Finally, he expressed concern about whether the agency would truly represent all Jewish interests, including those of Jews in Germany; the groups clamoring for trusteeship had sidelined the surviving communities and DPs. The commission revised its proposal, established a formal membership corporation called Jewish

Cultural Reconstruction, Inc. (JCR) to serve as trustee, and waited for a high-level decision on restitution policy.[55]

In the meantime, specific cases arose that set important precedents. One involved the YIVO collection. Following the rules of restitution, these materials would have been returned to Poland, the country of origin, but the Jewish community in Vilna had been destroyed. In this instance, Koppel Pinson argued, place was not the relevant consideration; YIVO understood itself as a diasporic institute. "Books properly belong where they can be at the disposal of a living Jewish community and Jewish scholars," he wrote, "not where all that remains are mute tombstones and only the faintest traces of a formerly flourishing Jewish community." Military government and the State Department ultimately agreed. YIVO was an international organization headquartered in New York that had lobbied for these materials early. Seymour Pomrenze himself arranged for their transfer. Appointed a short-term representative of the LCM, he returned to Offenbach in June 1947 with "a spectacular array of military orders," recalled Lucy Dawidowicz. "He made things bustle at the Depot as I'd never seen before." Three freight cars with seventy-six thousand items were quickly loaded, and the collections finally made their way to New York.[56] Although seen at the time as a special case, the argument made for YIVO could be extended to the nonidentifiable and ownerless works.

A daring theft of valuable Jewish manuscripts at Offenbach, one that violated American restitution policy and rules of military conduct, also created facts on the ground. In spring 1946, Judah Magnes sent scholar Gershom Scholem and bibliographer Abraham Yaari to Europe to secure Jewish materials for the Hebrew University library. Delays and visa problems forced Yaari to return home, but Scholem finally arrived at Offenbach in July 1946. Touring the OAD for the first time with Pinson, he lamented the Americans' achievement as a hindrance to his objectives. "We are entirely *too late*," he exclaimed in his journal. "Something could have been done a few months ago, if we had sent the right people to them." Although wanting to help, Isaac Bencowitz was a US military officer who was only prepared to do so much. "About all the things that are important to us in the Land of Israel he said: 'Forget about it!'" Scholem grumbled. The frustrated scholar sat in the Torah Room, examining and organizing the Hebrew manuscripts, marking them by value with roman numerals; there were only about four hundred, and he considered few exceptional. Scholem turned to Pinson, believing him most able to deal with the military authorities and "take the really *precious* things away from here." As Pinson wrote his wife, "we have worked out some bold schemes here that I will tell you about [at] home."[57]

Was one of those schemes to steal the manuscripts and rare books? Five months after Scholem's visit, on December 30, 1946, Rabbi Philip Bernstein, the Jewish adviser to the military governor, and his aide, US Army chaplain Herbert Friedman, came to Offenbach for an inspection. Accompanying them was Isaac Bencowitz, who had returned from his three-week trip to Palestine, where he saw Magnes and Scholem; he was briefly managing the OAD before going home. After the visit, Bencowitz directed his secretary to write up a standard receipt for five boxes with eleven hundred items to be transferred to the American Jewish Joint Distribution Committee. Friedman returned later that day, signing the receipt "Koppel S. Pinson"—although Pinson had left Germany months earlier. He then removed five wooden boxes stenciled with the word "Scholem" and loaded them onto a JDC truck. This was no loan of unremarkable books. Rather the boxes contained 366 rare items from the Torah Room that Scholem had marked I and II, which Bencowitz ordered packed and sealed that October. Friedman transported the books temporarily to the JDC warehouse, then took them by train to Paris as personal luggage. He had intended to turn them over to the Jewish Agency there for transit to Palestine, but officials feared reprisals if discovered; they helped Friedman move the boxes for shipment from Amsterdam. On April 21, the American consulate in Jerusalem reported they had arrived at the Hebrew University. If there is no proof that Scholem directed this operation, signs point to him as having inspired the theft.[58]

Within days of taking over the OAD, Horne discovered the disappearance of the boxes, even as the military's Criminal Investigation Division had begun looking into black-market activities at Offenbach concerning books and food supplies. The CID agent and Horne "together uncovered about half the story." Friedman initially denied any wrongdoing—he had not signed the receipt and the boxes contained only "grammars and light reading matter"—but he then confessed his actions to General Clay. Eventually Friedman and Bencowitz gave sworn testimony that "they together conceived and carried out" the plan. The Inspector General recommended they be discharged from the service and given a strong reprimand. Mitigating the situation, in his view, was that the two men had acted not "by any desire of mercenary gain but rather because of a strong personal conviction that these rare books and manuscripts were the property of the Jewish race and therefore should belong in the Hebrew University."[59]

The situation was a political minefield. "Matter highly confidential," American government officials urgently cabled the Jerusalem consulate, asking it to gain custody and inventory the stolen works. They wanted "details of identifying marks, book-plates, etc., which might be of additional value in determining the provenance and restitutability of the items in-volved." Indeed, a number were of known ownership—"not unidentifi-able materials as at first supposed"—belonging to Russian museums and libraries, Italian and Austrian collectors, and noted rabbi Joseph Breuer. The acting library director of Hebrew University made a contents list but did not provide the additional information. Military government officials sharply disagreed about what to do. Many wanted the boxes immediately returned, but in June 1947 Clay decided to leave them in Jerusalem for the time being. Despite his earlier qualms, he now expected a trustee agency for Jewish materials to be appointed, and it would determine the dispo-sition of the boxes. "Meanwhile, I think they are in safe hands," he said. Bencowitz and Friedman's unlawful behavior had been transmuted into an act of communal restitution.[60]

Whether Clay was comfortable with this is another matter. Months after the theft had been swept under the carpet, he told the story to two journalists, who wrote up the piece for *Stars and Stripes*. Exaggerating the theft, they reported that eleven hundred items worth three to five million dollars, including irreplaceable manuscripts and documents, had been ille-gally removed. Clay explained they would stay in Jerusalem, until military government received claims from their original owners, "who have not yet been heard from." He seemed to shrug off the incident, commenting that the great majority of the items would "wind up in Palestine, anyway." The article sharply contradicted him, stating "this is impossible under present MG regulations."[61]

It took many months for those regulations to be changed. Finally, in February 1949, the US government recognized Jewish Cultural Reconstruction, Inc. as the legal trustee of the remaining Jewish cultural property. JCR was made responsible for any final identifications and for distributing unrestitutable books. Preparing to close the OAD, the military government turned over three hundred thousand Jewish books and ten thousand ceremonial objects to the organization. The remaining materials went to the Wiesbaden Collecting Point, where the State Department assumed responsibility for restitution. When the transfer was completed at the end of May, JCR representative Bernard Heller threw a party for the Germans and DPs, praising their work at the depot: "I perceive a desire on *your* part to undo—as far as was in your power—a great wrong."[62]

Ironically, after all the effort to secure the Jewish cultural legacy housed in Offenbach, JCR's representatives found a disappointing mix of materials, "broken sets, remnants of private or public collections, with not a single collection which seemed an intact unit." Scholem's dour view was that 30 percent was of "no cultural and practical value whatsoever" and should be thrown away or left to the Jewish communities in Germany. He and Arendt believed, with good reason, that many Jewish cultural treasures were elsewhere. The Gestapo and ERR had sent looted books eastward to Czechoslovakia, storing them in castles and in the Theresienstadt concentration camp, the so-called model ghetto. Jewish collections had been incorporated into German libraries and universities, concealed by private hands, and evacuated with other property. In a Frankfurt bunker used by the military government for storage, Scholem found two rooms packed with books and pamphlets, in which "whole cases of Judaica have somehow found their way into the so-called non-Jewish material." He wondered how to "get the Hebrew manuscripts from the German public libraries by hook or by crook, possibly as a matter of spiritual atonement policy." Hampering JCR's efforts to claim these works was Military Government Law No. 59, issued in November 1947, which established a policy providing for the restitution of identifiable property to former owners within Germany.[63]

Hannah Arendt went to Germany in the winter of 1949–1950, in part to check into JCR's operations, but primarily to go on a collecting mission. She described a day searching for hidden treasures in Munich: "At 8:30 in the morning, meeting in the Municipal library with a former Gestapo-official (who, however, never was a Nazi! . . .); then a meeting with 2 guys from the trade unions who also hunt after their own libraries. Then we all [went] together to the ruins of the Wittelsbacher Palais because we suspect that there is still a cache. There great caution because stones are loose, climbing over rubble." She repeatedly asked Jewish communities to give up their own collections, which proved "one of our most complicated problems." Having dismissed their future in Europe, she thought Jewish survivors did not need large numbers of books or religious objects; she commented harshly on the custodians of Jewish books who acted as though they owned them, as well as the dealers who sold them for profit. They saw the situation quite differently. Resisting Arendt's entreaties, the Hamburg *Gemeinde* president excoriated the international Jewish agencies for not aiding the city's Jews. As long as they "do not help in the reconstruction of Hamburg community life," he would "oppose every attempt to get Jewish things out of Hamburg." Her colleague Joshua Starr had made similar requests on an earlier visit to Berlin. Although a go-between presented him as "the Israeli shaliah"—a legal emissary—German Jews had already encountered many collectors who aroused their suspicion. "I departed in good time," Starr reported, "before I could be exposed as just another snoopy and kleptomaniac American."[64]

Meanwhile, JCR had to deal with the books in its charge. Although the majority were unidentifiable, forty-five thousand contained identifying marks. These were not from "the great and famous private libraries of the European Jewish scholars," but rather a single book or two belonging to an unknown individual. One of Horne's final acts as OAD director was to compile lists of these volumes. Offenbach began to receive inquiries from all over the world about books lost during the Nazi era and war. Exiles and family members of those murdered in the Holocaust specified markings, bindings, and other unique characteristics, or simply provided titles, believing "their unmarked books *must* be among the large quantities we handle," a JCR agent commented. After seeing a newspaper article, one man wrote from New York about twenty volumes of a Talmud "stolen by the Nazis with my general luggage" in the Netherlands; he added that they had also taken his aunt, who was later killed in Auschwitz. Another drew the book stamp of his father's "very valuable, partly irreplaceable" library and, stating that he was an American citizen, asked for Horne's help. Mindful of the growing number of claims, Theodore Heinrich, long involved with Offenbach and at this time a US cultural advisor in Germany, believed JCR should search for the owner of every volume before it was deemed unclaimed property. Arendt refused, agreeing only to advertise the names of people who owned six or more volumes. This was in part a matter of practicality, but also reflected JCR's belief in communal restoration: Arendt had earlier complained that the "temptation to return books with stamps simply to the former owner is very strong indeed," a striking statement given JCR's agreement with the US government to do precisely that.[65] In this way, many identifiable books de facto came to be treated as those without discernible markings.

Jewish Cultural Reconstruction apportioned 38 percent of the books to the United States and 45 percent to Israel, which received the most valuable and unique items. It sent the balance to organizations in Africa and Latin America; only 11,814 returned to Germany and none to Eastern Europe. In the United States, JCR distributed books mainly to theological seminaries, yeshivas, and other Jewish institutions. A number went to leading universities and to the Library of Congress, in recognition of the role of the government and civil institutions in the restitution effort. JCR asked recipients to place a bookplate in each volume, as an emblem of travail and rescue, "so that it may not be forgotten that these particular items are but the surviving relics of the great spiritual tradition of European Jewry," which the United States and Israel would carry on. By the end of 1952 it had largely completed its work. No one, it seems, questioned JCR's judgment in making the distribution.[66]

Seymour Pomrenze and Isaac Bencowitz carefully documented their work at the OAD, creating photographic histories in two albums that put forth a particular interpretation of its historical and moral significance. The two men probably collaborated on the first album, covering Pomrenze's directorship; the second spanned May to November 1946, with Bencowitz in command. A small number were assembled by hand, with slight variations, and distributed to government officials and others. These albums have shaped the memory of this extraordinary effort.[67]

Volume One opens with "first impressions," long shots of the warehouse piled with wooden boxes, overflowing shelves, and stacks of desecrated Torah scrolls. Subsequent pages follow the cycle of OAD's activities: Materials arrive by truck and train, crates and loose books are taken in and processed. Manual laborers sort books, appear with boxes they have packed and sealed, and break for a noontime meal. Chaplain Isaiah Rackovsky stands in the stacks examining books for the JDC loan, as if in a library, and Jewish ceremonial objects are neatly shelved in the Torah Room. The second volume offers a fuller portrayal. Here is Offenbach's cast of characters: Bencowitz, his deputy Rouben Sami, the German administrative staff at their desks, and a host of visitors, including scholars, restitution officers, and counterintelligence agents. The section on operations

Figure 7.8. An orderly group of German employees return from lunch to work at the OAD. National Archives at College Park, Still Picture Branch (260-PHOAD-II).

highlights both the rapid sorting process—thirty thousand books separated by origin into "East" and "West," and ten thousand books identified by library stamp daily—and the painstaking labor of two men reassembling the jumbled catalog cards of one hundred looted libraries. Officials pose with shipments, trains, and barges, making restitution visible. Nevertheless, a wide shot reveals, over three hundred thousand unidentifiable books still await "an unknown ultimate destination."[68]

The *OAD Photographic History* serves as Offenbach's testament and pledge to fulfill its restitution mission. Bencowitz understood the OAD's work as an undoing of Nazi violence, the "antithesis" of the ERR. He assembled a third album from loose photographs he had found scattered in the OAD, which documented Rosenberg's agents in action and an exhibit of antisemitic propaganda. An ERR map showing the influx of loot from all over Europe to Berlin inspired him to draw his own stylized map, with Offenbach at the center and arrows pointing outward to Spain, France, Holland, Italy, and elsewhere, "reversing the flow started by the Einsatzstab Reichsleiter Rosenberg."[69]

From displacement, disarray, and defilement to order and restoration, the *Photographic History* conveys little sense of the uncertainties of this massive undertaking, the challenges of the work process, the fraught emotions amidst masses of Jewish books, and the questions swirling around the problem of identification and restitution. Only rarely do the images capture something other than the procession of efficient work and orderly output—when the photographer's eye caught something more. On the occasion of the final shipment to Holland, Major Graswinkel poses formally, a troubled look as he stares at the camera, partially shrouded in his dark uniform. Among a group of workmen preparing a barge for departure, one man, shirtless and emaciated, turns to the camera with an impenetrable expression. Other people took photographs that convey a different sensibility: a picture of Koppel Pinson with shyly smiling coworkers at the Rothschild Library, a snapshot by Theodore Heinrich of a Christmas party at the OAD. Kurt Röhrig, a photographer for the celebrated firm Dr. Paul Wolff & Tritschler, made a series of images of Offenbach's Torah scrolls, menorahs, and other treasures in 1948, commissioned by Heinrich; highly aestheticized, they give a sense of individual dignity and purpose to the employees. But the moments hinting at the human costs of cultural exile and renewal are few. Unintentionally, it is the three volumes of *ex libris* and book stamps that have this effect. Meant to be memorized as a practical means of identification—from generic stamps marking Jewish communal institutions, to myriad fanciful and prosaic bookplates bespeaking

Figure 7.9. The image of the worker in the foreground disrupts the photograph's caption in the *OAD Photographic History*, "on the way home at last." National Archives at College Park, Still Picture Branch (260-PHOAD-II).

Figure 7.10. Christmas meal among officers at OAD, 1948. University of Regina (89-44 b92f1057).

Figure 7.11. Worker carefully handling a Torah scroll, in a Dr. Paul Wolff & Tritschler photograph. Courtesy of the University of Regina (98-44 b94f1077). Copyright unknown.

individual taste and personality—together they evoke a vanished Jewish world and its brutal destruction.[70]

The Americans who worked at Rothschild and Offenbach found it both a profound experience and a crushing weight. Most had lived in the world of books and learning, and the collecting points, haunted by Nazi violence to that world, tested their capacities. "I feel more humble than ever. I know less than I ever knew," Koppel Pinson wrote his wife as he sailed home and pondered his year in Germany working with the DPs and the looted books. "I experienced what chaos means, what occupation means, what winning and losing a war means. The facts I shall have to assemble from books and libraries. But the feeling and the psychological understanding that I shall be able to infuse into these facts will undoubtedly be enriched by the experiences I had." For Isaac Bencowitz and Lucy Dawidowicz, the books inevitably conjured the dead. In an extant journal fragment, Bencowitz explained how he would pick up each book tenderly, imagining the people

Figure 7.12. Page of bookplates from looted Jewish libraries in *Ex Libris Found Among Looted Books in the Archival Depot*, an album produced to help OAD employees identify books. University of Regina (89-44 b82f974).

who once owned and read it, the yeshivas they attended and towns in which they had lived, the volumes "whispering a tale of yearning and hope since obliterated." Dawidowicz felt revulsion when she entered Offenbach, where the books were "orphaned and homeless mute survivors," "inanimate remnants with a smell of death." "Every surviving book from that world had become an historical document, a cultural artifact, specimen, and testament of a murdered civilization," she wrote. Yet driven by "obsessive fantasies of rescue," she toiled many weeks more than she had planned. Laying "to rest those ghosts of Vilna," she finally was "ready now to start a new life."[71]

When Goodman looked at the books, he saw European cultural heritage, wondering at the rare treasures he had been privileged to rescue. "It was history not from a book and no books would ever capture it," he said, echoing Pinson. After Goodman resigned and left Offenbach for the last time, he thought about his final years in Germany, from Nazi concentration camps to the perplexities of military government. Living hand-to-mouth, hungry and exhausted, in a tattered suit and worn shoes, he went home to his family in Götzenhain, not far away. "I knew it was the beginning of the end of my direct contact with Deutschland," he recalled. "I felt strangely American . . . I felt free."[72]

The book restitution mission was a unique operation in the American occupation in Germany, all the more so for being unforeseen. The Monuments Men, scholars, and book experts who came together at Rothschild and Offenbach felt a duty to the looted books and deep sense of the human suffering they represented. Through ingenuity and tenacity, they gathered, identified, and returned masses of them to the countries from which they had been stolen. For those in the American government, the fate of the unidentifiable books was enmeshed in international politics over US relations with Palestine and Israel and the emerging Cold War. But they also demanded a moral and just response. The orphaned volumes, whose Jewish owners were dead or unknown, raised profound questions about the inadequacy of a restitution policy that only recognized national claims and individual rights to cultural property. Criticizing these limitations, Jewish organizations, scholars, and military officers put forth an argument for cultural restitution tied to concepts of collective identity and serving the purpose of psychological and spiritual wholeness.[73] At Offenbach, institutions of the American government, military, culture, and civil society managed to navigate both these older and newer ideas of restoration. They did so not in a situation of order and command but one marked by contingency and uneven results: seven months of disarray, frustrations, and paralysis at the Rothschild Collecting Point; ten months of decisive action at the Offenbach Archival Depot; another fallow period and burst of activity in 1947 and 1948; then finally the distribution of the last residue of materials. Many decades later, the problem of looted books and their restitution remains part of the unfinished business of World War II.

Conclusion

After the war the information hunters and collectors picked up the threads of their lives. The scholars among them mainly pursued academic careers, with Adele Kibre a notable exception; she moved to Italy and Spain, resuming her research and microfilming manuscripts for American scholars. The librarians found opportunities in library management, information science, and international projects. Some, like David Clift, Jesse Shera, and Frederick Kilgour, became postwar leaders in the field. A number, including José Meyer, Manuel Sanchez, and Jacob Zuckerman, continued to work with foreign acquisitions, international libraries, and cultural heritage. Those who had gone abroad retained indelible impressions. Composer Ross Lee Finney even began writing twelve-tone works to express the troubling emotions sparked by the war. Reuben Peiss looked back on the Library of Congress Mission as a "miracle . . . which actually made real what had been only a half-believed dream."[1] After the war, he worked in a State Department intelligence agency and then taught library science at the University of California at Berkeley until his death in 1952. He was one of the few who experienced firsthand how a far-reaching endeavor encompassing intelligence gathering, mass confiscation, collection building, the destruction of Nazi publications, and restitution of looted books had grown out of the conditions of World War II.

Although on the margins of the war's great events, these missions made an imprint on the postwar world of books and information. In some ways, they suggest a direct line from wartime experience to postwar initiatives: These activities spurred the international collections of American research libraries, served as an experiment in information science, and offered a prototype for open-source intelligence gathering. However, the collections themselves—the physical publications, micro-film reels, and other materials—took a different trajectory. For years they left only traces until questions of accountability were raised about them at the end of the twentieth century. The wartime acquisitions programs of librarians, scholars, and the military thus left an ambiguous legacy, befitting the vexed and makeshift circumstances in which they took place.

The OSS and military efforts to acquire open-source intelligence propelled and focused advances in library and information science already underway. As Frederick Kilgour stated, "The Second World War introduced a new kind of information service."[2] The rapid expansion of the wartime federal government, its research ties to industry and academe, and the scramble to acquire international publications overloaded existing systems of information management and retrieval. Anticipating users' needs, of-fering quick access to material, and finding ways to pull together dispa-rate bits of information were crucial for intelligence work. OSS library specialists developed indexing, abstract, and translation services for war agencies, used microfilm for rapid reproductions, and even experimented with computers for information retrieval. In this way, the concept of infor-mation, novel and embryonic before the war, gained traction when it was linked to the new intelligence arm of the state.

A number of those involved in the wartime acquisition missions be-came pioneers of postwar library and information science. Kilgour drew upon his OSS experience to design new information technologies. He brought together Yale, Columbia, and Harvard libraries in a joint com-puterization project, then moved to Ohio State, where he developed the Online Computer Library Center in 1967. Starting from a small number of terminals and telephone modems connecting a handful of college libraries, OCLC eventually produced WorldCat, the largest online bibliographic data-base and infrastructure for interlibrary loan. For Kilgour, World War II had been the starting point for these innovations.[3]

Others followed a path into information science that led in part through their library war work. They moved information science away from its utopian roots in the documentation movement toward the prac-tical use of library automation in government, industry, and higher edu-cation. Librarian of Congress Luther Evans and Jesse Shera, head of the OSS Central Information Division, revived the American Documentation Institute, which had faltered in the 1930s and 1940s. Mortimer Taube and Scott Adams, experts in science and medical bibliography who served briefly in the LCM, created new computer-based systems of cataloguing and retrieval. Taube even founded a commercial firm offering information services. Eugene Power, who had microfilmed enemy publications and rare foreign books during the war, made the reproduction of limited editions for specialized needs an important niche of scholarly publishing. His company University Microfilms International ultimately became the global information powerhouse ProQuest. The postwar information revolution involved many elements, including telecommunications, computerization, mission-driven science, research and development, and cybernetic theory. World War II was the stimulus for library work to become part of that revolution.[4]

The IDC program of acquisition offered a model for collecting open sources for postwar intelligence. The early managers of the CIA believed that 80 percent of intelligence came from foreign publications, radio, and people with general knowledge, although they focused especially on monitoring communications and broadcasting. The State Department created a publications procurement program that was similar to the IDC's operations in neutral cities. Manuel Sanchez was an official in this program, but most of the wartime collectors did not continue to acquire open sources for government agencies.[5]

The collecting missions also contributed to a growing orientation among American libraries toward internationalism, in which gaining foreign holdings was deemed essential to American global power. The rejection of intellectual isolationism by such library leaders as Archibald MacLeish and Luther Evans led to the Library of Congress Mission, which was a first run for their vision of cooperative acquisitions. Driven by military decisions more than specific library needs, the LCM was a short-term project that ended when the international book trade was restored. However, a revamped Farmington Plan, using commercial agents, acquired extensively in the late 1940s and 1950s, first in Europe and then around the world, helping to build up American libraries' foreign holdings rapidly. As repositories of the world's knowledge, American libraries were now seen as part of a new intellectual order, with the United States at the center of international cooperation and information exchange. This impetus grew stronger over time: by 1990 two-thirds of the books acquired annually by the Library of Congress were not in English. At the same time, the mix of altruistic and instrumental goals that characterized the wartime librarians also shaped their involvement in international cultural and information organizations after the war. Library of Congress officials worked closely with UNESCO in its early years. Verner Clapp, who oversaw the LCM's efforts from Washington, was involved in several UNESCO projects; LCM Berlin chief Jacob Zuckerman headed its Libraries Section; and Luther Evans became its director general in 1953. All supported the postwar reconstruction of the library world.[6]

Americans' internationalism had distinct limits, however, as may be seen in the afterlife of the Monuments Men, including the archivists and librarians involved in book preservation and restitution. They had demonstrated the possibilities of cultural rescue in wartime, and inspired many of the provisions in UNESCO's Convention for the Protection of Cultural Property in the Event of Armed Conflict, known as The Hague Convention of 1954. One directive required that armed forces at war include personnel trained in cultural protection. Although the United States helped draft the Convention and signed it, objections from the military during the Cold War delayed its ratification for over fifty years. It was finally ratified in 2008, five years after the destruction of Iraq's cultural heritage in the Second Gulf War.[7]

The missions' most palpable legacy, yet one largely unrecognized, was the books and documents themselves. After its founding in 1949, the Federal Republic of Germany claimed captured German archives as necessary for the new state to function and West Germans to understand the Nazi past. These were returned in the 1950s, after the United States had undertaken a vast project to microfilm them.[8] In contrast, IDC microfilms of enemy publications were dispersed among different government agencies, and no complete run exists in the US National Archives. Propaganda and resistance literature collected during the war by José Meyer and others were pasted into scrapbooks at the Library of Congress and identified only as the X Collection; digital copies of the scrapbook pages but not the complete texts are on the Internet Archives.

For many years the confiscated Nazi publications and unidentifiable looted Jewish books attracted little notice, except from scholars and students of German and Jewish studies. Jewish Cultural Reconstruction had intended their distribution to be beneficial in Jewish religious education, although it is hard to know whether, in fact, those books were widely used in the United States. German collectors, émigrés, and institutions made periodic claims for restitution to the Library of Congress, and the State Department took up the remaining work of the MFAA unit under the supervision of Ardelia Hall. These efforts, while important, remained limited in scope, and the vast records of looting and confiscation went largely untapped.

Controversies about library acquisitions during World War II resurfaced with the rising Holocaust consciousness of the late twentieth century. The Department of Justice's Office of Special Investigations, founded in 1979 to investigate and prosecute Nazi offenders, had begun to examine questions of looted assets in the 1990s. Bill Clinton established the Presidential Advisory Commission on Holocaust Assets in the United

States (PACHA) in 1998 to "develop an historical account of the valuables that came into the hands of the Federal government." A team of historians, archivists, lawyers, and other experts worked intensively over a two-year period, conducting primary source research to investigate the fate of cultural and financial property. The National Archives formed a working group to identify its extensive records and make them available. For those most closely involved, the commission offered a rare instance of the US government seeking to come to terms with its past. Stuart Eizenstat, the Clinton administration official behind this effort, described it as a necessary "moral accounting of this lingering ledger of grief." President Clinton praised it as an effort "to finish the business of the 20th century."[9]

Among the looted assets scrutinized were the books brought to the United States by the LCM and JCR. Acting on a suspicion voiced at the Interagency Working Group on Nazi Assets in December 1996, the Office of Special Investigations opened an inquiry into the LCM's conduct. A report by Robert G. Waite in 1997 absolved the Library of Congress of wrongdoing. Two years later, the PACHA further examined the Mission and JCR's handling of confiscated and looted books. Some PACHA staff seem to have understood their charge as a search for malfeasance. One study entitled "Looted Books" mixed documented cases of individual theft with coincidences, speculation, and a selective reading of the evidence; it even reported hearsay from "a confidential source within the Library of Congress" who had related what "someone in the Hebraic Section told him." The analysis muddled important distinctions between the LCM's acquisitions, the restitution practices at the OAD, and the final disposition of books by JCR. The staff worked on a short deadline, which made their task of historical reconstruction extremely challenging. Although Librarian of Congress James Billington considered the report an attack on the library's integrity, one particular charge was investigated: that there were numerous looted books in the Hebraic Section. The Library of Congress ordered an examination of 125,000 volumes published in Europe from 1933 to 1945 and housed in that section. JCR had sent 5,708 volumes to the Library of Congress, but the shelf reading found only 2,300 of them; many did not have the JCR bookplate. There were also about 150 Hebraic volumes, stolen by Nazi organizations, that had entered the library through other means, most likely by the LCM.[10]

The PACHA's final report, *Plunder and Restitution* (2000), tiptoed around accusations of wrongdoing and culpability. Instead, the Library of Congress and the commission found a way to make these books visible, with the aim of honoring the books' owners, victims of the Holocaust, and the JCR's rescue mission. A virtual library marked their provenance in the electronic catalogue as the "Holocaust-Era Judaic Heritage Library," with a historical note about how JCR acquired them. These new entries recognized the books as a collection that shared the experience of war, looting, and genocide, as well as a sense of communal restoration. To the PACHA, they served the purpose of "moral accounting," even if they did not result in restitution to the individuals whose libraries had been taken decades earlier.[11]

Since 2000, there have been renewed efforts to identify these books and their histories. The Conference on Jewish Material Claims Against Germany (Claims Conference), founded in 1951, brought new attention to looted works by compiling a *Descriptive Catalogue of Looted Judaica* in 2009. Their survey showed, dismayingly, how few university libraries and Jewish institutions in the United States—let alone those in other countries—could identify their JCR books. Most research libraries had integrated the majority of volumes into their general collections, where they could not be located. Some Jewish libraries and colleges had run into financial problems and subsequently disappeared or were merged into other institutions; JCR collections were sometimes sold to raise money and others were lost.[12] Increasingly librarians and scholars have sought to discover and recognize these books, not only for the purpose of restitution but because they represent a significant part of the history of World War II and the Holocaust.

The document hunters and book collectors who brought these works to the United States would cheer on these efforts. They believed their missions would help win the war and ensure a democratic and peaceful future. They collaborated closely with the state, its intelligence function, war agencies, and military operations. They saw these as essential alliances, a view perhaps more difficult to hold today. Whatever the mixed motives and moral ambiguities of these missions, librarians, scholars, soldiers, and spies took on the challenges of books and information in wartime, and in the process helped to save knowledge and culture threatened by war.

Epilogue

I have lived with a rare book for nearly half a century—Baruch Spinoza's *Renati Des Cartes Principiorum Philosophiae, Pars I & II*, published in 1663 by the printer Johannem Riewerts in Amsterdam. My father gave it to me when I was learning high school Latin, and it has accompanied me from suburban Chicago to Philadelphia, with many points in between. He had received it in the early 1950s, from his oldest brother who was then sick and dying. Reuben Peiss had hoped to be a philosopher, but his life followed a different path, into librarianship and then, through the strange fortunes of war, into intelligence work and mass acquisitions abroad. But his early interests never faded, and this book must have been of great value to him. As my father observed, "Spinoza was his guy." I never thought much about the book, except to appreciate its aura of rarity, until I started upon this research. Where had it come from? How had Reuben Peiss acquired it, and from whom?

I brought the volume to Michael Ryan, at that time the rare books librarian at the University of Pennsylvania. Looking it over, he commented, "This is rather *rare*, you know." It was Spinoza's first published book, an exposition of Cartesian philosophy, and the only one in his lifetime that carried his and the printer's own names. The moment of appreciation and appraisal passed when he said the book had come from the Schaffgotsch library in Warmbrunn (now Cieplice), Silesia, a library that had been plundered at the end of World War II. The Spinoza was a looted book and raised familiar questions of provenance and restitution, now quite intimately.

Schaffgotsch was a long-standing aristocratic family of Lower Silesia, in what was once part of the German state and is now in southwestern Poland. Dating to the eighteenth century, the Schaffgotsch library held eighty thousand volumes, with strengths in theology, literature, philosophy, and natural history, as well as collections of coins, minerals, and weapons. In 1943 and 1944, when German authorities moved collections from Berlin eastward to protect them from Allied bombing, they filled the grand Schaffgotsch residence with displaced books and art. As the Soviet forces gained ground in early 1945, the custodians of the collections were ordered to pack them up and send them west. The most valuable art and cultural treasures were evacuated, but much was left behind. The Red Army seized the Schaffgotsch residence and forced the family to leave. The library was pillaged during this chaotic time.[1]

There are many unanswered questions about the Schaffgotsch library in the final days of the war, including who took the Spinoza volume. A family member or German expellee fleeing Warmbrunn? A Russian soldier or administrator with access to the library? No American troops came to this site, so it was not taken by a T-Force or the MFAA. Without that information, it is hard to determine how Reuben Peiss acquired the Spinoza, but there are several possibilities. He may have bought the book from a German bookseller or collector he had met in his work, using the common postwar currency of cigarettes and rations. He traveled all over the American zone of occupation and frequently to Berlin, where there was a robust black market. He may have heard about the volume and sought it out; information about such valuable items circulated among American intelligence agents, journalists, and others working in occupied Germany. He may have received the book as a gift from one of his Russian counterparts, with whom he worked closely on the operation getting books out of Leipzig, or from friends who knew his scholarly interests. He may have taken it, although most likely not from the Offenbach Archival Depot, where it does not appear on lists of rare books.

The books that were not pillaged lost their identity as the Schaffgotsch library collection. Under the Potsdam Agreement, most of postwar Silesia became part of Poland, its large German population forcibly expelled. The "castle libraries," as Hannah Arendt called them, were nationalized under the Communist regime, and such aristocratic residences were taken over for other purposes. The Schaffgotsch home is now part of the Jelenia Góra branch of the Wrocław University of Technology. Its surviving collections reside in the National Library of Poland in Warsaw.[2]

This single volume—its history so full of questions and gaps—stands on my shelf as a reminder of the social lives and secret lives of books. Not simply inanimate objects, books are highly mobile, taking up residence in our homes and memories. "Books have their destinies," goes a Latin saying, and as Walter Benjamin once commented, they are enmeshed in a "mysterious relationship" with their owners.[3] This rare book binds together the radical seventeenth-century philosopher, expelled from the Jewish community for his modern ideas, to a German aristocrat collecting in the spirit of the Enlightenment. Remarkably, it survived the pillaging in Silesia and destruction of the intellectual life it embodied, found its way into the hands of a twentieth-century American librarian who revered Spinoza, and came into mine, bringing home the fraught world of information hunters and book collectors in World War II.

NOTES

ABBREVIATIONS

AJA	American Jewish Archives
ALA	American Library Association
BAEF	Belgian-American Educational Foundation
CAP	Cooperative Acquisitions Project
COI	Coordinator of Information
CRL	*College and Research Libraries*
DSI	Division of Special Information
ERA	Education and Religious Affairs
HHPL	Herbert Hoover Presidential Library
HI	Hoover Institution
HIA	Hoover Institution Archives
ICD	Information Control Division
IDC	Interdepartmental Committee for the Acquisition of Foreign Publications
JASIS	*Journal of the American Society for Information Science*
JASIST	*Journal of the Association for Information Science and Technology*
JCR	Jewish Cultural Reconstruction
LC	Library of Congress
LCM	Library of Congress European Mission
LJ	*Library Journal*
LQ	*Library Quarterly*
MFAA	Monuments, Fine Arts, and Archives Section, US Army
NACP	National Archives at College Park, MD
NYPL	New York Public Library
NYT	*New York Times*
OAD	Offenbach Archival Depot
OMGUS	Office of the Military Government, US Zone (Germany)
OSS	Office of Strategic Services
PACHA	Presidential Advisory Commission on Holocaust Assets in the United States, William J. Clinton Presidential Library
QJCA	*Quarterly Journal of Current Acquisitions*
TNA	The National Archives (UK)
WJC	World Jewish Congress

PROLOGUE

1. Alfred Hessel, *A History of Libraries*, trans. Reuben Peiss, memorial ed. (New Brunswick, NJ: Scarecrow Press,1955), viii.
2. Reuben Peiss, "Mr. Voge's circular," n.d., folder: ULS Revision, Harvard Library Catalogue Department, Serial Division, Subject File, ca. 1919–1949, UA III 50.8.113.10.9, Harvard University Archives.
3. Frederick G. Kilgour to Keyes D. Metcalf, November 5, 1942; Metcalf to Kilgour, November 9, 1942, box 56, folder: Kilgour, F.G., UA III 50.8.11.3, Records of the Director of the Harvard University Library, Keyes D. Metcalf, 1937–1955, Harvard University Archives.
4. Peiss to Andrew Osborn, November 18, 1943, box: Corr. with Staff Members, folder: Peiss, Reuben, Library Catalogue Department, UA III.50.8.113.3.8; Peiss to "Auntie," December 1, 1944, personal collection.
5. H. Gregory Thomas business card with note to Allen W. Dulles, x/12-44, box 25, folder IDC, Entry 190, Bern-OSS-Op29OSS, OSS Records, RG 226, NACP.
6. Ross Lee Finney, *Profile of a Lifetime: A Musical Autobiography* (New York: C. F. Peters, 1992), 140; Scott Adams interview, conducted by Carol Fenichel, March 20, 1980, Medical Library Association Oral History Project, 33.

INTRODUCTION

1. On libraries in World War I, see Wayne A. Wiegand, *"An Active Instrument for Propaganda": The American Public Library During World War I* (Westport, CT: Greenwood Press, 1989). On World War II, John B. Hench, *Books as Weapons: Propaganda, Publishing, and the Battle for Global Markets in the Era of World War II* (Ithaca, NY: Cornell University Press, 2010); Patti Clayton Becker, *Books and Libraries during World War II: Weapons in the War of Ideas* (New York: Routledge, 2005); Molly Guptill Manning, *When Books Went to War* (Boston: Houghton Mifflin Harcourt, 2014).
2. General Orders No. 100: The Lieber Code, The Avalon Project: Documents in Law, History, and Diplomacy, Lillian Goldman Law Library, Yale Law School, Articles 36–38, http://avalon.law.yale.edu/19th_century/lieber.asp. John Fabian Witt, *Lincoln's Code: The Laws of War in American History* (New York: Free Press, 2012). Yael A. Sternhell, "The Afterlives of a Confederate Archive: Civil War Documents and the Making of Sectional Reconciliation," *Journal of American History* 102 (2016): 1025–50; Philip P. Brower, "The U.S. Army's Seizure and Administration of Enemy Records Up to World War II," *American Archivist* 26 (1963): 191–207.
3. On British intelligence, Richard J. Aldrich, *Intelligence and the War Against Japan: Britain, America and the Politics of Secret Service* (Cambridge, UK: Cambridge University Press, 2000). Among many works on the OSS, see Barry M. Katz, *Foreign Intelligence: Research and Analysis in the Office of Strategic Services, 1942-1945* (Cambridge, MA: Harvard University Press, 1989); Christof Mauch, *The Shadow War Against Hitler: The Covert Operations of America's Wartime Secret Intelligence Service* (New York: Columbia University Press, 2003); George C. Chalou, ed., *The Secrets War: The Office of Strategic Services in World War II* (Washington, DC: National Archives and Records Administration, 1992); Robin W. Winks, *Cloak & Gown: Scholars in the Secret War, 1939-1961* (New York: Morrow, 1987).
4. See Pamela Spence Richards, *Scientific Information in Wartime: The Allied-German Rivalry, 1939-1945* (Westport, CT: Greenwood Press, 1994); Astrid M. Eckard, *The Struggle for the Files: The Western Allies and the Return of German Archives After the Second World War* (Cambridge, UK: Cambridge University Press, 2012); Brett

Gary, *The Nervous Liberals: Propaganda Anxieties from World War I to the Cold War* (New York: Columbia University Press, 1999).

5. See Robert V. Williams and Ben-Ami Lipetz, eds., *Covert and Overt: Recollecting and Connecting Intelligence Service and Information Science* (Medford, NJ: Information Today, Inc., 2005); Colin B. Burke, *Information and Intrigue: From Index Cards to Dewey Decimals to Alger Hiss* (Cambridge, MA: MIT Press, 2014). For context, see W. Boyd Rayward, ed., *European Modernism and the Information Society* (Aldershot, UK: Ashgate, 2008); Alex Wright, *Cataloguing the World: Paul Otlet and the Birth of the Information Age* (New York: Oxford University Press, 2014); "The Science of Information, 1870-1945: The Universalization of Knowledge in a Utopian Age" symposium, University of Pennsylvania, February 23–25, 2017, http://repository.upenn.edu/science_of_information/.

6. On cooperative acquisition, Ralph D. Wagner, *A History of the Farmington Plan* (Lanham, MD: Scarecrow Press, 2002).

7. Among many important studies, see Lisa Moses Leff, *The Archive Thief: The Man Who Salvaged French Jewish History in the Wake of the Holocaust* (New York: Oxford University Press, 2015); Dana Herman, "*Hashavat Avedah:* A History of Jewish Cultural Reconstruction, Inc." (PhD diss., McGill University, 2008); Jonathan Rose, ed., *The Holocaust and the Book: Destruction and Preservation* (Amherst: University of Massachusetts Press, 2001); Elisabeth Gallas, *A Mortuary of Books: The Rescue of Jewish Culture after the Holocaust* (New York: NYU Press, 2019).

8. For background, see Lynn H. Nicholas, *The Rape of Europa: The Fate of Europe's Treasures in the Third Reich and the Second World War* (New York: Knopf, 1994); Elizabeth Simpson, ed., *The Spoils of War: World War II and its Aftermath: The Loss, Reappearance, and Recovery of Cultural Property* (New York: H.N. Abrams/Bard Graduate Center, 1997); Michael J. Kurtz, *America and the Return of Nazi Contraband: The Recovery of Europe's Cultural Treasures* (Cambridge, UK: Cambridge University Press, 2006); Leslie I. Poste, "The Development of U.S. Protection of Libraries and Archives in Europe during World War II" (PhD diss., University of Chicago, 1958).

9. The American orientation to European culture is suggested in Janice Radway, *A Feeling for Books: The Book of The Month Club, Literary Taste, and Middle-Class Desire* (Chapel Hill: University of North Carolina Press, 1997); Donald C. Meyer, "Toscanini and the NBC Symphony Orchestra; High, Middle, and Low Culture, 1937-1954," in *Perspectives on American Music, 1900-1950*, ed. Michael Saffle (New York: Garland, 2000); Gilbert Allardyce, "The Rise and Fall of the Western Civilization Course," *American Historical Review* 87 (1982): 695–725.

10. John Gimbel, *Science, Technology, and Reparations: Exploitation and Plunder in Postwar Germany* (Stanford, CA: Stanford University Press, 1990). See also Eckard, *Struggle for the Files*; Robert Wolfe, ed., *Captured German and Related Records, A National Archives Conference* (Athens: Ohio University Press, 1974).

11. Frank Biess and Robert G. Moeller, eds., *Histories of the Aftermath; The Legacies of the Second World War in Europe* (New York: Berghahn, 2010), 1. *Plunder and Restitution: The U.S. and Holocaust Victims' Assets: Findings and Recommendations of the PACHA and Staff Report* (Washington, DC: GPO, 2000); Stuart Eizenstat, *Imperfect Justice: Looted Assets, Slave Labor, and the Unfinished Business of World War II* (New York: Public Affairs, 2003).

CHAPTER 1

1. Archibald MacLeish to William J. Donovan, December 8, 1944, box 6, Archibald MacLeish Papers, Manuscript Division, LC, Washington, DC.

2. MacLeish to Donovan, March 24, 1941, MacLeish Papers; William J. Donovan, "What are We Up Against? There is a Moral Force in Wars," radio address, March 26, 1941, *Vital Speeches of the Day*, vol. 7, 386–389, www.ibiblio.org/pha/policy/ 1941/1941-03-26a.html. Douglas Waller, *Wild Bill Donovan: The Spymaster Who Created the OSS and Modern American Espionage* (New York: Free Press, 2011); Bradley F. Smith, *The Shadow Warriors: O.S.S. and the Origins of the C.I.A.* (New York: Basic Books, 1983), 3–94.

3. Scott Donaldson, *Archibald MacLeish: An American Life* (Boston: Houghton Mifflin, 1992).

4. Felix Frankfurter to Franklin D. Roosevelt, May 11, 1939, box 8, MacLeish Papers; David C. Mearns, "The Brush of the Comet: Archibald MacLeish at the Library of Congress," *Atlantic Monthly* 215 (May 1965): 90; Archibald MacLeish, *A Time to Act* (Boston: Houghton Mifflin, 1943), 166. MacLeish's writings on libraries are collected in *Champion of a Cause: Essays and Addresses on Librarianship*, comp. Eva M. Goldschmidt (Chicago: ALA, 1971). See also Nancy L. Benco, "Archibald MacLeish: The Poet Librarian," *Quarterly Journal of the Library of Congress* 33 (July 1976): 232–249; David C. Mearns, "The Story Up to Now," *Annual Report of the Librarian of Congress for the Fiscal Year Ending June 30, 1946* (Washington, DC: GPO, 1947), 219–227.

5. Donovan to Roosevelt, "Memorandum of Establishment of Service of Strategic Information," June 10, 1941, Box 128, COI, President's Secretary's File, Franklin Delano Roosevelt Presidential Library, www.fdrlibrary.marist.edu/_ resources/images/psf/psf000509.pdf. Frederick J. Stielow, "Librarian Warriors and Rapprochement: Carl Milam, Archibald MacLeish, and World War II," *Libraries & Culture* 25 (Fall 1990): 513–533. See also Brett Gary, *The Nervous Liberals: Propaganda Anxieties from World War I to the Cold War* (New York: Columbia University Press, 1999), ch. 4; Waldo Heinrichs, "The United States Prepares for War," in *The Secrets War: The Office of Strategic Services in World War II*, ed. George C. Chalou (Washington, DC: National Archives and Records Administration, 1992), 8–18.

6. Lisa Gitelman, *Paper Knowledge: Toward a Media History of Documents* (Durham, NC: Duke University Press, 2014), 53–82; William A. McHugh, "'To Advance the Boundaries of Knowledge': The *Union List of Serials* and the Provision of Resources for Research," Graduate School of Library and Information Science, *Occasional Papers*, no. 214 (University of Illinois, April 2008).

7. Edward Barrese, "Review: The WPA Historical Survey," *American Archivist* 44 (1981): 161. Jane Aikin Rosenberg, *The Nation's Great Library: Herbert Putnam and the Library of Congress, 1899-1939* (Urbana: University of Illinois Press, 1993), 37; Sargent B. Child, "What is Past is Prologue," *American Archivist* 5 (Oct 1942): 217– 227. On archives and the nation-state, see Stefan Berger, "The Role of National Archives in Constructing National Master Narratives in Europe," *Archival Science* 13 (March 2013): 1–22.

8. Douglas Waples and Harold D. Lasswell, *National Libraries and Foreign Scholarship* (Chicago: University of Chicago Press, 1936). On fears about propaganda, see Gary, *The Nervous Liberals*.

9. Gary, *The Nervous Liberals*, ch. 3; Christopher Simpson, *Science of Coercion: Communication Research and Psychological Warfare, 1945-1960* (New York: Oxford University Press, 1994); Timothy Glander, *Origins of Mass Communications Research During the Cold War: Educational Effects and Contemporary Implications* (Mahwah, NJ: Lawrence Erlbaum Associates, 2000); David W. Park and

Jefferson Pooley, eds., *The History of Media and Communication Research: Contested Memories* (New York: Peter Lang, 2008).

10. Alex Wright, *Cataloguing the World: Paul Otlet and the Birth of the Information Age* (New York: Oxford University Press, 2014); W. Boyd Rayward, ed., *European Modernism and the Information Society: Informing the Present, Understanding the Past* (Aldershot, UK: Ashgate, 2008); Trudi Bellardo Hahn and Michael K. Buckland, eds., *Historical Studies in Information Science* (Medford, NJ: Information Today, Inc., 1998); Pamela Spence Richards, *Scientific Information in Wartime: The Allied-German Rivalry, 1939-1945* (Westport, CT: Greenwood Press, 1994), ch. 1; Rayward and Buckland have done pioneering research on early information science: see W. Boyd Rayward, "The Origins of Information Science and the International Institute of Bibliography/International Federation for Information and Documentation (FID)," *JASIS* 48 (1997): 289–300; Michael K. Buckland, "What is a 'Document'?" *JASIS* 48 (1997): 804–809. On early information overload, see Ann M. Blair, *Too Much to Know: Managing Scholarly Information before the Modern Age* (New Haven, CT: Yale University Press, 2011).

11. "World Congress of Universal Documentation, Paris, August 16-21, 1937," box 56, folder: Science Service Documentation Institute 1934-41, Lydenberg, Hopper and Beals General Correspondence, New York Public Library Archives, NYPL, Astor, Lenox, and Tilden Foundations. W. Boyd Rayward, "The International Exposition and the World Documentation Congress, Paris, 1937," *LQ* 53 (July 1983), 254–258; Phillip Kinsley, "Wells Launches Project to Pool World Learning," *Chicago Daily Tribune*, Oct 30, 1937. For a critique of Wells, see W. Boyd Rayward, "H.G. Wells's Idea of a World Brain: A Critical Reassessment," *JASIST* 50 (1999): 557–573.

12. Thomas D. Walker, "*Journal of Documentary Reproduction*, 1938-1942: Domain as Reflected in Characteristics of Authorship and Citation," *JASIS* 48 (1997): 361. Watson Davis, "How Documentation Promotes Intellectual World Progress," *Science News Letter* 32 (October 9, 1937), 228–230; Claire K. Schultz and Paul L. Garwig, "History of the American Documentation Institute—A Sketch," *American Documentation* 20 (1969): 152–160; Eugene B. Power, *Edition of One: The Autobiography of Eugene B. Power* (Ann Arbor: University Microfilms International, 1990).

13. American Documentation Institute, Organization Meeting minutes, March 13, 1937, 6, box 56, folder: Science Service Documentation Institute; Power, *Edition of One*, 109. Clifton Dale Foster, "Microfilming Activities of the Historical Records Survey, 1935-42," *American Archivist* 48 (Winter 1985): 45–55; Walker, "*Journal of Documentary Reproduction*, 1938-1942," 361–368. On librarians' embrace of microfilm, see Nicholson Baker, *Double Fold: Libraries and the Assault on Paper* (New York: Random House, 2001).

14. Alan Kramer, *Dynamics of Destruction: Culture and Mass Killing in the First World War* (New York: Oxford University Press, 2007), 6–30; Mark Derez, "The Flames of Louvain: The War Experience of an Academic Community," in *Facing Armageddon: The First World War Experienced*, eds. Hugh Cecil and Peter Liddle (London: Leo Cooper, 1996), 617–629.

15. P. J. Philip, "Louvain Dedicates Library in Peace," *NYT*, May 7, 1928. On the politics of rebuilding, see Tammy M. Proctor, "The Louvain Library and US Ambition in Interwar Belgium," *Journal of Contemporary History* 50 (2015): 147–167. See also Frank Pierrepont Graves, "The Story of the Library at Louvain," *Scientific Monthly* 28 (February 1929): 132–142; Allanson Shaw, "Old Louvain Now Rises from the Ashes of War," *NYT*, December 27, 1925.

16. Procter, "Louvain Library and US Ambition." See also Pierre de Soete, *The Louvain Library Controversy: The Misadventures of an American Artist* (Concord, NH: Rumford Press, 1929). The Latin phrase was "furore Teutonica diruta, dono Americano restitute."

17. "100,000 March Here," *NYT*, May 11, 1933. Guy Stern, "The Burning of the Books in Nazi Germany, 1933: The American Response," *Simon Wiesenthal Center Annual* 2 (1985): 95–113; J. M. Ritchie, "The Nazi Book-Burning," *Modern Language Review* 83 (1988): 627–643; Patti Clayton Becker, *Books and Libraries During World War II: Weapons in the War of Ideas* (New York: Routledge, 2005).

18. "Bibliocaust," *Time*, May 22, 1933, 21; Walter Lippman, "German's Book Bonfire," *Literary Digest* 115 (May 27, 1933): 14–15; Joseph Roth, "The Auto-da-Fe of the Mind," in *What I Saw: Reports from Berlin*, trans. Michael Hoffman (New York: Norton, 2003), 207–209. For American protests in the 1930s, see "A Columbia 'Book Purge,'" *NYT*, May 13, 1936, 9; September 20, 1938, 10.

19. "The War on Books," *LJ* 65 (June 1, 1941): 515–516; "Letter from England," *LJ* 65 (June 15, 1941); 527–528; "Gleaning," *LJ* 66 (December 15, 1941): 1083; "Plymouth Library Damaged," *LJ* 66 (July 1941): 626; W. C. Berwick Sayers, "Bombing of the Books," *LJ* 66 (October 1, 1942): 821. David A. Lincove, "Activists for Internationalism: ALA Responds to World War II and British Requests for Aid, 1939-1941," *Libraries & Culture* 26 (1991), 499, 487–510.

20. Thomas P. Fleming to Harry Miller Lydenberg, January 10, 1940; Lydenberg to Archibald MacLeish, January 12, 1940, Correspondence, Sept. 1939–August 1941, Joint Committee on Importations Papers, Rare Books and Manuscripts Library, Columbia University. H. M. Lydenberg, "Foreign Importations," *LJ* 64 (November 1, 1939): 814; *LJ* 66 (February 1, 1941): 13.

21. ALA to Cordell Hull, April 2, 1940, Joint Committee on Importations Papers. Lydenberg to MacLeish, March 18, 1940, box 64, folder: NYPL, Dr. Harry M. Lydenberg, Director, Sept. 1, 1939 to Oct 1. 1941, UA III 50.8.11.3, Records of the Director of the Harvard University Library, Keyes D. Metcalf, 1937–1955 [Metcalf Records], courtesy of the Harvard University Archives. A. A. Berle to MacLeish, March 12, 1940, container 392, Coop. w/Government, ACQ 5-3-2, Records of the LC Central File, MacLeish-Evans, LC Archives, Manuscripts Division, LC.

22. Walter A. Hafner to Lydenberg, June 26, 1940; Lydenberg, "Committee on the Importation of Foreign Periodicals (Statement Number Four)," August 27, 1940; Fleming to Lydenberg, September 3, 1940, Joint Committee on Importations Papers. Lydenberg memorandum, June 22, 1940; Metcalf to Lydenberg, July 11, 1940, box 64, folder: NYPL, Lydenberg, Metcalf Records.

23. Arthur M. Schlesinger Jr., *A Life in the Twentieth Century: Innocent Beginnings* (Boston: Houghton Mifflin, 2000), 212, 241. Lydenberg to MacLeish, April 12, 1940, box 64, folder: NYPL, Lydenberg, Metcalf Records. John P. Marquand, *So Little Time* (Boston: Little, Brown, 1943), 15. For a brilliant discussion of intellectuals' anticipation of war, see Paul K. Saint-Amour, *Tense Future: Modernism, Total War, Encyclopedic Form* (New York: Oxford University Press, 2015).

24. Archibald MacLeish, "Libraries in the Contemporary Crisis" (1939), in *Champion of a Cause*, 21–22. Archibald MacLeish, *The Irresponsibles* (New York: Duell, Sloan & Pearce, 1940). See also Stielow, "Librarian Warriors and Rapprochement."

25. Archibald MacLeish, "Of the Librarian's Profession"; "The Librarian and the Democratic Process," in *Champion of a Cause,* 43–53, 61–67.

26. *P.L.C. Bulletin* 11, no. 3 (December 1940): 1–3; "The Library—1941," *LJ* (January 15, 1941): 65. See also "Our National Decisions," *LJ* (September 1, 1940): 695; "Safeguarding Cultural Objects," *LJ* 66 (August 1941): 654. Jane Aikin, "Preparing

for a National Emergency: The Committee on Conservation of Cultural Resources, 1939-1944," *LQ* 77 (2007): 257–285; Lincove, "Activists for Internationalism," 489–490. On the PLC, see Rosalee McReynolds and Louise S. Robbins, *The Librarian Spies: Philip and Mary Jane Keeney and Cold War Espionage* (Westport, CT: Praeger Security International, 2009), 53–64.

27. Directive, Eisenhower to All Commanders, December 29, 1943, in *Civil Affairs: Soldiers Become Governors; United States Army in World War II, Special Studies*, ed. H. L. Coles and A. K. Weinberg (Washington, DC: Center of Military History, US Army, 1992), 417. On the development of law and policies to protect cultural sites in war zones, see John Fabian Witt, *Lincoln's Code: The Laws of War in American History* (New York: Free Press, 2012); Lynn Nicholas, *The Rape of Europa: The Fate of Europe's Treasures in the Third Reich and the Second World War* (New York: Knopf, 1994); Roger O'Keefe, *The Protection of Cultural Property in Armed Conflict* (Cambridge, UK: Cambridge University Press, 2006). See also *Report of the American Commission for the Protection and Salvage of Artistic and Historic Monuments in War Areas* (Washington, DC: GPO, 1946).

28. Binkley quoted in Ralph D. Wagner, *A History of the Farmington Plan* (Lanham, MD: Scarecrow Press, 2002), 57–58. "ACLS Conference on Microcopying Research Materials in Foreign Repositories, Preliminary Memorandum," June 5–6, 1940, Farmington Plan Documents, *1940-1953*, vol. 1, 49, 4, UA III 50.29.40.26, Metcalf Records.

29. "ACLS Conference," 5, 42; Julian P. Boyd to Archibald MacLeish, July 4, 1940, in Farmington Plan Documents, 63. Power, *Edition of One*, 122–128.

30. Boyd to MacLeish, July 4, 1940, in Farmington Plan Documents, 58, 63. On library cooperation, see Wagner, *A History of the Farmington Plan*. See also Andrew Abbott, "Library Research Infrastructure for Humanistic and Social Scientific Scholarship in the Twentieth Century," in *Social Knowledge in the Making*, ed. Charles Camic et al. (Chicago: University of Chicago Press, 2011), 43–88.

31. Rudolf Hirsch, "Philadelphia's War Documentation Service," *Special Libraries* 31 (October 1940): 369–370. Sherman Kent, "War Collection," *Yale Alumni Magazine*, May 22, 1940, box 2, folder 27, Yale in World War II Collection, Manuscripts and Archives, Yale University Library; Kent, *Reminiscences of a Varied Life* (San Rafael, CA, 1991), 183; "Yale in Drive for Literature Bearing on War," *NYT*, November 5, 1939, 57. Karl Brown, "War Materials in Libraries," *LJ* (December 1, 1939): 942–943.

32. "Hoover Library on War, Revolution and Peace, Note Prepared by H. H. Fisher, Acting Chairman, Hoover Library," October 10, 1944, BAEF Subject Files, Collecting Activities, Corr., 1944–1946, BAEF Records, HHPL. Peter Duignan, "The Library of the Hoover Institute on War, Revolution, and Peace, Part 1. Origin and Growth," *Library History* 17 (March 2001): 3–19.

33. "Professor Ralph Lutz's European Trip, 1939, for the Hoover Library, Germany," n.d., reel 11, Micro 860/US Mss 21AF, Louis Paul Lochner Papers, Wisconsin Historical Society. Ralph Haswell Lutz diary, 1939, box 11, Ralph Haswell Lutz Papers, HIA. Nina Almond, "Hoover Library Collecting in Germany," ca. 1946, reel 11. See also Charles B. Burdick's hagiographic *Ralph H. Lutz and the Hoover Institution* (Palo Alto: Hoover Institution Press, 1974), 136–137.

34. Lutz to Harold H. Fisher, September 27, 1939, box 1, folder: Correspondence, Fisher, H.H., 1934–1939, Perrin C. Galpin Papers, HIA. Lutz to Harry E. Lutz, October 8, 1939, box 10; diary, 1939, Lutz Papers.

35. Lutz to Fisher, November 9, 1939, box 10, Lutz Papers.

36. Lutz to Fisher, November 9, 1939. Raymond Henle, Oral History Interview with Dr. Ralph H. Lutz, September 15 and 26, 1967, Oral History Collections,

HIA. "Report of Commitments, Expenditures and Travelling Expenses of Ralph H. Lutz on a collecting trip for the Hoover Library," BAEF Subject Files, Collectors, Lutz, Ralph.

37. Henle, Oral History Interview with Lutz.

38. José Meyer to Archibald MacLeish, August 10, 1940, June 11, 1940, August 22, 1940, Martin A. Roberts to Meyer, September 7, 1939; Meyer to Roberts, November 18, 1939, Container 395, Meyer, José, ACQ 5-6-10, LC Central File.

39. Meyer to Verner W. Clapp, Sept 6, 1940, ACQ 5-6-10.

40. Meyer, "Booktrade and Libraries in France, August-September 1940"; Meyer to MacLeish, October 18, 1940, ACQ 5-6-10. Meyer, "Libraries, Learned Institutions, Schools, Books, etc. in Occupied France, October-December 1940," X Collection, Pamphlet no. 56, X-D761, LC; I am grateful to Beatriz Haspo for making this report available. See also Natalie Zemon Davis, preface, *Liste Otto: The Official List of French Books Banned Under the German Occupation, 1940* (Cambridge, MA: Harvard College Library, 1992), iii-ix.

41. Meyer, "The Booktrade in France, August 1940"; "French Libraries, Publishers and Booksellers under the German Occupation" [ca Aug. 1940], ACQ 5-6-10; "Libraries, Learned Institutions." Karl Frank to Rudolf Schleier, March 15, 1941, Botschaft Paris 1377, Politisches Archiv des Auswärtigen Amtes; my thanks to Jennifer Rodgers for documents on Frank.

42. "French Libraries, Publishers and Booksellers"; "Libraries, Learned Institutions." Some of Meyer's documentation may be found in LC, X Collection 92, X-D761, no. 56–76, Internet Archives, https://archive.org/stream/xcollection92#page/n117/mode/2up.

43. MacLeish to Roosevelt, October 9, 1940; Meyer to MacLeish, December 15, 1940, ACQ 5-6-10. Edgar Ansel Mowrer, "Libraries of Paris Purged by Gestapo in Campaign to Nazify French People," *Los Angeles Times*, October 17, 1940, 4.

44. Interview with Wilmarth S. Lewis by Jesse H. Shera, 1975, William Sheldon Lewis Papers (MS 1324), Manuscripts and Archives, Yale University Library; William Langer to Lewis, November 5, 1943, WSL Interests, Washington, Wilmarth Sheldon Lewis Archives, Lewis Walpole Library, Farmington, CT. Sherman Kent, "Prospects for the National Intelligence Service," *Yale Review* (Autumn 1946): 120; W.W. Rostow, "The London Operation: Recollections of an Economist," in *The Secrets War*, ed. Chalou, 56. On the growth of R&A and its connection to the academy, see Barry M. Katz, *Foreign Intelligence: Research and Analysis in the Office of Strategic Services, 1942-1945* (Cambridge, MA: Harvard University Press, 1989); Robin W. Winks, *Cloak & Gown: Scholars in the Secret War* (New York: Morrow, 1987).

45. "Suggested Memorandum Explaining the Part Which the LC Will Play in Connection with the Office of Coordinator of Defense Information" (n.d.), Container 748, DSI, folder 4; John Wilson to Luther Evans, November 24, 1942, folder 3-3; MacLeish to Donovan, June 29, 1941, folder 4, LC Central File. On the DSI, see Gary, *The Nervous Liberals*, 163–165; Anthony Cave Brown, ed., *The Secret War Report of the OSS* (New York: Berkeley Publishing, 1976), 48.

46. Donovan to MacLeish, July 30, 1941, Container 748, folder 4; MacLeish to James F. Baxter, August 26, 1941, folder 1997, Entry 146, Miscellaneous Washington Files, OSS Records, RG 226, NACP. See also Sherman Kent, *Reminiscences*, 183–195.

47. Lewis to MacLeish, August 13, 1941, folder: MacLeish, Archibald, WSL Correspondence, Lewis Archives; Wilmarth Sheldon Lewis, *One Man's Education*

(New York: Knopf, 1967), 287, 334–335. Karen Peltier, "Description of the Card Files in the LWL" (TS); my thanks to Susan Walker for this document. On the CID, see Jennifer Davis Heaps, "Tracking Intelligence Information: The OSS," *American Archivist* 61 (1998): 287–308. On the links between Lewis's collecting and intelligence work, see William H. Epstein, "Counter-Intelligence: Cold War Criticism and Eighteenth-Century Studies," *ELH* 57 (1990): 63–99; George E. Haggarty, "Walpoliana," *Eighteenth-Century Studies* 34 (2001): 227–249; Winks, *Cloak & Gown*, 96–110; Geoffrey Wheatcroft, "Walpole: The House and the Letters," *New York Review of Books* 63 (February 25, 2016): 33–34.

48. Ernest S. Griffith to MacLeish, June 28, 1941, Container 748, DSI, folder: General 1941–1945.
49. "The proposal has been made . . .," October 20, 1941, folder 1813, Entry 146, RG 226.
50. Griffith to MacLeish, October 21, 1941, Container 748, DSI, folder: 3-1. "The proposal has been made." Committee on Materials meeting, October 7, 1941, September 30, 1941; "Memorandum on Decisions of the Committee on Foreign Publications," September 27, 1941, folder 1814; "Notes on Conference Held September 26, 1941 in Dr. Langer's office," folder 1622, Entry 146, RG 226.
51. William J. Donovan, "Memorandum for the President," December 22, 1941; "Interdepartmental Committee on Foreign Publications," December 16, 1941, Records of the Office of the Director, M1642, Roll 22, RG 226.

CHAPTER 2

1. IDC Outpost Letter no. 4, April 16, 1945, IDC/Washington, Monthly Reports and Outpost Letters, 1943–1945, Entry 67, IDC, Stockholm Outpost, OSS Records, RG 226, NACP.
2. Interview with Frederick G. Kilgour, Medical Library Association, Oral History Committee, May 11, 1985; Kilgour interview with author, Chapel Hill, NC, April 3, 2003.
3. Lt. R. J. Lefebvre to C.W. Barnes, August 22, 1942, folder 1813, Entry 146, Miscellaneous Washington Files, RG 226; Wallace Deuel, "Chapter 34, IDC," n.d., 8–16, box 95, folder 2, Entry 99, OSS History Office File, RG 226.
4. "Suggested Procedure for Foreign Photographers, C.O.I.," March 24, 1942, box 13, folder 7, Entry 1, Office of the Chief, General Correspondence, 1942–1946, RG 226.
5. William J. Donovan, "Memorandum for the President," May 29, 1942, Office of the Director, M1642, roll 42, RG 226. "London War Diary," vol. 1, 1–6, 64; vol. 2, 42, History of the London Office, M1623, roll 3; Allan Evans, "Microfilm," December 18, 1942, M1623, roll 4, RG 226. Eugene B. Power, *Edition of One: The Autobiography of Eugene B. Power* (Ann Arbor: University Microfilms International, 1990), 134–136. Lucia Moholy, "The ASLIB Microfilm Service: The Story of its Wartime Activities," *Journal of Documentation* 2 (1946): 147–173. See Pamela Spence Richards, "Information Science in Wartime: Pioneer Documentation Activities in World War II," *JASIS* 39 (1988): 301–306; Pamela Spence Richards, *Scientific Information in Wartime: The Allied-German Rivalry, 1939-1945* (Westport, CT: Greenwood Press, 1994); Isabelle Tombs, "Scrutinizing France: Collecting and Using Newspaper Intelligence during World War II," *Intelligence and National Security* 17 (2002): 105–126. Nelson MacPherson, *American Intelligence in War-Time London: The Story of the OSS* (London: Frank Cass, 2003).

6. *Oakland Tribune*, February 9, 1926. I am deeply grateful to Eric Andersson for providing extensive information about his great-aunt Adele Kibre.

7. Adele Kibre, "Microphotography in European Libraries," *Journal of Documentary Reproduction* 4 (1941): 161, 162.

8. "Along El Camino Real with Ed Ainsworth," *Los Angeles Times*, April 20, 1940. Power, *Edition of One*, 105.

9. Kibre, "Microphotography in European Libraries." Kibre to T. A. M. Jack, February 19, 1941, December 8, 1941, Documents 9528, Letters and Pamphlets Relating to European Anti-Fascist Resistance, Second World War, Imperial War Museum, London.

10. Kibre to Jack, December 8, 1941, July 17, 1941.

11. Power, *Edition of One*, 138. Donovan to G. Howland Shaw, February 16, 1942, file 103.91802; Donovan to Secretary of State, April 18, 1942, file 124.58/56, Central Decimal File, 1940-44, Department of State Records, RG 59, NACP. My thanks to Richard Peuser for these documents. "Estimated Requirements for Personnel Services, Justification" (n.d.), 9, folder 66, Entry 146; Adele Kibre, Entry 224, OSS Personnel Files, 1941-1945, RG 226.

12. Cecil Parrott, *The Tightrope* (London: Faber & Faber, 1975), 161–167, 172–173, 192. Stockholm Press Reading Bureau, July 1941–Dec 1942, HS 2/258; Stockholm, Press Reading Bureau, Organisation and Staff, 1942–1943, FO 898/153, TNA. Donovan to Secretary of State, April 18, 1942. C. G. McKay, *From Information to Intrigue: Studies in Secret Service Based on the Swedish Experience, 1939–1945* (London: Frank Cass, 1993), 101-106.

13. Kibre to Geoffrey Kirk, September 2, 1942, folder: Ministry of Information, Entry 63, IDC Stockholm Correspondence, 1942–1945, RG 226. The Anglo-American Microfilm Unit's output of 3,188 reels and documentation of its activities are housed in the British Library and are uncatalogued. My thanks to Ed King and Stephen Lester, respectively former and current head of the newspaper division, for allowing me to examine the Microfilm Unit's textual records. Ed King, "IDC Stockholm Unit in WWII," May 3, 2010 (TS).

14. Kilgour to Kibre, December 1, 1942, February 14, 1944, April 8, 1944, folder: IDC/Washington Correspondence, Entry 64, IDC Correspondence Received from Washington, London and Paris. Kibre to Kilgour, April 11, 1944, folder: IDC Washington Correspondence, Entry 63.

15. "R&A London War Diary," vol. 1, 70. Kilgour to Kibre, November 12, 1943, May 31, 1943, IDC/Washington Correspondence; Ralph H. Carruthers to Kibre, May 14, 1945, folder: IDC/Paris, 1945, Entry 64.

16. Kilgour to Kibre, May 31, 1943; Kibre to Evans, September 12, 1942, September 23, 1942, folder: IDC/London, Entry 63. John H. Moriarty, "The IDC," November 10, 1942, container 392, IDC, ACQ 5-4, Records of the LC Central File, MacLeish-Evans, LC Archives, Manuscript Division, LC. Dr. Knud Ditlef-Nielsen and Professor S. Huppert were marked "illegal" in folder: IDC/Stockholm (personnel), Entry 63.

17. "R&A London War Diary," vol. 1, 71–72.

18. Carruthers to Kibre, May 14, 1945; Kilgour to Kibre, November 12, 1943. Anglo-American Microfilm Unit Newspaper List, 1942–1943; "Denmark Underground Publications Borrowed from the Danish Exposition"; "II Publications B Periodicals, Note: British Press Reading Bureau Subscription List, Revised October 1, 1943," British Library Newspaper Division. On the saboteur, Kibre to Langer, October 26, 1943, addendum July 23, 1945, Airgrams, Entry 207, Field Station Files: Stockholm IDC, RG 226. Power, *Edition of One*, 138, 150.

19. Kibre to L. Randolph Higgs, September 10, 1945, folder: L. Randolph Higgs, Entry 63. Anglo-American Microfilm Unit Newspaper List, 1942-43. Seventh Interrogation Center, "Preliminary Interrogation Report, Source: Hoffmann, Rolf," June 25, 1945, World War II Nuernberg Interrogation Records, M1270, RG238, fold3.com/image/231974370.

20. Carruthers to Kibre, March 30, 1944, April 22, 1944, Kilgour to Kibre, December 13, 1944, folder: Correspondence to Stockholm, Entry 73, ETO General Correspondence, 1944–1945, RG 226. Carruthers to Kibre, June 8, 1944, folder: IDC/London, Entry 64.

21. Reuben Peiss to K. D. Metcalf, October 20, 1943, box 81, folder: Reuben Peiss, UA III 50.8.11.3, Records of the Director of the Harvard University Library, Keyes D. Metcalf, 1937–1955, Harvard University Archives.

22. [n.au.] to Ed, April 21, 1944, folder 15, Entry 197A, Field Station Special Funds Finance Records, RG 226. On wartime Lisbon, see Neill Lochery, *Lisbon: War in the Shadows of the City of Light, 1939-45* (New York: Public Affairs, 2011); Ronald Weber, *The Lisbon Route: Entry and Escape in Nazi Europe* (Lanham, MD: Ivan R. Dee, 2011).

23. [n.au.] to Argus, July 23, 1943, box 30, folder 16, Entry 92, COI/OSS Central Files, RG 226. On Garbo, see Ben Mcintyre, *Double Cross: The True Story of the D-Day Spies* (New York: Crown, 2012).

24. Ronald Campbell, "From Lisbon to Foreign Office," March 27, 1942, HS 6/987; "Extract from Report on Abwehr Organization; Report on Portugal," July 28, 1945, KV 3/175, TNA. Neville Wylie, "An Amateur Learns his Job? Special Operations Executive in Portugal, 1940-1942," *Journal of Contemporary History* 36 (2001): 441–457.

25. Ambrose E. Chambers to Wallace B. Phillips, March 31, 1942, box 2, folder 6; Argus to Regis, November 16, 1943, box 30, folder 16, Entry 92. On Lisbon operations, see Kermit Roosevelt, ed., *War Report of the O.S.S.* (New York: Walker & Co, 1976), 31–37.

26. Solborg to Goodfellow, cable, June 1, 1942, WN 14222, Corr. between Washington and Portugal, Entry 210, Classified Sources and Methods; W.A.R., "Portugal, Progress Report No. 1," July 25, 1942, box 78, folder 18, Entry 92; W.C., August 14, 1942, box 388, folder 8, Entry 210; J. Ray Olivera to Chief, OSS West European Division, May 6, 1943, box 30, folder 16, Entry 92; James H. Rand III to Olivera, August, 12, 1942, box 388, folder 8; H. Gregory Thomas to Fred, May 29, 1943, box 30, folder 16.

27. Whitney H. Shephardson to Francis P. Miller, May 24, 1943, box 9, folder 87, Entry 92; '423' to Mr. Brown, May 25, 1944, folder 988, Entry 148, Field Station Files, Lisbon, RG 226. "Office of Soporific Sinecures, Regurgitation and Metabolism Branch, R&A No. 00½, 1 April 1945," folder: OSS Clippings, William Leonard Langer Papers, Harvard University Archives.

28. Manuel Sanchez to John H. Moriarty, April 30, 1943, container 396, folder: Sanchez, Manuel, ACQ 5-6-13, LC Central File.

29. Peiss to Allen Dulles, November 3, 1944, folder: from Bern, Entry 73; Norbert Gallary to Chief, SI, "Report on Field Conditions," May 12, 1945, box 6, folder 303, Entry 99.

30. Carruthers to Langer attn. Kilgour, November 15, 1943, folder 1160, Entry 146, RG 226. Kilgour to Carruthers, cable, February 18, 1943, folder: Outgoing Plain Text, Carruthers, Entry 88, Overseas Cable File, Lisbon, RG 226.

31. Peiss to Kilgour, April 11, 1944; September 20, 1944; Peiss to Carruthers, April 28, 1944, folder: from Lisbon, Entry 73. Ledgers, July 1943-October 1944, folder 5, Contracts (Commercial Houses), Lisbon, Entry 197A.

32. Sanchez to Verner W. Clapp, October 15, 1943, Miscellaneous S-W, box 2, folder: Sanchez, Manuel, LC Central File. Peiss to Carruthers, June 27, 1944; Peiss to Kilgour, May 23, 1944, folder: from Lisbon.

33. Langer to James F. Rogers, "Excerpt from letter dated November 5, 1942 from RHC," February 5, 1943, folder 39, IDC 1943, Entry 145, R&A Branch Chief Files, RG 226. Saint to Argus and V/48, "English Technical Books for Germany," November 2, 1943, WN 19062, Entry 210.

34. Sanchez to Moriarty, April 15, 1943, April 30, 1943; Sanchez to Clapp, October 15–30, 1943, ACQ 5-6-13. Clapp to Sanchez, October 15, 1943, Box 33, folder: Sanchez, Manuel, LCM and CAP, 1942–1957, Records, Manuscript Division, LC. Ralph D. Wagner, "Manuel Sanchez: Librarian Behind the Lines," *American Libraries* 20 (November 1989): 962–964.

35. Sanchez to Moriarty, June 4, 1943, Miscellaneous S-W; Sanchez to Moriarty, June 30, 1943, ACQ 5-6-13. On sales to LC, see Invoices-Livraria Portugal-Series A-Want-List, Series E, box 26, LCM Records.

36. Sanchez to Moriarty, June 30, 1943; July 15, 1943, ACQ 5-6-13.

37. Sanchez to Clapp, July 1, 1943. Sanchez to Moriarty, August 15, 1943; Sanchez to Clapp, October 15–31, 1943.

38. Sanchez to Clapp, October 15, 1943. Sanchez to Clapp, November 5, 1943, ACQ 5-6-13. "Relations with the Americans and the British," n.d., 5, WN 12984, Entry 210.

39. Sanchez to Moriarty, August 31, 1943, ACQ 5-6-13.

40. Peiss to Carruthers, September 29, 1944, folder: from Lisbon. "IDC Monthly Report for February, 1945," Monthly Reports and Outpost Letters, 1943–1945, Entry 67.

41. John K. Fairbank, *Chinabound: A Fifty-Year Memoir* (New York: Harper & Row, 1982); Paul M. Evans, *John Fairbank and the American Understanding of Modern China* (New York: Basil Blackwell, 1988), 72–104. George N. Kates Papers, Archives of American Art, Smithsonian Institution. I am grateful to Robert M. Sargeant for information about his father Clyde Sargeant, telephone conversation, July 6, 2012.

42. "Estimated Requirements for Personnel Services, Justification," 4. Robert I. Crane to T. M. Nordbeck, "Field Trip," March 16, 1945; Nordbeck to Langer attn. Kilgour, "Trip to China, April 7, 1945, folder: Washington-Outgoing, Entry 61, IDC New Delhi Outpost, Correspondence, 1944–1945, RG 226. Kilgour to Members of the IDC and Far Eastern Advisory Group (FEAG), "Excerpts from Letters Recently Received from George Kates in Chungking," March 25, 1944, 2, box 32, folder 1, Entry 1.

43. "Bombay IDC 'Operations,' Informal Report by T/Sgt. Wayne M. Hartwell," [July 25, 1945], folder: Washington–Outgoing; Herold J. Wiens to Joseph E. Spencer and T. M. Nordbeck, "Visit to Chengtu and Sian by Lieutenant Wiens to discuss situation with bookbuyers," May 4, 1945, folder: Chungking, Entry 61; "Estimated Requirements for Personnel Services; Justification," n.d., folder 66, Entry 146.

44. C. F. Remer to Langer, December 24, 1942, folder 1820, Entry 146. Kilgour to IDC and FEAG, "Excerpts from Reports of George N. Kates in Chungking," April 4, 1944, box 32, folder 1, Entry 1. IDC Outpost Letter no. 4, April 16, 1945.

45. Kilgour to IDC and FEAG, "Excerpts from Letters," March 25, 1944; Kilgour to IDC and FEAG, "Excerpts from Reports," April 4, 1944.

46. Wiens to Richard P. Heppner and Spencer, "Proposed establishment of system for gathering enemy publications through Bishop Megan from Sian," [May 1945], folder: Chungking, Entry 61; Wiens to Spencer and Nordbeck, "Visit to Chengtu and Sian." On Megan, see Eileen J. Christensen, *In War and Famine: Missionaries in China's Honan Province in the 1940s* (Montreal: McGill-Queen's University Press, 2005). On Buck's role, see Kilgour to IDC and FEAG, "Excerpts from Letters," March 25, 1944.

47. Nordbeck to Kilgour, "Field Trip of R.I. Crane," March 17, 1944; Crane to Nordbeck, "Field Trip," March 16, 1945. Kilgour to Nordbeck, "Reporting," [April 10, 1945]; Margaret Fieldman, "Robert Irwin Crane," January 24, 1945, box 2, folder 8, Entry 1. On the X-2 investigation, see Nordbeck to Kilgour, May 30, 1945, box 1, folder: Washington—Outgoing, Entry 61. See also Robert I. Crane, "U.S.-India Relations: The Early Phase, 1941-1945," *Asian Affairs* 15 (Winter, 1988–1989): 189–193; John L. Hill, "Obituaries, Robert I. Crane, 1920-1997," *Journal of Asian Studies* 57 (May 1998): 633–634.

48. Thomas to Carib, June 29, 1943, box 30, folder 16, Entry 92. Belin to Langer, August 12, 1943.

49. Langer to Donovan, July 8, 1942, M1642, roll 42. IDC, "Request to the Bureau of the Budget for Supplementary Funds for a Subject Indexing Unit for April–June 1943 and for 1944," March 26, 1943, 11, folder 1058, Entry 146.

50. Moriarty, "The IDC"; IDC, "Meeting of 9 October 1942 Minutes"; "Meeting of 20 July 1943 Minutes," ACQ 5-4.

51. Jesse Shera to John A. Wilson, December 28, 1942; John L. Riheldaffer to Langer, July 14, 1942, folder 1813, Entry 146. Faustine Dennis, "IDC Subject Index to Foreign Publications," August 17, 1943, ACQ 5-4.

52. Kilgour to Donovan; IDC Outpost Letter no. 4, April 16, 1945.

53. Kilgour to Kibre, October 22, 1943, IDC/Washington Correspondence. Kilgour to Louis Ream, "IDC Budget Request (Revised) for 1944–45," January 20, 1944, folder 1057, Entry 146. Deuel, "Chapter 34, IDC," 20. Kilgour to Members of IDC, March 24, 1944; IDC Outpost Letter no. 2, March 1945.

54. Executive Secretary to IDC, Report, May 28, 1943, 4, Monthly Reports and Outpost Letters, Entry 67.

55. IDC Outpost Letter no. 4, April 16, 1945. [n.au.] to Argus, June 22, 1944, July 3, 1944, folder 981, Entry 148.

56. Carruthers to Kilgour, November 15, 1943; "Carruthers" [1943], folder 14, Entry 197A. Peiss to Carruthers, April 28, 1944, March 6, 1944, folder: from Lisbon. Peiss to Kilgour, April 11, 1944.

57. Carruthers to Kilgour, December 2, 1943, folder 1160, Entry 146. Peiss to Carruthers, April 28, 1944.

58. Carruthers to Kilgour, December 2, 1943; Kilgour to Langer, "Excerpt from a recent letter from Carruthers," August 17, 1943, folder 39, Entry 145.

59. W. L. Melton Jr. to John C. Hughes, October 20, 1943; Melton to Kilgour, November 25, 1943, box 30, folder 17, Entry 92. Carruthers to Kilgour, December 2, 1943.

60. Eric Andersson e-mail to author, July 12, 2004. "Reuben Peiss, A Memorial," in Alfred Hessel, *A History of Libraries*, trans. Reuben Peiss (New Brunswick, NJ: Scarecrow Press, 1955), ix–xi.

61. Nordbeck to Kilgour, March 5, 1945, folder: Washington–Outgoing, Entry 61.

62. John K. Fairbank to Kilgour and C. F. Remer, November 4, 1942, folder 1818; Remer to William L. Langer, "Comments from Fairbank on material available in Chungking," December 24, 1942; Fairbank to Kilgour, "Opportunities for

O.S.S. and Indec in New Delhi," folder 1820, Entry 146. William A. Kimbel to Langer, November 13, 1942; L. C. Irvine to James R. Murphy, October 19, 1943, box 30, folder 18, Entry 92. Langer to Robert B. Hall, May 3, 1944, folder 1219, Entry 146.

63. David G. Mandelbaum to Kilgour, "Indec Affairs, New Delhi," May 18, 1944, folder 1226, Entry 146. Mandelbaum to Langer, attn. Burton Fahs, "South Asia Section Letter," May 20, 1944, box 32, folder 1, Entry 1. See also Mandelbaum, Entry 224, OSS Personnel Files. Fairbank to Kilgour, no. 6, September 13, 1942.

64. Kilgour to IDC and FEAG, "Excerpts from Letters," March 25, 1944.

65. Ibid.

66. IDC," Request to the Bureau of the Budget for Supplementary Funds," 10; Kilgour to Ream, "IDC Budget Request," 22. Richards, *Scientific Information in Wartime*; Kilgour interview with author.

CHAPTER 3

1. Harold C. Lyon, "Operations of 'T' Force, 12th Army Group, in the Liberation and Intelligence Exploitation of Paris, France, 25 August–6 September 1944" (Fort Benning: Advanced Infantry Officers Course, 1948–1949), 22–24, 32, 36. Saul K. Padover to Chandler Morse, Harold Deutsch et al., September 11, 1944, box 2, Entry 81, ETO Correspondence of the OSS Mission to Germany, 1944–1945, OSS Records, RG 226, NACP.

2. For pathbreaking works on these missions, see Astrid M. Eckert, *The Struggle for the Files: The Western Allies and the Return of German Archives After the Second World War* (Cambridge, UK: Cambridge University Press, 2012); John Gimbel, *Science, Technology, and Reparations: Exploitation and Plunder in Postwar Germany* (Stanford, CA: Stanford University Press, 1990). See also Brian E. Crim, *Our Germans: Project Paperclip and the National Security State* (Baltimore: Johns Hopkins University Press, 2018); Franklin M. Davis, "The Army's Technical Detectives," *Military Review* 28 (May 1948): 12–17.

3. Frederick B. Alexander Jr., "The Operations of 'T'-Force (Target Force), 42d Infantry Division from Wurzburg, Germany, through Munich, Germany, 31 March–15 May 1945" (Military Monograph, Ground General School, October 1949), 3–4. *G-2 Section, Headquarters, 6th Army Group, Final Report, World War II* (n.d.), 48, 51. Eckert, *Struggle for the Files*, ch. 1. On the British teams, see Sean Longden, *T-Force: The Race for Nazi Secrets, 1945* (London: Hatchette, 2009). See also Report of the General Board, United States Forces, European Theater, "Organization and Operation of the Theater Intelligence Services in the European Theater of Operations," Study no. 14 [1945]. For instructions on gathering enemy documents on the eve of the war, see Shipley Thomas, *S-2 in Action* (Harrisburg, PA: Military Service Publishing Co., 1940). My thanks to Mark Bergman for information on the organization of military intelligence.

4. George W. Overton, "Activities with OSS 'T-Force' in Strasbourg," January 5, 1945, box 3, Entry 81, RG 226.

5. Allan Evans, "T-Forces in the ETO," November 4, 1944, box 2, Entry 81. Alexander, "Operations of 'T-Force,'" 5; *G-2 Section Final Report*, 50–51; Jack Hochwald, "The U.S. Army T-Forces: Documenting the Holocaust," *American Jewish History* 70 (March 1981): 379–380.

6. "T-Forces in the ETO" [Oct/Nov 1944], 4, box 2, Entry 81. Lyon, "Operation of 'T-Force,'" 50. Europe-Africa Division Outpost Letter no. 2, February 17, 1944, 4–6, folder 1371, Entry 146, Miscellaneous Washington Files; Chandler Morse

to William Langer, June 17, 1944, folder: London II, Entry 1, Office of the Chief, General Correspondence, RG 226. Baker to Chief R&A, October 11 1944; Edward A. Tenenbaum to Just Lunning, November 28, 1944, box 2, Entry 81. Third US Army, *After Action Report*, 1 Aug. 1944–9 May 1945, vol. 2, pt. 3, 54, 25.

7. Chandler Morse to Col. D. K. E. Bruce, Progress Report, R&A Branch, 1–15 October 1944 (Oct 16, 1944), folder 1374, Entry 146; Morse to Langer, June 17, 1944; R&A, "London War Diary," 112, History of London Office, M1623, Roll 3, RG 226.

8. Combined Services Detailed Interrogation Centre, "Printing and Publishing in Germany, Extract from PW Paper 31," n.d., IDC Interrogations of Prisoners, Entry 66, IDC Stockholm Outpost, German POW Interrogation Reports about Art, Archives and Publications in Germany, RG 226.

9. Index of Jews Whose German Nationality Was Annulled by the Nazi Regime, 1935–1944, and New York Passenger List, October 15, 1937, Ancestry.com; Electronic Army Serial Number Merged File, 1938–1946, World War II Enlistment Records, RG 64, NARA. MacLoeb Books advertisement, *NYT*, January 24, 1943; March 21, 1943. Perrin C. Galpin to Nina Almond, November 10, 1943, BAEF Subject Files, Collecting Activities, Correspondence and Memoranda, Almond, Nina, BAEF Records, HHPL; "Theater Service Record," September 20, 1945, Max Loeb, Entry 224, OSS Personnel Files, RG 226.

10. IDC, "Interrogation of Friendly Prisoners of War," RAL 142, January 16, 1945, IDC Interrogations of Prisoners Re Art, Archives and Publications, Entry 66.

11. Frederick G. Kilgour to Reuben Peiss, December 20, 1944, folder: Correspondence to Bern, box 5, General Correspondence, 1944–1945, Entry NM-54 73, RG 226. Morse, "Award of Unit Commander's Certificate of Merit," June 29, 1945, Loeb, OSS Personnel Files. "London War Diary," 112, 227.

12. IDC, "Archives, Libraries, Booktrade & Publishing Industry; Friendly German Prisoner of War Interrogations," Report No. 44, January 17, 1945; Report No. 58, January 30, 1945, WN 11622, Entry 210, Classified Sources and Methods, RG 226. "Interrogation of Friendly POWs," 1. On the book trade in the Third Reich, see Jan-Pieter Barbian, *The Politics of Literature in Nazi-Germany: Books in the Media Dictatorship*, trans. Kate Sturge (London: Bloomsbury, 2013).

13. "Archives, Libraries, Booktrade & Publishing Industry," Report No. 39, January 9, 1945; Report no. 55, January 26, 1945, WN 11622. "Interrogation of Friendly POWs," 1.

14. "Interrogation of Friendly POWs," 17.

15. "Archives, Libraries, Booktrade & Publishing Industry," Report No. 35, January 3, 1945, Entry 66. IDC, "Interrogation of Friendly POWs," 30–31. "Archives, Libraries, Booktrade & Publishing Industry," Report No. 77, February 12, 1945; Report No. 36, January 5, 1945, WN 11622.

16. "Archives, Libraries, Booktrade & Publishing Industry," Report No. 48, January 19, 1945, Report No. 73, February 5, 1945, WN 11622. See also "Interrogation of Friendly POWs," 22–24.

17. "Archives, Libraries, Booktrade & Publishing," Report No. 68, February 2, 1945; Report No. 26, December 16, 1944, WN 11622.

18. Archives, Libraries, Booktrade & Publishing Industry," Report No. 63, January 31, 1945; Report No. 44, January 17, 1945; Report No. 65, February 1, 1945, WN 11622. "Interrogation of Friendly POWs," 25, 33. On the OSS Art Looting Investigation Unit, see Michael Salter, "A Critical Assessment of US Intelligence's Investigation of Nazi Art Looting," *Journal of International Criminal Justice* 13 (May 2015): 257–280.

19. "Interrogation of Friendly POWs," 28, 20, 14, 26.

20. Ibid., 20–21.

21. Allan Evans, "T-Forces in the ETO." Dwight C. Baker, "Monthly Report on T Force," September 26, 1944, box 2, Entry 81.

22. Baker, "Special Report on Collected Materials from Paris Targets," September 30, 1944, box 31, folder 1, Entry 1; Tenenbaum to Lunning, November 28, 1944. Deutsch to Bruce, "Progress Report, R&A Paris, 16–30 November 1944," December 1, 1944, 6–7, folder 1374, Entry 146.

23. Morse to Bruce, "Progress Report, R&A Branch 1-15 Oct 1944." Deutsch to Bruce, "Progress Report," December 1, 1944.

24. Ross Lee Finney to Gretchen Finney, September 13, 1944, folder 19; October 5, 1944, folder 21; November 23, 1944, folder 23; Finney to Ross Finney, Jr., October 15, 1944, folder 22, box 2, Series 1, Correspondence, 1916-1996, Sub-Series 1, Personal, Ross Lee Finney Papers, JPB 04-15, Music Division, NYPL for the Performing Arts. On Finney, see Paul Cooper, "The Music of Ross Lee Finney," *Musical Quarterly* 53 (January 1967): 1–21; Ross Lee Finney, *Profile of a Lifetime: A Musical Autobiography* (New York: C. F. Peters, 1992).

25. Finney to Gretchen Finney, October 4, 1944, folder 21; September 12, 1944, folder 19; October 21, 1944, folder 22, Finney Papers.

26. Finney to Gretchen Finney, October 4, 1944. Morse, "Award of Unit Commander's Certificate of Merit to Pfc Stanley Rubint," June 27, 1945, Stanley Rubint, OSS Personnel Files; Stanley Rubint, Electronic Army Serial Number Merged File; U.S. Naturalization Record Index; New York Passenger Lists, Ancestry.com.

27. Finney to Gretchen Finney, October 19, 1944, October 18, 1944, folder 22; December 11, 1944, folder 24; October 31 [November 1], 1944, folder 23, Finney Papers.

28. Kilgour to David H. Clift, Report no. 2, November 25, 1944, IDC/London, Correspondence about Acquisition from Washington, London, and Paris, 1942-45, Entry 64, RG 226.

29. Finney to Gretchen Finney, November 16, November 21, November 18, 1944, folder 23, Finney Papers. Peiss to "Auntie," December 1, 1944, in author's possession, with thanks to Saul Pasternack for this letter.

30. Kilgour to Clift, November 25, 1944, 3–4, IDC/London, Entry 64; IDC, "Minutes of Meeting of 29 June 1945," 2, box 2, folder 8, Entry 1. Finney to Gretchen Finney, December 2, 1944, folder 24; Deutsch to Bruce, "Progress Report, R&A Paris, 1-15 November 1944," November 16, 1944, folder 1374, Entry 146. See also Kenneth Peacock and Ross Lee Finney, "Ross Lee Finney at Eighty-Five: Weep Torn Land," *American Music* 9 (Spring 1991): 16.

31. Finney to Gretchen Finney, February 6, 1945, folder 27, Finney Papers. Peacock and Finney, "Ross Lee Finney at Eighty-Five," 14.

32. "Meeting at War Office: 12 Dec. 44"; "Treatment of German Records and Archives," Control Commission for Germany, Policy–Planning–DMI's Working Party, FO 1050/1411, TNA.

33. "Field Program of the Intelligence Services Staff, R&A/ETO (FWD)," February 21, 1945, 1, box 3, Entry 81. Alexander, "The Operations of 'T'-Force," 19.

34. Alexander, "The Operations of 'T'-Force," 16; "Field Program of the Intelligence Services Staff," 1.

35. "Draft Minutes of Meeting held on 16 February 1945," February 19, 1945, 1–2, FO 1050/1411.

36. Sherrod East in Robert Wolfe, ed., *Captured German and Related Records: A National Archives Conference* (Athens: Ohio University Press, 1974), 4.

37. Hilary Jenkinson to G. W. White, "Comments on Eclipse Memorandum No. 7: Section IX," December 16, 1944; "Meeting at War Office: 12 Dec. 1944," FO 1050/1411. On Jenkinson's work and influence, see Paul Saint-Amour, *Tense Future: Modernism, Total War, Encyclopedic Form* (New York: Oxford University Press, 157–176; John Ridener, *From Polders to Postmodernism: A Concise History of Archival Theory* (Sacramento: Litwin Books, 2009), 41–68; Reto Tschan, "A Comparison of Jenkinson and Schellenberg on Appraisal," *American Archivist* 65 (2002): 176–195.

38. "Present Situation in regard to the treatment of Captured Enemy Archives during the Operational Period," Annexure 3, G-2 Records: SHAEF, Organization T-Force, September 1944–July 1945, WO 219/1986, TNA. "Meeting held by M.I. 17 on handling of documents in Germany during and after Hostilities in Room 350 on 1st February, 1945," FO 1050/1411.

39. Third US Army, *After Action Report*, 55. *G-2 Section, 6th Army Group, Final Report, World War II* (n.d.), 42–43. Report of the General Board, "Organization and Operation of the Theater Intelligence Services."

40. C. H. Noton to Brigadier E. J. Foord, "Information Conclusions Arising from a C.I.O.S. Group 7 Trip," June 16, 1945, PRO 30/95/15, TNA; Francis P. Miller to Chief, Special Sections, "Report on ECLIPSE Meeting of G-2 Officers from Armies at EAGLE (Main), Friday, 6 April 1945," April 9, 1945, FO 1050/1411.

41. "Meeting held by M.I. 17," 12.

42. Kilgour to Peiss, December 20, 1944, folder: Correspondence to Bern; Lucy Reynolds to Clift, January 16, 1945; Reynolds to Ralph H. Carruthers, February 2, 1945, folder: Correspondence to Paris, box 5, Entry NM-54 73.

43. "Field Program of the Intelligence Services Staff, R&A/ETO (FWD)," 9–10. Carruthers to "All Outposts and Washington–IDC," April 9, 1945, 4, IDC/London, Entry 64. Carruthers to Kilgour, April 8, 1945, IDC, box 1; Carruthers to Peiss, August 23, 1944, folder: Correspondence to Lisbon, box 5, Entry NM-54 73. IDC Outpost Letter, no. 5, May 1, 1945, IDC Monthly Reports and Outpost Letters, 1943–1945, Entry 67.

44. *G-2 Section, Final Report*, 49. Overton, "Activities with OSS 'T-Force' in Strasbourg"; Lewis Allbee to Harold Deutsch, December 12, 1944, box 2, Entry 81. Leonard J. Hankin to Hans Helm, "Report on Strasbourg Documents Mission," December 19, 1944; Hankin to Deutsch, December 29, 1944, folder: Hankin–T-Force, box 8, Entry NM-54 73.

45. Overton, "Activities with OSS 'T-Force' in Strasbourg."

46. "Far Eastern R&A Documents Collection in Cologne and Bonn," n.d.; Rubint to Finney, March 13, 1945; Hankin, "Report No. 1 from Cologne," March 12, 1945; Hankin, "Report No. 2 from Cologne," March 23, 1945, box 3, Entry 81.

47. "Far Eastern R&A Documents Collection in Cologne and Bonn"; Hankin, "Report No. 2 from Cologne." Carruthers to Kilgour, April 8, 1945, folder: Restitution of Collections (returned), Box 33, LCM and CAP, 1942–1957, Records, Manuscript Division, LC, Washington, DC.

48. Hankin to Deutsch, March 29, 1945, box 3, Entry 81.

49. Lloyd D. Black, "Report of Trip to Leipzig Area May 16–27 by Team #11A," May 31, 1945; Woodrow Borah, "Field Trip 13–28 May, etc.," June 4, 1945, box 3, Entry 81.

50. Rubint to Deutsch, June 12, 1945; Loeb, "Report of Operation of T-Force," June 6, 1945, box 3, Entry 81.

51. Borah, "Field Trip 12–28 May."

52. Loeb to Carruthers, May 20, 1945; Loeb, "Report of Visit to Frankfurt (Main) on 15 May, 1945"; Loeb, "Report of Operation of T-Forces," May 26, 1945, Box 3, Entry 81.

53. Black, "Report of Trip to Leipzig Area, May 16–27"; Deutsch to Langer, June 9, 1945, box 3, Entry 81; Borah, "Field Trip 13–28 May."

54. Borah, "Field Trip 13–28 May"; Loeb to Carruthers, May 20, 1945; Loeb, "Report of Operation of T-Forces," May 26, 1945.

55. Frederick L. Ryan, "Report on the Prussian State Library visited July 18," July 23, 1945, box 3, Entry 81. Deutsch to Langer, June 9, 1945.

56. Borah, "Field Trip 13-28 May"; IDC Outpost Letter no. 11, August 1, 1945, Entry 67. Deutsch to Col. Joseph O'Malley, "Evaluation and Utilization of Documentary Materials in the Future Russian Zone," box 24, folder 2, Entry 1.

57. Peiss to Deutsch, "Interim Report of Progress–Huckleberry Operation," June 25, 1945; Peiss to Deutsch, "Preliminary Investigations in the Vicinity of Weimar," June 1, 1945, box 3, Entry 81.

58. Peiss to Deutsch, "Preliminary Investigations." Borah to Deutsch, "Field Trip, Latin American Section of Northern Team, 2-14 June," June 16, 1945, with attachment "Institut für Aussenpolitische Forschung, Sondershausen," June 12, 1945, box 3, Entry 81.

59. Eugene B. Power, *Edition of One: The Autobiography of Eugene B. Power* (Ann Arbor: University Microfilms International, 1990), 149–150.

60. "Progress Report, R&A/Germany, 1–30 September, 1945," October 1, 1945, box 2, Entry 81.

61. Longden, *T-Force*, 103. Rubint to Jack Ashcraft, "Report on Strasbourg Operations," December 31, 1944, box 2, Entry 81. On Soviet trophy loot, see Patricia Kennedy Grimsted, "The Road to Minsk for Western 'Trophy' Books: Twice Plundered but Not Yet 'Home from the War,'" *Libraries & Culture* 39 (Fall 2004): 351–404; Konstantin Akinsha, "Stalin's Decrees and Soviet Trophy Brigades: Compensation, Restitution in Kind, or 'Trophies' of War?" *International Journal of Cultural Property* 17 (2010): 195–216.

CHAPTER 4

1. Harry M. Lydenberg to Keyes D. Metcalf, Juy 4, 1945; Luther Evans to Secretary of State, July 17, 1945, Container 400, folder: LCM, ACQ 5-11, Records of the LC Central File, MacLeish-Evans, LC Archives, Manuscript Division, LC. For important background, see John Cole, "The Library of Congress Becomes a World Library, 1815-2005," *Libraries & Culture* 40 (2005): 385–398; Pamela Spence Richards, *Scientific Information in Wartime: The Allied-German Rivalry, 1939–1945* (Westport, CT: Greenwood Press, 1994); John Conoway, *America's Library: The Story of the Library of Congress* (New Haven, CT: Yale University Press, 2000); Gary E. Kraske, *Missionaries of the Book: The American Library Profession and the Origins of United States Cultural Diplomacy* (Westport, CT: Greenwood Press, 1985). See also Reuben Peiss, "European Wartime Acquisitions and the Library of Congress Mission," *LJ* 71 (1946): 863–876.

2. Harry M. Lydenberg, "Notes on the talk by Luther Evans," October 6, 1945, box 60, folder: LC, Evans, Luther H., UA III 50.8.11.3, Records of the Director of the Harvard University Library, Keyes D. Metcalf, 1937–1955, Harvard University Archives.

3. Mason Hammond to Keyes D. Metcalf, April 22, 1944, box 31, folder: Hammond, Capt. Mason, Metcalf Records. "Memorandum on Hoover Library Collection Activities as of May 1, 1946," 19, BAEF Subject Files, Collecting Activities,

Corr. and Memoranda, 1944–1946, folder: HI, BAEF Records, HHPL. Charles E. Dornbusch to F.M., October 23, 1944; Dornbusch to F.M., January 26, [1945]; Stanley R. Pillsbury to Karl Küp, June 7, 1944, box 7, folder: D. O., Hopper, Correspondence WWII, General Library Staff, A-K, Franklin F. Hopper Papers, NYPL Archives, NYPL, Astor, Lenox and Tilden Foundations.

4. Harvard College Library, Order Department, Annual Report, 1942–1943, 1-2, box 36, folder: Annual Report, 1942–1943, Metcalf Records.

5. Frederick G. Kilgour to Adele Kibre, September 20, 1943, IDC/Washington Correspondence, Entry 64, IDC Correspondence Received from Washington, London and Paris, OSS Records, RG 226, NACP. Peiss, "European Wartime Acquisitions," 864.

6. "Documents sent by F. B. Ludington in preparation for meeting on International Cultural Relations, Feb. 11–12, 1942," 2, box 3, folder: IRB Organization and Policy Memoranda, ALA International Relations Committee Papers, Rare Books and Manuscripts Library, Columbia University. Office of Alien Property Custodian, "Report on Periodical Republication Program," November 1, 1945; Eugene A. Tilleux, "Withdrawal by the Custodian from the Periodical Republication Program; Some Elements of the Program Involved," May 25, 1945 (Washington, DC: US Office of Alien Property Custodian, 1945). "Report of the Meeting to Discuss the Proposed Project of Reprinting Foreign Research Materials . . . , Thursday, Dec. 2, 1943," box 61, folder: ALA-Joint Committee on Importations; Eugene Power, "Plan for Cooperative Reproduction of Wartime Publications," June 1945, box 61, folder: Foreign Purchases, Metcalf Records. Douglas Waples and Harold D. Lasswell, *National Libraries and Foreign Scholarship* (Chicago: University of Chicago Press, 1936). Carol A. Nemeyer, *Scholarly Reprint Publishing in the United States* (New York: R. R. Bowker, 1972), ch. 4.

7. Lydenberg to Carl Milam, Metcalf, and Charles H. Brown, April 16, 1945, box 15, Library Director's and Librarian's File, Metcalf Records.

8. Wouter Nijhoff Jr., to Metcalf, July 31, 1945; Nijhoff to Brown, September 14, 1945, box 78, folder: Nijhoff, Wouter, Metcalf Records. Reuben Peiss to W. Bedell Smith, November 1, 1945, box 29, folder: Publications, Stored, LCM and CAP, 1942–1957, Records, Manuscript Division, LC. See also Hendrik Edelman, "Nijhoff in America: Booksellers from the Netherlands and the Development of American Research Libraries—Part I," *Quærendo* 40 (2010): 166–226; B. H. Wabeke, "Dutch Underground Publications," *QJCA* 4, no. 2 (February 1947): 3–7. On Hafner's efforts in Paris, see Ross Lee Finney to Gretchen Finney, February 10, 1945, February 12, 1945, folder 7, box 2, series I, Correspondence, 1916–1996, Sub-Series 1, Personal, Ross Lee Finney Papers, JPB 04-15, Music Division, NYPL for the Performing Arts; Walter A. Hafner, "The French Book Situation," *LJ* 70 (January 15, 1945): 77. Librarie E. Droz to Gertrude M. Sullivan, March 1, 1945; Brown to Robert S. Morison, February 17, 1945, box 61, Folder: Foreign Purchases.

9. Metcalf to Thomas P. Fleming, March 22, 1945, November 22, 1944, folder: ALA-Joint Committee on Importations; Metcalf to Lydenberg, May 28, 1945, box 61, folder: LCM to Europe, Metcalf Records. William Warner Bishop to Flora B. Ludington, August 19, 1943, box 1, folder: IRB Correspondence 1942-44, ALA International Relations Committee Papers. Archibald MacLeish, Metcalf, and Robert B. Downs, "Forty-five replies were received," October 12, 1944, box 17, folder: ARL Committee on Postwar Competition, Metcalf Records. On library competition in World War I, see Keyes DeWitt Metcalf, *My Harvard Library Years,*

1937–1955 (Cambridge, MA: Harvard College Library, 1988), 203–204. Lydenberg to D.H. Arneson, November 11, 1944, RS 7/1/6, box 18, folder: Office of War Information, ALA Archives at the University of Illinois at Urbana-Champaign.

10. Archibald MacLeish, "A Challenge and a Program for American Libraries," [Oct 1942], Farmington Plan Documents, Vol. I, 79–80, 82, UAIII 50.29.40.26, Metcalf Records. Keyes D. Metcalf and Edwin E. Williams, "Proposal for a Division of Responsibility among American Libraries in the Acquisition and Recording of Library Materials," *CRL* (March 1944): 105–109. Ralph D. Wagner, *A History of the Farmington Plan* (Lanham, MD: Scarecrow Press, 2002).

11. Metcalf to Edward R. Stettinius, May 12, 1945, box 61, folder: LCM to Europe.

12. Felix Reichmann to Evans, June 28, 1945, box 33, folder: Reichmann, Felix; Sargent B. Child to Evans, July 12, 1945, box 33, folder: Child, Sargent, LCM Records. James L. Williams, "Disposal of Certain Duplicate Documents," July 16, 1945, box 16, folder: LCM (USFET), Foreign Records Seized, Records Relating to the Acquisition and Disposition of German Records During and After World War II, RG 242, NACP. Harold C. Deutsch to William L. Langer and Chandler Morse, "Report on Activities in Washington, July 14–26," July 26 1945, 6, box 24, folder 2, Entry 1, Office of the Chief, General Correspondence, OSS Records, RG 226.

13. Lydenberg to Metcalf, August 7, 1945, Container 400, folder: Association of Research Libraries, ACQ 5-11-1, LC Central File.

14. Evans to James T. Babb, September 17, 1945, ACQ 5-11-1. Cole, "The Library of Congress Becomes a World Library."

15. Frank Monaghan to Metcalf, August 31, 1945, box 61, folder: Foreign Purchases. Lydenberg to Metcalf, August 5, 1945, Container 392, folder: cooperation with government, ACQ 5-3-2, LC Central File.

16. Peiss to Verner W. Clapp, December 27, 1945, box 32, folder: Peiss, Reuben; Lucius D. Clay to Bradley Dewey, July 15, 1945, box 33, folder: Child, Sargent; CG USFET Main to War Dept., incoming classified message, December 4, 1945, box 10, unmarked folder, LCM Records.

17. Child to Evans, September 26, 1945, box 33, folder: Stuurman, Douwe; Evans to H. H. Fischer, October 4, 1945, box 29, folder: Policy, Hoover Library, LCM Records. For a summary of the arrangement, see Evans to Kenneth C. Royall, January 9, 1946, Box 23, folder U, Harry Miller Lydenberg Papers, Manuscripts and Archives Division, NYPL.

18. Peiss to Kilgour, October 27, 1945, box 10, folder: Commendations, LCM Records; Evans to Babb, October 18, 1945, ACQ 5-11-1.

19. Peiss to Clapp, November 1, 1945, box 32, folder: Reports, Peiss, Reuben, LCM Records. See also Peiss to W. Bedell Smith, "Storage and Shipment of publications being held in the ETO," November 1, 1945, box 29, folder: Publications, Stored, LCM Records; Peiss, "European Wartime Acquisitions."

20. HQ USFET, Eisenhower for Evans, outgoing restricted message, November 8, 1945, box 11, folder: LCM Cables, Outgoing; Peiss to A. G. Stahl, August 28, 1945, box 5, folder: Agent—Berlin—Duncker & Humblot, 1945–1946; "Telephone Conference between Mr. Peiss and Mr. Clapp, 31 October 1945," box 14, folder: Telecons, LCM Records.

21. Child to Evans, September 26, 1945; Peiss to H. W. Helm and F. N. Saur, September 28, 1945, box 29, folder: Policy Program Planning; Peiss, "Memorandum to All Representatives of the LCM," January 23, 1946, box 32, folder: Reports, Peiss, Reuben, LCM Records.

22. "Telephone Conference," 31 October 1945; "Mr. Peiss and Mr. Taube, Washington 1-1-1, December 27, 1945," 13; "Telephone conference between Mr. Peiss and Mr. Clapp," TC 4739, November 9, 1945, box 14, folder: Telecons.

23. Max Loeb to Peiss, "Report on T-Force Operation in Northern Bavaria, 26–30 Sept.," September 30, 1945, box 9, folder: Alfred Rosenberg Collections; Loeb to Peiss, "Report of activities during December 1945," January 8, 1946, box 34, folder: Targets, LCM Records.

24. Jacob Zuckerman to Friedel Zuckerman, January 7, 1946, January 6, 1946: I am grateful to Miriam Intrator and Alex Zuckerman for sharing these letters and Josef Nothmann for translations. On Zuckerman's background, see Harry N. Rosenfield to Salo Baron, July 24, 1947, box 39, folder 3, Salo W. Baron Papers, M0580, Department of Special Collections, Stanford University Libraries. On his important work for UNESCO, see Miriam Intrator, *Books Across Borders: UNESCO and the Politics of Postwar Cultural Reconstruction, 1945-51* (Basingstoke, UK: Palgrave Macmillan, 2019).

25. Child to Evans, September 26, 1945. Douwe Stuurman, *A Rhodes Scholar's View of Nazi Germany*, Oral History by David E. Russell (Davidson Library Oral History Program, 1982), OH 13, Department of Special Collections, University of California Santa Barbara Library; telephone conversation with Yvonne Pine (Stuurman's niece), March 14, 2014.

26. Peiss to Metcalf, January 4, 1946, box 81, folder: Reuben Peiss, Metcalf Records. Peiss to Clapp, October 14, 1945, November 1, 1945, box 32, folder: Reports, Peiss; Peiss to Clift, October 19, 1945, box 31, folder: Clift, David H., LCM Records.

27. "Telephone Conference Between Mr. Peiss and Mr. Clapp," TC-4930, November 29, 1945, box 14, folder: Telecons; "Telephone conference," November 9, 1945. Lydenberg to Metcalf, January 20, 1946, box 15, folder: ALA, Lydenberg, 1945-Aug. 1, 1946, UAIII 50.8.11.10, Metcalf Records. Phyllis Dain, "Harry M. Lydenberg and American Library Resources: A Study in Modern Library Leadership," *LQ* 47 (October 1977): 451–469.

28. Richard S. Hill, "Concert Life in Berlin Season 1943-44," *Notes*, 2nd Ser., 1 (June 1944): 13–33. Charles Warren Fox, et al., "Richard S. Hill: A Reminiscence," *Notes*, 2nd Ser., 18 (June 1961): 369–380; Dena J. Epstein, comp., "Buying Music in War-torn Germany with Richard S. Hill," *Notes*, 2nd Ser., 37 (March 1981): 503–519.

29. Lydenberg to Harvey and Sally Basham, March 24, 1946, box 1, folder Ba-Be, Lydenberg Papers. David H. Clift to Eleanore Clift, February 3, 1946, January 20, 1946, box 3, folder: Eleanore Clift, 1946, David H. Clift Papers, 1927–1972, Series 2/44/24, ALA Archives.

30. "Notes, Berlin—5 February 1946," box 30, folder: Regulations: Instructions—Directives, LCM Records. D. Clift to E. Clift, February 3, 1946.

31. Reuben Peiss, "Report on Europe," *CRL* (April 1947): 115. Clift to Clapp, April 4, 1946, box 31, folder: Clift, David H. Epstein, "Buying Music," 505. Hill to Ed Waters, May 4, 1946, Dena J. Epstein Papers, Center for Black Music Research, Columbia College Chicago.

32. Peiss to Clapp, August 5, 1946, box 32, folder: Reports, Peiss; "Notes, Berlin—5 February 1946."

33. Peiss to Clapp, August 5, 1946.

34. "Interview with Dr. Broermann on January 20, 1946," box 5, folder: Duncker & Humblot; Clift to Clapp, March 1, 1946, box 31, folder: Clift, David H.; Lydenberg

to Peiss, February 23, 1946, box 32, folder: Lydenberg, Harry M., LCM Records. Peiss, "Report on Europe," 114.

35. F. A. Brockhaus to Lydenberg, April 4, 1946; Lydenberg to Clapp, January 17, 1946, box 5, folder: Agents, Brockhaus, F. A. Fleming to Peiss, August 31, 1946, 2, box 31, folder: Reports, Fleming, Thomas P., LCM Records.

36. Richard S. Hill, "Report on Acquisition of Music," February 23, 1946, box 33, folder: Reports, Zuckerman, J.; Epstein, "Buying Music," 505. Hill to "Harold [Spivacke] and Ed[ward Waters], etc.," April 5, 1946, box 3, folder: Music, General, LCM Records. Richard S. Hill, "Buying Music in Germany," *QJCA* 4 (November 1946): 15–25.

37. Hill to Harold and Ed, April 5, 1946, 2, 5; Hill to Ed Waters, May 4, 1946, Epstein Papers. Vincent Giroud, *Nicolas Nabokov: A Life of Freedom and Music* (New York: Oxford University Press, 2015), ch. 10.

38. Hill to Harold and Ed, April 5, 1946, 6–7. Walter Hinrichsen to Harold Spivacke, November 23, 1945; Peiss to Clapp, May 25, 1946; Richard S. Hill, "Postmortem to Mr. Peiss on arrangements for acquisition of Peters publications," May 22, 1946, box 3, folder: Music, General. William Lichtenwanger, "Walter Hinrichsen, 23 September 1907–21 July 1969," *Notes* 2nd Ser., 26 (March 1970): 491–493.

39. Zuckerman to Peiss, report no. 3, n.d., box 33, Reports, Zuckerman.

40. Dr. Alfred Hildebrandt to the American Government in Frankfurt, 16 Sept [1945]; Lydenberg to Peiss, January 30, 1946; Hildebrandt to A. F. Zahm, November 4, 1946, box 8, folder: Hildebrandt Collection, LCM Records. On the collection, see Richard Eells, "Aeronautics," *QJCA* 4 (August 1947): 25–26.

41. Peiss to Stuurman, "Library of Dr. Ludwig Mach," December 28, 1945, and earlier reports in box 8, folder: Ludwig Mach Library; Peiss to Metcalf, July 25, 1946, box 34, folder: Harvard, LCM Records.

42. Peiss to Metcalf, June 24, 1945, box 61, folder: Foreign Purchases. Albert C. Gerould to Verner W. Clapp, June 25, 1945, Box 31, folder: Gerould, Albert C., LCM Records. Max Loeb had learned of the Leipzig materials a month earlier but his report was classified; Loeb, "Continuation of Report on T-Force Operation," May 21–23, 1945, box 3, Entry 81, OSS Mission to Germany, RG 226.

43. Peiss to Metcalf, July 24, 1945. Babb to Evans, September 21, 1945, ACQ 5-11-1. Clarence E. Mitchell, Order, April 24, 1945, box 5, folder: Agents, Harrassowitz, Otto; "The German Book-trade at the Time of Occupation by the Allied Military Government," box 32, folder: Peiss, Reuben.

44. Hans Harrassowitz to Lydenberg, March 27, 1946, box 5, folder: Agents, Harrassowitz, Otto. Peiss to Clapp, February 13, 1946, box 32, folder: Peiss, Reuben. Gerould to Milam, June 2, 1945, box 4, folder: ALA, Milam, Metcalf Records.

45. Child to Evans, February 5, 1946, box 31, folder: Child, Sargent; Lydenberg to Metcalf, April 2, 1946, box 32, folder: Lydenberg's files, LCM Records. Zuckerman to Clift and Lydenberg, March 12, 1946, box 33, Folder: Reports, Zuckerman.

46. Peiss to Mortimer Taube, August 12, 1946, August 16, 1946, box 32, folder: Reports, Peiss; Peiss, "Memorandum concerning export problem," July 6, 1946, box 30, folder: Regulations: Exports and Imports, LCM Records. "Reminiscences of Hellmut Lehmann-Haupt: Lecture, 1967 [A Bookman's Odyssey]," March 17, 1967, 28–29, Columbia Center for Oral History Archives, Columbia University Libraries. Douglas Waples, *On the March: A Short Autobiography for Friends and Family* (Washington Island, WI, 1967), 7.

47. Joseph Groesbeck, "Report of tour of duty with the LCM, 24 March–30 Sept. 1946," October 1, 1946; Groesbeck to Evans, October 3, 1946, box 31, folder: Reports, Groesbeck, Joseph, LCM Records.

48. Peiss to Taube, August 16, 1946. Peiss to Clift, telegram, August 9, 1946, box 67, folder 938, Librarian, Yale University, Records (RU 120), Manuscripts and Archives, Yale University Library.

49. Peiss to Clapp, October 15, 1946, box 3, folder: LCM, RS 97/1/32, Scott Adams Papers, 1920–1981, ALA Archives.

50. Lydenberg to Evans, April 25, 1946. Taube to Clapp, November 2, 1946, box 33, folder: Reports, Taube, Mortimer. Peiss to Dr. Eppelsheimer, October 16, 1946; Peiss, "Memo for MT," October 20, 1946, box 7, folder: Bibliography. Scott Adams, "Comments on the LCM," December 6, 1946, box 30, folder: Reports, Adams, Scott, LCM Records.

51. Clapp to Metcalf, May 9, 1946, box 16, folder: CAP, General, Harvard; Clift, Memorandum for Mr. Stuurman, Mr. Zuckerman, Mr. Fleming, June 13, 1946, box 1, folder: Acquisitions, general, LCM Records.

52. Peiss, "Memorandum to all Representatives," January 23, 1946; Peiss, "Memorandum to All Detachments," June 17, 1946, box 16, folder: Confiscated material; Peiss, "Disposition of German publications now impounded in Lisbon," February 27, 1946, box 1, folder: Acquisitions, general, LCM Records.

53. "Samlung Rehse," box 9, folder, Rehse Library, LCM Records.

54. Metcalf to Peiss, October 23, 1945, box 81, folder: Reuben Peiss, Metcalf Records. "Conference between Mr. Peiss and Mr. Clapp," 17 September 1945; "Telephone Conference Between Mr. Peiss and Mr. Clapp," November 29, 1945, 7, 9. Peiss to Clapp, September 21, 1946, box 7, folder: Eher Verlag, 1946. Don C. Travis to Chief, MFAA Section, August 31, 1946; Max Lederer, "Raw Material of History" (n.d.), box 9, folder: Rehse Library, LCM Records.

55. Peiss to Clapp, September 21, 1946; Peiss to [Stuurman], "Miscellaneous Notes Concerning Munich Operation, February 2, 1946," box 8, folder: Ludwig Mach Library.

56. Stuurman to Peiss, "Material now on hand and being readied for shipment," February 14, 1946, box 1, folder: Acq: clearances, shipments; Stuurman, "Weekly Report 6 Jan–12 Jan 46," January 14, 1946, folder: Ludwig Mach Library. Stuurman, "The Nazi Collection: An Appraisal," box 8, folder: Nazi Material; see also Douwe Stuurman, "The Nazi Collection: A Preliminary Note," *QJCA* 6 (November 1948): 21–22. Cf. LC's most notorious wartime acquisition, Timothy W. Rybeck, *Hitler's Private Library: The Books That Shaped His Life* (New York: Knopf, 2008).

57. Hill, "Report on Acquisition of Music"; Hill to David H. Clift, "Films," 7, March 9, 1946, box 9, folder: UFA Films, LCM Records.

58. Peiss to W. J. Muller, July 12, 1946, box 8, folder: Himmler Collection, LCM Records. Himmler's library should not be confused with the Himmler Collection of archival records at the US National Archives. Hill to Clift, "Films," 4. Vanderbilt to Peiss, January 30, 1946, box 9, folder: Ullstein photographic collection; Peiss to Evans, March 23, 1946, box 16, folder: Confiscated material. Zuckerman to Clift, March 15, 1946; Richard S. Hill, "Report 26–Berlin," April 13, 1945, box 33, folder: Reports, Zuckerman.

59. *Annual Report of the Librarian of Congress, 1946* (Washington, DC: GPO, 1946), 261–268. Clapp to Peiss, April 9, 1946, box 16, folder: Confiscated material; "LC Holdings Captured Enemy Documentation," February 15, 1950, box 16, folder: Complaints, LCM Records.

60. Peiss to Zuckerman, June 18, 1946, box 9, folder: Hans Reich Library; Lucy Reynolds to Peiss cable, September 22, 1945, box 11, folder: LCM Cables, Outgoing, LCM Records. Verner Clapp misleadingly claimed to the US High Commissioner for Germany that Loeb had purchased the library from Reich before he was a member of the LCM; Clapp to F. S. Hannaman, June 10, 1953, folder: Hans Reich Library. R. Lechner and W. V. Steiner to Luther Evans, February 19, 1949 (trans. Max Lederer, April 6, 1949), box 31, folder: Max Loeb; Herbert Reichner to Evans, April 14, 1947, folder: Complaints.

61. Peiss to Loeb, June 10, 1946, box 27, folder: personnel; Taube to Loeb, November 8, 1946, box 31, folder: Max Loeb; Taube to Clapp, November 11, 1946, box 33, folder: Reports, Taube. Clift to Lydenberg, July 23, 1946, July 31, 1946, box 2, folder C, Lydenberg Papers.

62. Taube to Clapp, November 8, 1946. Kenneth D. Alford, *Allied Looting in World War II: Thefts of Art, Manuscripts, Stamps and Jewelry in Europe* (Jefferson, NC: McFarland, 2011).

63. Peiss to Evans, March 23, 1946, box 16, folder: Confiscated material; Peiss, "Status of LCM to Germany—Summary Report," May 8, 1946, box 32, folder: Reports, Peiss. Jacob Zuckerman to LCM, April 23, 1946, folder: Reports, Zuckerman.

64. Peiss to Evans, March 23, 1946.

65. Peiss to Clay, October 23, 1946, box 29, folder: Policy Proposals, 1946; Peiss to Clapp, December 4, 1946, box 6, folder: Order No. 4.

66. Taube to Clapp, November 21, 1946, box 33, folder: Taube, Mortimer; Janet Emerson to Luther H. Evans, "Report of the Secretary of the LCM," October 20, 1947, box 31, folder: Emerson, Janet, LCM Records.

67. Peiss, "Report on Europe," 11; Peiss, "European Acquisitions"; *LC Information Bulletin*, June 8-14, 1948, Appendix, 11; Hill, "Buying Music in Germany," 25.

CHAPTER 5

1. "Times to Publish Goebbels' Diaries," *NYT*, January 25, 1948; Willard Shelton, "U.S. Asks How Hoover Got Goebbels Diary," *PM*, March 3, 1948.

2. George H. Nash, *Herbert Hoover and Stanford University* (Stanford, CA: Hoover Institution Press, 1988), 109. Perrin C. Galpin to Jan Karski, April 17, 1945, box 10, folder 10, Jan Karski Papers, HIA. H. H. Fisher, "Memorandum on Collecting in Europe," October 12, 1944, BAEF Subject Files, Collecting Activities, Corr., 1944–1946, BAEF Records, HHPL. Peter Duignan, "The Library of the Hoover Institution on War, Revolution, and Peace, Part I," *Library History* 17 (March 2001): 3–19. See also Gary Dean Best, *Herbert Hoover: The Post-Presidential Years, 1933-1964*, vol. 2 (Stanford, CA: Hoover Institution Press, 1983), 285–293; Glen Jeansonne, *Herbert Hoover, A Life* (New York: New American Library, 2016), 315–378. The name of the library changed over time: from the Hoover War Collection (1922–1937) to Hoover Library on War, Revolution and Peace (1937–1948); since 1957, it is part of the Hoover Institution on War, Revolution and Peace. For simplicity's sake, I refer to it throughout as the Hoover Library.

3. Louis Chevrillon to Herbert Hoover, October 24, 1945, BAEF Subject Files, Collectors, Chevrillon, Louis. Jacques van der Belen to Galpin, October 19, 1944; Madame L. Swaelus-Godenne and van der Belen to Gentlemen, February 2, 1945; to H. H. Fisher, April 26, 1945, BAEF Subject Files, Collections Sought, Belgian Collection, 1944–1948. "Inventory of a collection of documents originating from the NAZI 'Propaganda Abteilung Belgien,'" BAEF Subject Files, Collecting Activities, Corr., Almond, Nina.

4. Fisher to Grace E. Fox, June 3, 1944, Collecting Activities, Corr., 1944-46. Stephen Mizwa to Galpin, October 31, 1944; Fisher to John P. Gregg, October 20, 1944, BAEF Subject Files, Collectors, Gregg, John P. Fisher, "Memorandum on Collecting in Europe." *NYT*, March 24, 1945, 7.

5. Jan Karski, *Story of a Secret State: My Report to the World* (1944; rpt. London: Penguin, 2011), 260–261. Galpin to Fisher, March 21, 1945, BAEF Subject Files, Collectors, Karski, Jan, 1945 March–May. Bertrand M. Patenaude, *A Wealth of Ideas: Revelations from the Hoover Institution Archives* (Stanford, CA: Stanford University Press, 2006), 154–156; Cissie Dore Hill, "Jan Karski and the Hoover Institution," *Hoover Digest*, no. 4 (October 30, 2000), www.hoover.org/research/jan-karski-and-hoover-institution.

6. Karski to Galpin, n.d., box 10, folder 10, Karski Papers. Karski to Galpin, February 3, 1946, BAEF Subject Files, Collectors, Karski, 1946, Jan.–Feb. Galpin to Fisher, July 22, 1946, Collectors, Karski, 1946 July–Nov. Alexander Piskor to Fisher, November 10, 1945, Collectors, Karski, 1945 December. G. G. Hay to Hoover, March 15, 1946; "Gold Stuck to his Skin," *Evening Standard*, March 5, 1946; Karski to "Dear Sir," March 7, 1946, Collectors, Karski, 1946 March–June.

7. Merrill Spalding to "My Dear Chief," October 18, 1944, Collectors, Spalding, Merrill T., 1944. Fisher to Galpin, October 13, 1944; Spalding to Galpin, April 7, 1945, May 29, 1945; "Excerpts from letter to Harold Fisher, March 30, 1945," Collectors, Spalding, 1945; Fisher, "Memorandum for Mr. Spalding," October 11, 1944, Collecting Activities, Corr., 1944–1946.

8. William Heimlich, "In the first place" [ca. 1976], 40, folder 74093-10.V, William Heimlich Collection, HIA. On postwar conditions, see William I. Hitchcock, *The Bitter Road to Freedom: A New History of the Liberation of Europe* (New York: Free Press, 2008); Atina Grossman, *Jews, Germans, and Allies: Close Encounters in Occupied Germany* (Princeton, NJ: Princeton University Press), 2007.

9. John Brown Mason to Fisher, August 2, 1945, BAEF Subject Files, Collectors, Mason, John Brown, 1945. Fisher to Frank E. Mason, August 26, 1946, HI Collecting Activities of Frank E. Mason, 1946, Frank E. Mason Papers, HHPL. Albert Gerould to Verner W. Clapp, August 4, 1945, box 31, folder: Gerould, Albert C., LCM and CAP, 1942–1957, Records, Manuscript Division, LC. See also Galpin to Fisher, October 18, 1945; Fisher to Galpin, October 22, 1945, Collectors, Mason, John Brown. "Comment and Historical News," *Pacific Historical Review* 15 (March 1946): 132.

10. Frank E. Mason to Ellen Mason, August 20, 1945, August 29, 1945, Germany: Corr. and Memoranda, 1945 Aug.; Mason to Ellen Mason, September 11, 1945; Mason to "Brothers Snevily and MacNeil," September 13, 1945, box 4, Germany, Corr. and Memoranda, 1945 Sept. 1–15; Diary no. 4, 1945 (Sept.6–9) Berlin; Mason to Hoover, July 25, 1945, HI Collecting Activities of Frank E. Mason, 1945. "Memorandum for Mr. Hoover" [March 19, 1948], Goebbels Diary Corr., 1947-48, Mason Papers. Col. William F. Heimlich Oral History, vol. 1, session 1, HHPL; Raymond Henle, "Oral History Interview with Louis Paul Lochner, Hilde S. (Mrs. Louis) Lochner, participating," March 2, 1968, part 1, 32, Oral History Collection, HHPL. Louis P. Lochner, *Always the Unexpected: A Book of Reminiscences* (New York: Macmillan, 1956). On US war correspondents, see Steven Casey, *The War Beat, Europe: The American Media at War Against Nazi Germany* (New York: Oxford University Press, 2017).

11. Heimlich, "In the first place," 25, 28–30, 36. William F. Heimlich, "The Eagle and the Bear, Berlin, 1945-50," n.d., 31, 32, 57, 62, folder 74093-10.V, Heimlich Collection, HIA.

12. Mason to Ellen Mason, August 20, 1945. Mason to Hoover, August 27, 1945, Germany: Corr. and Memoranda, 1945 Aug.; Mason to Hoover, "Documents," September 1, 1945, Germany: Corr. and Memoranda, 1945 Sept. 1–15. The AP's Willy Brandt was not the German chancellor of the same name. On Frydman, see Lisa Moses Leff, *The Archive Thief: The Man Who Salvaged French Jewish History in the Wake of the Holocaust* (New York: Oxford University Press, 2015).

13. Heimlich Oral History, vol. 1, HHPL, 5. Mason to Hoover, "Documents." Mason, 1943–1947 Diary, August 19–24, 1945 entries, Mason Papers.

14. Mason, Diary no. 5, 1945 (Sept. 10–14) Berlin-Frankfurt, September 14, 1945. Hoover to Louis P. Lochner, November 13, 1945, BAEF Subject Files, Collectors, Lochner, Louis, 1946 Sept.–Dec., BAEF Records. For the investigation of Brandt, see "Vetting of Willy Erwin Hermann Brandt," January 8, 1946; Intelligence Section, ICS, OMGUS, "Circumstances Surrounding the Investigation of Willy Brandt," January 24, 1946; Louis P. Lochner, "1946" [May & July, 1946]; Willy Brandt, "a confession" [1946], reel 3, Micro 860/US Mss 21AF, Series General Correspondence, Louis Paul Lochner Papers, Wisconsin Historical Society. This history has recently come to light: Harriet Scharnberg, "Das A und P der Propaganda: Associated Press und die nationalsozialistiche Bildpublizistik," *Zeithistorische Forschungen/Studies in Contemporary History* 13 (2016):11–37.

15. "Excerpts from letter to Harold Fisher." HQ USFET to War Dept. G-2 for LC for Evans, September 8, 1945, box 11, folder: LCM Cables, Outgoing; Luther H. Evans to Ralph E. Doty, September 18, 1945, box 29, folder: Policy, Hoover War Library, LCM Records. Evans to Robert P. Patterson, February 26, 1946, box 51, folder: Hoover War Library, UA III.50.8.11.3, Records of the Harvard University Library, Keyes D. Metcalf, 1937–1955, Harvard University Archives.

16. Hoover to Clayton Bissell, October 29, 1945; Bissell to Hoover, December 13, 1945, BAEF Subject Files, Collections Sought, Germany, 1945. On military assistance to Mason, see Lochner to Hoover, September 8, 1946, reel 11, Lochner Papers.

17. Hoover to Patterson, May 16, 1946, BAEF Subject Files, Collectors, Lochner, 1946 Jan-Aug. Galpin to Fisher, February 14, 1946, BAEF Subject Files, Collecting Activities, LC Joint Effort, 1944–1945. "Telephone Conference Between Mr. Peiss and Mr. Clapp," TC5575, February 9, 1946, box 14, folder: Telecons, LCM Records. On Hoover's food mission, see Best, *Herbert Hoover*, 286–299.

18. *New York Tribune* clipping, March 18, 1946, BAEF Subject Files, Hoover, Herbert, Trips, Europe 1946; "Memorandum on Hoover Library Collection Activities as of May 1, 1946," Collecting Activities, Corr. and Memoranda, 1944-46; Galpin to Charles Delzell, March 8, 1946, Subject Files, Collectors, Delzell, Charles. Charles F. Delzell, "War and Anti-Fascism: A Personal Memoir," April 21, 1989, UA Biographical Files, Special Collections and University Archives, University of Oregon Libraries.

19. Galpin to Edgar Rickard, April 13, 1946; Van Der Belen to Rickard, April 10, 1946, Hoover, Trips, Europe 1946.

20. Hugh Gibson diary, April 13, 1946, vol. 1, March 17–April 26, 1946, Hugh Gibson Papers, HIA, https://digitalcollections.hoover.org/objects/51424.

21. Reuben Peiss to Harry M. Lydenberg, February 11, 1947, box 5, folder P, Harry Miller Lydenberg Papers, Manuscripts and Archives Division, NYPL. Lochner to Hoover, September 8, 1946; *Christian Science Monitor* clipping, March 21, 1947, BAEF Subject Files, Clippings and Press Releases, 1924–1961; "Memorandum on Hoover Library Collection Activities as of May 1, 1946."

22. Peiss to David H. Clift, May 23, 1946, box 16, folder: Confiscated material, LCM Records. Patterson to Hoover, June 13, 1946, Collectors, Lochner, 1946 Jan.-Aug. "Vita, Daniel Lerner," September 1, 1946, BAEF Subject Files, Collectors, Lerner, Dan, 1946. Lerner would go on to become a leading expert on mass communications and modernization; see Hemant Shah, *The Production of Modernization: Daniel Lerner, Mass Media, and the Passing of Traditional Society* (Philadelphia: Temple University Press, 2011), 31–57.

23. Lochner to Hoover, September 8, 1946, September 24, 1946, September 13, 1946, October 9, 1946, October 1, 1946, reel 11, Lochner Papers.

24. Lochner to Hoover, August 1, 1946, August 17, 1946, August 23, 1946, reel 11. "Oral History Interview with Louis Paul Lochner," 41–42.

25. Lochner to Hoover, September 28, 1946, August 30, 1946, reel 11.

26. Lochner to Hoover, September 24, 1946. Daniel Lerner to Fisher, December 22, 1946, box 7, folder 20, Daniel Lerner Papers (MC 336), Archives and Special Collections, Massachusetts Institute of Technology (MIT). For examples of PWD documents, see Daniel Lerner, *Sykewar: Psychological Warfare against Germany, D-Day to VE Day* (New York: George W. Stewart, 1949).

27. Lerner to Fisher, March 30, 1947, box 7, folder 21, Lerner Papers, MIT.

28. Lerner to Fisher, March 30, 1947. Lerner to Fisher, January 5, 1947, BAEF Subject Files, Collectors, Lerner, 1947 Jan.-March.

29. Lerner to Fisher, December 22, 1946; December 1, 1946, box 7, folder 20, Lerner Papers, MIT.

30. Brandt to Bernice Miller, February 13, 1946, Collecting Activities of Frank E. Mason, 1946. Leo D. Fialkoff to Chief of Intelligence, ICS, "Report on Berlin Black Market and German Attitudes towards It," September 20, 1945, box 82, folder 17, Daniel Lerner Collection, HIA. Lochner to Fisher, September 24, 1946, reel 11, Lochner Papers.

31. Michael Barnett, *Empire of Humanity: A History of Humanitarianism* (Ithaca, NY: Cornell University Press, 2011), 104–117; Philipp Baur, "From Victim to Partner: CARE and the Portrayal of Postwar Germany," in *Die amerikanische Reeducation-Politik nach 1945*, ed. Katharina Gerund and Heike Paul (Bielefeld: Transcript Verlag, 2015), 115–140; Susan Levine, "'The Moral Challenge of Abundance': Humanitarianism and the Rise of the Food Aid Complex After World War II," unpublished paper, October 16, 2015. My thanks to Susan Levine for information on CARE and postwar food aid.

32. Lochner to Hoover, August 23, 1946. Lerner to Fisher, February 16, 1947, Collectors, Lerner, 1947 Jan. –March.

33. Lochner to Hoover, September 8, 1946. Lerner to Fisher, February 16, 1947.

34. Lerner to Galpin, January 19, 1947, Collectors, Lerner, 1947 Jan. –March. Lochner to Peiss, October 10, 1946, box 31, folder: Lochner, Louis P., LCM Records. Lerner to Fisher, May 24, 1947, Collectors, Lerner, 1947 April-Sept. Mortimer Taube to Verner Clapp, October 16, 1946, box 31, folder: Reports, Lochner, Louis P., LCM Records. RGS, "Memorandum for the Record," November 28, 1947, no. 1440, Entry #UD 282-BB, Foreign Records Seized, Material Accumulated for a Conference on Captured German and Related Records, RG 242, NACP.

35. Lochner to Fisher, September 24, 1946. Lerner to Galpin, January 19, 1947, Collectors, Lerner, 1947 Jan.–March; Lerner to Fisher, February 16, 1947.

36. On the diaries' history, see Astrid M. Eckert and Stefan Martens, "Glasplatten im märkischen Sand: Ein Beitrag zur Überlieferungsgeschichte der Tageseinträge und

Diktate von Joseph Goebbels," *Vierteljahrshefte für Zeitgeschichte* 52 (2004): 479–526; Elke Frölich, "Einleitung," in *Die Tagebücher von Joseph Goebbels*, ed. Elke Frölich, Part III, 1923-45 (Munich: K. G. Saur, 2008).

37. On Frank Korf's role in the investigation, see Patricia Kollander, '*I Must Be a Part of This War': A German American's Fight against Hitler and Nazism* (New York: Fordham University Press, 2005), 177–194.

38. "Signed Statement of William F. Heimlich, Berlin, February 18, 1948," binder I (February 28, 1948); Hermine Herta Meyer to Daniel G. McGrath, March 30, 1948; "Interrogation of William Friel Heimlich by Miss Hermine Herta Meyer, Mr. K. Frank Korf and Mr. George H. Elkan," February 21, 1948, binder II (March 30, 1948), box 1, K. Frank Korf Papers, HIA.

39. Meyer to McGrath, March 30, 1948.

40. "Interrogation of Mr. Erwin Richter," February 23, 1948; "Interview with Robert Breier," February 23, 1948, binder II, Korf Papers.

41. Alice Kapp supplementary statement, February 24, 1948; Meyer to McGrath, March 30, 1948, Binder II. Janssen's later account is slightly different; see Werner Hanni, FBI Report, "The Goebbels Diaries, Character of Case, APC Matter, Testimony of Harry H. Janssen," June 16, 1948, folder 2, FBI Case No. 114–182, Record Group 65, Federal Bureau of Investigation Records, NACP. See also Kollander, *I Must be a Part of This War*, 182.

42. Interrogation of William Heimlich, March 16, 1948, Binder II. "Signed Statement of William F. Heimlich"; Meyer to McGrath, March 30, 1948. On Heimlich's activities, see Donald P. Steury, ed., *On the Front Lines of the Cold War: Documents on the Intelligence War in Berlin, 1946-1961* (Washington, DC: CIA History Staff, Center for the Study of Intelligence, 1999), 53–54, 62–64.

43. Robert G. Lawrence, FBI Report, Lt. Col. Hans Helm interview, June 2, 1948, file 114-4, folder 2; Frederic D. Vechery, FBI Report, Francis A. Saur interview, July 12, 1948, file 114–21, folder 1, FBI Case No. 114–182.

44. Gibson diary, February 19, 1947, vol. 3, February 2–22, 1947, Gibson Papers, https://digitalcollections.hoover.org/objects/51425. Gerald J. Driscoll, FBI Report, June 16, 1948, folder 2, FBI Case No. 114–182.

45. Interrogation of William Heimlich, March 16, 1948, February 21, 1948.

46. "Transcript of Telephone Conversation between Frank E. Mason, Eldorado 5-0963 and William F. Heimlich at Berlin 263381, Wednesday, February 18, 1948, 10:30 a.m.," Goebbels Diaries Corr., 1950, Feb. 1–15, Mason Papers; Heimlich to Mason, February 20, 1948, reel 40, Lochner Papers. "Signed Statement of William F. Heimlich"; Interrogation of William Heimlich, March 16, 1948.

47. "Transcript of Telephone Conversation," 4; "Draft by Frank E. Mason," January 22, 1950, reel 40.

48. Hoover to Heimlich, February 20, 1947, reel 40; Lochner to Hoover, September 24, 1946, reel 11, Lochner Papers. Sigrid Schultz, "Bewildering German Tales Offered to U.S. Publishers," *Chicago Tribune*, December 1, 1946.

49. Meyer to McGrath, March 30, 1948.

50. Orville Prescott, "Books of the Times," *NYT*, April 21, 1948; "Diary Kept by Goebbels Damns Him," *Los Angeles Times*, May 2, 1948; Allen W. Dulles, "A Brilliant Distorted Mind," *NYT*, April 25, 1948; "The Goebbels Diaries," *NYT*, March 15, 1948.

51. J.A. Carlson to [Clyde] Tolson, "The Goebbels' Diaries," Office Memorandum, U.S. Government, December 2, 1948, folder 1, FBI Case No. 114-182; "Goebbels Diaries at Stake in Suit," *NYT*, May 18, 1950; Harold I. Baynton to Howard Watson

Ambruster, May 26, 1950, reel 40. David L. Bazelon, Vesting Order 13111, Paul Joseph Goebbels, *Federal Register* 14 (April 9, 1949), 1730, HeinOnline. "On Confirmation of Nomination of Harold I. Baynton, of Nevada, to be Assistant Attorney General, Friday, June 16, 1950," 45–50, Goebbels Diaries, Statement before Senate Judiciary Committee, Mason Papers.

52. Galpin to Fisher, "Re: Goebbels Diary," March 9, 1948, BAEF Subject File, Collections Sought, Goebbels Diary, 1947–1948. Frank Mason to Fulton, December 19, 1949, reel 40. Driscoll to J. Edgar Hoover, "The Goebbels Diaries; Alien Property Custodian Matter," June 16, 1948, folder 2, FBI Case No.114-182. Lochner, *Always the Unexpected*, 318–319. On Heimlich at RIAS, Nicholas J. Schlosser, *Cold War on the Airwaves: The Radio Propaganda War Against East Germany* (Urbana: University of Illinois Press, 2015), 31–32, 45.

53. Mason to Mark Reardon, et al., July 6, 1977, box 5, Goebbels Diaries, Corr., 1949-77, Mason Papers. "On Confirmation of Nomination of Harold I. Baynton"; "Goebbels Diaries at Stake in Suit"; "Senate Hearings End on Book on Goebbels," *NYT*, June 24, 1950.

54. Galpin to Lochner, July 24, 1946, Collectors, Lochner, 1946 Jan.–Aug. Peter Duignan, ed., *The Library of the Hoover Institution on War, Revolution, and Peace* (Stanford, CA: Hoover Institution Press, 1985), 7.

CHAPTER 6

1. Dwight D. Eisenhower to Marvin A. Miller, June 11, 1946, World War II National Defense Subject File, 1940–1946, RS 2/4/60, box 4, National Socialist Publications [NS Pubs], folder 1, ALA Archives. For scholarly discussions of this policy, see Margaret F. Stieg, "The Postwar Purge of German Public Libraries, Democracy, and the American Reaction," *Libraries & Culture* 28 (spring 1993): 143–164; Kathleen J. Nawyn, " 'Striking at the Roots of German Militarism': Efforts to Demilitarize German Society and Culture in American-Occupied Württemberg-Baden" (PhD diss., University of North Carolina, Chapel Hill, 2008), 383–409.

2. "Read No Evil," *Time*, May 27, 1946, 31; Kathleen McLaughlin, "Allies to Wipe Out all Pro-Nazi Books," *NYT*, May 14, 1946, 1. For Order No. 4, see *Enactments and Approved Papers of the Council and Coordinating Committee*, vol. 3, March-June, 1946, 131–132, https://www.loc.gov/rr/frd/Military_Law/Enactments/Volume-III.pdf.

3. Ralph A. Ulveling and Carl H. Milam telegram, May 14, 1946, box 4, NS Pubs, folder 1.

4. JCS 1067, https://en.wikisource.org/wiki/JCS_1067; Feliks Gross, "Educational Reconstruction in Europe," *American Sociological Review* 8 (October, 1943): 548. James F. Tent, *Mission on the Rhine: Reeducation and Denazification in American-Occupied Germany* (Chicago: University of Chicago Press, 1982); Earl F. Ziemke, *The U.S. Army in the Occupation of Germany, 1944-1946* (Washington, DC: Center of Military History, 1975); Frederick Taylor, *Exorcising Hitler: The Occupation and Denazification of Germany* (New York: Bloomsbury, 2011).

5. Grayson N. Kefauver and John W. Taylor, "Control of Educational Institutions in Germany," August 23, 1944, box 5, folder: Control of Education, Information and Publishing; M.M. Knappen, "Memorandum on the Background of ERA Sections, particularly Religious Affairs," 12, box 10, folder: ERA Division History; G.R. Gayre, "Special Report on the Education Working Committee," May 7, 1944, box 37, folder: Re-education of Germany Working Party, Richard Thomas Alexander Papers, #9796, University of Virginia Library. Kurt Jürgensen, "British

Occupation Policy after 1945 and the Problem of 'Re-educating Germany,'" *History* 68 (1983): 225–244.

6. "Textbooks in Germany American Zone," August 1946, 1, box 27, folder: MG Reports, ERA, Alexander Papers. Marshall Knappen, *And Call It Peace* (Chicago: University of Chicago Press, 1947), 63–70.

7. Daniel Lerner, *Sykewar: Psychological Warfare against Germany, D-Day to VE-Day* (New York: George W. Stewart, 1949). Larry Hartenian, *Controlling Information in U.S. Occupied Germany, 1945–1949: Media Manipulation and Propaganda* (Lewiston, NY: Edwin Mellen Press, 2003).

8. OSS, "Five German Writers Discuss What to Do with Germany," January 18, 1945, 1-A-3, *U.S. Occupation of Germany: Educational Reform, 1945-1949* (microform, Bethesda, MD: Congressional Information Service, 1991); Lucius D. Clay, *Decision in Germany* (Garden City, NY: Doubleday, 1950), 281. Franz Neumann, et al., *Secret Reports on Nazi Germany*, ed. Raffaele Laudani (Princeton, NJ: Princeton University Press, 2013), 96, 103. Brett Gary, *The Nervous Liberals: Propaganda Anxieties from World War I to the Cold War* (New York: Columbia University Press, 1999); Christopher Simpson, *Science of Coercion: Communication Research and Psychological Warfare, 1945-1960* (New York: Oxford University Press, 1994); Daniel Pick, *The Pursuit of the Nazi Mind: Hitler, Hess, and the Analysts* (New York: Oxford University Press, 2012).

9. Douglas Waples, "Communications," *American Journal of Sociology* 47 (1942): 917. John V. Richardson Jr., "Douglas Waples (1893–1978)," *Journal of Library History* 15 (Winter, 1980): 76–83. Steven Karetsky, *Reading Research and Librarianship: A History and Analysis* (Westport, CT: Greenwood 1982); Susan E. Israel and E. Jennifer Monaghan, eds., *Shaping the Reading Field: The Impact of Early Reading Pioneers, Scientific Research and Progressive Ideas* (Newark, DE: International Reading Association, 2007).

10. Douglas Waples, "Disposal of Objectionable Materials," June 1, 1945; Guy Della Cioppa to Waples, July 3, 1945, folder: ACA Order No. 4, Entry A1 259, ICD Records, Publication Control Branch, OMGUS Records, RG 260, NACP. For a brief description of his war work, see Douglas Waples, *On the March: A Short Autobiography for Friends and Family* (Washington Island, WI, 1967).

11. Summary Outline of Field Manual for Publications Officer, [c. 1945], 3, box 5, folder: Control of Education, Alexander Papers. R. J. Percival, "Control of German Libraries," April 3, 1945, folder: Policy—Libraries, Education and Cultural Relations Division Records, Education Branch, RG 260.

12. *Adaptation of German Propaganda Controls*, July 22, 1944, box 4, folder: Civil Affairs Guides, Alexander Papers. Jan-Pieter Barbian, *The Politics of Literature in Nazi-Germany: Books in the Media Dictatorship*, trans. Kate Sturge (London: Bloomsbury, 2013), 142–145, 279–289, 357–358.

13. "Discussion," April 12, 1945, Policy—Libraries. O.P. Echols, "Draft: Removal of Nazi Literature from German Homes," July 5, 1945, AG 461, Confiscation of Nazi Literature, Entry A1 25, U.S. Occupation Headquarters Records, Adjutant General Decimal File, RG 260. See also Percival, "Control of German Libraries."

14. Edward C. Breitenkamp, *The U.S. Information Control Division and Its Effect on German Publishers and Writers, 1945 to 1949* (Grand Forks, ND: University Station, 1953).

15. *Handbook for Military Government in Germany, Prior to Defeat or Surrender* (SHAEF, 1944), paragraphs 829–830, https://history.army.mil/reference/Finding%20 Aids/Mil_gov.pdf. R. R. Chesnutt, "Conference of Education and Religion Officers

of Bavaria," 3-A-262; George S. Patton, Opening of Libraries, September 20, 1945, 3-A-253, *U.S. Occupation of Germany*. Robert Murphy to Secretary of State, September 8, 1945, Container 392, folder: Cooperation with government, ACQ 5-3-2, Records of the LC Central File, MacLeish-Evans, LC Archives, Manuscript Division, LC.

16. O. P. Echols, "Draft: Removal of Nazi Literature." "Removal of Nazi Books from German Homes," July 3, [1945], 350.09, ICD Records, Executive Office Central Decimal File, RG 260. For British perspectives, see "Purging of Nazi Literature," vol. 1, FO 1050/1366, TNA.

17. Breitenkamp, *U.S. Information Control Division*, 12. "Discussion," Policy—Libraries.

18. Psychological Warfare Division, SHAEF, *An Account of Its Operations in the Western European Campaign, 1944-1945*, n.d., 83.

19. Dr. Noole to the Military Government, Wuppertal, May 31, 1945, *ETO Report, MFAA for 1945*, RG 239, M 1944, http://fold3.com/image/270074346.

20. Stephen Spender, *European Witness* (London: Hamish Hamilton, 1946), 155, 153. Eisenhower cable to OMG for Bavaria, November 6, 1945, AG 461. Nawyn, "Striking at the Roots of German Militarism," 386–392.

21. Eric Feiler, "Public Library Survey in Nürnberg," August 10, 1945; J. Rothman, "Copy of Report on Libraries from Heidelberg," August 3, 1945; M. S. Pratt, "Public Library Survey [Regensburg]," August 7, 1945, German Libraries—Reports, ICD Records, Publication Control Branch. Reuben Peiss, "Allied Control Authority Order No. 4: Its Background and History," November 1, 1946, box 6, folder: ACC Order No. 4, LCM and CAP, 1942-57, Records, Manuscript Division, LC; Knappen, *And Call It Peace*, 75–76, 82–84. Ziemke, *US. Army in the Occupation*, 318–319; Bianka J. Adams, *From Crusade to Hazard: The Denazification of Bremen Germany* (Lanham, MD: Scarecrow Press, 2009), 17.

22. James F. Tent., ed., *Academic Proconsul: Harvard Sociologist Edward Y. Hartshorne and the Reopening of German Universities, 1945-1946: His Personal Account* (Trier: WVT, 1998), 16–17. Zonal Textbook Committee at Lubbecke Minutes, January 22, 1946, 2, 3-B-39, *U.S. Occupation of Germany*. Spender, *European Witness*, 152.

23. Spender, *European Witness*, 154, 176–177.

24. Knappen, *And Call It Peace*, 164. "Report of the ACC for Germany to the Council of Foreign Ministers," February 3, 1947, 17, box 9, folder: Demilitarization Reports, Alexander Papers.

25. *Foreign Relations of the United States, 1946* (Washington, DC: GPO, 1969), vol. 5, 661–663. W.H.A. Bishop, Unofficial Information Services Control Meeting, December 8, 1945, folder: ACA Order No. 4, Entry A1 259. "Purging of Nazi Literature," FO 1050/1366.

26. Mr. Heath to Ambassador Murphy, n.d., folder: ACA Order No. 4, Entry A1 259. Lt. Col. Charles W. Sole, "Report on Preparation of Brief for CONL/P(46)31, Confiscation of Literature and Material of a Nazi and Militarist Nature," May 22, 1946, AG 461.

27. ACA Coordinating Committee, "Draft Order for the Confiscation of Literature," April 4, 1946, folder: E-11, US Element Records, Activities of the DIAC & ACA, RG 260.

28. Miles Rieber to Aime J. Forand, June 5, 1946, NS Pubs, folder 4. "Memorandum to Mr. Clift from Mr. Travis, Munich Operations—February," March 9, 1946, 2, box 6, folder: Agents, MUEKO, LCM Records. Dorothy Thompson, "Education or Book Burning," *Forum* 104 (September 1, 1945): 42–43. Felix

Reichmann, "Disposition of Objectionable Literature," December 27, 1945, folder: Reichmann to This Outpost, OMGWB, Records of the Publication Officer, Karlsruhe, RG 260.

29. Stephen Vincent Benét, *They Burned the Books* (New York: Farrar & Rinehart, 1942), 12. Rosamond Cruikshank to Franklin Spier, April 27, 1943, and promotional materials in box 6, folder: Burning of the Books, 1943, Council on Books in Wartime Records, Rare Books and Special Collections, Princeton University Library. Guy Stern, "The Burning of the Books in Nazi Germany, 1933: The American Response," *Simon Wiesenthal Center Annual* 2 (1985): 95–113; John B. Hench, *Books as Weapons: Propaganda, Publishing, and the Battle for Global Markets in the Era of World War II* (Ithaca, NY: Cornell University Press, 2010), 4–6, 44–54.

30. Julian Park radio broadcast, May 11, 1943, box 6, folder: Burning of the Books; Alfred Kantorowicz, "The Burned Books Still Live," *NYT Magazine*, 7 May 1944, 17; Eleanor Roosevelt, "My Day, May 11, 1943," *Eleanor Roosevelt Papers Digital Edition* (2017), www.gwu.edu/~erpapers/myday/displaydoc.cfm?_y=1943&_f=md056492; MDL, "Talking Shop," *Wilson Library Bulletin* 19 (May 1945): 632.

31. Edward P. Morgan, "Allies Outpurge Nazis," *Chicago Daily News*, May 14, 1946. William Henry Chamberlin, "Bigger and Better Book Burnings," *Wall Street Journal*, May 24, 1946; "New Bonfires of Books in Reich Deplored Here," *Baltimore Evening Sun*, May 17, 1946 clipping, NS Pubs, folder 3; "Burning of German Books Decreed," *Christian Century* 63 (May 29, 1946): 677.

32. C.H.M., "Confidential, Conversation with Dr. Evans," May 21, 1946, NS Pubs, folder 3; L. Felix Ranlett to Owen Brewster, June 13, 1946, NS Pubs, folder 1. Louise S. Robbins, *Censorship and the American Library: The American Library Association's Response to Threats to Intellectual Freedom, 1939-1969* (Westport, CT: Greenwood Press, 1996), ch. 1.

33. David M. Merriell, "Voice of the People," "On Burning Books," *Chicago Tribune*, May 27, 1946; "In Nazi Footsteps," *Chicago Tribune*, May 15, 1946.

34. J. Emlyn Williams, "Allies Push Purge of German Culture," *Christian Science Monitor*, May 15, 1946. *Minneapolis Daily Times*, May 30, 1946, NS Pubs, folder 1.

35. Keyes D. Metcalf to Howard C. Petersen, May 31, 1946, box 51, folder: Horan, Maj., UAIII 50.8.11.3, Records of the Director of the Harvard University Library, Keyes D. Metcalf, 1937–1955, Harvard University Archives. "From Clay for Echols (Eyes Only)," May 31, 1946, in *The Papers of General Lucius D. Clay, Germany, 1945-1949*, ed. Jean Edward Smith (Bloomington: Indiana University Press, 1974), vol. 1, 225, 224–226. H. M. Lydenberg to C. H. Milam, August 8, 1946, NS Pubs, folder 1.

36. Robert P. Patterson to John Haynes Holmes, June 13, 1946, NS Pubs, folder 4. Edward T. Peeples to Anna Louise Myers, June 25, 1946, folder: ACA Order No. 4, Entry A1 259. "From Clay for Echols," 225.

37. Reuben Peiss, "Memorandum of Interview with Brigadier General George S. Eyster, June 12, 1946," PACHA, *Clinton Digital Library*, http://clinton.presidentiallibraries.us/items/show/30060. Peiss, "Final Summary Report as Chief of the LCM as of November 30, 1946," December 4, 1946, 9–10; Peiss, "Memorandum: Conversation with General Clay, Berlin, June 13, 1946," box 7, folder: ACC Order No. 4, LCM Records.

38. Scott Adams, "Comments on the LCM," December 6, 1946, box 30, folder: Adams, Scott, LCM Records. Reuben Peiss, "Order No. 4," *LJ* 72 (March 1, 1947): 372–374.

39. Teletype conferences, July 13, 1946, box 15; June 10, 1946, August 28, 1946, box 14, folder: teletypes; Clapp to Peiss, October 4, 1946, box 30, folder: Regulations, LCM Records.

40. Peiss, "Final Summary Report," 11, 9–12. Peiss to Clay, October 23, 1946, box 29, folder: Policy Proposals; "Memo of conversation with Don Travis," July 9, 1946, box 6, folder: ACC Order No. 4, LCM Records. Joe Groesbeck to Lydenberg, July 23, 1946, IRO Subject Files, RS 7/1/6, box 15, folder: LCM, ALA Archives.

41. Lt. Col. Robert A. Reese, "Instructions for Disposal of Confiscated Material of a Nazi and Militarist Nature," August 10, 1946, 3-A-66, *US Occupation of Germany*.

42. "First Report on Confiscation of Nazi-Militaristic Literature," July 20, 1946, folder: Confiscation & Disposal of Literature, Education and Cultural Relations Division Records, Education Branch, RG 260. Bayer.Staatsminister für Unterricht und Kultus, Munich, memo, June 8, 1946; Rektor der Phillips-Universität, Marburg, to OMG Frankfurt, June 11, 1946, box 2, folder: Books, Banned, Alexander Papers.

43. Adams, "Comments on the LCM." John B. Rhind and Elisha I. Greifer, "Report of the ERA and ODIC Representatives Visit to the Laender re Disposal of Confiscated Literature," February 4, 1947, folder: Confiscation & Disposal of Literature.

44. Rhind and Greifer, "Report of the ERA and ODIC Representatives"; "Initial Report on Württemberg-Baden, January 24, 194[7]," folder: Confiscation & Disposal of Literature; "Interim Status Report on the Confiscation of Literature and Material of a Nazi and Militarist Nature," September 22, 1946, AG 461. Nawyn, "Striking at the Roots of German Militarism," 405–409.

45. L.D. Gresh to Don C. Travis, April 18, 1947; Travis, "Memorandum for Dr. Gresh, Disposal of Nazi Literature," January 14, 1947; Gresh to Director, ERA Division, OMGWB, May 16, 1947; "Report of the Board for the Disposition of Nazi and Militaristic Literature," August 25, 1947, folder: Confiscation & Disposal of Literature. "Library Orientation, Education and Cultural Relations Division, 6-21 July 1948," August 31, 1948, 10, box 15, folder: Education Mission to Germany, Alexander Papers.

46. "Report of TDY J. A. Horne on Present Status of Archives and Libraries in Land Bavaria," September 9, 1946, 5, Munich Central Collecting Point, RG 260, M1946, fold3.com/image/270061577. E. F. D'Arms and H. W. Ehrmonn, "Education Mission to Germany," November 4, 1946, 3-B-268, *US Occupation of Germany*.

47. *Report of the U.S. Education Mission to Germany*, Department of State, Publication 2664, European series 16 (Washington, DC: GPO, 1946), 8. Bernice E. Leary, "A Report on Children's Books and Reading," June 1947, 4, box 4, folder: Children's Books and Reading, Alexander Papers. Delbert Clark, "German Textbook Hails Militarism," *NYT*, January 18, 1947. Richard T. Alexander to W. F. Russell, January 5, 1948, box 14, folder: ALA, Education and Cultural Relations Division Records. *Report of the Military Governor*, no. 34, May 1947–April 1948, 13, box 28, folder: MG Reports, Alexander Papers. "Library Orientation," 3.

48. See Anne Kornhauser, *Debating the American State: Liberal Anxieties and the New Leviathan, 1930-1970* (Philadelphia: University of Pennsylvania Press, 2015); James T. Sparrow, *Warfare State: World War II Americans and the Age of Big Government* (New York: Oxford University Press, 2011). Hal Foust, "Americans Duck 'Nazi' Label in Literary Purge," *Chicago Tribune*, August 11, 1946.

49. "Books to Burn," *Pittsburgh Courier*, May 25, 1946, 6; "In Nazi Footsteps."

50. Sumner Sewall to Chief of Staff, October 17, 1946; Howard E. Wilson to Clay, October 7, 1946, AG 461.

51. Julian P. Boyd, "A Landmark in the History of Library Cooperation in America," *CRL* 8 (April 1947): 106. [James T. Babb] to Dan Lacy, September 13, 1948, box 67, folder 939, Librarian, Yale University, Records (RU 120), Manuscripts and Archives, Yale University Library. Robert B. Downs, "Wartime Co-Operative Acquisitions," *LQ* 19 (July 1949): 157–165. Ralph D. Wagner, *A History of the Farmington Plan* (Lanham, MD: Scarecrow Press, 2002).

52. Tuesday Morning Meeting Minutes, May 6, 1947, May 25, 1948, June 1, 1948, June 2, 1948, box 10, University of Pennsylvania Library Records, UPB55, University Archives, University of Pennsylvania. Rudolf Hirsch to Lacy, April 2, 1948, April 16, 1948; Lacy to Hirsch, May 3, 1948; Lacy to Evans, June 3, 1948, box 16, folder: Confiscated material, LCM Records. Hirsch to Waples, March 16, 1945, ACA Order No. 4, Entry A1 259. Charles David, "Introduction," *The Library Chronicle of the Friends of the University of Pennsylvania Library* 40 (Winter 1974): 9–14.

53. Boyd, "A Landmark in the History," 106. Boyd to Charles W. David, May 31, 1948; Boyd to Metcalf and Ralph E. Ellsworth, May 15, 1948, and correspondence in box 61, folder: ARL, LCM German Books, Metcalf Records. Benjamin Fines, "Librarians Plan Censorship Fight," *NYT*, June 16, 1948. See Hermina G. B. Anghelescu and Martine Poulain, eds., *Books, Libraries, Reading, and Publishing in the Cold War* (Washington, DC: LC Center for the Book, 2002); Greg Barnhiser and Catherine Turner, eds., *Pressing the Fight: Print, Propaganda and the Cold War* (Amherst: University of Massachusetts Press, 2012); Robbins, *Censorship and the American Library*.

54. Peiss to Metcalf, June 1, 1948; Boyd to Metcalf, May 21,1948, box 61, folder: ARL, LCM German Books.

55. Staff Memorandum, February 1948, vol. 1, No. 2, Cooperative Programs, Box 8, Penn Library Records. Richard Thomas Alexander Jr. Interview by G. Kurt Piehler and Brian Puaca Jr., Veterans Oral History Project, Center for the Study of War and Society, University of Tennessee, Knoxville, October 1, 2004, 7–8.

CHAPTER 7

1. Seymour J. Pomrenze, "The Restitution of Jewish Cultural Treasures after the Holocaust: The OAD's Role in the Fulfillment of U.S. International and Moral Obligations (A First Hand Account)," Proceedings of the 37th Annual Convention of the Association of Jewish Libraries, Denver, 2002. Koppel Pinson, "A Report on Jewish Cultural Treasures and Their Part in the Educational Program of the AJDC," June 13, 1946, Koppel S. Pinson Collection, Magnes Collection of Jewish Art and Life, University of California, Berkeley.

2. On the U.S. military and restitution, see Michael J. Kurtz, *America and the Return of Nazi Contraband: The Recovery of Europe's Cultural Treasures* (Cambridge, UK: Cambridge University Press, 2006); Leslie I. Poste, "The Development of U.S. Protection of Libraries and Archives in Europe during World War II" (PhD diss., University of Chicago, 1958); Robert G. Waite, "Returning Jewish Cultural Property: The Handling of Books Looted by the Nazis in the American Zone of Occupation, 1945 to 1952," *Libraries & Culture* 37 (2002): 213–228; Markus Kirchhoff, "Looted Texts: Restituting Jewish Libraries," in *Restitution and Memory: Material Restoration in Europe*, ed. Dan Diner and Gotthart Wunberg (New York: Berghahn Books, 2007), 161–188. On Jewish restitution efforts, see Dana Herman, "*Hashavat Avedah*: A History of Jewish Cultural Reconstruction, Inc." (PhD diss., McGill University, 2008); Mark Glickman, *Stolen Words: The Nazi*

Plunder of Jewish Books (Lincoln: University of Nebraska Press, 2016); Elisabeth Gallas, *A Mortuary of Books: The Rescue of Jewish Culture after the Holocaust* (New York: NYU Press, 2019); Elisabeth Gallas, "Locating the Jewish Future: The Restoration of Looted Cultural Property in Early Postwar Europe," *Naharaim* 9 (2015): 25–47.

3. Lynn H. Nicholas, *The Rape of Europa: The Fate of Europe's Treasures in the Third Reich and the Second World War* (New York: Knopf, 1994); Kurtz, *America and the Return of Nazi Contraband.*

4. John Walker, "Report on the Preservation and Restitution of European Works of Art, Libraries and Archives," July 10, 1945, 1, American Commission for the Protection and Salvage of Artistic and Historic Monuments in War Areas [Roberts Commission] Records, RG 239, M1944, roll 34, NACP.

5. "The American Commission for the Protection and Salvage of Artistic and Historic Monuments in War Areas, Special Meeting, July 27, 1944," 11, M1944, roll 5. Fred W. Shipman to William D. McCain, April 9, 1945, no. 109, Entry UD 282-BB, Foreign Records Seized, Material Accumulated for a Conference on Captured German and Related Records, RG 242, NACP. Eleanor Mattern, "World War II Archivists: In the Field and on the Home Front," *Library & Archival Security* 24 (2011): 61–81.

6. Jerome Michael to J. H. Hilldring, June 5, 1946, box 39, folder 3, Salo W. Baron Papers (M0580), Dept. of Special Collections, Stanford University Libraries. Hohe Schule, "Library for Exploration of the Jewish Question," Document 171-PS, n.d., PACHA, *Clinton Digital Library*, http://clinton.presidentiallibraries.us/items/show/29910. Sem C. Sutter, "Looting of Jewish Collections in France by the Einsatzstab Reichsleiter Rosenberg," in *Jüdischer Buchbesitz als Raubgut: Zweites Hannoversches Symposium*, ed. Regina Dehnel (Frankfurt am Main: Klostermann, 2006), 120–134; Patricia Kennedy Grimsted, "Roads to Ratibor: Library and Archival Plunder by the Einsatzstab Reichsleiter Rosenberg," *Holocaust and Genocide Studies* 19 (Winter 2005): 390–458; Jonathan Rose, *The Holocaust and the Book* (Amherst: University of Massachusetts Press, 2001); Elizabeth Simpson, *The Spoils of War: World War II and Its Aftermath: The Loss, Reappearance, and Recovery of Cultural Property* (New York: Harry N. Abrams, 1997).

7. Mason Hammond, Carrier Sheet, "Institut zur Erforschung der Judenfrage," June 24, 1945; Hammond, "Library of Yiddish Scientific Institute," June 23, 1945; Sol Liptzin and Max Weinreich to Eugene N. Anderson, May 7, 1945, Central Collecting Points Records: OMGUS Headquarters, RG 260, M1941, roll 9. HQ 3rd US Army G-5 Section, "Semi-Monthly Report of MFAA, for Period Ending 15 April 1945," April 17, 1945, 16, M1944, roll 23.

8. Joseph Gutmann, *My Life of Jewish Learning; In Search of Jewish Art, the Forgotten Image* (New York: Hunter College, CUNY, 2002), 4; Grace Cohen Grossman, "The Skirball Museum JCR Research Project: Records and Recollections," in *Neglected Witnesses: The Fate of Jewish Ceremonial Objects During the Second World War and After*, ed. Julie-Marthe Cohen with Felicitas Heimann-Jelinek (Nr Builth Wells, Wales: Institute of Art and Law, 2011), 329–330. Abraham Aaroni and Julius H. Buchman, "Europe's Jewish Cultural Material," *National Jewish Monthly* 61 (May 1947): 309–311. My thanks to archivist Joe Weber for sharing relevant documents from the Abraham Aaroni Papers, 1944–2003, SC-15278, Jacob Rader Marcus Center, AJA, Cincinnati, Ohio.

9. Mason Hammond to W. Douglas Cooper, "Collections at Hungen," August 22, 1945, Records of the MFAA Section, OMGUS, RG 260, fold3.com/image/

290369332. Jochen Stollberg, "City and University Library of Frankfurt am Main," in *International Dictionary of Library Histories*, vol. 1, ed. David H. Stam (Chicago: Fitzroy Dearborn, 2001), 268–271.

10. Glenn H. Goodman, *Thoughts and Memories* (unpublished TS, 1986), 369–370, 373, 384; I am deeply grateful to Susan Josephson for sharing part of her father's memoir and for helpful biographical details (e-mail, April 21, 2016). See also Glenn Goodman, File 29278, International Tracing Service Records, United States Holocaust Memorial Museum, Washington, DC; *Ohio State Lantern*, October 22, 1947; January 13, 1949, 7; July 13, 1951, 3; October 14, 1975, 2, http://go.osu.edu/lanternarchives. On interned American civilians, see Mitchell G. Bard, *Forgotten Victims in Hitler's Camps* (Boulder, CO: Westview Press, 1994).

11. Goodman, *Thoughts*, 374, 382, 411. Walter W. Horn to Hammond, "Transfer of books and ceremonial objects from the Rosenberg Institute . . . to the rooms of the former Rothschild Palais," July 20, 1945, RG 260, M1941, fold3.com/image/291849790.

12. George E. B. Peddy, "MFAA Report for July 1945," August 7, 1945, fold3.com/image/231979843; A. R. Richstein, "MFAA Status of Collecting Point Report," October 5, 1945, Central Collecting Points Records: Wiesbaden, RG 260, M1947, fold3.com/image/231980208; "Partial List of Libraries and Collections," July 25, 1945, RG 260, M1949, fold3.com/image/290371368. See also Julius Buchman, "Weekly MFAA Report," August 15 to October 9, 1945, Activity Reports ('illegible' folder), RG 260, M1947. Although Aaroni and Zorach Warhaftig stated there were no Hebrew experts at Rothschild, Buchman and Richstein indicate otherwise. Warhaftig to Dr. J. Robinson, January 18, 1946; Aaroni to Dr. Federbusch, March 4, 1946, box 39, folder 9, WJC Papers, MS 361, AJA.

13. Glenn H. Goodman, "Rosenberg—Institut für Judenforschung! Repositories in Hungen, Oberhessen" [1945], Records of MFAA Section, fold3.com/image/290371305.

14. Goodman, *Thoughts*, 382, 424–426; Buchman, "Weekly MFAA Report," August 22, 1945, fold3.com/image/231979926.

15. Lucy Dawidowicz, *From That Time and Place, A Memoir, 1938-1947* (1989; rpt. New Brunswick, NJ: Rutgers University Press, 2008), 314; Leslie I. Poste, "Report of Inspection of Offenbach Collecting Point," November 2, 1945, Central Collecting Points Records: OAD, RG 260, M1942, fold3.com/image/232104992.

16. Goodman, *Thoughts*, 398, 424–425. H. De la Fontaine Verwey, "The Bibliotheca Rosenthaliana during the German Occupation," *Omnia in Eo, Studia Rosenthaliana* 38/39 (Leuven, Belgium: Peters, 2006), 61–72.

17. Poste, "Report of Inspection"; A. R. Richstein, "MFAA Status of Collecting Point Report," December 5, 1945, RG 260, M1947, fold3.com/image/231969701; Seymour Pomrenze to Oliver W. Holmes, December 16, 1945, folder 100, Entry UD 282-BB. The number of books in Rothschild is disputed, ranging from 130,000 to 250,000.

18. Aaroni and Buchman, "Europe's Jewish Cultural Material," 309; "Suggestions for how to continue work in the Collecting Point," n.d., RG260, M1949, fold3.com/image/290371258; although this memorandum has no author, it comports with Goodman's description of Feldmüller's plan, in *Thoughts*, 403–407.

19. Kurtz, *America and the Return of Nazi Contraband*, 47–86.

20. Cecil Roth, Opening Address, Conference on Restoration of Continental Jewish Museums, Libraries and Archives, London, April 11, 1943, box 30, folder 1, Baron

Papers; "Jewish Culture," *Times Literary Supplement*, March 11, 1944, RG 239, M1944, fold3.com/image/270101783; Gallas, "Locating the Jewish Future."

21. See Herman, *Hashavat Avedah*; Elisabeth Gallas, "Documenting Cultural Destruction: The Research Project of the Commission on European Jewish Cultural Reconstruction," in *Als der Holocaust noch keinem Namen hatte*, ed. Regina Fritz et al. (Vienna: New Academic Press, 2016), 45–62. On Arendt, see Natan Sznaider, *Jewish Memory and the Cosmopolitan Order: Hannah Arendt and the Jewish Condition* (Cambridge, UK: Polity, 2011), 40–66; Dov Schidorsky, "Hannah Arendt's Dedication to Salvaging Jewish Culture," *Leo Baeck Institute Year Book* 59 (2014): 181–195.

22. L. C. Pinkerton to Secretary of State, "Jewish Cultural Material Saved from Nazi Hands," May 16, 1945, no. 1451, Entry UD 282-BB. [Judah L. Magnes] to Simon Rifkind, November 30, 1945, RG 260, M1949, fold3.com/image/290371317. Dov Schidorsky, "The Salvaging of Jewish Books in Europe after the Holocaust: The Efforts of the Hebrew University and of the Jewish National and University Library," in *Jüdischer Buchbesitz als Raubgut*, 197–212.

23. Theodor H. Gaster to Luther Evans, December 30, 1945, box 3, folder 5, Col. Seymour J. Pomrenze Papers (P-933), American Jewish Historical Society, Center for Jewish History, NY. Verner W. Clapp to Sargent B. Child, November 6, 1945, no. 1451, Entry UD 282-BB.

24. Goodman, *Thoughts*, 418. J. H. Buchman, "Weekly MFAA Report," September 12, 1945, RG 260, M1947, fold3.com/image/231979954.

25. Koppel S. Pinson, "Report of the Educational Director of the AJDC Committee in Germany and Austria for November 1945," Pinson Collection. Pinson to Hannah Arendt, November 23, 1945, box 39, folder 3, Baron Papers. On Jewish DPs and refugees, see Atina Grossmann, *Jews, Germans, and Allies: Close Encounters in Occupied Germany* (Princeton, NJ: Princeton University Press, 2007); William I. Hitchcock, *The Bitter Road to Freedom: A New History of the Liberation of Europe* (New York: Free Press, 2008).

26. Staff Cable Control Outgoing Message [Lucius D. Clay], December 15, 1945; Simon H. Rifkind to Clay, January 7, 1946; Clay to Rifkind, January 12, 1946, RG 260, M1942, roll 5.

27. Paul Vanderbilt, "Memorandum on removal of books from the Rothschild library building . . . for use in Displaced Persons Camps," December 28, 1945, RG 260, M1949, fold3.com/image/290371273; Pomrenze to Oliver W. Holmes, March 13, 1946, no. 318, Entry UD 282-BB. Ralph E. Brant, "Administration and Operations of the OAD," February 2, 1946, RG 260, M1942, fold3.com/image/232101790.

28. Pomrenze to Holmes, March 13, 1946. S. L. Temko, "MFAA Status of Collecting Point Report," January 5, 1946, RG 260, M1947, fold3.com/image/231970368.

29. Pomrenze to Holmes, March 13, 1946. See also Sargent Child, "Comments on Report Concerning Offenbach Collection Point, 2 Feb. 1946," February 19, 1946, RG 260, M1949, fold3.com/image/290371104. On the MFAA's exhibitions and parties, see Theodore A. Heinrich to Mother and Dad, November 6, 1946, file 154; to Dick and Nancy, November 9, 1946, file 918, Theodore A. Heinrich Papers, Special Collections, University of Regina, Regina, Canada.

30. Horn to Hammond, July 20, 1945; Goodman, *Thoughts*, 409, 378. Walter I. Farmer, *The Safekeepers: A Memoir of the Arts at the End of World War II* (Berlin: Walter de Gruyter, 2000), 94–99.

31. Goodman, *Thoughts,* 378. "Report No. 1," "Suggestions Concerning the Future of the Offenbach and Rothschild Library Collecting Points," n.d., RG 260, M1949, fold3.com/image/290371633; Glenn Goodman is the likely author of these reports. Everett P. Lesley and Clyde K. Harris, "Duties and Projected Operations, MFAA Branch, Det. E-6," January 23, 1946, 6, RG 260, M1947, fold3.com/image/231980666. Pomrenze, "Restitution of Jewish Cultural Treasures."

32. Albert A. Mavrinac, "MFAA Status of Collecting Point Report," February 2, 1946, RG 260, M1949, fold3.com/image/290371127.

33. Pomrenze to Holmes, March 13, 1946. Colonel S. J. Pomrenze Interview with Grace Cohen Grossman, August 14, 1989, box 5, folder 2, Pomrenze Papers.

34. "Report of a short managing-meeting of the OAD on 13th March 1946"; Glenn Goodman, "Meals," March 7, 1946, RG 260, M1942, roll 2. S. J. Pomrenze, "Offenbach Reminiscences and the Restitution to the Netherlands," in *The Return of Looted Collections (1946-1996): An Unfinished Chapter,* ed. F. J. Hoogewoud et al. (Amsterdam: The Symposium, 1997), 10–18; Goodman, *Thoughts,* 422–423.

35. Paul Vanderbilt to Luther Evans, March 25, 1946, no. 1453, Entry UD 282-BB. Poste, "Development of U.S. Protection."

36. OAD Monthly Report, March 1946, RG 260, M1942, roll 9.

37. Pomrenze Interview, August 14, 1989, 17. Poste, "Development of U.S. Protection," 35–57. OAD Monthly Report, May 1946; OAD Monthly Report, June 1946, roll 9; OAD, *Library Markings Found among Looted Books in the Archival Depot,* roll 12; *Ex Libris' Library Bookplates,* roll 13, RG 260, M1942. Farmer, *Safekeepers,* 99.

38. [Baron] to Jerome Michael, November 11, 1946, box 39, folder 2, Baron Papers. Lucy Schildkret to Dr. Weinreich, June 17, 1947, box 55, folder 4; February 16, 1947, folder 3, Lucy S. Dawidowicz Papers, P-675, American Jewish Historical Society, New York; Nancy Sinkoff, "Lucy S. Dawidowicz and the Restitution of Jewish Cultural Property," *American Jewish History* 100 (January 2016): 140. See also Glickman, *Stolen Words,* 210–211; David Fishman, *The Book Smugglers: Partisans, Poets, and the Race to Save Jewish Treasures from the Nazis* (Lebanon, NH: University Press of New England, 2017).

39. "Recap of Civilian Personnel Who Are Paid from Local Ex-Enemy Economy," April 23, 1946, RG260, M1942, fold3.com/image/232162714. Pomrenze Interview, August 14, 1989. Personal communication, Jennifer Rodgers, May 16, 2016, on DPs employed at ITS. On suspicion of DPs, see Hitchcock, *Bitter Road to Freedom,* 312–338. On theft of books by German employees, see Astrid Eckert, *The Struggle for the Files: The Western Allies and the Return of German Archives after the Second World War* (New York: Cambridge University Press, 2012), 54–55.

40. On the Jewish visitors, see OAD Monthly Reports for May through August, 1946, RG 260, M1942, roll 9. Goodman to Captain Bencowitz, April 26, 1946, RG 260, M1942, fold3.com/image/232162566.

41. Child to Luther Evans, February 20, 1946, box 31, folder: Child, Sargent, LCM and CAP, 1942–1957, Records, Manuscript Division, LC; "Suggestions concerning the future of the Offenbach and Rothschild Library Collecting Points"; *Economic Status Land Greater Hesse, June 1946,* 28, file 1097, Heinrich Papers. OAD Monthly Report, July 1946, 5, estimated that about 25% of nonidentifiable material was "not of Jewish significance"; figures varied through the history of the collecting points. See also Philip Friedman, "The Fate of the Jewish Book During the Nazi Era," *Jewish Book Annual* 13 (1957/8): 3–13; Robert G. Waite, "Returning Jewish Cultural Property."

42. Jacob Zuckerman to David H. Clift, February 14, 1946; Zuckerman to Clift, February 18, 1946; Zuckerman to LCM, April 23, 1946, box 33, folder: Reports, Zuckerman, J.; Clift, "LCM Report, 16 April to 15 May 1946," May 15, 1946, 5–6, box 31, Reports: Clift, David H., LCM Records. Pinson, "Report on Jewish Cultural Treasures." "U.S. Mission Finds 425,000 Jewish Books," clipping, February 26, 1946, box 39, folder 9, WJC Papers.

43. [Bencowitz] to Zuckerman, May 16, 1946, RG 260, M1942, roll 4; [Bencowitz] to Pomrenze, June 3, 1946, box 3, folder 5, Pomrenze Papers. Bencowitz, "Analysis of Personnel Requirements of the OAD," October 14, 1946; "Personnel Recommendation," October 28, 1946, roll 2; OAD Monthly Report, September 1946, roll 9; November 1946, roll 10, M1942.

44. Heinrich to Mother and Dad, January 1, 1947, March 23, 1947, file 155, Heinrich Papers. Heinrich, "Promotion of Mr. Joseph A. Horne," August 21, 1947, roll 2; OAD Monthly Report, January 1947, roll 10, M1942. Dawidowicz, *From That Time and Place*, 314. For a fascinating study of Horne, see Cynthia Staples, "Interludes," *Words and Images,* https://wordsandimagesbycynthia.com/2014/06/03/update-interlude-toc/.

45. Heinrich to Mother and Dad, February 18, 1947, file 155. Horne to Ted [Heinrich], August 20, 1947, fold3.com/image/114/232178697; Horne to Joe [Pomrenze], August 18, 1947; Horne, "Inspection of Burg Oberhaus, Passau, August 19, 1947, RG 260, M1942, fold3.com/image/270112873. OAD Weekly Report, 17–22 February [1947]; OAD Monthly Report, August 1947, RG 260, M1942, roll 10. Poste, "Development of U.S. Protection." 378. Horne to E. G. Lowenthal, August 23, 1947, 81 HQ Files: Jewish Libraries and Books, Wiener Library (Cengage Learning, 2007).

46. Joseph A. Horne, "Visit of Dr. Grummach [sic]," March 4, 1947, M1942, fold3.com/image/232161003. Hellmut Lehmann-Haupt, "Dr. Grummach's [sic] visit," November 20, 1946, M1949, fold3.com/image/290371729.

47. Schildkret to Mrs. Buchman, May 12, 1947; Schildkret, "Conference of the Central Historical Commission. Not for general circulation," May 16, 1947, box 55, folder 4, Dawidowicz Papers. Dawidowicz, *From That Time and Place*, 314–324. For a full analysis, see Sinkoff, "Lucy S. Dawidowicz," 117–147.

48. OMG Hesse, OAD Monthly Report, January 1949, Annex D, 4, RG 260, M1947, fold3.com/image/114/232053589.

49. Pinson to Magnes, March 11, 1946; Pinson to Baron, March 13, 1946, Pinson Collection. Pomrenze to Baron, May 15, 1946, box 31, folder 6, Baron Papers. The Hebrew phrase from Proverbs is translated "charity saves from death."

50. Pinson to Magnes, March 11, 1946. Seymour Pomrenze report, Commission on European JCR Minutes of Meeting, June 26, 1946, box 3, folder 8, Pomrenze Papers.

51. Magnes to Pinson, May 3, 1946, Pinson Collection. On Allied restitution policy, see Michael J. Kurtz, *America and the Return of Nazi Contraband.*

52. Director, Acquisitions Department to Luther Evans, August 6, 1946, box 34, folder: Restitution of "unrestituted materials" (Jewish Books), LCM Records. Reuben Peiss to Lucius Clay, July 6, 1946, RG 260, M1949, roll 3. On the UNESCO proposal, see Miriam Intrator, *Books Across Borders: UNESCO and the Politics of Postwar Cultural Reconstruction, 1945-1951* (Basingstoke, UK: Palgrave Macmillan, 2019), ch. 5.

53. Michael to Hilldring, June 5, 1946. Luther Evans to Jean Thomas, June 17, 1946, box 34, folder: Restitution of "unrestituted materials." For a full discussion, see Gallas, *A Mortuary of Books.*

54. Vanderbilt to Evans, March 25, 1946. "Telephone Conference between Mr. Peiss and Mr. Clapp," TC 5436, January 24, 1946, box 14, telecons, 1945–1946, LCM Records.

55. Clay to AGWAR cable, June 15, 1946; Clay to AGWAR for WDSCA, July 24, 1946; October 16, 1946, M1942, roll 5. Michael to Hilldring, November 9, 1946, box 43, folder 5, Baron Papers.

56. Pinson to L. Bancel LaFarge, March 28, 1946, Pinson Collection. Dawidowicz, *From That Time and Place*, 325. On the restoration of YIVO's materials, see Sinkoff, "Lucy S. Dawidowicz"; Herman, "*Hashavat Avedah*."

57. Scholem quoted in Noam Zadoff, *Gershom Scholem: From Berlin to Jerusalem and Back*, trans. Jeffrey Green (Waltham, MA: Brandeis University Press, 2018), 115–116. Pinson to Hilda Pinson, July 13, 1946, Pinson Collection. "Report of Prof. G. Scholem on his mission to Europe . . . concerning the libraries of the Diaspora" [Sept. 15, 1946], box 58, folder 9, Baron Papers. My thanks to Noam Zadoff for insights into Scholem, the OAD, and LCM.

58. Richard F. Howard to Wesley C. Haraldson, "OAD," May 27, 1947; Haraldson to Ambassador Murphy, Mr. Heath, and Mr. Steere, May 2, 1947, box 130, file 400B, Classified General Correspondence, Entry 2531-B, Foreign Service Posts, State Department Records, RG 84, NACP. Cf. Herbert A. Friedman, *Roots of the Future* (Jerusalem: Gefen Publishing House, 1999), 106–112; Herbert Friedman interview, June 12, 1992 (RG-50.030*0074), 30–33, US Holocaust Memorial Museum. The number of items removed is disputed.

59. Howard to Haraldson, May 27, 1947; Horne to Major Born, January 22, 1947; "Hebrew Manuscripts Given to AJDC" (handwritten notes, n.d.); Howard, "Report and Request for Investigation," February 20, 1947, RG 260, M1947, roll 11. Haraldson to Murphy, Heath, and Steere, May 2, 1947.

60. [Donald R.] Heath to American Consulate Jerusalem telegram, April 1947; L. Wilkinson to General Clay, May 17, 1947; Horne to OMGUS Econ. Div., Restitution Branch, MFAA Section, January 30, 1947; Clay to Wilkinson, June 7, 1947; Wilkinson, "Material wrongfully sent from OAD and presently at Jerusalem," May 27, 1947; Dispatch No. 132, American Consulate General Jerusalem, July 24, 1947, RG 260, M1947, roll 11.

61. Robert Haeger and Bill Long, "Lost EC Treasure Found in Palestine," *Stars and Stripes*, December 9, 1947, file 1055, Heinrich Papers.

62. Bernard Heller, "A report of what we have accomplished" [1949], box 43, folder 5, Baron Papers. "Recovery and Distribution of Jewish Cultural Treasures through the JCR," September 25, 1950, box 39, folder 14, WJC Records. Dana Herman, "*Hashavat Avedah*"; Gallas, *A Mortuary of Books*.

63. "Recovery and Distribution," 2. Gershom Scholem to Joshua Starr, August 30, 1948, box 43, folder 7; "Special Report by Prof. G. Scholem on 'The Non-Jewish Books in Frankfurt,'" September 14, 1950, box 232, folder 5, Baron Papers. See also Marie Luise Knott, ed., *The Correspondence of Hannah Arendt and Gershom Scholem*, trans. Anthony David (Chicago: University of Chicago Press, 2017), 101–109. On looted books in Eastern Europe, see Patricia Kennedy Grimsted, "Tracing Patterns of European Library Plunder: Books Still Not Home from the War," *Jüdischer Buchbesitz als Raubgut*, 139–167.

64. Hannah Arendt to "Dear Professor" [Baron], January 24, 1950; Arendt, Field Report No. 12, December 1949, 6; Field Report No. 18, February 15–March 10, 1950, 3; "Report on Berlin, February 11-18, 1950," box 232, folder 5; Joshua Starr, "Cultural Property in Berlin and the Soviet Zone," Field Report No. 6, April

8, 1949, box 231, folder 17, Baron Papers. Grossman, *Jews, Germans, and Allies*, chs. 3–4.

65. "Recovery and Distribution," 3; E. G. Lowenthal, Field Report No. 10, October 1949, box 232, folder 5, Baron Papers. Elieser Curt Fuld to "Collecting Point for Books," March 31, 1948, RG 260, M1949, fold3.com/image/295527690; William Wolf to Director, OAD, November 12, 1948, file 947, Heinrich Papers. Many individual claims are documented in these records. Arendt, Field Report No. 12, 7; Field Report No. 15, February 10, 1950, box 232, folder 5, Baron Papers.

66. "Recovery and Distribution," 3; Wolf Blattberg, "Recovering Cultural Treasures," *Congress Weekly*, October 30, 1950, 5–6; JCR, "World Distribution of Books, July 1, 1949–January 31, 1952," box 231, folder 18, Baron Papers.

67. Pomrenze Interview, 1989, 24. F. J. Hoogewoud, "The Nazi Looting of Books and its American 'Antithesis': Selected Pictures from the OAD's Photographic History and Its Supplement," *Studia Rosenthaliana* 26 (1992): 158–192.

68. *OAD Photographic History*, vols. 1 and 2, 1946, RG 260, M1942, roll 11. The photograph albums, with slight variations, are also in the Heinrich Papers. For digital reproductions, see Yad Vashem Digital Photo Collection and Pomrenze Papers.

69. *The Einsatzstab Reichsleiter Rosenberg (ERR) of which the OAD Has Become the Antithesis* (album), RG 260, M1942, roll 11. *OAD Photographic History*, vol. 2.

70. *OAD Photographic History*, vol. 2; photograph at Rothschild Library, Offenbach Depot Operation, 1945–1946 Armistice Scrapbook, Pinson Collection. Christmas 1948 photograph, file 1057; Dr. [Paul] Wolff & Tritschler photograph, 1948, file 1077; *Ex Libris Found Among Looted Books in the OAD*, file 974, Heinrich Papers. On this point, see Kirchhoff, "Looted Texts," 163–164.

71. Pinson to Hilda Pinson, August 20, 1946. Bencowitz quoted in Leslie I. Poste, "Books Go Home from the Wars," *LJ* 21 (December 1, 1948): 1702. Dawidowicz, *From That Time and Place*, 326. Bencowitz's full journal is apparently lost; the wording suggests it was retrospective rather than contemporaneous.

72. Goodman, *Thoughts*, 417, 436, 434–435.

73. See Elazar Barkan, *The Guilt of Nations: Restitution and Negotiating Historical Injustices* (Baltimore: Johns Hopkins University Press, 2000); Sznaider, *Jewish Memory and the Cosmopolitan Order*.

CONCLUSION

1. Reuben Peiss to Harry M. Lydenberg, May 8, 1947, "P" folder, box 5, Harry Miller Lydenberg Papers, Manuscripts and Archives Division, NYPL.

2. Interview with Frederick G. Kilgour, Medical Library Association, Oral History Committee, May 11, 1985, 6.

3. Interview with Frederick G. Kilgour; Frederick Kilgour, "Origins of Coordinate Searching," *JASIS* 48 (1997): 340–348.

4. Claire K. Schultz and Paul L. Garwig, "History of the American Documentation Institute—A Sketch," *American Documentation* 20 (April 1969): 152–160. Tracisio Zandonade, "Social Epistemology from Jesse Shera to Steve Fuller," *Library Trends* 52 (Spring 2004): 810–832. Jennifer Heaps, "Tracking Intelligence Information: The OSS," *American Archivist* 61 (1998): 287–308; Lisa Gitelman, *Paper Knowledge: Toward a Media History of Documents* (Durham, NC: Duke University Press, 2014). Scott Adams interview conducted by Carol Fenichel, March 20, 1980, Medical Library Association Oral History Project. Eugene B. Power, *Edition of One: The Autobiography of Eugene B. Power* (Ann Arbor: University Microfilms International, 1990).

5. Hamilton Bean, *No More Secrets: Open Source Information and the Reshaping of U.S. Intelligence* (Santa Barbara, CA: Praeger, 2011), 39; Sherman Kent, *Strategic Intelligence for American World Policy* (Princeton, NJ: Princeton University Press, 1949), 4, 74–76, 133–139. Colin B. Burke, *Information and Secrecy: Vannevar Bush, Ultra, and the Other Memex* (Metuchen, NJ; Scarecrow Press, 1994); Burke, *Information and Intrigue: From Index Cards to Dewey Decimals to Alger Hiss* (Cambridge, MA: MIT Press, 2014).

6. John Y. Cole, "The International Role of the LC: A Brief History," *LC Information Bulletin* 49 (1990): 15–18. Céline Giton, "Weapons of Mass Distribution: UNESCO and the Impact of Books," *A History of UNESCO: Global Actions and Impacts*, ed. Poul Duedahl (Basingstoke, UK: Palgrave Macmillan, 2016), 49–72; Miriam Intrator, *Books Across Borders: UNESCO and the Politics of Postwar Cultural Reconstruction, 1945-1951* (Basingstoke, UK: Palgrave Macmillan 2019).

7. Elizabeth Simpson, *The Spoils of War: World War II and its Aftermath: The Loss, Reappearance, and Recovery of Cultural Property* (New York: Harry N. Abrams, 1997); Bianca Gaudenzi and Astrid Swenson, "Looted Art and Restitution in the Twentieth Century—Towards a Global Perspective," *Journal of Contemporary History* 53 (2017): 491–518; Patty Gerstenblith, "Beyond the Hague Convention," in *Cultural Awareness in the Military: Developments and Implications for Future Humanitarian Cooperation,* eds. Robert Albro and Bill Ivey (Basingstoke, UK: Palgrave Macmillan, 2014), 83–99.

8. Astrid M. Eckert, *The Struggle for the Files: The Western Allies and the Return of German Archives After the Second World War* (Cambridge, UK: Cambridge University Press, 2012).

9. Andrew J. Bacevich, "The World According to Clinton," *First Things*, June 1999, https://www.firstthings.com/article/1999/06/the-world-according-to-clinton; Stuart Eizenstat, *Imperfect Justice: Looted Assets, Slave Labor, and the Unfinished Business of World War II* (New York: Public Affairs, 2003).

10. Robert G. Waite's report is in PACHA, "Waite, Robert—"Looted Books'," *Clinton Digital Library*, https://clinton.presidentiallibraries.us/items/show/29349; see also Waite, "Returning Jewish Cultural Property: The Handling of Books Looted by the Nazis in the American Zone of Occupation, 1945 to 1952," *Libraries & Culture* 37 (Summer 2002): 213–228. PACHA, "Murphy, Greg; SHR 99-014 Looted Books (PCHA) [7]," *Clinton Digital Library*, https://clinton.presidentiallibraries.us/items/show/28321.

11. PACHA, *Plunder and Restitution: The U.S. and Holocaust Victims' Assets: Findings and Recommendations of the Presidential Advisory Commission on Holocaust Assets in the United States and Staff Report* (Washington, DC: GPO, 2000).

12. Conference on Jewish Material Claims Against Germany (Claims Conference), *Descriptive Catalogue of Looted Judaica,* https://www.scribd.com/document/111635738/Descriptive-Catalogue-of-Looted-Judaica. Anders Rydell, *The Book Thieves: The Nazi Looting of Europe's Libraries and the Race to Return a Literary Inheritance*, trans. Henning Koch (New York: Viking, 2017).

EPILOGUE

1. Rafał Werszler, "Donośląska Biblioteka Schaffgotschów: Lokalizacja, Księgozbiór, Wnętrza, Meble," *Perspectiva* 9 (2010): 232–256, perspectiva.pl/pdf/p17/15Werszler.pdf. Andrew Demshuk, *The Lost German East: Forced Migration and the Politics of Memory, 1945-1970* (New York: Cambridge University Press, 2012). Patricia Kennedy Grimsted, "A Silesian Crossroads for Europe's Displaced

Books: Compensation or Prisoners of War?" in *The Future of the Lost Cultural Heritage: The Documentation, Identification, and Restitution of the Cultural Assets of World War II Victims*, ed. Mečislav Borák (Prague: Tilia, 2006), 133–169. "Looting of Art Objects in Poland," Gunter Grundmann Interview (Feb. 1947), Restitution Research Records, OMGUS Records, RG 260, M1946, roll 118.

2. Paulina Buchwald-Pelcowa, "The National Library's Historial Collections," *Polish Libraries Today*, vol. 5 (National Library Warsaw, 2001), 20; "National Library of Poland," *International Dictionary of Library Histories*, ed. David H. Stam (London: Routledge, 2001), 545–548.

3. Walter Benjamin, "Unpacking My Library," *Illuminations* (New York: Schocken Books, 1969), 61.

INDEX

For the benefit of digital users, indexed terms that span two pages (e.g., 52–53) may, on occasion, appear on only one of those pages.